Impro for Storytellers

Keith Johnstone

Routledge / Theatre Arts Books
New York

First published in 1999
by Faber and Faber Limited
Published in the USA by
Routledge / Theatre Arts Books
29 West 35th St
New York, NY 10001

Photoset by Parker Typesetting Service, Leicester
Printed in England by Clays Ltd, St Ives plc

An earlier version of this book was first published by
Loose Moose Theatre Company, Canada, as
Don't Be Prepared – Theatresports for Teachers, in 1994

A CIP record for this book
is available from the Library of Congress

ISBN 0 87830 105 4

10 9 8 7 6 5 4 3 2 1

Contents

Introduction ix

1 Theatresports 1
Origins, 1 – *Theatresports at Loose Moose*, 2 – *Theatresports by Stealth*, 6 – *Teaching the 'Form'*, 7 – *In at the Deep End*, 11 – *Disaster is Unavoidable*, 12 – *The Sticky Stage*, 12 – *The Magnetic Stage*, 13 – *Challenges*, 13 – *The Warning for Boring*, 16 – *Misbehaviour*, 18 – *Using Audience Volunteers*, 20 – *Mime*, 21 – *Why is Theatresports a Comic Form?*, 22 – *Types of Player*, 23 – *What Theatresports Can Achieve*, 23

2 Audience Suggestions 25
No One Cares, 25 – *Laughter Misleads*, 26 – *Traps*, 28 – *Rejecting Suggestions*, 28 – *Scene Sale*, 29 – *Use Restraint*, 29

3 Trouble with Feedback 31
Getting Educated, 31 – *Fools' Paradise*, 31 – *Destructive Feedback*, 33 – *Being 'Over-cheered'*, 33 – *Group-Yes*, 34 – *Flashlight Theatre*, 36 – *The 'Seen Enough' Game*, 36 – *Theme and Forfeit*, 39 – *Gorilla Theatre*, 42 – *Micetro Impro*, 49

4 Spontaneity 55
'Here Be Monsters', 55 – *Being a Chameleon*, 55 – *No Syllabus*, 55 – *Progressive Desensitization*, 56 – *Paradoxical Teaching*, 56 – *Tug-o'-War*, 57 – *Giving Presents*, 58 – *Evaluating the Work*, 59 – *Playing Tag*, 59 – *On Not Making the Rules Clear*, 60 – *Blame Me*, 60 – *Drop Dead, Keith*, 61 – *Volunteers, and Failure*, 61 – *When Students Fail*, 62 – *Forcing Failure*, 63 – *Don't Punish Yourself*, 64 – *Be Average*, 64 – *Sport Versus Show-business*, 66 – *The Wrong Risks*, 67 – *Dullness is Deliberate*, 68 – *Being 'Original'*, 69 – *The Imagination*, 72 – *Prodigies*, 73

5 Impro for Storytellers 75
*Journey without Maps, 75 – Action and Interaction, 76 – On Not
Being a Hero, 78 – Moral Decisions, 78 – Circles of Expectation, 79 –
Point, 80 – Justification, 81 – Mysteries, 82 – Breaking the Routine, 84
– Fun with Tilting, 89*

6 Making Things Happen 101
*Blocking, 101 – Being Negative, 113 – Wimping, 114 – Cancelling, 118 –
Joining, 118 – Gossiping, 118 – Agreed Activities, 120 – Bridging, 120 –
Hedging, 123 – Sidetracking, 123 – Being Original, 124 – Looping, 124 –
Gagging, 125 – Comic Exaggeration, 127 – Conflict, 128 – Instant
Trouble, 128 – Lowering the Stakes, 128 – Consequences, 129*

7 Story Games 130
*Creating Games, 130 – Word-at-a-Time, 131 – What Comes Next?, 134
– Non-sequential Lists, 142 – Link the Items, 144 – Verbal Chase, 144 –
The Boris Game, 145 – Keyboard Game, 151*

8 Being There 155
*Three-word Sentences, 155 – One-word Sentences, 155 – The Hat-
Game, 156 – Making Faces, 162 – The Vampire, 168 – Leave for the
Same Reason, 169 – Dubbing, 171 – Invisibility, 178 – The Ghost
Game, 181*

9 Some Filler Games 183
*The Die Game, 183 – Emotional Goals, 184 – Endowments, 185 – Freeze
Games, 186 – Guess the Phrase, 187 – The No 'S' Game, 188 – A Scene
without . . ., 189 – Sideways Scenes, 189 – Yes-But, 190*

10 Procedures 192
*Blind Offers, 192 – Justify the Gesture, 193 – He Said/She Said, 195 –
Substitution Impro, 199 – Moving Bodies, 200 – The Arms, 202 – The
Dwarf, 204 – The Giant, 204 – Adjective, 204 – Wide Eyes, 204 – Wide
Mouth, 206 – Tempo, 207 – Sound Scape, 208 – You're Interesting,
209 – Boring the Audience, 211 – Wallpaper Drama, 212 – Straight Men,
213 – Gibberish, 214 – Status, 219 – The Kinetic Dance, 232 – Party
Endowments, 233 – Sandwiches, 236 – The King Game, 237 –
Master–Servant, 240 – Slow-motion Commentary, 241 – Verse, 245 –*

The Klutz, 246 – *Advancing (And Not Advancing)*, 248 – *Hitting with Balloons*, 254 – *Beep-Beep*, 260

11 **Serious Scenes** 264
Substituting Phrases, 264 – *Love and Hate*, 265 – *Emotional Sounds*, 268 – *Mantras*, 270 – *Alfred Lunt*, 274

12 **Character** 275
Who Are We?, 275 – *Changing the Body Image*, 276 – *Machines*, 277 – *People Machines*, 277 – *Being Animals*, 278 – *Obsessions*, 280 – *Fast-Food Laban*, 283 – *Fast-Food Stanislavsky*, 285

13 **Miscellaneous Games** 302
Bell and Buzzer, 302 – *Scenes with Fingers*, 302 – *People as Objects*, 303 – *Dennis's Puppet Show*, 304 – *Changing the Object*, 304

14 **Entertainment Games** 307
Stealing, 307 – *The Knife Game*, 308 – *Hand on Knee*, 310 – *Spasms*, 314 – *Paper-Flicking*, 316 – *Speech Defect Game*, 317

15 **Technical Stuff** 320
Judges, 320 – *Penalties*, 325 – *Counting Out*, 326 – *Waving the Lights Down*, 327 – *Scoring*, 327 – *Three Seldom-used Versions of Theatresports*, 328 – *The Five Theatresports Matches in Current Use*, 329 – *Rules of Theatresports*, 331

16 **Afterthoughts** 337
The Body, 337 – *The Mind*, 338 – *The Sexes*, 338 – *Quality*, 339 – *Great Audiences*, 340 – *Great Improvisers*, 341 – *Getting Jaded*, 341

Appendix One: Fast-Food Stanislavsky Lists 343

Appendix Two: A Selection of Tilt Lists 354

Appendix Three: More Filler Games 362

Appendix Four: Notes I've Given 369

Index of Games 373

Introduction

Benjamin Constant was aged four when his tutor suggested that they invent a language. They went around the estate, naming everything, and working out a grammar, and they even invented special signs to describe the sounds. Ben was aged six before he discovered that he'd learned Greek.[1]

We were warned that Algebra was going to be really difficult, whereas Einstein was told that it was a hunt for a creature known as 'X' and that when you caught it, it had to tell you it's name. K.J.
Make learning a beloved activity . . . – *Laszlo Polgar*

I was embarrassed that I could be identified in the twilight by my strange walk, that I couldn't catch, that I threw like a girl, that if you put me into water I sank. I thought that my ideas weren't worth listening to (not realizing that my speech was often unintelligible). I was so socially inept that if I forgot something I'd have to walk around the block to fetch it – not wanting to be seen as a lunatic striding aimlessly about.

'Posture training' might have helped but the gym teacher favoured the athletes; singing would have improved my breathing, but I was told just to open my mouth in time with the others; relaxation exercises could have loosened me up, but I was urged to 'try harder'. Our teachers wanted us to bring 'honour' to the school and if Quasimodo had been a fine cricketer they'd have been delighted, but they'd have done nothing about the hump.

One might imagine that social pressure would remove aberrations; but contact with other people is stressful (our blood pressure goes up every time someone enters the room), and whatever lowers our anxiety soon becomes engrained. If a fake smile does the trick, or a tight mouth, or planning what to say instead of listening, we'll repeat this behaviour until we're convinced that it's 'us', just as we believe that our posture and our voice are 'us'.

I remember being held in 'detention' and fuming at the school's refusal to help me: 'So I can't get my tongue round the words, so I lumber like a bear – why isn't that my teachers' responsibility? What's so important about the number of sheep in Tierra del Fuego in 1936 compared to being human? What about relationships? What about shyness? What about fear? Why complain that I needed speech therapy but not tell me what it is or how to get it?' I was so engrossed that when the hour was up I had to be told several times to leave.

I yearned for something that might have been called *Drama as Self-improvement*, and I was right to yearn for it. If my weight could have been shifted on to my bones my muscles wouldn't have had to keep holding me up. And if I could have learned to 'let go', and to speak clearly, I wouldn't have been so tormented.

Geography students can have tight eyes, and maths students can slur their speech, and this isn't thought relevant, but drama has to consider the whole person. A drama teacher (who isn't overwhelmed by some mammoth production at the end of the school year) can let students experiment with different 'selves': the shy can become confident, and the hysterical more at ease. No academic who understands this can dismiss drama as 'one of the frills'.

I enlisted in a two-year crash course established to replace teachers exterminated in the war (I wasn't 'good enough' to enter a university). There was no remedial work for voice or posture, and when I began teaching I soon lost the ability to speak. Many hours spent at the Golden Square Hospital – round the corner from where William Blake used to live – taught me to add sounds that I'd never noticed, and alerted me to flaws that I'll take to my grave.

By happenstance I've spent my life teaching the skills that my teachers had ignored. I encourage negative people to be positive, and clever people to be obvious, and anxious people not to do their best. People are surprised when I give as much attention to the 'klutzes' as to the 'talented' players.

George Devine (pronounced D'veen) was Artistic Director of the Royal Court Theatre and he employed me to run the script department, to supervise the theatre's educational work, and to direct plays.

Groups of sixth-formers came for week-long visits. They met the artists and staff, and attended shows in the evening (including professional wrestling). Two of Her Majesty's Drama Inspectors (John Allen and Ruth Foster) sat in on a 'final discussion' where twelve eighteen-year-old males stared at me, glumly unresponsive. I said that other groups had loved being at the theatre, but 'I hear you're only interested in how much money people earn.'

I kept provoking the group until one growled: 'Theatre's no use, so why bother learning about it?'

I said: 'Theatre is about relationships. Why don't I teach you how to pick up girls?'

Two of them closed in on me, one red in the face and the other ashen, but I couldn't remember which colour precedes physical attack. They were shouting in despair that 'picking up girls' was an ability that you either had or you didn't have. Suddenly they were all talking furiously, and saying how strange it was to be at a place where people liked their work and cared about things other than money, and how they were destined for rotten stinking jobs that didn't interest them. Then they homed in on the inspectors, and raged about their repressive school. The meeting was supposed to end at four-thirty but they were still at it at seven-thirty.

This impressed the inspectors and for years I gave workshops at the Ministry of Education's Summer School for Drama Advisers (at Strawberry Hill) and to groups of Advanced Drama Teachers for the Greater London Council. I taught the Royal Shakespeare Company's Theatre-Go-Round summer school each year, and gave hundreds of demonstrations in schools and colleges.

The Royal Academy employed me until I left England, and since then I've given courses at theatre schools in many countries, including some fifteen years at the Danish State School (on and off). When the International School of Theatre Anthropology (ISTA) devoted a summer school to the study of improvisation, they invited Dario Fo, Grotowski and myself each to give a week of workshops.

People are surprised that I'm still excited about teaching, but why shouldn't I be when I've hardly scratched the surface?

When Devine founded the Royal Court Theatre Studio he invited me to teach there. The advertisement offered 'refresher courses' to all members of 'the theatrical profession', but I had no idea what I was supposed to refresh.

I admired actors who were 'alive', moment by moment (unlike those from the 'Theatre of Taxidermy'), so I pinned up a list of 'Things My Teachers Stopped Me From Doing' and used it as a syllabus. My teachers had felt obliged to destroy our spontaneity, using techniques that had proved effective for hundreds of years, so why not reverse their methods? I had been urged to concentrate on one thing at a time, so I looked for ways of splitting the attention; I had been taught to look ahead, so I invented games that would make it difficult to think past the next word. 'Copying' had been called cheating, so I made people imitate each other. Funny voices had been anathema, so I encouraged funny voices. 'Originality' and 'concentration' had been prized so I became notorious as the acting coach who shouted 'Be more obvious!' and 'Be more boring!' and 'Don't concentrate!'

Many of these 'reversals' are now known as 'classic' games (as if they came from ancient Greece) and they worked so well that we were soon laughing all day long. But were we really so amusing? I didn't know of any other improvisation in England (except some Stanislavsky classes), so the only way to validate the work was to go onstage with a pride of improviser lions.

Devine wanted the processes of theatre to be visible to everyone (in disagreement with his friends like Olivier, who wanted to 'preserve the magic'), so there was usually at least one observer watching my classes. The British Council sent along any foreigners who wanted to see new methods of actor training (because who else would have welcomed them?), and my improvisation group (the Theatre Machine) was soon invited to tour abroad. When the work was good, the reviews compared us to Chaplin and Keaton.

NOTES

1 He grew up to write *Adolphe* and become a lover of Madame de Stael.

1 Theatresports

Origins

Theatresports was inspired by pro-wrestling, a family entertainment where Terrible Turks mangled defrocked Priests while mums and dads yelled insults, and grannies staggered forward waving their handbags (years passed before I learned that some of the more berserk grannies were paid stooges).

The bouts took place in cinemas (in front of the screen) and the expressions of agony were all played 'out-front'. No theatre person could have believed that it was real, and nor could anyone with a knowledge of anatomy. Jackie Pallo explains how he would climb up one of the posts and then crash down on to his prone victim – 'landing with my knee across his throat. He would go into convulsions, and so would the ladies at the ringside. Everybody would be happy. But if my knee had hit his throat with my weight and the impetus of my jump from the post behind it, the poor lad would have ended up on a slab.'[1]

Wrestling was the only form of working-class theatre that I'd seen, and the exaltation among the spectators was something I longed for, but didn't get, from 'straight' theatre – perhaps because 'culture' is a minefield in which an unfashionable opinion can explode your self-esteem.

John Dexter and William Gaskill (two of Devine's directors) shared my fleeting interest in wrestling, and we fantasized about replacing the wrestlers with improvisers, an 'impossible dream' since every word and gesture on a public stage had to be okayed by the Lord Chamberlain. He was a Palace official who gutted plays of any ideas that might disturb the Royal Family, and who was actually a coven of ex-Guards officers. I wanted one of them to sit at the side of the stage and blow a whistle if anything untoward seemed likely to occur, but the spectators would have chased him out of the theatre.

It was embarrassing to have visiting Russians commiserate with us over our lack of freedom. The best theatre in England (Joan Littlewood's

Theatre Workshop) was punished because one actor had imitated Churchill's voice, and another had walked across the stage carrying a board 'at a phallic angle'. Even comedians needed Royal approval for every proposed word and 'significant gesture'. Had wrestling been recognized as theatre, every throw, posture and expletive would have needed permission. Gaskill and the Board of the English Stage Society hastened the demise of this 'nannying' when they courageously presented plays by Edward Bond uncut.[2]

In spite of this censorship, the Theatre Machine was soon performing on public stages (once a week at the Cochrane Theatre, for example). I was giving comedy classes in public and the Lord Chamberlain was reluctant to open that can of worms, but Theatresports – a competition between teams of improvisers – could not be presented as 'educational'. It was just a way to liven up my impro classes until I moved to Canada, where we played it at the Secret Impro Theatre in a basement at Calgary University and then at the Pumphouse Theatre.

In the early days we gave the money back if we performed badly, and the audiences would leave the theatre searching for positive things to say – 'I liked *that* scene', '*She* was good!', 'I liked the Pecking-order' – and they'd come back to see another show, curious to know what a satisfactory performance was like.

I demonstrated the game in Vancouver (where I found an excellent theatre for it), and in Europe, and it's since spread all over the world. Eleven countries competed at the Calgary Winter Olympics, and our international summer school attracts students from over twenty countries. The Chairman of the Californian State Arts Council wrote to our funding bodies and to the Canada Council to say that our work was so valuable that they'd fund us from California if their mandate permitted.

Theatresports at Loose Moose

Loose Moose is the theatre that I founded (with Mel Tonken) in Calgary. It had been a cattle auction house and was designed so that farmers could be close to the stage and have an unimpeded view; hence the half-circle of steeply raked seats. So it was perfect for improvisers: an acting space where we could lie down and still be seen.[3]

It's two minutes past eight on a Sunday evening and the smell of popcorn tells you that you're in the presence of something populist. The opening music starts, and the spectators begin to cheer as a follow-spot weaves over them. It settles on the Commentator, who stands in front of a scoreboard high up to the right of the semicircle of the audience.

He/she welcomes the spectators and breaks the ice, perhaps asking them to: 'Tell a stranger the vegetable that you most hate!' or 'Tell someone a secret you've never told anyone!' or 'Hug the stranger closest to you.' (I'm amazed that our spectators will agree to hug each other.)

Perhaps they'll be asked to do a Mexican wave: if so, this is best led by an improviser standing centre-stage. The Commentator now becomes a disembodied voice that eases any difficulties, explains the finer points, and tells you if you've left your car headlights on. This voice can comment briefly without being intrusive, whereas emcees have to speak in paragraphs to make their interruptions seem worthwhile.

'Can we have the traditional boo for the Judges!' says the Commentator.

This is a way of giving the audience permission to boo later on (should the urge take them).

Three robed Judges cross the stage to sit in the moat that surrounds our acting area. Bicycle horns hang around their necks (these are the 'rescue horns' used to honk boring players off the stage). Their demeanour is serious, it being less fun to boo light-hearted people.

On a typical night the Commentator might introduce: 'a ten-minute challenge match played by two of our rookie teams. Give the Aardvarks a big hand . . .'

Three or four improvisers scamper on from the side opposite their team bench. This allows us a view of them as they cross the stage.

'And now, a round of applause for the Bad Billys!'

Teams at Loose Moose can sink into semi-obscurity in the two-foot-deep moat around the stage, but many groups feature their teams, lighting them at all times, and sometimes sitting them across the rear of the stage, facing front, where they are forced to sustain fixed expressions of glee (this is typical of 'Game-Show Theatresports', in which the emcee is the star and the players may be of no more consequence than the volunteers at 'give-away' shows on TV).

'A Judge and two team captains to the centre,' says the Commentator.

A coin is tossed, and perhaps the winner will create some benevolence by saying: 'You make the first challenge.'

A player crosses into 'enemy territory', and says: 'We, the Aardvarks, challenge you, the Bad Billys, to the best scene from a recent movie!' (or whatever).

'We accept!' say their opponents.

Each team improvises their 'movie' scene (challengers going first), and the Judges award points by holding up cards that range from one to five: five means excellent, one means bad, and a honk from a rescue horn means 'kindly leave the stage'. Challenge follows challenge until an agreed time is reached.

Sometimes there are 'one-on-one' challenges, in which players from the opposing teams perform together – perhaps in a 'one-on-one love scene to be judged on sincerity and truth' (one-on-one scenes may involve several players from each team). Challenges can be to anything (at the discretion of the Judges) – for example, Bruce McCulloch's challenge to 'the best scene completed in the length of time that I can submerge my head in a bucket of water'.

Scenes may drag, just as in conventional theatre, but we hope that anything tedious will be cut short by a 'Warning for Boring' (a honk from a rescue horn), and if the Judges honk a scene that everyone is enjoying there'll be mass outrage. I remember being a Judge with Suzanne Osten at Unga Klara, and witnessing her amazement at the fury generated by the Stockholm theatregoers. I asked her to turn and look at them and she saw all these happy Swedes yelling their heads off.

Penalties involve sitting for two minutes beside the scoreboard with your head in a wicker penalty basket. On rare occasions the Judges will penalize a member of the audience, perhaps for shouting an obscenity. The audience member never refuses – the peer pressure is enormous.

This beginners' game is usually followed by a fifteen-minute Free-Impro in which a 'trainer' gives a class (exactly as I did with the Theatre Machine in the sixties). This can be interesting in a quite fresh way, and the audience enjoys being initiated into the 'secrets'.

The Free-Impro is usually followed by a Danish Game (so called because I developed it in Denmark at a time when we wanted to emphasize the international appeal of Theatresports). The Judges leave, and an 'Ombud' explains the penalty basket (if it hasn't already been used), and tells the spectators that after each pair of challenges they'll be asked to shout the name of the team that 'did the best scene'. He/she drills them into yelling as loudly as possible. Some prissy Theatresports groups ask the audience to hold up coloured cards to indicate the team they prefer, but that's gutless compared to shouting a team's name as loudly as you can.

After each pair of challenges, the 'Ombud' reminds the spectators of the scenes they've just been watching (because laughter interferes with transfer from the short-term memory). 'Did you prefer the love scene in which the Executioner eloped with the Prisoner? Or the love scene in which the aged Janitor said a tearful farewell to his broom? On the count of three – One! Two! Three!'

The winners earn five points, and a new challenge is issued.

Sometimes there has to be a re-shout, and team names may have to be yelled separately, but even if we had a 'decibelometer' or whatever, we'd never use it. Yelling *en masse* is good for the soul.

Teams add variety by challenging to scenes in mime, or in gibberish, or in verse, or in song, and so forth, while the Sound Imps (Sound Improvisers) supply thunder, or explosions, or blue-grass music, or 'The Ride of the Valkyries' or punk rock, or 'The Dance of the Sugar Plum Fairy', or 'vampire music', or love themes, or flushing toilets, or whatever else is appropriate.

In every American city you can see improvisers performing with just a few chairs: not even with a desk, or a table, or with a door to slam on the way out. I blame this on mime-influenced ideas, and on 'bar-pro' (impro in bars where the stages are usually minuscule). Whenever possible I surround the players with tables covered with junk – a golf-cart, beds and bedding, wheelchairs, a boat that they can 'row' about the stage, and whatever. On tour the Theatre Machine used to raid the prop rooms – borrowing, for example, the massive Hansel and Gretel's cage from the Vienna Opera (and then not using it).

'Scenographies' are supplied by 'Snoggers', who lurk backstage ready to roll tumbleweed across the stage for a Western scene, or to drape chairs with 'mylar' for a scene in heaven.[4] They'll fold back the carpet to reveal the taped outline of a body (to establish a crime scene), or lay a black-painted ladder on the stage to indicate a 'railroad track', or they'll stand on opposite sides of the stage holding up baskets to establish a gymnasium. Audience volunteers are sometimes conscripted: I once saw fifty people run on to the stage and lie down and make sucking noises while the improvisers pretended to be duck hunters wading through a swamp.

After an hour we take a fifteen-minute break, and then our best improvisers play a Revised Match in which the winners of each challenge get an extra scene in which to pile up more points; this enables the audience to see more of the 'hottest' team.

Our audience are out of the theatre by ten o'clock at the very latest, and if the performance has gone well, you'll feel that you've been watching a bunch of good-natured people who are wonderfully cooperative, and who aren't afraid to fail. It's therapeutic to be in such company, and to yell and cheer, and perhaps even go on stage with them. With luck you'll feel as if you've been at a wonderful party; great parties don't depend on the amount of alcohol but on positive interactions.

Loose Moosers are computer experts, or doctors, or pizza cooks, or City workers, and so on. Few of them intend to earn a living using their impro skills, and nor do I encourage it, yet our alumni write for and/or perform in shows like *Saturday Night Live*, and *Roseanne*, and they work as writers and script consultants, as well as being actors and stand-up comedians. Their success has resulted in many senior players leaving Calgary, and the matches at Loose Moose are sometimes run almost entirely by teenagers who provide the music, the lighting and the commentary, and run the concessions, and so forth.

Teens who would despise any conventional 'cultural' performance will go through considerable hardship to take part in our shows because impro is 'daring', and because they get to practise exactly those interpersonal skills that they are so desperate to improve. Their self-confidence and 'grace under fire' are the abilities that posh English schools struggle to instil.

Theatresports by Stealth

Let's say that students in an impro scene are gabbling away and paying no attention to each other (because if they listened to what was being said they might be obliged to alter). You might slow them down by saying that the first student to use a word that includes an 's' loses the game; for example:

— 'Good morning, Dad.'
— 'You came in very late last night, Joan!'

Dad loses (because the word 'last' contains an 's'). Of course, if he'd been paying attention, he could have said something like: 'You came in very late . . . er . . . long after midnight, Joan!'

Students enjoy this game more if you split them into two teams and award the winner of each 'round' five points. They will now be playing a version of Theatresports.

Add more games. Say that the first player to kill an idea loses; for example:

- 'You seem out of breath. Been running?'
- 'It's my asthma . . .'

This asthma attack loses because it rejects the idea about running.

Or add a game in which you lose if you say anything that is not a question.

- 'You want to interrogate me?'
- 'You're a suspect, aren't you?'
- 'Shall I sit down here?'
- 'That's my chair.'

The suspect wins.

Ask two Team Captains to pick three or four players each. Appoint a scorekeeper, and three Judges. Ask these teams to challenge to anything that occurs to them (at the discretion of the Judges); for example, to the best master–servant scene or to an 'Indian leg-wrestle', or to the most frightening scene – whatever. Encourage the onlookers to root for their teams and tremendous enthusiasm can be released.

Give each Judge a set of scorecards from one to five, and a bicycle horn that they can honk to end boring scenes. Later on you can add a Commentator (preferably with a microphone) and you can appoint 'teckies' (sound-and-lighting improvisers) and 'snoggers' (scenographers). If you introduce the ideas piece by piece the students will feel that they thought up the game themselves.

In good circumstances, competition generates a desire to improve technique, and the teacher becomes a resource for students who are eager to master the skills – an excellent teaching situation.

Teaching the 'Form'

I'm teaching Theatresports in class, and the Fat Cats and the Aardvarks are being introduced by a Commentator, and are crossing the stage to their team benches.

I interrupt: 'Don't straggle in like separate individuals. Be attentive to each other. Be visibly a group. Don't look isolated.'

They try again.

'Better!' I say. 'But you look nervous.'

Another attempt.

'Now you look arrogant. We preferred you the first time!'

'So what are we to do?'

'Keep imagining that the spectators are even nicer than you expected. Experience a little shock of pleasure each time you look out front. Don't "demonstrate" this, just "experience" it, and trust that your positive feelings will be transmitted subliminally.'

I might ask them to imagine that they've been kept in a box full of wood-shavings all week, and that this is their one chance to be fully alive. Or I might get them to enter with their eyes narrower than usual – this will almost certainly make them feel hostile – and then I'll try for the 'rebound' effect.

'Enter again, but this time let your eyes be wide open!'

Wide-eyed students see everything in a positive light, and huge energy can be released. They'll seem less afraid of the 'space' around them, and they're likely to stop 'judging themselves'. Remove defences in life and you increase anxiety: remove them onstage and anxiety diminishes.

I get the Commentator to say: 'Can we have the regulation "boo" for the Judges!'

Two Judges cross the stage to their 'bench', while a third goes centre-stage to supervise the coin toss.

'You should all stay together,' I say.

'This saves time.'

'But then we don't see the Judges as "one organism". Cross the stage as a unit and take your places while the audience hiss and boo. Then the Commentator can cut into the booing by saying: "Head Judge to the centre for the coin toss, please!" ' (This 'Head Judge' is a fiction – one Judge must not be able to boss the other two about.)

The Fat Cats win the toss, and one of them mumbles: 'What about a master–servant scene?'

I cut in: 'You're young, you're healthy, you aren't crippled! Stride to the other half of the stage and hurl your challenge in a clear voice. Be formal; announce: "We, the Fat Cats, challenge you, the Aardvarks, to the best master–servant scene!" The voice is not just to be heard, it's a whip that disciplines the spectators. Be dynamic! Forget this Hamlet stuff of feeling queasy before the duel!'[5]

Two Fat Cats come onstage and I stop them instantly. 'What message are you giving to the audience?'

'We hadn't started!'

'But you're looking uptight! This tells the spectators that you don't want to play.'

'But we do want to play!'

'Then express some pleasure!'

They try again, and again I stop them.

'Didn't we look cheerful?'

'You were grinning away like bad circus performers!' (All teeth and tight eyes.) 'And what about your team-mates who stayed on the bench? What were they doing?'

'We weren't doing anything,' they protest.

'So what message does that give? You look as if you're relieved to have escaped a task! That won't create much benevolence!'

This time they all leap up, fighting to see who plays the scene.

'That displays you as selfish! Be eager, but be good natured enough not to mind if someone else gets to play.'

Next time they hit the stage like a wave. Two go happily back to the bench while the others scramble to drag on a table and chairs.

'Never rush when you set up the props or the furniture. Just be efficient.'

'But we don't want to keep the audience waiting.'

'The audience doesn't like players who seem stressed. They want you to be visibly in control. Theatre is an expression of vitality, but it's also a cave where human beings should feel secure.'

A master–servant scene establishes a besieged castle, and I stop them after a couple of sentences. 'Let's say that the scene is over and the Judges are slow in giving their score – what does the Commentator do?'

'Tell them to hurry up?'

'That's a bit high status. Say: "And the Judge's scores are . . ." If nothing happens, drop hints. Say quietly: "The Judges are taking their time over this decision", or: "The audience are getting restive." Never seem bossy or aggressive.'

I ask them to imagine that the Fat Cats have performed well.

Each Judge holds up a three card.

'But if it went well – why not a couple of fours? Don't be afraid to be criticized for scoring high!'

The Aardvarks leap onstage to present their scene.

'Wait!' I say: 'That's how the other team arrived. Isn't there some other way to express good nature and playfulness?'

They're baffled.

'Wish your colleagues good luck. Shake hands with them. Pretend they're boxers and that you're their seconds. Towel them. Mime putting gum-shields in their mouths. Announce them as the "Undefeated Winners" at this particular game. Let them sign autographs. You can't convey good nature, courage, affection and playfulness by being obedient!'

'But won't the Judges start to count us out?'

'I hope so [anything for variety] but when they do, just start the game!'

They are about to launch into their master–servant scene.

'Just a moment. There's a table and two chairs onstage, but that was the previous scenography. How about working on an empty stage? Or why not drag on the boat? Why not invite some audience members on to the stage and have them be distorting mirrors in a fun-fair.'

They remove the furniture while their team-mates sit in the moat and look bored.

'Whoa! Be eager to assist your colleagues [even if they're members of the other team]. This is theatre, not the work-a-day world where people are mean spirited and drag themselves about with "marks of woe".'

The Aardvarks begin their scene.

'Wait!'

'What now?'

'The other scene was set in a castle, and so is this one. Why not be two lighthouse keepers playing golf? Or God being massaged by one of the angels? Never repeat what the other team did unless they were so incompetent that you can say: "We'll show you how they should have played that scene!"'

We move on.

'Let's imagine that the Aardvarks have performed an uninspired scene. Will the Judges please score it.'

Each Judge holds up a one card.

'But if the scene was only worth a one, why were we watching it? Honk boring players off the stage. Don't let them burble on.'

It's the Aardvarks' turn to issue a challenge.

'We, the Aardvarks, challenge you, the Fat Cats, to a game requiring verbal skills.'

'That's like asking us to compare a pole-vaulter with a shot-putter. The audience wants to see the players competing in the same event.'

'All right, we challenge you to "an experience while hitch-hiking" told by an audience member!'

'We accept!'

'I'll give you a story,' I say. 'I was hitch-hiking once and I couldn't get a ride for hours, but then I saw a flying saucer and thumbed it down.'

They prepare to act this out.

'You believe that rubbish?'

'No.'

'Why accept something that you could have made up yourselves?'

'But why should a story from the audience have to be true?'

'Because then the spectators will be imagining the effect on the person who volunteered it. And you can ask them how accurate you were.'

We move on.

'Let's say that the Aardvarks have performed an amazingly funny scene. What do the Fat Cats do?'

'An even funnier scene.'

'But the audience were rocking in their seats – can you compete with that? Why not offer something slow, something serious, something "emotional"?'

I put two students centre-stage, and turn to the players on the bench: 'This scene is going splendidly – what do you do?'

'Join it!'

'But if it's going splendidly, you probably aren't needed. Stay on the bench and try to find a way to end it!'

'End it when it's going well?' they snort.

'A scene that ends when the audience is howling with laughter will get fours and fives, but if you eke it out lingeringly, you'll get a lower score. But let's suppose that a scene is going badly – what then?'

'Get on-stage and help them.'

'Absolutely! Or shout advice! Or grab the mike and add a commentary! Or mime sweeping them off the stage! Or plead with the Judges to honk a rescue horn. Or enter as Doctors and take them back to the asylum! Or as Impro-Police who arrest them for cruelty to the audience.'

If a team is 'honked off' the stage, make sure that they stay good natured. Professional actors are very likely to express anger or resentment, but no one admires this, or wants to invite them home after the game.

In at the Deep End

The first Theatresports in Vancouver was played in the evening after a two-day workshop. I introduced the concept in the last hour and suggested that the students phone a local theatre for permission to play a match that night after the regular performance. The theatre agreed, and the audience were invited to stay and had a wonderful time (as did the players).

In contrast, groups that study in private, and who are determined to 'get it right', usually give up; yet had they been thrown in front of an audience they might have had a great adventure. And some skills can't be mastered in private (like staying good natured while being publicly trashed).

So my advice is:

- Find Judges who will throw you off when you're boring.
- Play a match in public *before* you know what you're doing.
- Keep the first matches mercifully short (twenty minutes is ample and can seem like hours when you are uninspired).
- Screw-up with good humour.
- 'Lick your wounds'; practise the skills; plunge in again.

In a school context, performing in public may mean playing in front of another class, or during the lunch-hour, or challenging another school.

Disaster is Unavoidable

The first time a group works in public they may be so humble, so vulnerable, that the audience's heart goes out to them. Next time, or the time after, they'll leap onstage without a trace of humility, and the audience will say to itself: 'So they think they're funny? Let's see them prove it!' and the glory turns to ashes.

Yo-yoing between arrogance and humility when you're a beginner is as inevitable as falling off when you learn to ride a bike.

The Sticky Stage

A beginners' team is onstage with nothing to offer. Will they end their scene so that they can calm down and try again? No they won't – because they're too proud to admit defeat. But what if they did become inspired? Will they end the scene then? Not when they're basking in the warm sunshine of the audience's approval! Yet this approval can't last for ever, and when it's gone they'll be ashamed to slink off. So they're stuck, and will soon be searching desperately for a laugh to end on. This is tedious for the audience, and yet weak Judges will collude in this, thinking, We've got to give them a chance. This removes the great advantage of Theatresports, which is that dead scenes are given a quick burial.

The Magnetic Stage

Players sitting on the team-bench feel left out, so they leap in, not realizing that they should have been shouting advice, or providing sound effects, or waiting for an opportunity to wave the lights down.

I attended a match where even the 'offstage' team was constantly onstage ('being helpful to the other team'), and I was told that 'having everyone onstage is "democratic"'. Not so at Loose Moose where an experienced improviser will sometimes play against a four-person team.

'Wouldn't your audience love to see a solo performer thrust onstage and having to survive?'

'That would be "shining"!' they said. ('Shining' means showing off.)

'But it's thrilling to see a human being who is at the centre of attention, and who is without fear. Solo violinists, or magicians, or jugglers aren't shining!'

Arrogant players feel that they've failed if they're playing a submissive role, or are waiting on the bench. They leap onstage to share the glory whether they're needed or not, and yet the world's drama is based on scenes between two people. It's very difficult to find a good three-person acting scene because the third character is usually functioning as some sort of spectator – and why should improvisation be any different? Scenes that involve all the players should be the exception, not the rule.

Challenges

Issuing challenges: Keep a certain formality. Challenges should seem important. (If the players can't take the game seriously why should the onlookers?) And be brief. Most challenges are self-explanatory. If you neglect something essential – for example, that a 'miss-grab' loses a Hat-Game – the Commentator or a Judge can clarify this.

Challenge to anything: Many teams only challenge to games (and to the same games), but unexpected and unheard-of challenges keep the players alert. Challenge to novelties like a spelling-bee, or to the most convincing impersonation of a celebrity, or to the best scene with an audience member, or to the best scene directed by the other team. Take risks. Challenges that seem stupid, incomprehensible or repetitive can always be rejected (at the discretion of the Judges).

Some groups want to ban challenges that 'always fail' (there was once a move to veto the He Said/She Said Game, but if we avoided every game that a group disliked, the difficult ones would never be mastered. The problem lies not in the games, but in weak Judges who let uninspired scenes drag on. If the players are boring (which they will be if they're screwing up a game), throw them off.

Great teams brain-storm to find new challenges; for example: to the funniest joke, to the best one-minute radio drama played in the dark (this gives our audience a chance to cuddle), to the best scene featuring an object chosen by the other team (at the Olympics, Calgary offered a live goat[6]), to the best scene using an audience volunteer (off-limits to beginners because volunteers must be treated with love and generosity and this takes skill), to the best enactment of a folk tale (with an audience volunteer as the Hero), to the best love scene with a tragic ending, to the best excuse, to the best lie, to the best exposure of an injustice, to the best revenge, to the best escape, to the most com-passionate scene, to the best use of the other team (e.g., as a blob in a science-fiction movie, as furniture, as bowling balls), to the most serious, positive, truthful, romantic, horrific, or boring scene (the Danes at the Olympics presented an unforgettable 'most boring consummation of a marriage'), to a family relationship, to a scene with pathos, and so on.

Great teams set themselves goals like including audience volunteers in every scene, or playing each scene in gibberish, but when teams only challenge to Theatre Games (and to the same games week after week) this creates the same monotony as soup followed by soup followed by soup. Games are for providing contrast, and should be interspersed between stories, or between challenges to 'the best religious scene', or 'to the most psychotic scene', or whatever.

The need for variety: Wonderful challenges are sometimes created in the heat of the moment, but when inspiration fails, each challenge is likely to resemble the one before. A scene in which someone asks for a job is followed by another scene in which someone asks for a job. Some groups try to solve this by issuing vague challenges; for example: 'We challenge you to a scene involving physical skills', but then Theatresports moves further away from sport (because there's less direct comparison between the teams). The Audience team[7] would avoid such problems by shouting: 'The book! The book!' in pretended panic, and run to open a book in which they had written possible challenges. If you create such a book, write verbal challenges in one column, physical challenges in another, solo challenges in another, and so on.

Duration of challenges: Some groups expect every scene to last for six minutes (or whatever), but this diminishes variety. Others assume that a scene that lasts a quarter of an hour is better than one that lasts thirty seconds. I've seen matches in which not one scene pleased the performers, and yet they struggled to make them all last for at least six minutes. It would have been better to say: 'This is garbage! Can we start again!'

Avoid 'lock-ins': Don't trap yourself by announcing what will happen unless you have to. For example: if the Commentator has said: 'And now for the final challenge', and the scenes are dreary, it becomes difficult for the Judges to add a further challenge. Another example: a Director set up a dramatic scene, and over-directed it by saying: 'You can only use three-word sentences.' It would have been better to add this instruction later in the scene – if it was needed.

Baulking: A challenge can be baulked at (refused) at the discretion of the Judges. Such baulks add variety and give the spectators something to discuss on the way home. Typical baulks might be: 'We want to baulk at that challenge on the grounds that everyone's sick of it!' Or: 'We think that challenge is too vague.' Or: 'We'd like to baulk unless they can make us understand what they mean!' Or: 'We've just had two scenes in verse. Does anyone really want them to be followed by two singing scenes?'

If a baulk is upheld, a fresh challenge must be issued, and if this should also prove unacceptable, the Judges must issue a challenge of their own.

Judges can also baulk. They can say: 'We object to that game!' (and give reasons); or they can drop hints, for example: 'If you'd like to baulk at that we'll be delighted to uphold you!'

I've seen Judges baulk at a challenge to 'the best suicide in slow-motion', asking that the challenge be made more general; for example, 'to the most interesting suicide'.

Baulks should never be accepted automatically; for example:

'We challenge you to the best scene involving a beard!'

'We baulk at that!'

'On what grounds?'

'On the grounds that they've got beards and we haven't!'

'Overruled!'

Correct! After all, a clean-shaven team could improvise beards from wigs, or a scientist could invent a hair-restorer so powerful that a SWAT team has to shave its way into him.

When three members of a team were sitting with their heads in penalty baskets (a rare occurrence), the fourth player baulked at a challenge to: 'the best four-person pecking-order'. This was overruled on the grounds that the audience would be delighted to see one person play four different characters (or working with three audience volunteers).

Players wishing to be cooperative will agree to be in scenes that hold not the slightest interest for them (or for us), but it's better to baulk than to collude in mutual self-destruction.

The Warning for Boring

He is terrified of becoming 'too respected', he explains, 'because they don't tell you when you are bad'.
Interview with Sir John Gielgud, *Guardian Weekly*, 8 November 1996

If a team receives a 'Warning for Boring' they have to end their scene and leave the stage (it's not a 'warning' but the real thing, but it sounds less insulting than a cry of 'boooorrring').

'Warnings' are given by a 'honk' of the rescue horn that each Judge wears around his/her neck. Before I bought these horns, 'warnings' were given by a zero card, but it feels less 'teachery' to be 'honked' off, rather than 'zeroed' off. (Judges can also end a scene by waving the lights down, as can the lighting operators or team members if they see a suitable moment.)

Even experienced players will plod on, hoping for inspiration that never comes. Our players will sometimes storm into our green room after a bad show saying: 'Where were the boring-calls when we needed them!' (as if forbidden to end boring scenes themselves), but there is a minority of players who so enjoy being the centre of attention that they don't care if they're tedious. I heard one say: 'I'm a performer – why should I care what the audience think?' (making me wonder about his sex life). Such players will complain that the warning is being given (or that the lights are fading), before people have lost interest, but could there possibly be a better time? The audience will howl with rage if a scene is honked unjustifiably, and this unites them with the actors against the Judges (good!), and yet selfish players will resent the 'injustice'.

'No Judge can be right all the time,' I say. 'And Theatresports is not a school where everyone's prestige depends on being marked correctly. After all, you're not being cast out into the tundra during a blizzard.'

'But don't you realize what a depressing effect the warning has on the audience?'

'It does if the players skulk off like whipped dogs, but it's heart-warming to see improvisers who are thrown off and stay good natured.'

'I didn't go through drama school to be told I was boring!'

'If you want to be dignified, why improvise?'

Handled ineptly, warnings can be brutal, but used properly they create benevolence. The spectators adore improvisers who can be thrown offstage and yet stay happy.

Accepting the Warning

At least one group softens the warning by saying that it just means 'that the players failed to see a possible ending'. This goes against the nature of sport. The spectators want to see boxers being knocked out, speed-boats flipping over, and improvisers being told unequivocally that their scene has failed. Boring means boring, and many scenes are boring after twenty seconds (already irredeemably stupid).

Instead of learning how to be rejected with good humour – which can take all of five minutes – many groups remove the warning, and other groups give the players two or three minutes to 'find an ending', perhaps signalling this by throwing in a towel, yet minutes of boredom may have preceded this (if the Judges are timid). Throwing in a towel shows an extraordinary greed for stage-time, because it admits defeat, and yet still demands a chance to 'wrap up the scene'. (Why 'wrap-up' something bad when you can flush it away instantly?) Another unsatisfactory solution is to impose time limits on all scenes, sometimes as little as one or two minutes ('unsatisfactory' because players should learn how to end scenes by themselves). I've even heard of Theatresports being advertised as 'no scene over ninety seconds', which might make some sense if the entire event only lasted for fifteen minutes, but why kill scenes that have a lot of power and energy? Perhaps weak judges had allowed boring scenes to drag on pointlessly, and the ninety-second rule was an act of desperation.

In the early days we were so protective of the players' feelings that a team kept possession of the stage until the third warning, and all warnings had to be unanimous. Then we threw teams off after the second warning. Finally, after much heart-searching, we decided that justice was less important than getting dead scenes off the stage, and we said that any Judge could end any scene at any time (without consultation), but even then dreary scenes were sometimes allowed to continue while the bored Judges toyed with their rescue horns but were reluctant to 'do the deed'.

These days the so-called Hell-Judges (improvisors who are sitting at the rear of the audience, see p. 324) can press a button when they're bored. This flashes a red 'Hell light' at the Judges' feet, and in the lighting booth. The official Judges can ignore this, but it's likely to shake them out of their apathy.

I could have invented more discrete ways to remove improvisers from the stage – as in 'comedy lounges' where the comedian has to leave when a picture lights up behind the bar – but I wanted the warnings to be blatant because I was tired of the audience that 'appreciates' theatre and says, 'I quite liked it', as if discussing a dubious egg.

Misbehaviour

My group, the Theatre Machine, gave hundreds of performances, and toured abroad, and yet we had no competitors. This puzzled me until I realized that we were presenting a continuing skirmish between me and the players; they would start one scene while I was setting up another; I would force them to complete undigested material, and they would retaliate by doing the opposite of whatever I was asking. There was always some craziness going on, and the result was about as academic as the films of Will Hay (a comedian who played a harassed schoolteacher). Other groups would have seen this byplay as 'not part of the show', and as 'not worth imitating', and yet it had changed a comedy class into a popular entertainment.

Had you attended the All-Star Show in Calgary – usually me 'fronting' four performers – you might have seen me whisper to them, after which the show would have noticeably improved. It might have seemed as if some profound advice was being given (maybe it was), but

I'd have been saying: 'Misbehave! Make my life difficult! Screw me up!'

At first, the average Theatresports team sees such 'misbehaviour' as an opportunity to ruin the work of its opponents. There'll be nothing good natured about it, and the audience will hate them. You can see such destructive misbehaviour when the players on the bench shout out irrelevancies which are meant to express their good nature, but which make them sound like ill-mannered drunks; yet if you misbehave brilliantly, the audience will adore you, and see you as playful 'children'. A team that insisted on getting penalties deliberately would be disruptive, but a team that earned a penalty by decorating the stage with flowers would be spreading 'good vibes'.

I'll give some examples:

- A scene ends, and one of the players pretends to trip into the moat as he leaves the stage.
- At the end of a Danish Game, both teams piled on top of the Ombud (emcee). Then one emerged with her and carried her backstage (this mock rape was not 'politically correct', but the audience roared its approval). If it had happened mid-game, it would have been intolerable.
- Norm Hitchcock 'lost a hat' in a Hat-Game and another scene was in progress before anyone noticed that he was still frozen in the same position. This happened fifteen years ago, but the memory still gives me pleasure.
- Roger Fredericks ate his bouquet during the medal presentation at the Calgary Olympics. This was far more entertaining than having to watch the winners stand to attention during a tedious speech (but please don't do this – 'shop' flowers are sprayed with noxious chemicals).
- A loser crossed the stage to the winning team, said, 'We'd like to present you with this plaque!', and stapled it to one of their foreheads (using an empty stapler and a plaque that was backed with sticky tape).
- A Commentator said, 'And tonight the technicians in the booth are naked!' The audience looked back at the booth and it seemed to be true (only the top halves of our technicians are visible).
- We decided to start the show with a 'warm-up' for the players, and the Commentator muttered, 'Nothing worse than a cold improviser.'
- A team gave coffee and doughnuts to the front row.
- A team said, 'We want to baulk at that challenge!'
  'On what grounds?'

'On the grounds that we think we'll lose!'

- A player who received a stupid answer from an audience member turned away, saying, 'I'll go over here and ask the more mature side.'
- Happy music introduced the Free-Impro and the players danced around the Trainer in a gleeful circle.
- A team raised fake scorecards and awarded mock-points to their rivals (it had been a wretched scene but they were giving it fives). The Judges called a 'time-out' and collected the cards. Had the team then produced another set of cards this would certainly have earned them a penalty for disrupting the game, and had they been awarding zeros, or ones, this would not have been an expression of good nature.
- An excellent way to misbehave is by offering more volunteers than are needed. If I'm leading a section of Free-Impro and I ask for two volunteers, sixteen people may dash on to the stage and pile on to the sofa. This creates good humour, and displays the performers as fearless (even if they aren't).
- At the Calgary Olympics, the British took the audience's photo, and later on they gave the camera to a spectator and posed for their own photograph. The Judges had to call the match to order, but from then on the audience was in love with the British.

If misbehaviour is understood, everyone becomes bolder. It works best if it's used to fill dead time. Avoid it and there'll always be something slavish about your work.

Using Audience Volunteers

Audience volunteers interest the spectators in a fresh way, and the time spent improvising with them doesn't feel like 'part of the show'. Never abuse them (as happens in stand-up comedy), and when they kill idea after idea – as they will – you must somehow manoeuvre them into being successful. Always be seen to be making them the centre of attention (they will be anyway, so you might as well take the credit for it). Give them free tickets or T-shirts, or tokens for the concessions. Treat them with love, courtesy and respect, and it's as if you've treated the whole audience with love, courtesy and respect; yet I've seen volunteers who were wandering about in a scene with the players ignoring them; who were asked to be the hero of an adventure which became an excuse for the players to shine; who were not introduced; who were not given prizes;

who were not thanked; who were not accompanied back to their seats.

Many groups work with audience volunteers a few times and then give up, but this may be because they treated them horribly. Another reason could be that the best time to invite volunteers on to the stage is when you don't need them, that is, when things are going really well. Any volunteer you get when things are going badly is a fool who is not worth having. Never let people volunteer each other, and never invite anyone who avoids your eye. Reject people who are over-eager.

Dennis Cahill sometimes clutches his head and does a 'Victorian mind-reader' act in which he senses that 'someone wants to volunteer' – then he plunges into the audience and emerges with someone who held eye contact with him.

Let volunteers open and close their mouths while the players dub their voices, or tell the players to be puppets, and have audience volunteers manipulate them in scenes (the 'puppets' providing the dialogue).

Be inventive. I've lain down on the stage and said that nothing will happen until we get eight volunteers to play a ten-minute Theatresports match. We listened to music until eight sheepish people emerged. The audience cheered everything they did with wild enthusiasm.

Mime

Improvisers will mime a door and step through the 'wall' beside it; their mimed cup will 'dissolve' into nothingness; they'll throw back their heads to 'quaff from a full tumbler' which would have drenched them if it contained liquid.

These 'mistakes' are messages that say: 'See how incompetent I am? This is not my "field". Ignore the mime – just enjoy the dialogue!'

This may reassure the performer but it doesn't please anyone else, so I shout things like: 'Take your time! Don't walk away from your "horse" before you climb off it! Where did the flowers go when you embraced your lover? Hold the cup level! Stop walking through her refrigerator!' And so on.

Some players avoid the problem by reducing mime to 'blips'. They'll go to the 'kitchen', gesticulate for a split second, and return holding a mimed cup of 'steaming coffee'.

'Slow down!' I say. 'The kettle can't possibly have boiled yet – you didn't even have time to fill it!' ('Blip' mime can be useful, but it shouldn't always be used.)

If students will mime as well as they can, they'll improve very quickly. If your mime seems unintelligible, tell the spectators what you were trying to convey and they'll love you for your humility.

If you're 'scrubbing the floor' or 'cleaning boots', or 'brushing someone's hair', try not to touch the actual surface. Work about an inch away. And never clench your fist tight if it's meant to be holding something that has bulk.

Mimed objects are sticky. Place a 'real' cup on a table. Now repeat this in mime, and it'll seem as if you set a mimed cup on to the table and picked it up again (the 'release' being so small that it went unnoticed). 'Over-release' mimed objects when you put them down or they'll seem stuck to you.

Why is Theatresports a Comic Form?

One reason is that comic improvisation is often as funny or funnier then rehearsed comedy. For example, when I'm giving workshops to a theatre company I might say, 'Let's invite the spectators to stay after your performance tonight so that we can improvise for them?'

The actors will agree happily, but when the time comes they'll be scared stiff. They needn't worry, though, because the audience will soon be howling with laughter, and far more violently than they would at comedies that may have taken months to rehearse.

If these are traditional European actors (trained in a stodgy intellectual way), they may sit up long into the night – hours after I'm fast asleep – trying to make sense of the audience's readiness to laugh. Perhaps they'll understand that people so love spontaneity that they were reacting as if watching a sporting event.

Another reason why public improvisation tends to be comic is that an evening of serious scenes would be like seeing a series of car crashes in which we empathized with the victims. Classical tragedy packages a tragic episode that may last only fifteen minutes, and Shakespearean tragedy uses poetry and clowning so that the misery won't exhaust us. Sometimes in a 'serious' impro class ice coats the walls and forms lumps in our stomachs so that we have to give up and go away. If we keened and howled our grief with the same passion that we laugh this might not happen, but the emotion stays locked up inside us. Hence there are film compilations like *The World of Chaplin* but none called *The Best of Ibsen*.

Types of Player

- *Bridgemasters* build 'bridges' to destinations that could have been reached in one stride.
- *Bulldozers* crash uncaringly or unknowingly through other players' ideas and scenes.
- *Directors* want to make all the decisions. They order other improvisers about and criticize them (some do this onstage: others confine it to the bench).
- *Dullards* make 'negative choices' and lower the stakes.
- *Gagsters* go for the laugh at the expense of all else.
- *Glibsters* resist emotional involvement (especially pathos). They may be skilled at pushing the action forward, but nothing 'touches' them.
- *Hysterics* are so excited that they're almost impossible to control (is that their intention?). They gabble incessantly, even if this means repeating the same phrase.
- *Passengers* accept ideas, but they won't 'drive' a scene forward. Every improviser should practise this skill – because sometimes it's fine to let someone else take the wheel.
- *Shiners* want to be centre-stage, even when the audience is bored stiff. Such 'star' behaviour may bear little relation to the players' actual achievement. Asked how the show went, they'll tell you how it went for them.
- *Gagsters*, *Glibsters* and *Passengers* can be useful; but *Bridgemasters*, *Bulldozers*, *Directors*, *Dullards*, *Hysterics* and *Shiners* can be a pest.
   Even the best improvisers revert to 'type' when they get rattled.

What Theatresports Can Achieve

Some people (often fervent capitalists and sports fans) condemn Theatresports on the grounds that it's competitive, but while 'straight' theatre encourages competition – and I could tell you stories that you'd hardly believe – Theatresports can take jealous and self-obsessed beginners and teach them to play games with good nature, and to fail gracefully.

   When Theatresports is played by people who've had minimal or zero contact with me, you may be seeing a copy of a copy of a copy – and with each step it will have become 'safer' and sillier, but when the players are experts, and the quality is reasonable, Theatresports can:

- alleviate the universal fear of being stared at;
- turn 'dull' people into 'brilliant' people (i.e. 'negative' people into 'positive' people);
- improve interpersonal skills and encourage a life-long study of human interaction;
- improve 'functioning' in all areas (as it says on the snake-oil bottles);
- develop story-telling skills (these are more important than most people realize);
- familiarize the student with the bones of theatre as well as the surface;
- give the stage back to the performers;
- allow the audience to give direct input, or even to improvise with the performers, rather than sit trying think up intelligent things to say on the way home

I hope that after using this book you'll agree that such claims are justified.

NOTES

1 Jackie 'Mr TV' Pallo, *You Grunt, I'll Groan* (London: Queen Anne Press, 1985). If you still have a trace of doubt about pro-wrestling being theatre, I should mention that a wrestler is being sued by World Champion Wrestling because his failure to appear for a series of bouts 'played havoc with the story-lines' (*Globe and Mail*, 5 May 1998).

2 People don't realize when works of art have been censored. I wanted Devine to freeze the action for the space of time that deleted material would have occupied, perhaps with a commentary describing what the spectators were missing. Movies could fill in the blanks with the face of the censor and his address and phone number.

3 Alas! We have now moved out of this splendid theatre and into a sometime cinema, where we have the same sight-line problems, etc. as other groups.

4 Sean Kinley transformed 'snogging' from a chore into an art form.

5 'But you wouldst not think how ill all's here about my heart . . .' etc. – lines that must have been added by an actor because the coming transitions are weakened if Hamlet is already depressed.

6 When Calgary was host to the Winter Olympics the International Olympic Committee funded a tournament with groups from many countries.

7 This team left Calgary to 'make good'. Several of them write and/or perform for major American TV shows, e.g., *The Kids in the Hall* and *Saturday Night Live*. They called themselves The Audience Team to spread the maximum confusion.

2 Audience Suggestions

'Who would you like us to be?'
Bored voice: 'Surprise us!'

'Give me an activity starting with an "L".'
Hostile voice: 'Leave!'

No One Cares

Asking the audience for suggestions before each scene is the only method
some groups know, but it pushes Theatresports towards 'light entertainment' (increasing the percentage of utter trivia), and can result in shows
in which there isn't one scene that the players actually want to be in.

I asked an emcee of the Boston Improvisation Group why he did this,
and he said (predictably) that he had to, 'or the audience wouldn't believe
we were improvising'. At that exact moment an elderly man interrupted
us, saying, 'Excuse me, but how much do you pay the people who shout
out the suggestions? And what could I earn in an average week?'[1]

Even then the emcee didn't seem to get the message that the
spectators believe even the worst scenes to have been rehearsed. This is
the agony of public improvisation, that on a bad night you are seen not
only as untalented, but as bereft of good taste and any common sense.

Why should an audience be expected to lower its standards if they
know that a show is unscripted? Would a disgusting meal taste better if
the waiter said, 'Ah, but the chef is improvising!' The truth is that people
come for a good time and nobody cares how the scenes are created
except other improvisers. Dario Fo was entertaining seventy thousand
people in a football stadium when lightning began ripping across the
sky, so he launched into an impromptu debate with God. Was he
improvising? Mightn't he have been basing it on old material? Who
cares? It must have been wonderful either way.

When the Theatre Machine strayed into 'old material', I would head
them off, not because they were 'cheating', but because fresh material is
more exhilarating.[2]

Laughter Misleads

'Who's giving the suggestions?'

'The audience, of course!'

'Take a look. Perhaps the suggestions are coming from a few malcontents who want to be funnier than you.'

Even malevolent suggestions are accepted if they get a laugh.

– What do I have?

– Worms coming out of your nose!

The actor mimes this, not realizing that it's an insult. In any audience there may always be a few individuals who are plotting your downfall – like those oafs who threw birdseed at Edna Squire Brown and Her Educated Doves (a striptease act).

An actor is sent out of earshot while the audience are asked for three activities to communicate to her. Male voices shout: 'Picking her nose!' 'Gutting a chicken!' 'Shaving her armpits!' These suggestions are made by men who want to see a woman humiliated, and yet they are accepted gleefully.

Request an activity when a performance is going really badly and someone will yell, 'Shovelling manure!' The players will then pretend to shovel manure.

When I fronted the Theatre Machine I would ask for a suggestion about once every hour (as a gesture of goodwill). This gave no chance for the 'wits' in the audience to get into a feeding frenzy. I'd never imagined that improvisers would one day be asking for suggestions before every scene and enslaving themselves to the whim of aberrant individuals. After all, who are the experts at setting up scenes? We are! Not some klutz in the audience who is just trying to get a laugh.

'But suggestions add variety.'

'But the same suggestions keep recurring: ask for a room in a house and someone will shout, "The bathroom." Ask for a profession and someone will shout, "Gynaecologist!" Ask for three objects after a Frankenstein scene, and you're likely to get "a scalpel" a "brain" and a "heart–lung machine" because that's where the audience's "head" is.'

Building a tower of suggestions almost guarantees that the scene will be a disaster, and yet this often happens when the first suggestion is felt to be unsatisfactory.

– What character should I be?
– The Easter Bunny!
  [*The improviser isn't inspired by this idea.*]
– And what's so special about this Easter Bunny?
– He's wearing scuba gear!
  [*This gets a big laugh because it's intended to screw him up.*]
– And what's the Easter Bunny's problem?
– He's got no legs!
  [*An even bigger laugh, and his colleagues come onstage like walking wounded, deluded into believing that the audience actually wants to see a scene with a paraplegic Easter Bunny wearing scuba gear.*]

Howie Mandel made fun of such improvisers in an American TV special:

'Who am I?' he said.
'A Doctor!' shouted a voice.
'And give me a place to be?'
'In a hospital!' (They liked him, they weren't trying to screw him up.)
'And what's my problem?'
'Your patient is dying!' (Negative, but not stupid.)
'And now tell me something funny to do!' he said sarcastically, and turned to something more interesting.

Self-revelation should be at the heart of improvising, but suggestions offer a way to hide the performers' true identities. 'Tickling a moose in shark-infested custard while licking food-stamps' will create utter rubbish, but it involves zero risk that anyone's secret self will be exposed.

Joan Rivers, thinking back to her youth, wrote: 'I had no consistent image of myself onstage – and never thought about it. There was no core to me, nothing that made it all the same girl. I was only trying to be a funny girl . . . The minute there was no laugh, there was no me – and the audience knew it instantly.'

Milt Kamen told her that 'comedy has to come from your centre, from who you really are . . .' but she found that this was 'still a concept too large, too all-encompassing, too frightening for me to grasp and make my own.'[3]

Start 'cold', and where will the ideas come from? From you, and then there's a chance that your inner demons may be released, and that's the price you pay for being an artist.

Traps

– Who am I?
– Copernicus!

One in five North Americans believe that the sun goes round the earth, so that's not helpful, but even if President Clinton or Donald Duck are suggested, can your imitation bear scrutiny?

Instead of asking 'Who am I?', ask for a 'profession', or for a 'relationship' (especially a family relationship), and reject any suggestion that fails to inspire you.

– Where am I?
– Bangladesh!

Bangladesh is 'funny' because it's associated with starvation but the improvisers don't feel competent to deal with 'starvation' on the spur of the moment, so the suggestion paralyses them.

Ask for a location that will inspire you, and reject any that don't (Derek Flores once accepted 'bathroom', but then exited through the mirror into an *Alice in Wonderland* universe).

'Can we have a place to end at?' This encourages the players to 'bridge', to 'mark time' until they achieve the agreed ending. This leads to dreary scenes.

'What's our problem?' If you insist on asking this, ask it before the audience knows the nature of the scene or saboteurs will shout, 'You can't swim!' for a scene about a Channel swimmer, or, 'You've got no legs!' for a scene about the Frog Prince.

Rejecting Suggestions

Ask, with just a trace of disapproval or boredom, 'Do people really want to see that?' Or say, 'We did that last week!', or 'We've done that so often.' If you're asked to be a proctologist (yet again), just say, good-naturedly, 'Not your profession, sir!' If you ask for a subject to improvise a poem on and you get 'existentialism', say cheerfully, 'Could someone suggest something I can understand?'

Never be ashamed to admit ignorance. One panicky player agreed to be a buzzard in a scene although she had no idea what a buzzard was (the Judges intervened).

Scene Sale

When I'm told that the spectators expect the scenes to be based on their suggestions, I say that it's because we've trained them that way, and that we've also trained them to make stupid suggestions.

I invented the Scene Sale as a way to affirm that the players are not the audience's slaves. Use it once and the audience understands instantly that a stupid idea that gets a laugh may be useless as the basis for a scene.

A player becomes an 'auctioneer' and gets the spectators to 'bid' for a scene, checking with the other players to see whether any suggestion inspires them.

- We want a suggestion that thrills us.
- Brazil!
- What does that mean? You want a scene in Brazil?
  [*The improvisers give it a thumbs down.*]
- Climbing a mountain?
- What do you want to happen on that mountain?
- You meet a yeti!
- Anyone want to accept that? What else are we offered.
- Your daughter arrives home with an old schoolfriend of yours.
- Er . . . Does anyone like that idea?
  [*The improvisers shake their heads.*]
- You're an old man, and the schoolfriend is even older than you are!
- And your daughter is only fifteen!
- We accept!

The enthusiasm that this creates among the actors gives a reasonable chance that the scene will be worth watching.

Use Restraint

Suggestions are overused, and are responsible for scenes that are dead at the starting gate, and they are used as an excuse for failure ('What can they expect if they ask us to put an elephant into panty-hose?').

We can go months without asking the spectators for a suggestion, and yet no one ever mentions the fact. The audience would rather see good scenes than sit watching players who are uninspired or stymied.

Never accept a suggestion that fails to inspire you, or that is degrading (it can hardly have escaped your notice that the 'putting an elephant in panty-hose' suggestion is anti-women).

If you accept a suggestion, do it. 'Birth' was accepted as an activity, but the scene was about a mother and a baby. 'Revenge' was accepted, but no one was revenged.

A suggestion may get a laugh, but don't assume that anyone wants to see a scene based on it. In general, the funnier the suggestion, the less use it's likely to be.

Repeat the suggestion clearly, even if you are sure that everyone has heard it. Audiences like you to exercise your authority: it makes them feel safer.

NOTES

1 The American actor Nat Warren White was with me and can confirm this.
2 When I gave workshops at Chicago's Second City Improvisation Theatre, the players asked for suggestions before the interval, and presented scenes based on them after the interval. I sat backstage with them while they found ways to adapt old material to the suggestions. This was their preferred method, and why not, if it gives good results? However, since then I've seen an interview with their touring company in which they said they were 'using the Loose Moose method of asking for suggestions immediately before the scene because it brought back the excitement'.
3 Joan Rivers with Richard Meryman, *Enter Talking* (New York: Delacorte Press, 1986).

3 Trouble with Feedback

Racine read his plays to his cook and rejected what she couldn't understand.

Getting Educated

When I was young we thought that we should 'educate the audience', but I began to suspect that the audience should be educating us.

'But, Keith, we have the knowledge!'

'No, we don't! We're just guessing, but they know when to laugh, and when to be silent, and when to weep, and when to unwrap their chocolates. They may not be able to verbalize their knowledge but they have it.'

(Lenny Bruce expressed the same idea when he said that, taken individually, each spectator may be an idiot, but when the audience react *en masse* it's a genius.)

'But, Keith, if the audience educate us we'll end up just doing "light entertainment." '

'Maybe. Maybe not.'

Fools' Paradise

Fighting the laughter creates benevolence, because when the audience laughs, it laughs in unison, whereas 'cheap laughs' fragment it.

It can be entertaining to watch clowns play the piano wearing boxing-gloves, but the novelty wears off. This is easy to understand, intellectually, but players are conditioned to be funny every time they walk on to a stage. They don't hear the trickle of the audience's tears, or the crackle of tiny goose-pimples, but they're responsive to every chuckle ('They're laughing! We must be on the right track!') Yet if the laughs don't come, and there's nothing on offer except gags, the players can be embarrassed for weeks.

The solution is to base Theatresports on storytelling. Stories hold the interest even when the audience aren't laughing, so it's unfortunate that the easiest way to get a laugh is by undermining the story. If your Oedipus has a dog called Rex and your Macbeth has a 'kilty conscience' then we're back to square one.

Laughter misleads. Sometimes it's just drunks, teenagers and other improvisers who are laughing, while the bulk of the audience sits with folded arms.

'But isn't laughter the whole point of Theatresports?'

'Wouldn't you like to make people weep?'

'Yes.'

'Wouldn't you like them to thrill with horror?'

'Of course.'

'Don't you want them awestruck? Filled with suspense? And compassion?'

'Absolutely!'

'Well that can't happen if laughter is the measure of all things!'

I'd like people to laugh so much that their warts 'ping' off, but they get exhausted. They need love scenes, or scenes with pathos, so that they can recharge their batteries. A show where you laugh more at the beginning than at the end is a disappointment. Moss Hart discovered this when the try-outs of his comedy *Once in a Lifetime* were such a disaster. Sam Harris enlightened him, saying with a sigh,

> I wish, kid, that this weren't such a noisy play . . . I've watched this play through maybe a hundred times, and I think . . . that it tires an audience out . . . Sure they laugh, but I think they're longing to see that stage just once with maybe two or three people on it quietly talking the whole thing over . . . Once this show gets under way nobody ever talks to each other. They just keep pounding away like hell and running in and out of that scenery . . .

Hart removed many jokes, and gave the audience spaces where it could rest, and the play became funnier; not 'funny all the time', but funny up to the final curtain. Moss said, 'All the old stumbling blocks that we had uselessly battered our heads against seemed to resolve themselves smoothly and naturally.'[1]

When I directed the Theatre Machine (from onstage) I wanted the spectators to laugh hysterically for the first few minutes so that they knew they were in our power; then I fought the laughter, easing up just before the interval, and only letting it rip for ten minutes at the end of the performance.

Gags are fine for fifteen minutes, but not for hour after hour, because even if they're 'fresh', it'll soon be like a 'banquet of anchovies', as some classical author said about reading Seneca.

Destructive Feedback

Pick your nose in life, and we'll discourage you, but do it on a stage, and some fools may laugh or even cheer and this 'validates' the behaviour. Drool on stage and a chuckle will encourage you to drool again. Should this process continue unchecked, you'll be known as 'the drooling comedian', which was not your ambition.

Rock stars are under similar pressures. If they move their hands near their pelvis the teeny-boppers will scream. This coaxes the unwary to move their hands nearer and nearer to their crotch until they're leaping about the stage clutching themselves (it's even become a fashion). Oprah Winfrey asked Michael Jackson why he did this and he said, 'I think it's just me,' unaware that audiences had conditioned him to do it.

Being 'Over-cheered'

I've seen Theatresports in fifty-seat theatres where everything the players did was received with whoops and shrieks (the few genuine members of the public were looking around as if they'd come to the wrong party). The players knew that their friends and fellow-improvisers were generating this phoney feedback and yet they were misled by it (just as painted lips and false eye-lashes work their magic although we're aware of the artifice).

There are processes in the audience that are very subtle: a growing identification with the players, an excitement that comes from wondering if the performance will be a success, the expectation of a miracle. This 'communion' is destroyed when a section of the audience cheers indiscriminately.

Long ago I saw a video of Robin Williams's stand-up performance in San Francisco where the audience so approved of him that he couldn't 'sense' them properly. He was like a fisherman in despair because the fish are leaping eagerly into his boat and yet not one of them is worth having. He did a 'comedian in hell' routine, and made 'penis' jokes, and after the show 'ended' he kept wandering back on stage, desperate for that moment-by-moment rapport when the audience responds with

exquisite sensitivity. Then he dragooned a volunteer to play improvisation games with him, which might have been thrilling had it been a
waitress – because everyone would have been genuinely interested – but
he chose another celebrity (John Ritter) and this compounded the
problem. He finally gave up and raced to his dressing room. The camera
lurched after him, and found him huddled in a corner. Asked 'how it
went' he said (as far as I remember), 'Great audience.'

Improvisers who are being over-cheered should do absolutely nothing
until people come to their senses.

Group-Yes

I had been mulling over descriptions of small aboriginal groups in which
decisions are made by total agreement, rather than by voting, so when I
arrived at class I asked the students to say, 'Yes!' to any suggestion,
explaining that the suggestions should come from everyone – that there
were to be no leaders: 'If you can't respond with genuine enthusiasm,
please leave the group and sit quietly at the side. We'll time how long the
group can sustain itself, so don't fake it! Is that agreed?'

'Yesss!'

'You promise not to say, "Yes!" to any suggestion unless you really
mean it?'

'Yesss!'

Rats will leave a sinking ship, but few improvisers will leave a sinking
scene, so perhaps I'll make them raise their rights hands and swear that
they'll leave the moment that they feel the slightest reluctance.

'You accept these conditions?'

'Yesss!'

'You want to begin?'

'Yesss!'

The improvisers then usually start with sequences like:

'Let's sit down!'

'Let's stand up!'

'Let's jump up and down!'

'Let's lie down and rest.'

'Let's sleep!'

'Let's dream!'

'Let's wake up!'

The cancelling of the dream may lose a few people, but the nature of the suggestions gradually changes, and begins to take the group on adventures.

'Let's wiggle our toes!'

'Let's wiggle our whole bodies!'

'Let's hug each other!'

'Let's be on a beach!'

'Let's swim!'

'Let's dive down deeper!'

Their first attempts will probably disintegrate in less than a minute, but the group soon learns to sustain itself, and as the negative ideas drop out, the energy increases, and they invent and reinvent 'sensitivity games' at breakneck speed.

I drag out those students who won't leave even though they're visibly unenthused, and afterwards I remind everyone that the game is an investigation of what the group wants, and that only if the players are honest will it give accurate feedback.

Some seemingly cooperative but 'clever' students wreck the game every time. They intend to unite the group, but their 'clever' suggestions are out of step, and suddenly they're alone. This rather shocking feedback trains them to be obvious, rather then 'clever'.

This game soon begins to resemble 'primitive' ceremonies; individuals are singled out, and hoisted high, and carried around, and sacrificed, and buried, and resurrected (if the group begins by isolating unpopular students, please move on to something else). About fifteen minutes into a Group-Yes drumming is likely to be 'discovered' (on the wall, on the floor, etc.). The noise can be tremendous so choose the place and time carefully, and insist that the players stay within the limits of the area agreed. If things are getting too wild, just shout, 'Let's sleep!' or 'Let's stop!' (The group can't get really out of control because they'd be unable to hear the suggestions.)

I played Group-Yes with large numbers of people at Fishponds (in Bristol), where sixty-member 'tribes' rampaged about the estate, alarming the groundsmen, and having separate adventures before reuniting and splitting off again.

When destructive suggestions are eliminated the players become friendlier and more sensitive to the needs of others, and the game has immense sustaining power. One class at RADA played Group-Yes for six consecutive one-and-a-half-hour lessons, beginning as they entered the room and continuing without interruption. They were getting something that they desperately needed but I felt guilty being paid to teach them.

Group-Yes becomes a performance game when it is used to generate stories. If you want to accelerate the stories for entertainment purposes, switch to *Yes! And* . . .

– Let's explore the forest!
– *Yes! And* . . .
– Let's go into the deepest part of the forest!
– *Yes! And* . . .
– Let's discover an old castle surrounded by thorn bushes.
– *Yes! And* . . .
– Let's make our way through the thorns!
– *Yes! And* . . .
– Let's explore the castle.
– *Yes! And* . . .
– Let's find a sleeping princess.
– *Yes! And* . . .

As I write, it occurs to me that we could have two or more Group-Yes Games in adjacent spaces, and that instead of dropping out, students who disliked a suggestion could join the other group. The group that gained the most members would be declared the winner.

The exhilaration attached to playing Group-Yes can give the students insights into how negative their habitual interactions are.

Flashlight Theatre

A game for small theatres. Loan each spectator a flashlight, and then switch off all the other lights. Now the performers can feel themselves getting brighter or duller according to how many people are interested in them. I'm proud of this 'invention' because it's so simple and 'to the point'. (Keep it short.)

The 'Seen Enough' Game

I've tried many ways to encourage a class to give instant feedback, including asking them to boo the players, and to throw things, but nothing worked until I thought of asking them to leave quietly when they'd seen enough – voting with our feet is very natural.

This works best in a room with two doors along one wall. Whatever the circumstances, I make sure that each student can make an easy exit; then I explain that each 'round' will be over when half of the onlookers have left (or are leaving), and that the winner will be the person who holds our attention for the longest time.

'You mean go out onstage alone?'

'Sure.'

'But what do I do?'

'Anything that holds our interest.'

There are unlikely to be any takers, unless I tempt them for a while.

'This is an advanced game,' I say. 'So we could postpone it till later, but if anyone's brave enough to volunteer, we'll time you, and if you can last fifteen seconds, we'll praise you.'

This reassures them because they believe (wrongly) that they can hold our interest for a lot longer than fifteen seconds. Then I say, 'After each attempt we'll ask people why they left. They don't have to have a reason, but if they can tell us what broke the thread, that will be valuable information.'

I might mention the group of Danish actors who were so enthralled by this game that they played it for an entire day; and I'll be overheard telling someone that it's usually the most popular students who are the first to try the game. I'll get a volunteer eventually (probably a man).

'What shall I do?'

'Do whatever you think will interest us, but don't start until our timekeeper says, "Go!" '

'Go!'

He rushes to get a chair, places it mid-stage and starts wrenching at his boot. 'Twelve seconds!'; says the timekeeper as half the class stands up to leave. I point out that if he'd fetched the chair in a reasonable manner, twelve seconds would have passed before he sat in it, and we'd have had time to wonder what he had in mind.

'Wasn't the boot interesting?'

'It could have been, but you were frantic.'

'I didn't want to bore you!'

'If you aren't interested in your boot, why should we be? It was like watching a movie on fast-forward.'

I make him repeat everything that he did at a third of the speed, and he becomes three times as interesting. The idea that speed can be boring is a revelation to him, even though the slowness of great clowns is legendary.

There'll soon be a flood of volunteers who tell stories and jokes, and who change emotion, or do whatever else they think will interest us (a striptease empties the room instantly). Someone sings and everyone exits after a couple of bars, but then someone else sings and we stay for second after second, so it's not easy to know the secret.

A characteristic of this game is that the onlookers leave in waves, rather than trickling out. Soft-hearted spectators may be reluctant to leave, but they will if I point out the moments when they suppressed the impulse.

After each round I prompt the player to ask individuals why they left. Some have no idea (nor do they need one since they're leaving on impulse) but others are very articulate, and the game becomes a thrilling investigation of why the threads of interest snap.

A player scratches herself and we leave almost immediately.

'Wasn't I interesting?'

'Why should we sit here watching you scratch?'

'But I was scratching in different places.'

'You were afraid to develop the scratching, so you got into a loop!' (A meaningless repetition.)

'But what should I have done?'

'Something obvious. Rub some anaesthetic cream into the itch and discover that it's made your entire leg numb so that you walk weirdly. Or discover a lump and find that you're growing another head.'

'Growing a second head is obvious?'

'If you've just discovered the lump, then it's obviously growing. And it would obviously be good if it was something that you communicate with.'

Another player takes off his boot, and gropes inside it. He mimes finding a small object and we're agog, but he throws it away and there's a mass exodus. When we return he points at someone: 'Why did you leave.'

'Because you "cancelled" the object, and then you didn't look as if you knew what to do!'

The threads snap when we realize that the performer is no longer involved in anything except a sort of bluff, and that there'll be no rabbit coming out of that particular hat. Hence we're likely to leave whenever a player completes or repeats an activity.

Let's imagine that you're the performer in this game. If you climb through a window we'll wait to see if there's some point to this action. Creep over to a safe and try to open it, and we'll be happy – unless we're bored by such a cliché – but if the safe fails to open, some people will exit. Others may leave if you find a second safe inside the first safe, and if you find a third safe inside that one, everyone will abandon you because they know that you're terrified to step boldly into the unknown future.

After a while, I let the students volunteer in pairs. This feels safer, but if they ignore each other, or kill each other's ideas, the room empties.

In the context of ordinary theatre, Seen Enough is a terrifying ordeal, but once a few players have taken the plunge, it's no more alarming than being caught when you're playing 'tag', and with practice you'll be able to improvise alone for minutes at a time, and still grip our attention.

I speed up the skills by commentating on what the audience expects to happen. For example: 'She's put her hands together – perhaps she's going to pray.'

The player prays to God for forgiveness.

'I wonder what God will do?'

And so on.

Afterwards, the player says, 'The idea that God should do something amazed me because I was thinking only of myself!'

Seen Enough is rather like street theatre in that the spectators feel no obligation to stay.

Theme and Forfeit

I directed the Loose Moose *All-Star Show* using four experienced improvisers, but whether the players were lovers, homeless people or priests, everything was reduced to light-hearted trivia (as per usual).

I suggested that we should announce a theme, and invite the audience to shout 'forfeit' if a scene failed to embody it. Such forfeits would involve serving at the bar during the interval (for a couple of minutes), or creating a modern dance, or apologizing sincerely to the audience, or whatever.

At first the players earned forfeit after forfeit, but this didn't depress anyone because the spectators were gleefully anticipating the moment when they would take their revenge, and players felt absolved.

Themes might include:

- Ecology
- Education
- Good families/bad families

- Taboos
- Justice (and injustice)
- Religion
- Romance and lust
- Crime and punishment

If ecology was the theme and the players just gossiped, the audience would give them a forfeit, so the way to survive was to incorporate the theme into the structure: a beetle with a white flag might try to surrender, or a choir of angels could be killed by herbicides. If the theme was religion, a chaste lover might remove his gloves and reveal that he had the stigmata, or an irate priest might climb in the window to harangue a married couple for using birth control.

If you've just watched a scene between two room-mates you're likely to set up a similar scene (because that's already in your mind). If you realize this is happening, or if you can't think of a way to embody the theme, ask for the 'title bucket'. This contains strips of paper with story titles written on them. For example:

- The Forbidden Door
- The New Neighbour
- The Babysitter
- The Slob
- The Terrible Revenge
- The Magic Ring
- The First Day
- The Landlord from Hell
- The Corrupt Judge
- The Sofa

Pick one at random and the combination of theme plus title is very likely to trigger ideas. The title of 'The Bridegroom', paired with 'Science Fiction' led a player to discover that she'd married an alien. The pairing of 'The Birth' with 'Athletics' inspired Derek Flores to enter by pushing the top of his head through a slit in the curtains with agonizing slowness, while someone added a sport-type commentary. 'The Sofa' plus the theme of 'Sex' inspired a scene in which a man arrived home with a woman and was getting along fine until the jealous sofa began insulting her in a voice that only he and the audience could hear. She fled as the sofa began to suck him into its upholstery. ('Keith' sofas have a concealed slit in the back that players can exit through.)

The forfeits are written on strips of paper (coloured paper for group forfeits and white for individual forfeits). We review them before each performance, adding new ones, and removing those that anyone objects to. Sometimes the players in a scene receive a group forfeit, and sometimes they select a scapegoat for an individual forfeit.

After each scene we ask, 'Did that do justice to the theme?' and if the spectators yell, 'RIGHT ON!' the players are awarded five points, but if they yell, 'FORFEIT' a scenographer presents the forfeit chalice. If the shout is unclear, award nothing.

No one sees the strip of paper that you select, so if at the last moment you can't face miming a striptease, or singing the National Anthem, you can invent your own punishment.

Here are a handful of typical forfeits:

- Improvise an epic poem on a theme suggested by the audience until they hiss and boo.
- Phone your mother (or father) and tell her about the wretched scene you just directed (from a cell-phone).
- Become very old and reminisce about your days as a young improvisor.
- Expose a personal secret.
- Describe a part of your body that you particularly dislike, and explain why.
- Get a 'firing-squad' from the audience and have them mime shooting you. (Another player can drill this squad.)
- Ask God to make you a better improviser.
- Wear the radio-controlled punishment collar during the next scene.[2]
- Shake hands with the audience as they exit the theatre. (We always make sure that someone receives this forfeit because it's such a friendly thing to do.)

The Lighting Imp provides a pool of light for the more verbal forfeits, and the Music Imp is likely to fade-in some appropriate music.

The best forfeits are popular for ever, but others are discarded. Keep them shorter than the scenes, and don't base them on improvisation games (we want them to add variety, not diminish it). Never let the audience know that you've okayed them in advance, and never say, 'Oh, I always get the same one,' or 'Oh, I hate this one!' If you display familiarity with them they seem a lesser punishment.

Our audience so loved yelling 'forfeit' that players who became experts at incorporating the theme would sometimes earn them deliberately.

Gorilla Theatre

I left the players of Theme and Forfeit to fend for themselves, but I returned after a few weeks to watch a performance and saw scene after scene crash and burn. Improvisers can't guarantee success, any more than a footballer can guarantee a great match, but the players who were waiting 'on the bench' were so unnerved that they were clutching their heads and staring at their feet. They weren't even looking for places to wave the lights down.

At 'notes' afterwards I suggested that we should replace Theme and Forfeit, with an 'event' in which the players would take turns directing each other. 'Directors' would be punished if their scene failed, and rewarded if it succeeded. This scheme to improve 'coaching' skills became Gorilla Theatre.

A large board to one side of the stage says:

MY SCENE IMPRO
THE PLAYER RESPONSIBLE
FOR THIS SCENE IS . . .

Below this is a slot into which players slide their names when they wish to direct their colleagues, perhaps demanding a scene in which a beggar is kicked and turns out to be Jesus, or a passionate love story in which someone makes the wrong choice.

Playing Gorilla

Three experienced players enter and (if there's no Commentator) one of them becomes a temporary emcee who welcomes the audience, explains the game, and announces that the winner will be awarded a week of 'quality time' with the 'Gorilla' (as though this was a great privilege). Last week's winner is then introduced, and enters hand in hand with someone wearing a gorilla suit, or perhaps one will be carrying the other. The 'Gorilla' is delighted to see the audience and goes 'ape', perhaps: shaking hands with the front row and showing great affection (or mixed feelings) for the player with whom it spent the previous week.

One of the players displays a flat plastic banana, and it's explained that the winner will be the player who receives the most bananas. The spectators are rehearsed in shouting 'BANANA' (for scenes that were well directed) or 'FORFEIT' (for scenes that weren't). The Gorilla brandishes the 'forfeit chalice' and two are read out as examples, perhaps: 'Stride arrogantly about the stage until the audience begs you to stop,' and: 'Redirect that miserable scene so that it works!' Most forfeits are identical with those from Theme and Forfeit.

Rock/paper/scissors is played to decide who directs first, and when a scene is over, the player least involved – certainly not the director – becomes the emcee, and asks: 'Did so-and-so direct that scene well? On the count of three . . . One! Two! Three!' (Never say, 'Was that scene worth a banana?' or the audience are likely to vote for the scene, and not for the directing of it.)

If 'BANANA' is shouted, the Gorilla fastens a flat plastic banana to the director's clothing, but if 'FORFEIT' is shouted, the Gorilla presents the 'forfeit chalice'. (A forfeit can't earn another forfeit or the audience might punish a performer for ever.) Even if a director gives up in mid-scene and says 'I'll take my forfeit now!' the vote should still be taken.

If the roar is indecipherable, take the vote again, and perhaps have separate shouts for 'BANANA' and 'FORFEIT'.

The pinning on of the first banana should be an important moment. Subsequent bananas can be more casual, but the pinning should always happen onstage because the spectators like to see their hero honoured. Never pin a banana on to yourself: another player (or the Gorilla) must do it for you. Don't 'bunch' the bananas or it'll be difficult to 'read' which director is ahead. If you don't want to pin (or Velcro) the bananas on to the players, construct a board that displays a row of half-peeled plywood bananas, one for each player, and lengthen the appropriate banana each time that one is awarded. Have a 'banana count' after the interval.

Players wishing to direct a scene put their name-card into the 'slot' (which may involve some confusion if several players are competing to direct). Don't let one name push another out of the slot so that it falls on the floor – this looks messy.

After a little under two hours' play (plus interval) the player with the most bananas is hugged by the Gorilla and the two of them rush into the foyer to say farewell to the spectators.

A Commentator can increase the interest by saying things like: 'If this scene fails, this will be so-and-so's fiftieth forfeit this season!' (Say it even if it isn't true.) Or point out that 'There are only ten minutes left in the match, and so-and-so still hasn't earned a banana!' In the absence of a Commentator the players can supply such information.

Gorilla is not intended for beginners, and even a good improviser may be a poor coach (although the game will gradually teach the skills).

The Loose Moose touring company has been presenting three-player Gorilla matches that last for fifty minutes.

Heat

'Heat' is a wrestling term meaning uproar among the crowd, and wrestlers create it by self-aggrandizement, and by seeming to pummel their opponent's perfectly healthy but heavily bandaged arm. In Gorilla Theatre it's usually generated, not by the scenes, but by the performers' behaviour between scenes and by their interaction with the directors.

Players need to give the audience permission to boo and cheer. They have to make themselves 'targets' by mock-confident announcements like: 'You thought that was a good scene? Wait until you see this one!' or: 'Now I'll show you something with emotional truth and dramatic power!'

Given a forfeit, you might incite the audience by saying, 'What for? You were laughing! You were crying! You were being entertained!'

One 'last-week's winner' entered with the Gorilla on a chain, and shouted arrogantly, 'The simian will be mine again!' This gave the spectators permission to 'hate' him, and yet his manner, and his use of the word 'simian', demonstrated that his 'aggression' was just a tease.

Sometimes one of the players will be a 'baddie' who says aggressive things like: 'That scene was worth a whole bunch of bananas! It wasn't? Who said that? Don't think you won't find your tyres slashed when you leave the theatre!'

Asked to make the audience weep, the players stood about looking miserable, but when the director was greeted by screams of 'FORFEIT', he pretended to be indignant.

'Well the scene didn't make us weep!' shouted an audience member.

'I'll make you weep!' shouted the director, with fake belligerence. Later on he was booed by some audience members as he was accepting a banana, so he said, 'You're all together now, but remember this – it'll be dark when you leave the building!' This threat was greeted with ecstatic cheers, and cries of 'take his banana away'.

Say, 'I will entrust you with this scene even though you totally screwed up the previous one!' or 'When this scene is over you will have the privilege of pinning the banana on me!' and the audience will be waiting to punish your arrogance, and yet, if the scene is good, they'll be just as eager to 'banana' you.

Observe how professional wrestlers excite their audience by pretending to be bestial, and/or lunatically arrogant. If you can whip the audience into a frenzy, it's almost irrelevant whether the scenes are good or bad, but it has to be clear that the players are 'just teasing', and that their fake 'aggression' is an expression of good nature. It can take several performances before some players strike the right balance.

Not every player should be a baddie. We need 'blue-eyed boys' (as the 'goodies' were called in English wrestling) who are 'pure' and 'moral', and who try to direct socially desirable scenes.

Taking the Vote
After each scene a player (not its 'director') consults the audience and says things like: 'So-and-so really fought to save that scene, but did he succeed?' or 'It sounds as if banana has the edge over forfeit!' or, ominously 'Rebecca was totally responsible for that scene.'

At the end of the game the other players congratulate the winner, shake hands, hug, and so on.

Directing the Scenes
Boldly announce the nature of your scene (so that we'll know exactly what you're struggling to achieve). For example: 'I want to see an out-of-work parent who is too poor to buy a Christmas present for a child,' or 'I want a scene with pathos in which someone is stood-up by their date and comforted by a fatherly waiter,' or 'I want a sadistic scene about a homeless ghost who pursues a cabinet minister and exposes the heartlessness of this brutal Government!' or 'I want you to chill our blood with a scene about a schoolteacher who creates a golem to keep discipline!'

Fight for the scene you want by throwing in dialogue, by starting it again, by recasting it, by ejecting someone and taking over their role (the ultimate insult in the professional theatre). The struggle to attain your vision is at the heart of Gorilla Theatre and makes it unlike any other form. Your romantic nineteenth-century scene where the players 'pine for each other but daren't even touch' is likely to be hysterically funny, rather than romantic – but whether you achieve your vision or not, there's a huge difference between a director who sets up an impro game and does nothing to ensure its success and a director who has a dream that he/she wants fulfilled. The spectators know this and vote accordingly.

When the directors have no idea what they want – apart from entertaining the audience – Gorilla Theatre becomes just another way of packaging the 'same old stuff'. But a struggle to achieve something worthwhile can be wonderful to watch.

Ending Scenes

On a good night everything works splendidly, but on a bad night the directors in Gorilla Theatre – in common with most improvisers – will allow boring scenes to grind on pointlessly. Only the most experienced directors have the self-discipline to bail out and cut their losses. We know this, because we've been inviting them to kill their scenes after thirty seconds without incurring a forfeit, and yet even when they know that there is nothing of the slightest interest on the stage, most of them will still opt to continue.

I'm working on this problem, but in the meantime the players can help by saying, 'Nothing's happening. What should I do?' or 'Help us! We're dying out here!' or 'Do you really think anyone is still interested?'

Or they can say, actor-like, 'What's my motivation?'

Fake quarrels can liven things up:

– Can't we kill this scene?
– Shut up!
– But it's not working!
– I'll make it work!

Other ways to curtail boring scenes include:

• Giving the director a Hell light (see pp. 18, 324).
• Having the teckies flicker and then dim the lights when a scene is tedious.
• Playing a submarine-diving 'whoop-whoop' siren, plus a high-pitched voice that chants, 'Scene in danger! Scene in danger!' getting gradually louder, and ending with 'Abandon scene! Abandon scene!'

Rationing the Directing Time

Current Gorilla at Loose Moose has four players and a Commentator.

Each player is allowed twenty minutes of directing time (*in toto*), and the Commentator keeps an eye on this, saying, for example, 'Ray's scene lasted three minutes and forty seconds – that leaves him eleven minutes of directing time in this game.'

This is working well and stops the scenes from dribbling on, but if the players start scheming to win by doing very short scenes I'll have to invent some device to correct this.

Directors are also being allowed to bail out of a scene that they think has died without receiving either reward or punishment.

The Commentator can help to whip the audience into a frenzy, keep the game moving and cover any blank spaces. So far we've been using Ray Gurrie, who is very experienced, and the results are excellent.

Notes I've Given

• Other players can assist the director – for example, by waving the lights down – but the audience still has to 'believe' that you're competing against each other.

• If the forfeit asks you to apologize for your existence, be sincere.

• The director accepted a stupid suggestion – why didn't the players protest?

• Never be gratuitously obscene.

• If you're looking for 'berries in a forest', and you're stupid/original enough to discover a supermarket with berries 'on sale', it should at least be staffed by witches.

• Always pretend that a week with the Gorilla would be delightful.

• Saying, 'Say something very witty to end the scene', has become a boring cliché.

Gorilla Moments

• Dennis, as a 'baddie', controlling the vote, hears 'FORFEIT' – and the audience rage and insist on a banana. Derrick says, with fake nobility, 'Yes, I take full responsibility for this scene. If you enjoyed it, please vote banana!'

• A bananaless player is teased by having a freshly won banana waved under his nose.

• A director apologizes: 'Well what could I do with someone like X screwing everything up?'

• A director says, 'I think the only way to make this scene work is to get in there and do it myself!'

• A director sets a scene in local bar – some spectators cheer so the director gets them on stage to be typical denizens of this bar.

• A director says, 'All my scenes this evening will express a moral conflict.' His scenes are good, but they don't express moral conflicts, and the spectators are delighted to give him forfeits.

• The audience loves to be controlled, and dominated, as when teenage Rebecca cracked a whip and told them, 'Pay attention, class.'

• Just before the vote a director appeals to the audience, saying, 'I'm doing my best. You treated me pretty brutally just now.'

• The setting-up of a scene is incompetent, and the players harass the director, saying in fake amazement, 'You're really prepared to take responsibility for this?'

• A player who receives a banana glows with pride, and shouts in amazement, 'They like me! They really like me!'

• Another player who receives a banana begins an 'Oscar Night' speech, saying, 'I'd like to thank my mother, my dentist, the Academy . . .' and so on.

• A director says, 'I want to see this as a good solid acting exercise – no screwing around!'

• A scene fails, but the 'noble' director wipes away a tear and says, 'It's all right! I'll never give up the struggle!'

• Players offer mock enthusiasm, crying, 'I'll be in this scene too!' and 'Pick me! Pick me!'

The Gorilla

Without a Gorilla the game is just 'my scene impro', but a Gorilla can add greatly to the spectacle. Purchase several costumes and launder them frequently. The 'fur' has to be shaggy. Commercial gorilla costumes can be ordered via carnival shops.

Gorillas spend time backstage cooling off, but they can help with the scenography, or they can give hats to the actors or hand them props. They can be in scenes as a 'rug', or an exhibit in a zoo, or as a low-key waiter, and so on (always in a supporting role). They should fill any dead space between scenes with their antics, perhaps creating pathos when an actor rejects a prop, or applauding when a player they like is awarded banana after banana.

An obedient Gorilla is useless. Gorillas have to misbehave. Encourage them to experiment. Tell them that they're expected to take risks, and that they're allowed at least two big mistakes in each show.

A Gorilla should be a memorable part of the show, but it mustn't become the star.

Micetro Impro

Micreto is another feedback game, but whereas Gorilla Theatre is for experts, Micetro can be played by a mix of experts and beginners, and the feedback is more precise.

It began at Utrecht where tickets had been sold for a performance at the end of a four-day summer school. All twenty-six students wanted to play Theatresports, even though this is one of the more difficult impro forms and half of them were novices. I decided to accept everyone, and then narrow the field in some way.

How to Play

You need a scoreboard with many horizontal grooves. Each groove holds a player's name-card, ready to be slid to the right, and each player wears the same athletic number as the groove that his name rests in (from ten to twelve players is the preferred number).

The Scorekeeper introduces the two directors who are sitting in the first row of the audience. He/she then explains that the spectators will reward each scene with a score from one to five, and gets the audience to practise clapping for a score of one (for scenes they hate), and for a score of five (for scenes they love). It's essential that they are made to clap for one, or they may be too polite to give such a low score. He/she then introduces the players who cross the stage and crowd into the moat opposite the scoreboard (i.e., they sit on the audience's left – if there's space for them).

The Scorekeeper retreats to the scoreboard (which is only lit between scenes), while a director picks numbered metal discs at random from a metal bowl (clanking them audibly into a second bowl) and shouting the numbers: 'Three, One, Six and Ten, please.'

These four players (or however many have been chosen) are given a scene, or a game, by the directors who shout in ideas, correct errors and wave the lights down (if the lighting improviser hasn't already made that decision).

At the end of a scene, the players go to the scoreboard side of the stage and the Scorekeeper asks the audience if they thought the scene was worth a one, or a two . . . and so on, up to five. Each player in a scene receives the same number of points, even if he/she had only walked-on as a waiter, or was just a voice from offstage (hence the built-in unfairness of this game). If there are lots of players – say twenty – there will have to be many group scenes in the first round (or the game will last for three hours) and this increases the unfairness. Towards the end of the game, two-player or solo scenes proliferate.

The Scorekeeper slides their name-cards the correct number of places along the slots, and more metal discs clink into the bowl as players are selected for the next scene. When all the players have crossed the stage (appeared in a scene) they rush back to begin Round Two. This crossing and recrossing of the stage tells the audience how each round is progressing, and if just one player remains to the audience's left, everyone realizes that there'll have to be a solo scene. Such scenes usually get higher scores because the spectators identify strongly with the solo players.

Sometimes the directors will ask the players of solo scenes, 'Do you have anything?' (i.e., any ideas for a scene), especially towards the very end of the game.

From Round Two on, we start to eject the hindermost: 'Numbers Five, Four and Seven are eliminated. Thank-you very much! Better luck next time!' say the directors. The losers cross the stage, shaking hands with each other, and wave cheerfully as the Scorekeeper calls for applause and removes their names from the board (I'd like their names to clank loudly into a bucket). Some go backstage to help with the scenography, and others join the audience, and with luck we'll have shed about half of the players by the interval (an hour into the game).

On rare occasions there may be ten 'laggards' all with the same score, and just one or two players who are ahead of them. In this case, delay the eliminations until the next round, or the game will be over almost immediately.

Sometimes extra players will join a scene to help out. If they came from the audience's right, then they would have already been scored for that round, but if they came from the audience's left, the directors (or the Scorekeeper) will say something like, 'Number Three and Number Eleven – do you want to be considered part of that scene?' This is asked before the vote, and there's often a significant pause as these players try to guess whether the scene will be scored low or high.

Eliminations continue until we can declare a winner (the 'Micetro'). Sometimes each of the last few players does a solo scene; a scene embodying several characters, perhaps, or in which a lawyer defends a 'criminal' audience member (or whatever). Then the Scorekeeper displays a five-dollar bill in a golden frame and says, 'If Betty', or whoever, 'doesn't really deserve this magnificent prize, clap now!' (The prize has to be derisory or the competition might be vicious.)

A few people applaud – as a joke – and then the audience is asked, 'But if you think she has really earned it, clap now!'

The audience cheer, and Betty is chaired on the other players' shoulders, and congratulated by everyone, while soap-bubbles are blown, the confetti machine spews out confetti, the follow-spot weaves about and the disco-ball rotates. The audience leave, almost always very happily, because Micetro almost always gets better and better as the game nears its end. Betty will probably stand at the entrance shaking hands with the spectators as they leave, accepting their congratulations. Some groups make fun of the Micetro – for example, by placing a fake cheese on his head as a crown – but this implies that they resent his/her success.

A strong player can be eliminated early on, and a beginner can be swirled along in the wake of a stronger player, but on average, the best players survive until after the interval. Over a number of games this feedback becomes so incontestable that players with inflated egos turn to other impro forms, or decide to take some classes.

Micetro develops the skills of beginners quicker than any other form because it's more effective to correct them mid-performance than to give notes afterwards. For example, a 'silly waiter' who ruins a delicate love scene can be sent back, perhaps again and again, until he/she presents something believable.

It's thrilling to see more and more of fewer but 'hotter' performers. Spectators will groan if a popular improviser is eliminated early, but that makes the game poignant (sometimes the favourite in a steeplechase falls at the first obstacle), but we lessen the chance of this by delaying the eliminations until after Round Two.

Directing for Micetro

The directors' responsibility for the quality of the work becomes clear as soon as they shout instructions, and perhaps even restart scenes. You might expect this to 'rattle' the improvisers, but these intrusions absolve them from blame, and when the directors are skilled Micetro is the least stressful form of public improvisation that we know. Sometimes the standard can be very high – recently the winner scored a five in every scene, and the runner-up was just one point behind. The directors alternate in setting-up scenes, but they are not in competition with each other. They work together to make things happen and to correct errors. Either can take over the direction at any moment (and might still throw ideas in if the scene falters). Sometimes they intrude so often that neither can remember which of them started the scene.

- If the actors are rushing things, say, '*Slow down!*' If they are discussing going somewhere, say, '*Get there!*'

  It's often enough just to say, '*Do it!*': 'You made Cecilia pregnant! You deserve flogging!'

  '*Do it!*'
- You may have to add ideas: if the players are in a garden, and just gossiping, say, '*Plant something!*' or '*Throw a hunk of meat to a cannibal plant!*' or '*Have a snake tempt you!*'
- Try to drag what's latent in a scene to the surface. For example:

- I'm starving.
- *Shoot something and eat it.*
- I'm very attracted to you.
- *Kiss him!*
- I've a terrible headache.
- *Operate on her brain!*

When two 'brothers' arrived to open their father's will, each greeted the other with a simultaneous cry of 'Mike!', so the director said, 'The will explains why you are both called Mike.'

- Enforce 'positive' attitudes (especially at the opening of scenes): 'God I'm tired.'

  No you're not! You feel particularly fit and well.

  Or: 'What a boring film that was.'

  Say, 'What a wonderful film that was!'
- Remove anything disgusting – we don't want scenes about vomiting or excretion.
- Veto 'clever' ideas.
- Look for a way to alter the balance that has been established between the characters.
- Remove stupidities.
- When something dramatic happens, make sure that the players react

to it. If they continue unchanged, return to the moment and enforce a change in them.

- If things are going splendidly, direct hardly at all.
- Never suggest something that's already about to happen so that you can take the credit.
- If there are two separate 'items' on a stage, bring them together. For example, if there's a book on the table, say, 'Read something from the book!' (And then say, 'Be altered by what you read!')
- Remember what has happened, and look for places to 'feed it back in' – this adds structure.
- Use corrective games: for example, if the players are gagging as a substitute for interaction, or are just burbling on, make them continue in gibberish, or in three-word sentences. If they are refusing to be controlled by each other, add the He Said/She Said Game.
- Eject characters who intrude unnecessarily.
- Force transitions by shouting, 'Recognize him!' or 'Weep!' or 'Leap on him and apologize!' and so on. A male boss was accused of being sexist by a female employee but the scene degenerated into gossip. The director should have shouted, 'Make a pass at her!'

Scenes that are going nowhere can be hurled into the future by brute force. For example: a woman was 'strolling along the beach with her father' who told her that he was going to die. Gloom set in and nothing happened, so the directors said, 'Do it!' The father collapsed and gasped that there was one thing she could do to save him. The spectators had the idea of incest so there was a huge laugh (incest is a popular theme on American talk shows), but this paralysed the players, so a director said, 'Send the daughter on a journey!'

'You have to climb a mountain,' gasped the father, 'and speak to the guru who lives in a cave at the top.'

They started to gossip about this, but a director propelled the daughter into the future by saying, 'Get there!' The daughter 'arrived at the base of the mountain' (wishing to delay the interaction), but was told: 'No! Arrive at the top. Meet an old hermit who lives in a cave.'

The hermit arrived but the scene stalled again – nothing happened – so a director told him to die, and he collapsed and gasped that there was just one way she could save him.

There was another huge laugh as the daughter realized that she was caught in a hall of mirrors (and because, at an unconscious level, the audience knew that the whole sequence was one long evasion of the incest theme).

I've seen Micetro reduced to utter tedium by directors who were either afraid to direct or who interfered when no help was necessary (the motto should be: 'Only fix it if it's broke!'). I've even heard of improvisers who are so greedy for stage time that they ask the newest and least experienced members of their group to direct them – so why bother?

I would have invented this form decades ago had I realized that the spectators could agree on a score. Hysterically funny scenes, scenes with genuine emotion (pathos), and scenes that tell stories get fours and fives, whereas players who are just being silly get ones and twos in spite of the laughter. This confirms my belief that laughter is misleading.

We spell it Micetro because this seems less pretentious than Maestro, and we can have tough little mice on the posters.

One of the pleasures of Micetro and of Gorilla (at Loose Moose) is that the players do all that they can to improve other people's scenes, so having fun is more important to them than winning. Self-obsessed and mean-natured improvisers should stick to conventional impro unless they can learn to be supportive.

The problem with Micetro is that it needs brilliant directors. Train some, and Micetro will be the most pleasant and least stressful of all impro forms for the players.

NOTES

1 Moss Hart, *Act One* (London: Random House, 1959).
2 This punishment collar belongs to a man who trains dogs and who lends it to us only occasionally, believing us to be 'weird'. We let an audience volunteer feel a ninety-volt jab, and then we fasten it around the offending player's neck, secretly unplugging it as we do so. The operator makes a 'bzzzz' sound as he presses the zapper – something no one ever remarks on – and the player leaps or writhes. It's important that the screams sound 'happy', so that the spectators don't feel pity.

4 Spontaneity

'Here Be Monsters'

When I began to teach impro I was told that human beings should always be 'in control', and that the rise of the Nazis had been caused by 'too much spontaneity' and by 'an upsurge of unconscious forces'. Religious students insisted that their swamis had forbidden them to have unpleasant thoughts, or explained that we were 'fallen creatures' who could never be trusted to act on impulse. Freudians fretted about the 'id', and defined 'art' as a symptom (even though there are cultures where it's abnormal not to be an artist). Goya's 'The sleep of reason . . .' was quoted by intellectuals unaware that reason is utterly merciless and it's the sleep of compassion that breeds monsters.

Being a Chameleon

If you're going to teach spontaneity, you'll have to become spontaneous yourself.

With a couple of exceptions, my teachers thought that the incentive should come from us, but the incentive has to be generated, or increased by the attitude of the teacher. If you're teaching mantras you have to be serious and 'stable', and to make the students feel 'awe'. If you're teaching clowning you might have to be a lunatic. It's never enough just to explain the games carefully and correctly, and then – if the students are unenthused – wish that you had better students.

No Syllabus

I visualize myself as coaxing students away from the rim of a wheel and towards the hub.

This makes a conventional syllabus impossible, since any spoke will do if it enthuses a particular group of students. If a spoke gets boring, I just move to a more interesting spoke. When students reach the hub, all spokes seem equally important and exciting.

Progressive Desensitization

Wolpe's cats were so frightened that they stopped eating unless they were fed away from his laboratory (no doubt with sufficient reason), but each day he moved their feeding dishes closer to the lab, and their phobia disappeared.

This inspired him to train phobic patients to stay relaxed while he presented them with the most harmless item in a 'hierarchy of fear'. If they were terrified of birds, he might ask them to imagine a very small feather in a country thousands of miles away. If they began to tremble he'd have to find something even less scary, but with luck they'd stay calm, and he could proceed to a slightly more alarming image. After ascending the hierarchy for a few weeks they might be able to confront a stuffed bird, and quite soon they'd be able to sit in a cage of live ones, but if they panicked (i.e. if the hierarchy was too steep) he would have to move them back many steps before proceeding again. This was exactly what I had observed in my own teaching, and I realized that my skill lay in coaxing my students into 'dangerous areas', without having them back off.

If it were practical, I'd feed beginners while they were improvising.

Paradoxical Teaching

The psychologist Dan Wiener[1] attended our summer school and told me I was using paradoxical psychology. This involves asking the patients to rehearse their symptoms, for example, to practise a nervous tic in the hope of bringing it under conscious control. This may be alarming for psychologists, fearful of sending their patients 'round the bend', but in impro the risks are non-existent – the students just become more objective, and better able to modify their behaviour. For example, if I want students to accept ideas, I'll ask them to kill ideas first, because then they'll recognize such negativity when it occurs 'accidentally'. 'Doing it wrong' puts everyone in a good mood.

Tug-o'-War

I ask each student to find a partner.

'Mime picking up a rope,' I say. 'Have a mimed tug-o'-war.'

I look out of the widow so that they can't scan me for signs of approval, and I hear them straining and gasping. After thirty seconds I turn back to see that no one has 'lost', but that some of the 'ropes' are getting longer.

'That's enough,' I say, and grasp the hand of a hefty-looking student so that we can pull against each other in a real tug-o'-war. Afterwards I say, 'How long did that take?'

'About two seconds.'

'So why did the mimed tug-o'-wars last nearly a minute with no winners or losers?'

I explain that their thinking applies to the 'real' world where there are palpable ropes, and genuine winners and losers, but that in the world of the stage we swim or sink together.

They laugh at the lunacy of trying to win a mimed tug-o'-war.

'Every group I've taught behaves like this,' I say. 'Except Zen monks. Normal people try to win, no matter how inappropriate the circumstances.'

Perhaps I'll tell them that when I explained this in Stuttgart, two students were so determined to 'win at losing' that they ran forwards and smashed their bald heads together. The class will laugh even more at this.

'Play the game again! But this time do whatever you think will please your partners. If they want to lose, pull them, and if they want to win, agree to be pulled. Observe the happy smile on the winners' faces. You'll have done them a kindness.'

I stare out of the window again but now I hear the sounds of people laughing and having a good time.

'Give in!' I shout, because some students are still heaving away at thin air. 'Lose! Be what your partner wants you to be. Unless you are willing to be changed you might as well be working alone!'

Maybe I get a smallish student to have a tug-o'-war against all the others.

'Who would an audience want to win?' I say, and the answer is obvious.

The student jerks the 'rope' and the rest of the class fall into a giggling heap. They are beginning to realize that losing can be at least as much fun as succeeding, and that failing good-naturedly puts everyone in a good mood.

Giving Presents[2]

I ask the class to mime 'giving presents to each other' in pairs, admitting that the game is suitable for three-year-olds, but 'please humour me'. Then I say, 'Be delighted with the presents. Say things like, "Oh that's just what I wanted!" Give more gifts! Keep exchanging them.'

Even in this simple transaction students will be trying to assert their identity; one who wants to be thought tough will give a skull, or a gun, or a sharpened bicycle-chain; whereas one wishing to be thought sensitive will give a book of sonnets, or a flower.

I get them to repeat the game (perhaps with other partners), but now I say, 'Don't define the present you give; define the present you receive, and make it something that you really want!'

This way is more pleasurable, and the presents become more interesting and varied. For example:

– I've got this for you.
– Oh! It's the coat I saw in the shop window. You're so kind. But I have a surprise for you!
– A mechanical bird! Does it sing?
– Press the button.
– Oh, how beautiful. But wait till you see what I've got for you.
– What is it? It's so heavy!
– Open it and see!
– An inflatable Parthenon! I was saving up for one!

And so on.

Defining the present they receive gives them the illusion that they're revealing less of themselves.

I'll refer back to this game when I'm teaching action and interaction, and especially when I work on text. Defining the present you receive is the secret of being a good listener. Peter Oscarson, the Swedish director, told me that he saw the last actor from Stanislavsky's company who was still working on stage. This ninety-year-old was hardly able to do more than shuffle about and raise his arms a little, but he 'listened' better than anyone Peter had ever seen. When Peter was introduced, his congratulations had to be written on a pad, because the man was as deaf as Beethoven.

Instead of telling actors that they must be good listeners (which is confusing), we should say, 'Be altered by what's said.'

Evaluating the Work

After a scene in pairs I might ask the players, 'Was the work good?'

This confuses them, so I say, 'Your work is good if your partner enjoyed working with you!'

This idea is strange to them (many beginners have no idea how anyone else feels).

'Keep checking up on your partners to make sure they're having a good time. Think of it this way: if you're good but no one wants to work with you, I doubt you'll improve; but if your work is inept and yet everyone wants you as their partner, you'll soon be one of the very best.'

Sometimes I'll say, 'You looked as if winning mattered more than enjoying the game, so we didn't like you!' or 'The scene should have been a disaster, but you gave your partner such a good time that we enjoyed watching you.'

Other evaluations can be made – for example, is the point of an exercise being achieved? – but when improvisers ignore their partners, I'll say, 'We're not going to praise you unless your partner is good.'

Playing Tag

If there's a large area of grass available, I might ask the students to play 'tag'. Some head for the horizon as if desperate to avoid being chased, and yet they'll insist that 'We like running.' It's as it they're trying to win by keeping away from the hunter (which amounts to a refusal to play). I explain that the players who risk being caught get the most pleasure (we knew this when we were children, but some of us have forgotten).

Perhaps some people are afraid that once they're 'it' they may never catch anybody, but good-natured students would never allow a 'hunter' to stagger into exhaustion, and a good coach would already have intervened (I'd have entered the game and allowed myself to be tagged).

Tag in Pairs can be played after a game of regular tag. The members of the group pair off, put their arms around each other and play tag (this became popular in educational drama). Each couple has to cooperate or they'll try to rush off in different directions. This releases far more laughter, and there's less anxiety about winning or losing (because no one's ego is on the line). Pairs should be evenly matched: we don't want a strong person yanking a weaker partner around.

Try playing Tag in extreme slow-motion. This is just the representation of a game (as is a mimed tug-o'-war), but compulsive 'winners' will speed up to catch someone, or to avoid the hunter. Such manoeuvres allow us another way to discuss inappropriate thinking.

On Not Making the Rules Clear

Nervous improvisers want to have the rules of a new game repeated several times, but I tell them that if they misunderstand me, they may invent a much better game. This makes them laugh, and they understand that I won't blame them if they screw-up.

Rather than explain games exhaustively – which implies that errors should not be made – it's better to correct errors as they occur.

Blame Me

When I worked with teachers in the early sixties, I'd wait until someone 'failed', and then I'd say, 'It's all my fault. I gave you the wrong game,' or 'I should have rescued you sooner! I'm so stupid!'

There's be a buzz of conversation as they discussed whether I was mad or incompetent, and then I'd remind them that I was supposed to be the expert.

'So if you're in trouble, tell yourself: "Keith got me up here, and he wasn't any help. What an idiot!" Or blame the situation, blame the class for having too many people in it, blame the noise from the air-conditioning, but never blame yourself.'

It would take a while before my behaviour persuaded them that I was serious.

'My mistake!' I'd say. 'I should have asked you to be altered when he insulted you!' or 'What am I thinking of! I should have taught you the Blind-Offer Game first!'

Accepting responsibility for the students' failures makes me seem very confident. Soon even shy students will volunteer, knowing that they won't be humiliated, and the class begins to resemble a good party rather than anything academic.

Drop Dead, Keith

Some players made split-second eye contacts with me, mid-scene, to check that they had my approval. I tried hiding behind the furniture, or wearing a bag on my head, but nothing worked until I hit on the idea of shouting: 'Say, "Drop dead, Keith!"' Students who are so worried about my opinion that they can't forget about me certainly won't want to insult me, so the eye contacts cease. (You'd better have a good rapport with your students before you try this.)

Another way to take their minds off me is to make them do exercises in pairs, and then repeat the exercise with new partners. Each new confrontation energizes them, and gives them something more interesting to think about.

Volunteers, and Failure

'Two volunteers!' I say. 'You and you!'

The class laugh and my 'volunteers' look a little sick.

'What's wrong?'

'Wrong?'

'You looked the picture of health before I dragged you out!'

I explain that 'looking sick' is a ploy to get sympathy if they screw-up, and to win them extra credit if they succeed. The class will almost certainly be laughing again, because each student had assumed that 'looking pathetic' was his/her own unique strategy.

Sometimes, beginners won't volunteer; they'll just sit there hoping I'll pick someone else. I tell them that I understand their caution: 'You want someone else to volunteer, so that you can profit from their example!'

They laugh in acknowledgment, and one says, 'Why should we volunteer when we don't know what we'll be asked to do?'

'That's the best time, because then you won't be scheming to show us how clever you are. It's always best to volunteer with a blank mind and see what happens.'

Still no response, so I explain that real learning means 'getting it wrong'.

This surprises them, so I explain further: 'You could memorize the instructions for how to walk on stilts, but you'd still have to learn by falling off.'

I might describe a training film that shows Tim Gallway coaching tennis. A student tells him that she has no accuracy, so he asks her to hit a ball into a bucket at the other end of the court.

'How close was it?' he asks.

She has no idea (she so detests her errors that she refuses to observe them), so he asks her to hit more balls and to say where each lands.

'Six feet to the left,' she says. And then, 'Four feet to the right!'

Each ball bounces nearer to the bucket until the fourth or fifth lands inside it.[3]

Or I might tell them about Kimon Nicolaides, who taught life-drawing, and who said that 'The sooner you make your first five thousand mistakes the sooner you will be able to correct them.'[4] Then I might add, 'Learn to ride a bike on grass so you don't lose any skin, and stand facing a bed when you learn to juggle so that you don't have to keep chasing the balls, and always try to improvise with people who understand that it's okay to screw-up. And remember that if you succeed brilliantly, you'll depress the rest of us, and then we'll never get any volunteers.'

If my attitude is playful, they'll be laughing at this – but some shy students may still look anxious. If so, I'll explain that 'Shy people should volunteer first because the longer you delay, the greater the chance that we'll have moved on to something else, or that another student will have just done exactly the thing that you were planning to do.'

Talking about volunteering can alter students' attitudes. They understand that their private hell is shared by everyone, and this gives them courage.

Try introducing certain games as 'advanced', and predict that the students will fail, but 'it'll be fun anyway'. This allows them to fail with honour, and it becomes easier to get volunteers (not more difficult, as one might have supposed).

When Students Fail

'You're not very good at this game,' I say. 'It'll take you twice as long to learn it!'

This treats their failure as survivable, whereas if I said, 'But you must master this!' I would be adding to their despair.

If students continue to fail, I'll say, 'Excellent! We've found something that's really difficult for you! What a great opportunity to improve your technique!' or 'How many times have you played this game?'

'Never!'

'And are you supposed to be good at it?'

'Well – not really . . .'

'So why shouldn't you screw-up?'

This makes students smile and cast off tension visibly.

Sometimes I'll announce the exact time it will take to master a skill:

'How long have you spent on this game?'

'We've just started.'

'It'll take you twenty minutes to become proficient.'

I say this as we're moving on to some other game (so who knows if it's true?), but the prediction implies that I'm sure they'll succeed.

Forcing Failure

Visitors to Loose Moose are often amazed at the boldness of our 'technicians' (the improvisers who are responsible for the lighting, scenography and sound).[5] These 'teckies' began their training by seeing themselves as assistants to the players, and they might have continued in this way, if I hadn't pestered them.

'No one's complaining about you!' I say. 'You're supposed to make several screw-ups per match. Theatresports is disposable theatre! What does it matter if you damage a few scenes?'

Caught between the players and the director the teckies might as well assert themselves. An improviser who opens a door may now be hit by a blast of organ-music; he kneels and 'crosses' himself and a stained-glass window fades-in. Two players glance at each other, and a love theme oozes around them, the lighting becomes romantic, a moon appears, our stars light up and our prop boat is pushed on; suddenly they're two lovers eloping across a lake, something which hadn't been in their minds at all. This union of sound, light, action and scenography is quite magical, but it can't be achieved by people who are timid.

I'll also abuse the Judges (within earshot of the players).

'Why so cautious? Get the scorecards up faster! Take risks! Who said you had to be perfect?'

This lessens the Judges' anxiety, and makes it difficult for the players to resent 'bad decisions'.

I seldom have to do my 'Why aren't you screwing-up?' performance these days, but it's how the tradition was established.

Don't Punish Yourself

At school a 'Buddhist' tranquillity would have got me smashed on the head, but if I gnawed my pencil and crunched up as if in agony, my teachers would perceive me as 'trying' and would either write the answer for me or veer off and torment someone else. This strategy kept me safe, but it didn't teach me anything, and it carried the risk that 'thinking' might become a 'forced activity', never again to be experienced as effortless.

A student frowns, and contorts with tension, so I ask him why he's doing this. The class is bewildered – no one has ever drawn their attention to such behaviour.

'If you looked twice as miserable, and tied yourself in even tighter knots, would you learn twice as quickly? I don't think so! Tight muscles are detrimental to learning, so stay happy! Stop promising yourself to "try harder"!'

'But I want to improve.'

' "Trying harder" can't make you spontaneous; it's like trying to slam a revolving door!'

Be Average

A student still looks up-tight, so I say, 'Are you trying your best?'

'Of course!'

'Is that a good strategy?'

'If I don't try I won't get anywhere.'

'If we saw mountaineers "doing their best" we'd know that they'd moved outside of their area of competence and were fighting for their lives. An admired team of gymnasts at the Olympics saw the gold medal receding, and they "tried" with all their might, and started to fall off the bars.'

'But how can I achieve anything worthwhile if I don't struggle for it?'

'Just be average!'

Consternation.

'Look at the room!' I say. 'Look at the chair! Now "try" to look at the room; "try" to look at the chair. Does it help? I don't think so. Touch your nose! Now do it again but this time "try" to touch it – did that improve the action? Hypnotists ask you to "try" to open your closed eyes, or your interlocked fingers, because the harder you "try" the less ability you have.'

'But I don't want to be mediocre!'

'Trying makes you mediocre. It's like running up the down-escalator.'

No comprehension.

'We only try when we don't trust the forces within us. Each brain organizes a universe out of the electro-magnetic flux – no brain equals no universe – so if we have this magical computer inside our skulls and yet feel that we can't draw, or compose a tune, or write a story, or improvise, we must be under some prohibition.'

Not a glimmer.

'Sometimes being average is the best possible strategy.'

Outrage.

'Anyone can walk a plank, but if it stretched across an abyss, fear might glue us to it. Our best strategy might be to treat the abyss as something ordinary (if that were possible) and to walk across in our average manner.'

'You mean if we were content to be average we'd be just as good as when we try harder?'

'Yes, or better, because "being average" allows automatic processes to take over, and there are parts of the brain that are infinitely more gifted than the social-self. Are there any athletes here?'

A few hands go up.

'When was your fastest time?'

They tell me.

'Were you trying your hardest?'

I get answers like, 'Funny you should ask, because I really had no idea how fast I was going.'

Such answers are almost routine (a world speed-skating champion used almost exactly those words in Calgary recently).

Here's a quote from *Maximum Performance* by Laurence E. Moorhouse and Leonard Gross (New York: Pocket Books, 1977):

> I took every opportunity I could to interview athletes who had just broken a world's record . . . I could predict almost exactly what each of them would say. The scenario went like this.
>
> 'I didn't feel well that day. I was nauseated and felt weak. As a matter of fact, it crossed my mind to ask the coach to scratch me from the event . . . I don't remember any particular moment during the

event. It all seemed so easy. At the finish, the way the crowd was cheering told me I had done well, but I had the feeling that if I had only tried a little harder I could have done much better.'

And yet it's obvious that 'forgetting' to try harder gave them their success. Try to make your arm immovable, absolutely rigid, and it'll be easy for me to move it – because half of its muscles will be assisting me. Allow only those muscles to operate that are needed to resist the force and it will be a third stronger.

I might tell my students about the weightlifter who broke the world record because he didn't realize that extra poundage had been added accidentally. Or I might mention the elderly heart patient who lugged one end of a 1,600-pound steel pipe off of a trapped child. Interviewed on TV, he said, 'Well, I saw what had happened so I lifted it off without thinking.'

The consciousness that we experience as 'ourselves' is a defence system against the intrusions of other people (why else would so much of our inner dialogue be concerned with manipulating their opinion of us?), but in life-or-death situations our good angel shoves us aside, slams time into slow-motion and does its damnedest to rescue us. If improvisers were content to be 'just average', and to 'go with the flow', this good angel could operate even when there wasn't a dire emergency, and we'd call this 'being inspired'. Of course, the 'intellect' has its uses, as a man discovered who leapt impulsively into a river to save a drowning child and remembered that he couldn't swim (but if he hadn't remembered he might have swum).

If 'trying harder' meant staying relaxed and happy while you spent more time with a problem, then it could be recommended, but it usually involves treating the mind as if it were constipated and had to have ideas squeezed out of it.

Improvisers who are 'determined to do their best' scan the 'future' for 'better' ideas, and cease to pay any attention to each other.

Sport Versus Show-business

Players who come from show-business assume that failure has no value. If so, I ask them:

- Which is the most famous tower?
- Which is the most famous space shuttle?

- Which is the most famous ocean liner?

I explain that it would be madness to turn the cameras away when a racing-car burst into flame, and that if we had to watch God playing golf – FORE! A hole in one. FORE! A hole in one! – we'd know we were in hell.

Show-business pastes over inadequacies with glitz and razzmatazz, but sport displays a tug-o'-war between success and failure. A scripted show would be wrecked if the scenography collapsed, and yet this could be the high point of an improvised show.

The excitement of sport is maximized when there's a fifty/fifty toss-up between triumph and disaster. This determines the height of the net, and the size and distance of goals, the rank of the boxers, and so on, and yet when I'm told that Theatresports has been 'adapted to the local conditions' I can be sure that the risks have been minimized; that there'll be pre-game meetings at which the teams agree on the challenges; that the Judges will be pussy-cats; and there'll be no Warnings for Boring; and so on.

I had intended to give the stage back to the performers, but when the model is show-business the director will be reinvented in the guise of an emcee who bosses the players about, gets laughs at their expense and becomes the star of the show. An Australian group timed their emcee and found that he talked for more than half the time. Stand-up comedians leech on to the role because the moment things begin to die (i.e. the laugher becomes exhausted) they can hand the show over to the players. Many Theatresports groups are really presenting a star emcee who is 'accompanied' by improvisers. It's as if I had invented tightrope-walking, and had returned to find that my students had lowered the rope to ground level.

Failure is part of any game, and unless this is understood, Theatre-sports will be a high-stress activity.

The Wrong Risks

We all have some special area that we reserve for 'risk-taking': we shop-lift, or hang-glide, or break the speed limit, or gamble, or get drunk, or procrastinate, or deceive our lovers, or climb mountains. But only fools take risks that are suicidal.

The improvisation stage should be one of those special areas, and yet I saw a match recently in which a player foolishly asked the audience, 'Who am I?'

Someone shouted, 'Margaret Atwood!'

Afterwards I said, 'Why did you accept "Margaret Atwood" if you had no idea who she is?'

'But I was taking a risk! Isn't that what you tell us to do?'

'Where's the risk when the chance of failure is one hundred per cent? You might as well dive into an empty pool screaming, "How's this for a riiiiissskkkk?" SPLAT!'

I coached five improvisers in a lunch-time show, making their task as easy as possible, yet that evening, when they worked without me, they made their task as difficult as possible.

I had warmed them up with the game in which the first player to use a word that included the letter 's' loses, but when they worked by themselves they banned the letter 'e' ('e' being the commonest letter). There were long pauses as they checked each word, and this created no trust, no good nature, no exhilaration, and no pleasure – only embarrassment.

I had followed this with Speaking in Three-word Sentences (another game that makes the players attend to what they're saying instead of rabbiting on), but they played the One-word version that I use to force physical solutions. They hadn't practised this, they didn't know its purpose, and they failed miserably.

It's as if they believed that the audience came to admire their cleverness, rather than to bask in their good nature and warmth and playfulness, but that's like assuming that the best sex involves standing up in a hammock. Perhaps players who can't fail gracefully are impelled to increase the difficulty so that their failure will seem forgivable ('I'm not really impotent, dear, it's just that the hammock is so unstable').

Dullness is Deliberate

Never kick over a row of Hell's Angels' motorbikes unless you're the hero of a movie.

Dullness is a set of procedures for ensuring that nothing untoward happens, and some people have no talent for it. They're forever in trouble and can tell you wonderful stories about their hazardous adventures.

Dullness can be a life-saver (never let a stranger tie you to the bed), but audiences pay to see its opposite, and they reward behaviour that they would condemn in real life, as when Antony Sher as Richard the Third hoisted the front of Lady Catherine's skirt with his crutch. No one wants W. C. Fields as their dentist, or Harpo as their blind date, but we'd enjoy being a fly on the wall.

If dullness is a technique, and we reverse it, it should be possible to transform a genius at being dull into a genius at being brilliant. Even training people to say 'yes' rather than 'no' can make immediate improvements. Let's say that I invite a cautious beginner to improvise, saying, 'Did you bring the parcel?'

Answering 'yes' would involve a loss of control, so the parcel will be seen as something to be got rid of. A typical response might be: 'Sorry, I forgot' or 'They said they'd send it tomorrow' or (more cunningly) 'Yes, I gave it to your mother.'

Turn these defensive answers into positive ones and something may happen:

'Did the parcel arrive?'

'Yes, shall I open it?' or 'There seems to be something alive in it!' or 'The time-machine? It's out in the hall. They want it back by last Thursday.'

The student would now be perceived as 'talented', yet it takes no more 'talent' to accept the parcel than it does to reject it.

Being 'Original'

Being 'original' and being 'stupid' are often identical. An improviser who is trying to be stupid will open a parcel and find a brick, but so will an improviser who is trying to be clever, because both know that no normal spectator could possibly want the contents of the parcel to be a brick. A scene started like this:

- Is that your bird?
- It's not a bird, it's a 'drib'. We call it a drib because it's very like a bird but it flies backwards.
- Really! My tac eats dribs.

Only players desperate to be clever could create such embarrassing stupidities.

Asked 'Is that your dog?' an improviser said, 'Actually, it's a leopard, but I rubbed the spots off!'

The audience groaned.

Another player was asked, 'What breed of dog is that?'

'I don't know – but it catches mice and goes meow!'

'The audience expect a dog, so I'll give them a cat' is the level of thinking involved, and yet if she'd responded normally there'd have been no problem.

– Your dog's very friendly. What breed is it?
– A German shepherd.
– Is it for protection?
– Well, I've seen the terrible stories in the newspapers.
– You'll have read about me, then?

When originality is seen as an avoidance of the obvious, creativity fizzles out. A player asked for an 'activity', and was given: 'Making an omelet!'

He pretended to be in a kitchen, and then, trying to be clever, he asked, 'Do we need eggs to make an omelet?'

'You just have to rub tobacco and cheese together!' said his partner, wanting to outdo him.

His heart sank, but his belief that he should accept ideas, no matter how moronic, condemned him to act out this foolishness. A Warning for Boring would have been a kindness, but the feeble Judges let them plough on.

Improvisers should learn to be 'obvious', because then things will happen. 'Stupidity' and 'cleverness' are devices that stop things from happening.

Let's say that I'm 'lying on a beach'. Eventually I'll need to relate to another 'item', so let's say that I see a crab. If there are two 'items' (me and the crab) the audience will want us to interact, so let's have the crab take my photo.

'Surely that's original?'

'The crab? What would you expect to find on a beach?'

'With a camera?'

'Perhaps it's a tourist.'

'You really think that a crab with a camera is obvious?'

'If I'm on the beach, then of course a crab is "obvious", and the audience will expect me to interact with it. Having it bite me would be negative, and a tiresome cliché, but having it take my photograph adds the mystery of why is this crab photographing me? The audience love mysteries that they believe will be resolved.'

'But a photographer crab wasn't in the mind of anyone in the audience.'

'Agreed, but it wasn't denying the audience anything that it wanted. Had the crab been an intrusion, it would certainly have been "original", but if a beach, why not a crab? Perhaps it's one that I befriended last year, or it could be in love with me (and I'd have to be very tactful and sensitive in order not to hurt its feelings), or it could have a little Nazi arm-band . . .'

'A crab with Nazi arm-band! And you don't call that original!'

'Well, obviously I have to have an attitude to the crab. Perhaps I'm Jewish.'

'But I don't think of ideas like that.'

'This is my obviousness, not yours, but how can you release your obviousness if you insist on being "original"? Being "obvious" means being your own person, not somebody else's, and it lets the spectators see you as brilliant and courageous, because they would be terrified to function so effortlessly.'

Some players excuse their 'originality' by arguing that they were using the first idea. For example, a vampire's coffin was opened:

'We forgot the stake!' said one player (afraid to move the scene forward).

'Use this!' said his partner, miming something large.

'What is it?'

'A giant tomato!'

This 'tomato' was later defended on the grounds that 'it was original', and that it was 'the first idea'.

'But that "first idea" was an attempt to wreck the story because you'd no idea what to do after you'd hammered the stake in!'

(The 'tomato' is an example of the talent needed to achieve dullness. Stakes are hard, and sharp, and spear-like – could you think up an exact opposite for a stake in a split second?)

Brains sort the world into categories; if I want to name something red I can say 'blood', or 'sunsets', or 'cherries', or 'a field of poppies'; if I want to name heavy things, I can say 'an elephant', 'a ton weight', 'the planet Jupiter', or 'a giant gerbil'. We interiorize 'lists' for the entire universe, and if I seize a 'first idea' from a 'how-to-be-original' list, I can kill any interaction stone dead.

'So we can't be original?'

'Of course you can. It's fine to tell the story of Red Riding Hood from the point of view of the wolf – as in the impro game called King-Kong: My Side – or to be a couple of sperm fighting your way through to the egg, or to have an intelligent conversation with your goldfish, or to be someone's canary, or to be a billionaire who buys precious objects in order to destroy them, or to be a tailor who vivisects people until they fit his suits. But you mustn't use "originality" to deny the audience things that have been promised them.'

The Imagination

I was born in a world so censored that it can hardly be imagined even by those of us who were born into it – can you believe that the grand piano in our school hall had skirts around its carved legs lest it arouse our lust? The horror of tenderness was such that a psychologist recommended no physical contact between parents and children except for a formal handshake first thing in the morning.[6]

Masturbation was thought to cause madness, but why madness rather than tennis-elbow? Admittedly, if you shut a madman in a cell, he's likely to start masturbating. But sane people thrown into jail are likely to comfort themselves in exactly the same way. The idea that masturbation causes insanity is based on the same mislogic that makes many people fear that 'crazy thinking' leads to insanity. It's their behaviour that classifies people as insane, not their thinking, so it's a pity that many perfectly sane people allow themselves only a narrow range of approved ideas.

Clowns, comedians and cosmologists enjoy the pursuit of 'crazy ideas'. Every new idea was crazy once (cooking your meat, wearing animal skins, flying to the moon), and 'lunatic thinking' (for fun) is part of being human, is the difference between soaring about in a limitless universe and being locked up in a grubby little room.

As we grew up we struggled to create a 'social-self' that would shield us against the onslaughts of other people. (I'm sure you'll remember glancing at your reflection in shop-windows to ensure that the lie was being maintained.) If we can perfect this, we'll hardly ever get laughed at against our will, but the imagination will be our enemy – because it refuses to present us as 'sensitive', or 'tough', or 'charming', or 'mature', or whatever else we're pretending to be.

I can demonstrate this antagonism by shouting disconnected nouns as loudly and quickly as possible: 'Cabbage! Match-box! Shoe-lace!

Electron! Lithium.' After just five words, I'm in trouble, because the word lithium seems so inexplicable that my social-self creates a log-jam so that I can check whether I'm 'giving myself away' (only now do I remember that it's a chemical that is given to psychotics).

Many dull people claim to have 'forgotten' their entire childhood (all those years when their thinking was 'not adult'), and their minds are like maps scrawled with 'Here Be Monsters', but their imaginations aren't dead, just frozen. Reassure them, and protect them while they are coaxed into 'forbidden areas', and a seething mass of lunatic thoughts will emerge that aren't dull in the least. The teacher has to establish such 'craziness' as a mark of sanity, so that instead of panicking, the students can 'join the club'. Laughter is a great help in making forbidden ideas so acceptable that the students have no need to snap back into numbness.

The best trick I know for releasing the imagination is to persuade the students that their imaginations have nothing to do with them.

'The imagination is a huge animal with a will of its own,' I say. 'Be interested in it, but accept no responsibility. You're not its keeper. Where do ideas come from, anyway? Why should I say "I thought of it", or "I thought of an idea", as if my creativity was something more than the acceptance of gifts from an unknown source?'

Ultimately students have to accept that the imagination is the true self (as William Blake knew), but it's not easy to grasp this nettle.

Prodigies

Laszlo Polgar decided to make his children into geniuses, and chess seemed a suitable discipline (although he wasn't a very good player). My information comes from a perhaps rather unsympathetic article in the *Guardian Weekly* (26 November 1989). Peter Lennon wrote:

> Polgar is against conventional schooling, he says, because 'it did not make learning a beloved activity; . . . Polgar's approach to learning is, he says, that 'the pleasure of the accomplishment must be several times as much as the experience of failure.' He claims to reject blind discipline. 'I have achieved discipline,' he says, 'by kindling interest in, and love for, the subject. I believe that early childhood is not at all early in respect of learning, not even of specialization.

If we believe that prodigies are born, not made, how can we explain his success? His three daughters were grand-masters while still in their teens, and the youngest, Judit, became the top-ranking woman player at age thirteen.

Retarded children are responding wonderfully to new teaching methods (we're having to revise our opinions of the capabilities of Down's syndrome children almost monthly). Computers are teaching the profoundly deaf to speak: Whales are balancing their trainers on their snouts and hurling them high into the air and not eating them. It seems reasonable to conclude that 'untalented' students could be accelerated to unheard-of levels of 'brilliance' if we could press the right buttons.

NOTES

1 Author of *Rehearsal for Life*.
2 See the chapter on spontaneity in Keith Johnstone, *Impro* (London: Faber and Faber, 1979).
3 In his book *Inner Tennis*, Gallway recounts how he asked a mediocre player to demonstrate how he would hit the ball if he were an expert. The man hit the ball perfectly, over and over again. Asked why he didn't always hit the ball that way, he said, 'Ah, but I don't think I can keep this up much longer.'
4 Kimon Nicolaides, *The Natural Way To Draw* (Boston: Houghton Mifflin Company).
5 The Stockholm City Theatre once sent a technician to study our technicians.
6 The paediatrician Dr Spock mentioned this. My family didn't even shake hands.

5 Impro for Storytellers

Storytelling is frightening (and exhilarating), because it involves a journey into the unknown. Abandon the struggle to tell stories and improvised comedy will be just another form of gutless 'light entertainment' (gravy without meat), and your best players will drift away in search of something more stimulating than the endless repetition of the same games.

A Dutch impresario, Jan de Blieck, arranged our first European tour.

'But the audience won't understand a word we say!'

'Why would they buy tickets if they can't speak English?'

Each time we arrived in a new country the word we could read on the posters – besides Theatre Machine – was 'mime'. Witticisms and verbal dexterities were useless. It was like playing to the deaf. It was sink-or-swim, and we 'swam' because I'd taught improvisation as a form of storytelling and you can show stories happening even if you can't use words.

(At Dubrovnik, we learned six words of Serbo-Croat, and the audience cheered whenever we used one, but on the next night they were unresponsive: no one had told us that the tickets had been bought by eight hundred Russians from a visiting cruise ship.)

Journey without Maps

My son is scowling at a piece of paper.

'What's that?' I ask.

'A semantic map!'

'A what?'

'I have to write a story and I'm supposed to map out everything that's going to happen so that my teacher can mark it. She says it'll stop me writing the wrong things.'

(He's aged ten and yet she's already destroying his pleasure in writing just as someone once destroyed hers.)

'Why not draw the map afterwards?'

'But how will I know what to write?'

'Have you ever been on the beach and discovered a cave?'

'Yes.'

'Did you go in?'

'Of course.'

'Well – writing a story can be like creeping into a forbidden house, or lowering a gigantic hook into a haunted lake.'

He likes this idea. 'But how do I begin?'

'Start with something ordinary and then have something mysterious happen.'

He goes away for a while, full of enthusiasm, but then he comes back disheartened, and says, 'I'm stuck!'

'What's your story about?'

'It's about a boy who has to write a story.'

'Is he in trouble?'

'No.'

'Well, stories are about people who get into trouble.'

He rushes off for a whole hour and comes back looking pleased. 'He's in such a mess. Now what?'

'Either rescue him or make him suffer more.'

'But how can I end my story?'

'Feed things back in that happened earlier. Where did your story begin?'

'At school.'

'Then why not work the school into the end of the story? Stuff you've mentioned earlier should be reincorporated.'

'Reincorporated?'

'Fed back in. Oroborus.'

'What's oroborus?'

'A snake eating its tail.'

Stories seem so well constructed that it's natural for teachers to assume that they were thought up in advance, but Gregor Samsa could have mated with another cockroach, and Humpty Dumpty could have been unscrambled by feeding him to a chicken.

Action and Interaction

When I was one of a group of young playwrights we could never agree on what was meant by 'dramatic action', but I would define it now as the product of 'interaction', and I'd define 'interaction' as 'a shift in the balance between two people'. No matter how much the actors leap about, or hang from trapezes, or pluck chickens, unless someone is being altered, it'll still feel as if 'nothing's happening'.

- I seduced your wife this afternoon.
- [*Pause*] Enjoy it?
- [*Pause*] Not really.

This would be an example of action if it was clear that the relationship between the characters was shifting.

Entering a strange restaurant by ourselves, we'll avoid anything that might make the customers stare at us, forks halfway to their mouths; we achieve this by making sure that we aren't worth a second glance (because a second glance would glean the same information as the first). Presenting a consistent exterior may have evolved as a way of showing predators that we aren't afraid of them, so it should be no surprise that beginners will always know who's ringing the door-bell (because being taken aback when they open the door would involve a transition to some other state). Asked to improvise in pairs, most will jog, or play cards, or waltz, or play Frisbee: they'll choose activities that allow them to stay 'intact'. This may fool the average coach into seeing them as 'working well together' but it's really a ploy to prevent change. Even players who are determined to 'shine' will be consistent; if they start loud, they'll continue loud; if they begin by flashing big false smiles, they'll end by flashing big false smiles.

One way to understand 'action' is to attend performances that are in a language that you can't understand. Some will be baffling, but if the characters are altered by what was said, you'll remember them as though they were speaking in English. Good theatre is like tennis in that the spectators look to see how a statement is received, whereas in bad theatre it won't be received.

Blatant refusals to be altered may occur in scene after scene (and the laughter at the thwarting will reinforce the behaviour).

- Oh no! I shot you!
- Lucky you were firing blanks.

Or:

- The kitchen's on fire!
- [*Bored voice*] Yes. I started it . . .

On Not Being a Hero

When in doubt, torment the heroine – *Sardou*

A hero is not just a miserable wretch stuck in a dungeon, or serving at the check-out in a supermarket. A hero suffers in pursuit of a goal (and yet I've seen shows in which the improvisers never pursued anything).

In one of the first classes that I ever gave someone shouted, 'Look out! There's a shark!'

His partner parried by saying, 'It's all right, it's just a piece of driftwood.'

In another scene a 'wife' said, 'I'm so glad you're home, dear, because there are strange noises coming from the basement.' Her 'husband' said, 'I keep telling you, dear, we don't have a basement!', which got a laugh, but now no one had to descend those frightening stairs.

Rejecting the role of hero keeps sending the players back to square one.

Players who reject the role of hero suffer the very real agony of being trapped in front of a bored audience.

Moral Decisions

All stories are trivial unless they involve a moral choice, and it can be especially thrilling to watch the hero make the 'wrong' choice (for example, Jack the Giant-killer selling the cow for a handful of beans).

Making a moral choice alters you, makes your character experience relief, or sadness, or despair, or whatever, so moral choices are avoided. Demanding a scene that illustrates a moral is ineffective, but asking for a scene in which *one* character makes a moral choice usually works. Here are some examples:

- Your car killed a pedestrian and you drove on without stopping. Beg, bribe, bully, or blackmail someone else to say that he/she was driving.
- Two hunters shoot a person in mistake for a bear. Will they bury the corpse secretly? Will they run away? Will they report it?
- Someone is blamed for your crime. Will you confess?
- Someone is drunk; will you take advantage of them?

- Will you let your drunken guest drive off into the night?
- Will you commit perjury to help a friend?

Circles of Expectation

The spectators create a 'shadow story' that exists alongside the improvisers' story. Storytelling goes well when there's a close match between the players' stories and the spectators' shadow stories.

Two players asked the audience, 'Where are we?'

They were told, 'Exploring an unknown planet!'

This created a 'circle of expectation' that includes man-eating plants, machines that obey the commands of extinct masters, and so on, but an 'astronaut' gasped in horror and said, 'Oh no! It's my mother!'

This killed the scene stone-dead (because even he had no interest in following up this idea). His 'mother' can't possibly have been in the minds of anyone watching, but he had construed 'being creative' as avoiding anything that might have occurred to a normal person.

The opposing team asked for a geographical location: 'Where are we?'

'In a desert!'

Arab hospitality, or Foreign Legionnaires, or Valentino in heat were 'inside the circle', but the desire to be 'original' led to a discussion about paper-clips.

Let's say that a 'clever' improviser plays a scene in which he converses with a worm on a forest path (the worm's voice being supplied from offstage). This creates a circle of legitimate expectation; perhaps it wants to be helped back on to the soil, or to find a friend, or to be moved further away from the nest of robins, but our improviser will drag in an idea from outside the circle. Perhaps the worm will be defined as a bookworm, because who expects a bookworm in the middle of a forest? But this establishes a new circle – perhaps it fell out of a book, but that's too 'obvious' – so the improviser will thwart the audience yet again by having the worm want to enter the Eurovision Song Contest, or be taken to the zoo so that it can make love to an elephant. Hence, the improviser becomes increasingly out of step, and the onlookers have less and less interest in what happens.

The players who stay within the circle seem the most original. A sexually liberated grandmother was asked for advice by her non-orgasmic granddaughter. She said, 'Here's something that I've always found helpful,' and went to the cupboard and mimed taking out a sex-education book. The audience groaned because they knew that this was intended to evade the problem (let the book do it), so I told her to scrap the sex book and drag out a Victorian vibrator operated by a foot-pedal. The audience laughed so much that we ended the scene, but afterwards the players claimed that this idea was an example of being 'original' – something I tell them not to be – so I explained that the spectators had laughed so much precisely because the idea was so blindingly obvious. They had been expecting a vibrator, and as granny was very old, what could be more 'in the circle' than a vibrator from the era before electricity became generally available?

The spectators' imagination works within the circle, but the improviser who tries to be 'original' is doomed to work outside the circle.

Point

'Little Red Riding Hood is taking a basket of cookies to her granny. She picks some flowers, and when she gets to granny's cottage, granny puts them in a vase.'

Any four-year-old will tell you that this is 'not a proper story', and any student of literature will explain that there has to be conflict; so let's add conflict.

'Little Red Riding Hood is taking a basket of cookies to her granny. She meets a wolf who eats her up. Granny is sad.'

Your four-year-old will still dismiss this as silly, because children come out of the womb knowing that 'point' is achieved not by conflict, but by the reincorporation of earlier events.

Question: why doesn't the wolf eat Red Riding Hood in the forest?

Answer: because if the wolf eats granny first we'll want to know what will happen when Little Red Riding Hood is 'fed back in'.

Feeding something back in from earlier in the story adds 'point' and creates structure. 'Point' can also be generated by reference to something outside the story, as when two 'hunters' captured 'Big Foot', who unzipped himself and climbed out of the suit:

'Harold! What are you doing out here in the woods dressed as Big Foot?'

'Oh, you know – Government Summer Work's Programme . . .'

Perhaps the easiest way to achieve 'point' is by reference to a previous scene, but it is likely to weaken the current scene, and is best when used as a 'gag' to achieve an ending. The improviser Chris Klein played a character who had trouble doing up a waistcoat that had lots of buttons. Later in the game he blundered through in a scene in hell, tormented for all eternity by this intractable waistcoat.

A pointless story is one in which the recapitulation is missing or bungled, whereas a perfect story is one in which all the material is recycled (although a 'perfect' story may be very dull unless the hero is abused in some satisfying manner).

Justification

An improviser established a living-room and asked the audience for an activity. Some saboteur shouted 'digging' (which got a laugh), so he began to dig, but the activity wasn't *justified*: he wasn't planning to hide a corpse under the floorboards, or trying to find out where the 'voices' were coming from, or retrieving buried treasure, so the activity was pointless and led nowhere.

News from neurology, and artificial intelligence, suggests that the personality is just one 'module' of the brain, and that it maintains the illusion of being 'in charge' by accepting responsibility for thoughts and actions that are generated by the other modules. This can be seen when we invent reasons for obeying post-hypnotic suggestions, or when the verbal hemisphere of 'split-brain' patients automatically justifies the decisions of the non-verbal hemisphere.

Such justification is never-ending, effortless and automatic. When a projectionist mixed up the order of the reels of a movie, my mind struggled to accept this as 'flash-backs' or 'art'. If an author describes cows who are arranging themselves on the hillside to spell out messages, it's almost impossible not to speculate that they're being controlled by aliens, or that a genius cow is pushing the others into position, or that the farmer is going insane, or that an elaborate practical joke is being played.

The best improvisers exploit this wired-in creativity by saying things like: 'I have an idea!' or 'Did you bring it?' even though their minds are a complete blank. Less skilful players have to know the reason for their ideas before they express them (for fear of being exposed as 'uncreative').

Asked to use a balloon as if it were a different object, beginners will 'think' what to make it into, and their minds may go blank, whereas if they picked it up it might become a telephone, and if they'd licked it, it might become an ice-cream. A dull improviser, confronted by a mimed mouse, won't 'see' it as wearing a tuxedo and holding a bouquet, because such dullards want to be sure that the ground is safe before they venture on to it. Brilliant improvisers step willingly into the void of the future: dullards who master this trick are no longer dullards.

Mysteries

Place anything, or anyone, on a stage and the spectators will think, Why should we be interested in this?

You don't need 'clever' idea to start a scene because whatever you do will be accepted as a mystery to be solved (justified). If you're pretending to climb a mountain, we'll want you to find a dead parachutist with a haversack full of money, or for God to give you some more suitable commandments. The mystery of why we should watch you 'changing a wheel' is solved when you fall in love with the stranger who stops to assist you.

Start dusting an armchair, and the spectators will give you their attention as a loan (that they expect to be repaid with interest), but if you finish dusting and wave the lights down, they'll feel cheated, no matter whether you dusted to music or managed to get a few laughs. They hoped that the mystery of why you were dusting would be solved, but no love letter or book of spells was found tucked into the upholstery, and the armchair did not say, 'Oooh! That's nice. Do it again!'

I'll create some 'mysteries', and allow some other part of my mind to justify them. Let's say that we have established a fisherman on a river bank. The spectators will be waiting for something to alter the fisherman:

- He takes out a worm and it cries, 'No! Stop it! Don't put that hook into me!'
  This adds the mystery of why does it talk?
- Perhaps the fisherman is about to hit a fish on the head when he notices that it looks exactly like his missing son.
- He hooks a dead body which adds the mystery of whose body it is, and why this should be significant.
- He sees himself sitting on the opposite bank.

Such 'breaks' start an inner process in us because our brains can't help imposing order on chaotic material.

I'll develop the first idea (the talking worm):

'You talk?' gasps the fisherman.

'We're not supposed to talk, not ever. But that hook, it's so cruel!'

'You mean all worms can talk?'

'Everything does!'

I'm in danger of becoming blocked, so I'll introduce something arbitrary: a shadow falls across the fisherman. I have no idea what this shadow may be, but an audience would want to know, and automatic processes will give me the answer, so I'll type that:

The fisherman looks up and sees Death standing over him . . .

My unconscious has done well here because there's obviously a connection between Death and the worm, but this needs to be made explicit:

The fisherman collapses in terror.

'Calm yourself,' says Death. 'I haven't come for you. I've come for the worm. Now fish!'

The fisherman presses the worm on to the hook, and casts it into the darkening waters.

An audience will want to know what Death wants the worm to catch. Anything can be fished up, but if I want a 'good' idea, I'll probably 'wimp' and refuse to 'think up' anything at all, so I'll type something completely obvious – that the fisherman catches a fish.

'Give it to me!' says Death.

'No!' says the fisherman, clutching the fish as if it was valuable (either 'yes' or 'no' would have pushed the story forward, but 'no' precipitates a crisis).

Death becomes utterly terrifying: 'You won't?'

This raises more mysteries: What will Death do? Why does the fisherman want to keep the fish?

Arbitrary leaps are integrated into a coherent structure, not by searching forwards (an error that has blocked many people), but by searching backwards. So what has been 'shelved'? The worm said that everything in the universe talks!

'Take it then!' cries the fisherman in terror.

But the whole universe roars, 'Don't give him the fish!'

This raises the stakes and by now even I want to know what happens.

Mysteries are time-bombs that are expected to detonate: for example, the princess's promise is a mystery that explodes when the frog cavorts in her bed; the footprint in the sand is a mystery that ticks away until Crusoe sees the cannibals. If the spectators lose confidence that any mysteries will be solved, the threads that grip their attention will begin to snap, which is why it's so difficult to win them back when they've lost interest.

Breaking the Routine

Breaking the routine frees the improviser from the treadmill of always needing a good idea.

Beginners feel uncreative when an activity nears completion. Some compensate by choosing a 'clever' activity like scuba-diving in boiling custard – but the audience says to itself, 'So they scuba-dived in boiling custard – what's the point?'

To solve this problem I defined anything that the improvisers were doing as a routine – poking the fire, reading this book, tracking a moose (whatever) – and I argued that the audience pays to see routines being broken. The routine of 'watering a flower' is broken when it says, 'Thank-you!' The routine of waking up in the morning is broken when you discover that you're in the wrong house.

A section from *Mr Bean's Christmas* might make this clearer. Mr Bean is stuffing a turkey that's as big as an ostrich, and he's making this action more interesting by crouching between its legs like a berserk gynaecologist. This is very funny, but if he completes the action of stuffing the turkey, he risks the 'so what?' response. He avoids this by losing his wristwatch inside it. Then his problem is how *not* to find the watch, so he pushes his head inside the turkey and gets stuck. If he managed to extract his head, we'd be a little disappointed, so he blunders about until he finds a knife with which to cut himself free. This is made more interesting by the arrival of his girlfriend. He covers the turkey with a towel, and as she doesn't really look at him (being occupied with parcels), she easily accepts him as a man drying his hair, but we'll still be disappointed if this routine of getting his head out of a turkey was completed, so the towel comes off and reveals this turkey-headed monster waving a knife, and she reacts as if she was in a horror movie.

Start any routine, ordinary or bizarre, and the spectators will watch patiently, hoping that you will 'break' it, and they see a routine that is not broken as an introduction to a routine that will be broken.

For example:

- The mirror tells the Queen that she is the most beautiful woman in the kingdom. This is introduction, since the act of looking in the mirror is completed (it would have been a 'break' if it was the first time that the mirror had spoken to her).

- One day the mirror breaks the routine by telling her that Snow White is now the most beautiful woman in the kingdom.
- The Queen tells the huntsman to kill Snow White and bring back her heart. This is introduction, since the instructions are completed, but the routine of 'killing Snow White' is broken when he sets her free and cuts the heart out of an animal instead.

Some everyday activities (routines):

- Reading a book
- Looking at the fire
- Calling the dog
- Mowing the grass
- Throwing stones into a lake
- Selling someone a suit

It takes no more 'talent' to break such routines than it does to write them down, and breaking them is a pleasure once the concept is understood; for example:

- You read a book that describes someone who is in exactly your situation. Then it tells you about a murderer who is breaking into a house, and you hear a crash of glass from downstairs.
- You are looking at the fire when you notice a love letter burning in the flames.
- You are calling the dog and something gigantic crashes towards you through the forest.
- You are mowing the grass and you accidentally sever a snake that gasps that it has a message for you.
- You are throwing stones into a lake and one stays in the air. It starts floating upwards and so do you.

Any routine can be broken in many ways. For example:

- You're reading a book when you find the lost will hidden between the pages.
- You're reading a book when you discover that your wife has underlined all the passages about hating men.
- You're reading a book that inspires you to murder your husband.

● You're reading a book that you discover is about you – do you dare to see how it ends?

● You're reading a book and you find that your guest has used a rasher of bacon as a bookmark.

I coached a scene in which a tailor sold a suit to a customer. The players took their time, and were pleasant to watch, but they felt uninspired.

'You can't think what to do?'

'We're stuck.'

'You see yourself as "needing a good idea", but I see you as completing the routine of "buying a suit" – so why not invite the tailor to the wedding?'

They obeyed me, but once the invitation had been accepted they were stuck again.

'Break the routine by saying, "There's a problem . . ."'

'Which of us should say it?'

'Either of you. It doesn't matter.'

'But we don't know what the problem is.'

'Nor do I, but saying, "There's a problem" presents a mystery that will gain you at least another fifteen or twenty seconds of spectator interest.'

The groom announced that there's a slight difficulty, and the tailor said, 'Really, sir?'

I pointed out how attentive the spectators were.

'But what now?' they say.

'Stay inside the circle created by the story. And what's inside the circle? The tailor, the suit and the wedding invitation, so why not say, "You look a healthy young man. I was wondering if you could assist me on the wedding night . . ."'

'But what if I was the one who said, "There's a problem"?' says the tailor.

'Say it, and trust that your brain, or God, or the Great Moose will supply a justification. Try it!'

They went back to the scene.

– There's a problem, sir.

– Indeed?

– Yes, sir – the suit's not for sale.

'Whoa!' I said. 'That doesn't make any sense, you've just sold it to him!'

'That's what my mind gave me.'

'Of course it did, because it wants to cancel the transaction so that nothing will have happened.'

'So what do I say?'

'Something positive. Something that takes the action forwards.'

'But I can't think of anything.'

'That's because you're trying to find the whole reel of cotton when all you need is a length of thread that you can follow. Your mind is refusing to introduce a mystery unless it knows how you will justify it, but any mystery will do so long as it stays within the circle of probability. You said that you owned the shop, so why not say: "I wonder if you would mind coming upstairs with me for a moment . . ." This will set so many thoughts going that it could win you thirty seconds of audience attention.'

'But why would I invite him upstairs?'

'How should I know? It's a mystery.'

'But supposing I can't solve it?'

'Take the risk! Aren't there two of you? Maybe your partner or one of your team-mates can solve it. Live dangerously!'

At some point, an attentive student will say, 'You tell us to be obvious, and not to be original, but isn't breaking the routine being original?'

I explain that 'being obvious' means staying inside the circle, whereas 'being original' is an attack in the inner consistency of a scene so as to derail it.

'Let's suppose your routine is "descending by elevator", and that your partner begins to do magic tricks. This has nothing to do with being in an elevator (it's been dragged in from outside the circle to impress the audience), but if you were trapped in the elevator, the performing of a magic trick would be "obvious", because it's plausible that the trapped passengers might be trying to entertain each other. Or let's say that you're "descending by elevator" when you notice that beneath "Main" and "Basement" is a button marked "H". Why not press it and descend straight into hell?'

'And that's not original?'

'It would be continuing the action of descending, so I'd call it obvious. Originality depends on the circumstance: if your action is "burgling a house", then playing the bagpipes would be original (so don't do it) but if you're a clown like Harpo Marx, then of course you should play the bagpipes. "Being obvious" means revealing something that was already latent.'

'It's very confusing.'

'Only because someone taught you to avoid the obvious.'

'But my own ideas aren't worth anything!' (What degradation this student has suffered!)

Someone interrupts: 'What's so special about being an improviser if the obvious choice is the one anyone could have made? Isn't "being obvious" the same as "being boring"?' (He hasn't understood a thing.)

'You must have noticed that the audience will often laugh from sheer pleasure when someone says something completely obvious. The obvious choice is the one you would have made if you hadn't been taught to be "clever", or "artistic". Your obviousness may seem worthless to you, but your obviousness is not mine, and it expresses your true self, whereas "being original" conceals your true self by substituting something previously defined as original.'

'But what if I really am original?'

'Or course you're original, and the more obvious an idea seems to you, the more clearly it will express your uniqueness, but if you try to be creative, you'll be forever dredging up the same fashionable stupidities.'

'You don't really believe that?'

'Let's say you're "sitting in the garden" when a worm tells you that it's hungry (its voice being supplied by someone offstage). An improviser who is striving to be original will say something really stupid like, "Why not eat me then?", because that can't possibly be in the mind of the audience.'

'But what would an obvious improviser say?'

'He could say, "Why don't you eat dirt like the other worms?", and the spectators would be delighted, because this idea would already have been bobbing about at the threshold of their consciousness.

'Let's say that your routine is "peeling a potato". You know intuitively that if you complete the action the audience will feel cheated. (Why go to the theatre to see someone peeling a potato?) Your impulse may be to abandon the potato in search of something more original, like answering the phone, or washing the dishes, but this reduces the potato to mere introduction.'

'How can answering the phone be original?'

'It's original because it side-tracks the action (drags it outside of the circle). The audience aren't interested in the phone, or in the washing-up: they're interested in the potato, and they want you to break the routine by some arbitrary step related to the act of peeling. Cut your hand and start looking for a bandage, or for the thumb you lopped off, and the audience will think, Ah! Now we see the point of the potato. Or have it shriek when you stick the knife in.'

'So it's wrong to search for "good ideas"?'

'There are no good ideas!'

'Of course there are!'

'Not in isolation. It's like talking about levers without saying what they're to be used for – a burned match might be better than a crowbar for righting a capsized beetle.'

The audience hope that the improviser is presenting them with an activity (a routine) with the intention of breaking it: routines that are not completed are seen as introductions to routines that will be completed.

The phrase 'blindingly obvious' suggests that everyone already knows that the obvious can be hard to grasp.

Fun with Tilting

Taking my comedy classes into public was a thrilling adventure, but every third session would crash and burn. This made me desperate to improve our chances, and I soon discovered that if two 'strangers' were 'feeding birds in the park' it might be helpful to stir things up by shouting things like, 'Realize that you knew each other at school!' or 'All the birds go to one person!', but it was hit and miss. Years would pass before I realized that frightened improvisers keep restoring the balance for fear that something may happen.

For example: if two gangsters are eating together and one says, 'I'm sorry, Louie, but the boss has ordered me to kill you!', Louie will probably maintain the balance by saying, 'But he told me to kill you!' The audience will laugh, reinforcing such behaviour, but the results will be disappointing.

Comic strips can give insights into tilting because the transactions are so simple: for example, a man throws a penny into a wishing-well, and a genie appears and materializes a woman for him. This delights the man until she runs off with the genie. His disappointment makes us feel that the time spent glancing through the strip was well spent, whereas had he just said, 'Thanks very much!' and walked off with the woman, the transaction would have seemed pointless. Of course, if a 'dominatrix' had chased the man with a whip while the genie rolled on the ground, helpless with laughter, or had the woman wished for an 'adonis' to replace the man, this would also have made the strip worthwhile.

I'm directing some beginners in Micetro, and a prison guard enters with a birthday cake for a prisoner's birthday. She blows out the candle and tells him that he's the nicest of all the prison guards.

'I know,' he says, and the audience laugh, which he takes as a signal that he's on the right track, but this response allows the relationship to continue unchanged, so I tell him to say, 'Am I really?'

This also gets a laugh, but it alters the level of dominance between them and makes him more sympathetic (we want improvisers to be vulnerable). They continue to interact but nothing's happening, so I tilt the balance by saying, 'Look at your watch – tell her it's time for her execution.'

They both became equally depressed – maintaining the balance.

'Don't both have the same reaction,' I say. 'Tell her it's not personal!'

She weeps, but he becomes resolute, but then he tilts the relationship again by becoming tearful and saying that he loves her and will help her escape. There is a lot of emotion. He unlocks the cell for her and as she steps out I say, 'Shoot her!'

He begins a long 'bridge', intending to kill her after lots of chat.

'No, no, go back to the moment when I said, "Shoot her!" Shoot her now, no explanation. Justify afterwards . . .'

He does this, but she just stands there, only willing to be wounded, and this wound is a purely verbal idea that doesn't change her in the least.

'Just die!' I shout.

He stands over her body looking blank.

'Look calmly at the audience and say something to them,' I say.

He looks out-front and breaks the routine of escaping by saying, 'It's kinder this way!' as the lights fade.

Audiences seem to know intuitively when a tilt is needed. One moment a platform can be enthralling, but then everyone will say – in unison – 'Tilt now!', as if we'd been born knowing exactly when a scene should move into the chaotic future.

What the Audience Wants

You know Aristotle says of tragedy that it must excite fear, if it is to be good. This is true, not only of tragedy, but of many other sorts of poetry . . . You find it in very good comedy – *Goethe*

Here are some of the terse descriptions of movies from the back of the *TV Guide*:

Family

Rebellious youth locks horns with his new step-father.

Teenager meets the father she never knew.

Teenager comes to terms with abusive parent.

Family member, presumed dead, turns up alive.

Daughter accuses her parents of sexual abuse.

Young girl, distressed by impending break-up of her parents' marriage, makes pact with the devil.

Crime

Woman is taken hostage by religious fanatic.

Cop pursues a deranged killer who was released through a legal loophole.

Young woman learns that her room-mate has deadly designs on her boy-friend.

Single mother discovers hit-man's next target.

Thief steals woman's diaries and woos her, using the secrets he knows about her.

Miscellaneous

Escaped mental patient poses as a doctor.

New Yorker dumps his bride on honeymoon to chase his dream girl.

Millionaire plans to hunt whichever of his guests turns into a werewolf at full moon.

Rape victim tracks down and kills her rapists.

Embittered ex-con seeks revenge on prosecutor.

Child-hating ex-wrestler becomes bodyguard to tycoon's pesky offspring.

These one-sentence descriptions imply relationships that will be altered, because we know, from experience, that the lawyer will be tormented by the embittered man, and that the ex-wrestler will turn into a lovable pussy-cat (and so forth), yet the chance of seeing such transactions in public improvisation is just about zero.

It's been argued that such 'serious' subjects are unsuitable for comedy, but one of the funniest scenes I ever saw was about someone dying of cancer; and Mack Sennett (of Keystone Kops fame) would see serious movies and then tell his writers the plots so that they could base comedies on them. Any event can be either funny or serious: it's a matter of attitude and style.

Some players claim to be above the use of such sensational material, but great dramatists aren't. I've never seen an improvisation in which a murderer is tormented by his victim's ghost (*Macbeth*); or in which a bureaucrat tells a nun that unless she sleeps with him he'll execute her brother (*Measure for Measure*); or in which a murderer stands astride the bleeding corpse while seducing the widow (*Richard III*). Such interactions are avoided because they would thrust the players into an unpredictable future, and yet 99 per cent of the earth's population would rather see 'an escaped mental patient posing as a doctor' than eight people in a desert talking about paper-clips.

– Why are you strapping me to the table, Doctor?
– Because God wants me to move your eyes to the top of your head so that you can always be watching him!

The pay-off for the spectators would be the terror of the patient, but defensive players would respond with some stupidity like, 'You mean like your eyes, Doctor?' or 'Oh, good! Then I'll be able to see when it's raining!'

Any theme in written drama, or popular with American talk-shows, should be acceptable as a theme for improvisers. If we avoid popular themes like incest, terminal diseases, rabid Nazis, family crises, ex-lovers stalking us, racism, religious bigotry, and so on, the result is a toothless theatre that gums the spectators into pointless laughter.

Platforms

The platform is the stability that precedes the chaos.

For example, it's interesting to see a road casualty being shovelled into an ambulance, but it's a lot more interesting when you realize it's someone you just had lunch with. This is why Odysseus discovers the cave with the huge cheeses before he meets the Cyclops, and why Circe invites his crew to a feast before she turns them into pigs.

James Bond and Indiana Jones movies may seem to refute this since they begin with stunts, and mayhem, but that's a spin-off from TV, where the mass audience will switch channels unless they're offered something cruel.

Audiences understand this, and they wait for Jones to give a boring lecture, or for Bond to be mildly flirtatious with Miss Moneypenny, because they know that this is where the story really begins. Non-stop excitement, explosions and stuntmen burning to death may seem more interesting than 'nothing', but the 'nothing' is essential. If Bond were to rape Miss Moneypenny on M's desk while M was tied to a chair, the movie would never recover (unless the camera drew back to show that the real M and the real Bond were watching a SMERSH propaganda movie, and even then they'd have to be slightly bored).

'I really don't think it's in our best interests to tolerate this sort of thing, do you, James?'

'I suppose not, sir.'

Continuous excitement is counter-productive but platforms don't have to be dull (any more than the SMERSH propaganda movie needs to be dull). The requirement is that there should be a stable relationship between the characters, but beginners would rather be couch potatoes watching TV than priests at an exorcism, or members of a bomb squad during a tea break. If they're 'in an office', it'll be in a generic office, never a specific office. Asked to be 'picnickers', they'll be in a generic field, never in a field outside a mental hospital, or on a hill where a cult is awaiting the end of the world. In 'jail' they'll sit on a bench and look depressed, even though it would be more fun to read the graffiti, or press the Room Service button and have the guard come in and beat them up.

Great improvisers have the opposite attitude: invited into someone's apartment, they'll say, 'Are those portraits of your ancestors?' or 'What are all the chains and whips for?' or 'Shot all these tigers yourself, did you?' This helps to create structure because audiences will expect such arbitrary details to be justified later on. If there are stuffed animal heads on the wall, and one head is covered by a silk scarf, 99 per cent of the spectators will be waiting for the host to leave the room so that the hero can look under it, and they like it to be someone he knows.

Let's say that I'm directing Micetro and that you've 'been invited into a stranger's home', and are exchanging pleasantries. I might strengthen the platform by shouting, 'Notice the science-fiction collection!' or 'Comment on the skull on the mantelpiece' or 'See the crucifix on the wall.'

The sci-fi collection could lead to the discovery that the entire universe is operated from a switch in the basement. If you picked up the skull, someone offstage could grab a mike and supply a voice for it. If the crucifix began to laugh, you could realize that your host was a demon.

Negating Tilts

I give beginners insight by asking them to negate or minimize tilts 'for fun'. Here are some popular techniques:

• *Already having the disturbing knowledge* – If a human head arrives in a parcel, a dull improviser can maintain the stability (and get a useless laugh) by saying something like, 'Who is it this time?' or 'It must be for the family at number ten!'

If a doctor says, 'Great heavens! Someone's implanted a control device in your brain!', the patient can wreck the tilt by saying, 'Yes, I'd like you to change the battery.'

When a player told an audience volunteer, 'I'm from the future – I'm going to be your baby!' she told him that she'd had a hysterectomy (volunteers are always defensive). This should have demolished him, but he tried to control her by saying that he'd brought a 'replacement womb' for her, and yet her 'hysterectomy' was a tilt that should have devastated him. Afterwards he claimed that he was 'trying to be original', but tilt-theory displays him as 'refusing to be altered'.

When it was agreed that a player would tilt a scene by telling his girlfriend that he was 'gay', she forestalled him by saying, 'Of course I've always known that you were homosexual!'

• *Skipping the 'platform'* – Beginners might think it effective to begin a scene by saying, 'I am from the future! Take me to Julius Caesar!' but this squanders a good tilt by using it as a platform. Perhaps attendants from a psychiatric hospital can arrive to capture this lunatic, and perhaps a further tilt can be achieved when you consider that the attendants are from the year 3006, but it would be better to start from a platform that was more stable.

• *Letting the platform anticipate the tilt* – A good tilt should be like dropping a large boulder into a small pond, but beginners will lead up to a tilt by discussing slavery before saying, 'I've sold you!'; or they'll talk about reincarnation before meeting their deceased parent who is now an alarm-clock. This reduces the boulder to a small pebble. For example, a doctor introduced the 'control device in the patient's brain' tilt by saying, 'Are you still getting the headaches?' And then: 'And dreams about being kidnapped by flying saucers?' And then: 'Perhaps they aren't dreams at all – perhaps the aliens really have inserted something into your head!' Followed by: 'I'd better take a look!'

This is like stabbing the neck muscles of a bull to ready it for the matador, whereas what we really want is for the bull to be catapulted into his bedroom in the early hours.

Platforms can be tailored to fit the tilt, so long as they don't imply the tilt. If a mad tattooist is to attack you, it's a mistake to discuss the rumours about a mad tattooist, but a stranger can admire your skin, and force you to strip, because the audience still won't know what's intended. (This applies to improvised scenes: longer narratives can certainly anticipate some of the tilts.)

Peter Oldring played a scene with an audience volunteer in which he displayed an amazing ability to befriend animals. He mimed petting the pigeons, he juggled the sparrows, he let the squirrels run around his shoulders and down the other arm, he cuddled a baby deer, and so forth. Then he applied a 'visitor from the future' tilt by explaining that he had travelled from a world where humans were at peace with nature. His ability to befriend wild animals made the tilt believable, and yet it could not have been anticipated, whereas if he'd led up to it by discussing time travel, the 'boulder' that was to be dropped into the small pond would have become smaller and smaller.

Forcing Tilts

I interrupt scenes to ensure that tilts are validated.

For example, a 'returnee from a package tour to Transylvania' tried to tilt a scene by saying, 'I keep having this urge to bite someone, Doctor!'

The audience saw the patient as a vampire, or a werewolf, and they longed for the doctor to be bitten, or at least be in peril, but he diagnosed a disease that made people's heads explode.

'You're the fifth one today. Looks like it's starting to burst right now!'

The patient staggered about, clutching his head (the doctor making no attempt to take cover), and the audience laughed, but the scene became stupid and boring. Before you dismiss this exploding head idea as moronic, consider how well the doctor had achieved his aim of 'not being altered', even to the length of ensuring that the patient didn't have a head to bite him with.

I coached a scene between a vampire and psychologist: 'I want blood!' said the vampire, and the psychologist offered her neck, saying, 'Oh, bite me, please!' which got a laugh (but then the scene went downhill). I took them back to 'I need blood!' and this time she said, 'You can suck the blood of my cat!'

No one will casually agree to have their pet sucked by a vampire (unless its owner is another vampire), so I returned them to 'I need blood!' and told the vampire to bite the psychologist. This time she ran around the table so that he couldn't catch her.

'Don't escape!' I shouted. 'Be frozen with terror! Get bitten! Scream!'

She did, and the scene shot forward like an arrow, but it would have been wrong to have seen her as 'untalented', or as 'failing to achieve her purpose':

- She had offered herself to be bitten as a way not to be changed.
- She had offered her cat as a way not to be changed.
- She had run around the table as a way not to be changed.

Afterwards she said that by saying, 'Bite me!' she was giving the spectators what they wanted, but I argued that they'd wanted the vampire to terrify her, whereas saying, 'Oh, well, bite me, then!' had left her in exactly the same state as before.

'So I shouldn't have let him bite me?'

'You should have been altered by the threat, but it looked like "business as usual". You looked like a wet-nurse for vampires!'

At present I'm using a bell to train improvisers to tilt platforms. It rings after thirty seconds and they must either abandon the scene or tilt whatever relationship has been established. For example: two students are in a library – ding – and then one says to the other, 'I've been stalking you!' or – ding – one says, 'I'm invisible to normal people. How come you can see me?' or – ding – one says, 'Someone's trying to kill you!'

This skill can be practised verbally with one player naming a scene or situation, and another player tilting it. For example:

- A honeymoon scene. Ding!
- The penis escapes and hides under the bed.
- A picnic in a field. Ding.
- One of the picnickers has a vision.
- Practising the piano. Ding!
- The furious composer climbs in the window.
- An execution. Ding.
- The victim catches the bullets in his/her teeth.

Tilt Lists

The idea of 'tilting' became 'graspable' by everyone when I pinned up a list of 'strangers on a park bench' tilts on the green-room wall. It was intended to liven up scenes in which an improviser would interrelate with a volunteer from the audience – feed the birds perhaps – and then leave. Such gossipy interactions can be interesting, but when such a park-bench scene has been presented about ten times it becomes Theatre for the Bland: the only risk is that the spectators may have seen it so often that they're sick of it.

Here are some tilts from my current park-bench list (either expressed as instructions, or as lines of dialogue):

- 'This was my favourite place before I died.'
- 'God (or Satan) sent me to find you.'
- One is a psychic who always knows that the other will say or do.
- One player is a visitor from the future.
- 'Everyone I talk to has bad luck.' (Bad things start happening to the other person instantly.)

If you used the 'favourite place before I died' tilt, a skilled improviser might pretend to put a hand through you, and then stagger back in horror (staring aghast at the hand). This would give the spectators the feeling that 'something happened', and as the scene is about mortality, it might even be remembered.

I'll improvise a tilt from a 'someone climbs in your window in the middle of the night' tilt-list. Perhaps Philip is asleep.

- Excuse me.
- Augh! What are you doing in my room?
- Hallo.
- Do I know you?
- Hardly.
- You're a thief!
- No, no! It's just that the window was open so I thought, Why not see who's there? Make a friend for life. Read the motto on my T-shirt – SAY YES TO ADVENTURE.
- But it's the middle of the night.
- I'll pay you!
- Pay me? For what?
- For your time. Look, my pockets are stuffed with money!
- I can't accept money from a complete stranger.
- We're not strangers – not any more. I'm Maurice! What's your name?

- Look, turn away.
- What for?
- I want to get out of bed and put some clothes on.
- No need to be embarrassed – you've got beautiful skin!
- Are you some sort of pervert?
- Yes, I get sexual excitement climbing in and out of windows. Just kidding! Where's the electrical outlet?
- What?
- Ah! Here's one!
- You wake me up in the middle of the night because you want to shave!
- Shave? Why would I want to shave? This isn't a razor. [*Tilt*] I'm the mad tattooist!
- [*Acceptance of the tilt*] Oh, no!
- It won't hurt – well, not much!
- Help! Help!
- Sissy!
  [*Maybe the tattooist wrestles Philip to the ground.*]
- I saw you at the swimming competition last night. What skin! I thought. What a canvas for my art! So I followed you home, running from tree to tree. It took me hours to work up the courage to climb through your window!
  [*Perhaps the intruder displays exquisite samples of his work on his own body.*]
- Why let some apprentice labour over you when you can have my skills gratis?
- [*Philip could agree to have an eagle tattooed on his shoulder and the scene could be tilted again by having the tattooist handcuff him to the bed face down (homosexual anxiety).*]
- What are you doing?
- [*Tilt*] I'm Beryl's husband!
- Oh, no!
- It'll go easier if you don't wriggle – how do you spell 'adulterer'?

This scene is sadistic enough to interest an audience, but unless the players are well trained, a policeman would climb in the window before the tattooing started, or Philip would try to sell advertising space.

There are now dozens of lists on the green-room wall, and it's quite usual for players to glance at them before going onstage. There's a danger that popular tilts like 'This was my favourite place before I died,' or 'I've sold you,' will be used again and again, but we ask our Judges to reject shop-worn tilts.

Tilt-lists allow the players to break taboos without feeling that they're revealing secret parts of themselves, so they can say, 'It wasn't my idea! It was on the list!'

Strong Tilts and Weak Tilts

A weak tilt presents no mystery; for example, if two improvisers meet on a park bench, and one sprains his ankle, this may change their relationship, but no mystery is involved, whereas if one had made the other throw sticks for him, this could be an unforgettable tilt, because is this a werewolf? Is this someone who is possessed by the spirit of a dog? Is he/she some sort of fetishist?

Or again, if an improviser gives birth in a taxi, this will alter her relationship with the taxi-driver but the spectators will think, So what?, whereas if it was the Pope who had the baby, this would demand an explanation.

Here are some weak tilts:

- The waiter struggles to open a bottle, and then someone helps him (the waiter is grateful).
- A boyfriend accidentally breaks his girlfriend's precious doll (she's distraught).
- Someone comes to view an apartment and rents it (the landlord is delighted with the sale).
- A dinner party is interrupted by an earthquake (the butler drops the turkey).

These can be turned into strong tilts by adding mysteries; for example:

- The waiter who can't open the bottle is approached by a demon who offers to open it.
- There is a tiny TV camera in the broken doll.
- The new tenant ties the landlord to a chair.
- A guest apologizes for the earthquake, saying, 'I'm sorry – I get these waves of anger occasionally!'

These mysteries arouse our curiosity, and we'll expect the players to solve them: the demon can be lusting after the waiter's soul, a spouse is spying on the lovers, the new tenant can be collecting people's brains, the guest who caused the earthquake could be God.

Abritrary Tilts

Tilts can be added arbitrarily. This encourages stronger platforms (absolving the players of the need to think ahead, and to 'be clever'). Players can easily make random tilts seem as if they were generated by the platform. For example, a director in Gorilla Theatre asked for a parent–child scene, and we saw a bad poet having his verses corrected by his daughter. Then a tilt written on a strip of paper was taken from a hat. It read: 'It's time I told you about the family curse!', so the father explained that for hundreds of years the men in the family had been doomed to be bad poets, and then he added a further tilt (and mystery) by saying that the curse could only be broken by a youngest daughter.

Just as tilt scenes can be a relief from too much gleeful stupidity, so gleeful stupidity can give relief from too many tilt scenes. We tried an evening of 'tilts' but gave up at half-time because we preferred more variety.

Coda

If a tilt gets a huge laugh, wave the lights down, unless the platform has been 'solid'. A good tilt can seldom redeem a feeble platform.

Challenges to 'the best tilt' are inadvisable because the audience won't understand the terminology.

See Appendix Two for tilt lists.

6 Making Things Happen

The improviser who does not tell stories is chained to the treadmill of always needing a 'better' joke.

Here's my current list of the methods commonly used to kill stories (i.e. to stop anything untoward from happening), although it's not 'set in stone'.

- Blocking
- Being negative
- Wimping
- Cancelling
- Joining
- Gossiping
- Agreed activities
- Bridging
- Hedging

- Sidetracking (confusing)
- Being original
- Looping
- Gagging
- Comic exaggeration
- Conflict
- Instant trouble
- Lowering the stakes

Learning to use these techniques for fun gives us insight into our defensive procedures (paradoxical teaching).

Blocking

– Will you take these cookies through the forest to Granny, please.
– But she's gone on vacation, Mummy.

You block when you want to stay in control.

– Like to come swimming?
– No thanks.

Some players are like wrestlers who won't allow their opponents to get the slightest grip:

– Coffee?
– Tea, please.

– Like a chocolate cookie?
– Have you got a plain one?

Some block their own ideas.

– Like a swim?
– Great!
– Sorry, I forgot – the pool's empty.

The spectators may laugh (because they like to see people thwarted), but they'll feel that nothing's happening.

Some blocking is almost undetectable; for example, an improviser 'feeds pigeons', and his partner says, 'I couldn't help noticing that you were eating that bird seed.'

He replies, 'Yes, it's corn-flakes.'

This gets a laugh (why?), but it blocks the implications that he's weird, that he thinks he's a bird, that he's about to migrate, that he gives flying lessons. It takes 'talent' to be so instantly 'dull'.

Not all negative answers are blocks; for example:

– You must be too tired to come up for coffee?
– Oh no! I'm fresh as a daisy.

Blocking can involve 'character', facial expressions, gesture, and so forth. For example: a man and a woman were sitting in a 'car' when her husband arrived and started to harangue her. The man became old, and established that he was just a hitch-hiker. He said afterwards that he was trying to be original, but I see him as avoiding interaction by refusing the role of lover.

There's a moot area between blocking and not blocking, so it's best to appoint a panel of three Judges and accept their decision. All blocking games should be played with elation.

Constructive use – to increase 'resistance'.

Both Block

If I ask beginners to kill ideas deliberately, they'll look depressed and palm me off with sequences like:

– Let's go fishing!
– Is that a cockroach?
– Would you like an ice-cream?
– I keep thinking it's Thursday.

'You're ignoring ideas, not killing them,' I say. 'Every idea must be shot down in flames.'

I start them again, and insist that they should 'be happy' and should play with elation.

– Let's go fishing.
– I don't feel like it.

This is still not a complete negation, so I interrupt to insist that they should be as happy as possible while making sure that each idea is forcibly rejected.

– I never fish! I detest fishing! Is . . . is that a cockroach?
– Cockroach? Not in my kitchen!
– Hah! The crud on the walls is an inch thick.
– Garbage! I scrubbed the whole place from top to bottom only yesterday.
– You didn't get out of bed yesterday.

These students are learning to be elated, even in adversity, and they'll start to notice blocking when it occurs elsewhere.

Both Block (Two Realities)
The players disagree on the locale of the scene, and each fights for his/her reality.

We played this game at the Royal Court Writers' Group in the 1950s. I've since read a Middle Eastern story in which a hunter enters a forest and meets a crazy old man who seems to inhabit a different universe, but when the hunter emerges the familiar world has gone for ever.

I'll improvise the beginning of such a scene.

– Er . . . Are you waiting for Percy?
– Who's Percy?
– What are you doing here then?
– I'm waiting for a bus.
– A bus?
– Where else would I wait?
– In my living room!
– Get out of the road!
– Take your hands off me!
– That truck nearly hit you!

- Look at you. You're trampling mud all over the carpet.
- You're mad!
- And you are trespassing!
- Trespassing?
- I'm phoning the police!
- Oh, you're one of those confounded mimes!
- A mime?
- Well, you're using a mimed telephone.

And so on, until they exit in rage, or until one gets sucked into the other's reality; for example:

- The sofa! It's spouting leaves like a bush!
- It is a bush!
- But . . . but . . . What's happening to the walls! Why – what am I doing at a bus stop in my pyjamas!

And so on. Having one join the other's reality is my idea. Left to themselves, players would see this as a defeat (like losing a mimed tug-o'-war).

First to Block Loses
- Got the suntan lotion?
- It's here. Shall I rub some on?
- I'll do it!

The second improviser wins.
Another example:

- Have you done your homework, Tommy?
- Here it is, sir.
- I see you failed to solve the last problem.
- It's over the page, sir.

The teacher wins.
Or imagine two priests:

- I thought you were praying, Father, kneeling on the ground like that. [*The second priest almost says that he was praying, but catches himself.*]
- Do keep your voice down, Father McMurphy. I'm watching a spotted nut-hatch!
- A rare bird indeed. Let me see through those binoculars.
- Just a moment . . . Why there's a whole flock of them!

The second priest loses because he is so full of his own ideas that he won't hand over the binoculars.

Improvisers who master this game can walk on a stage with blank minds and create stories by accepting whatever occurs.

– Haven't seen you lately.
– I've been away.
– Africa?
– Hunting crocodile.
– Still carrying the gun, I see.
– Yes. There's one stalking me. I killed its mate, and it's been following me ever since.
– What – here in Riley Park?
– Ssssh! Don't move! I thought I heard something.
– Behind the bush?
– Behind the shed.

The player who said, 'Behind the bush' wins, because his 'bush' was blocked by a 'shed'.

Divide the class into two teams, and let each cheer for its champion. Award five points when anyone lures their partner into blocking them. This will encourage them to make bolder offers. (If no ideas are killed, declare a draw, or say 'speed up'.)

Encourage the players to lure their opponents into killing their ideas – this encourages bolder offers. Return to this game sometimes, and point out how the skills are improving.

Don't let the players retreat into gossip.

Remove the Blocks
The coach removes any blocks that occur and the game continues.

I intervene to change negative responses to positive ones; for example:

'Are you enjoying the book?' says Ken.

'Not much,' says Paula.

I cut in and tell her to say, 'It's the most exciting book I've ever read!'

This makes her vulnerable. Her partner can say, 'What's exciting about a cookbook?' or 'So you're interested in exploring caves?' and the scene may slip 'out of her control'; Paula might have to improvise more daringly.

Tag Version

'Get in the car, Bill!' says Ann.

'I forgot to close the garage door,' says Bill, not wanting to be controlled.

'That's a block,' I say, and I replace Bill with Wole.

'Get in the car!'

'Shall I drive?' says Wole.

'No, I'll do it,' she says, so I replace her with Doris.

'Like me to drive, Doris?'

'But of course. You're a much better driver than I am, Wole.'

This game needs a skilled teacher – one who is aware of the blocks as they occur. And how do you become skilled? By coaching games like these and making errors.

Both Accept (Gibberish)

This game forces the players to respond to, and to make, physical offers. Students must be skilled at gibberish (see p. 214).

Alan shakes hands, and says, 'Draw dednob!'

He gestures towards the couch.

'Nosi nebneb?'

'Nesne jit tez,' says Beryl politely as she sits.

'Nagerc divad,' says Alan unscrewing the top of a mimed object and pouring liquid from it into two glasses. 'Nay rai cirtap!' he says, making a toast.

'Nay rai cirtap!' Beryl echoes.

She turns away and he mimes spitting his drink into the potted plant. (If she did the same she'd be 'joining' him, and blocking his idea.)

'Gook segleh!' she gasps, and sinks into unconsciousness. He presses an intercom and says, 'Nira callu!'

The door is thrown open and a woman enters, looks at the body on the sofa with satisfaction, and pays Alan.

'Nagrom,' he says, bowing submissively.

'Nos drahcir!' she says, snapping her fingers.

He mimes opening a window and traffic sounds fade in. You can be sure that the spectators will want to know what happens.

Both Accept (Mime)

– A sound wakes him.

– He wakes her.

– She hears it too.
– He throws open a cupboard.
– She finds a sliding door at the back of the cupboard.
– He expresses astonishment.
– She gestures as if wanting something.
– He mimes taking something from the drawer.
– She takes the mimed object and uses it as a flashlight.
– Both crawl into the space behind the cupboard. They stand up.
– She draws attention to something on the wall.
– He mimes pressing a button.
– They pretend that they are in an elevator that has started moving.
– She looks up as if watching the floor numbers changing.

And so on. As in the gibberish version, the players learn to pay careful attention to each other and to advance the story by non-verbal means. (Teach Blind Offers (see p. 192) first.)

'Sounds Good to Me'
Confine an improviser's dialogue to four positive acceptances; for example:

– Yes.
– Sounds good to me.
– I'll go along with that.
– Thank-you.

This game is useful for shy students, and for those who 'can't do improvisation', but their partners have to be skilled at driving a scene forward.

– My daughter said you wanted to speak with me.
– Yes.
– She tells me you wish to marry her!
– Sounds good to me.
– Is she pregnant?
– I'll go along with that!
– You stand there and tell me you've made by daughter pregnant!
   [*The 'yes-sayer' would prefer to say, 'It's not mine!' as a way of staying out of trouble, but the game forces him to agree.*]
– Yes!
– I'm not sure I like your attitude!

[*None of the four positive choices seems appropriate so there's no response.*]

— So! Just because you've made my daughter pregnant, you think an oaf like you is entitled to marry her?
— Thank-you.
— Perhaps you'd like to see around the castle?
— I'll go along with that.
— We'll start with the dungeons.
— Sounds good to me!

Try a paradoxical version using 'No!', 'Forget it!', 'You must be joking!', 'Drop dead!'

— So you want to marry my daughter?
— Forget it!
— I've brought you both a suitable house.
— You must be joking!

And so on.
Or try just two replies: 'Yes!' and 'Certainly'; or 'No!' and 'Never!'

One Blocks/One Accepts

— You're late!
— I lost the address.
— No you didn't! You're ill. You could hardly crawl up the stairs!
— I think I'm dying!
— Just a common cold!
— I'm glad to hear that!
— No you're not. You're a malingerer!
— [*Bursting into tears*] True! I'll leave!
— No you won't! You're trying to avoid military service.
— How did you know?
— I didn't! You just admitted it. Coward!
— Yes, I am!
— Rubbish! You're a hero. Step into in this machine.
— You're taking an X-ray?
— Certainly not. We have an agreement with the enemy to exterminate 50 per cent of our young men to save the expense of transporting them to the battlefield.
— You mean it'll blow me to pieces?

- Not at all. It shows you multiple reruns of old comedy shows until
  you commit suicide!
- That's terrible!
- No it isn't! You get a medal, and a military funeral.
- Full state honours?
- Are you joking? No, we freeze-dry you and stand you in a sentry box!
- At Buckingham Palace?
- You think we'd use corpses to guard the Royal Family? No, we'll prop
  you up outside a recruiting office in Chelsea.
- Chelsea?
- No, not Chelsea – Hammersmith. You've been issued with a rifle?
- Yes.
- No you haven't. That's a plastic replica. Step into the machine. No,
  don't go in there. Just testing you for obedience!

The 'acceptor' must not repeat everything, or nothing can happen.
The audience enjoy this stop–go interaction, so long as some sort of
story is being generated.

Accept but Make Negative Offers
The player who accepts makes negative offers that become positive when
they are reversed (there were a few of these in the last sequence). This
game is tough, but worth the effort. I teach it by prompting the negative
offers; for example:

- *Say, 'I'm glad you're my dad!'*
- I'm glad you're my dad!
- I'm not your dad. You were adopted.
- Adopted?
- Well, not exactly. We found you on the doorstep.
- *Say, 'So you don't know who my real parents were?'*
- So you don't know who my real parents were?
- Of course we do! There was a note!
- *Say, 'You should have kept it!'*
- You should have kept it!
- Of course I kept it! I've had it in my wallet ever since.
- *Say, 'I suppose they died years ago!'*
- I suppose they died years ago!
- Died? Certainly not. They're living down the street!

And so on. Here's another example (unprompted by me):

- Shall we have breakfast?
- Of course not. We're going hunting!
- So we're not taking the boat?
- Of course we're taking the boat! Launch it immediately!
- Like this?
- Not there! Paddle over to the quay so I can get in.
- Sorry, I'm such an idiot.
- I wouldn't be employing you if you were an idiot. Way don't you help me?
- You're so steady-footed, sir!
- Augh! [*Splash!*] Don't just stand there, pull me out!

The special pleasure of this game lies in seeing the 'aggressor' being shamelessly manipulated.

- Well, at least you've given up the hunt for the lake monster, sir.
- Given up! Rubbish. I won't rest another day until I have it stuffed and mounted in the gazebo! Pass me that harpoon!
- Shall I row, or shall we use the outboard motor, sir?
  [*Long pause while Sir hunts for a contradiction.*]
- Hoist the sail!

The one who accepts must use some discretion or they'll 'loop' intolerably. For example:

- Pass me that harpoon!
- This one, sir?
- No, the one on the wall!
- This wall, sir?
- No. The harpoon from the cupboard!
- The one your grandfather left you?
- Not that one!

This soon becomes tedious.

It's Tuesday (Over-accepting Offers)
Each player builds a tirade based on some innocuous remark.

Beginners tend to accept ideas rather timidly, so when an improviser at the studio began a scene by saying, 'It's Tuesday!' I told her partner, 'Over-accept that offer!' which baffled him, so I fed him the dialogue:

'Be aghast. Shout, "Great heavens! Don't you realize what day this is?" Take her by the shoulders and say, "It's my coronation! All my life I've waited for this day! I had the tattoos done, the circumcision's almost healed! Get me my robes!"'

Then I fed lines to his partner:

'Over-accept "Get my robes!" Burst into tears; fall on the carpet and go into tragic grief. Say, "But the robes are still at the cleaner's! I didn't think you'd need them! Those coupons arrived giving twenty per cent off, and I was trying to save money!"'

At the end of this tirade I said, 'Over-accept "save money!"'

'Save money,' he said angrily.

'Not anger!' I shouted. 'You were angry before. Try despair!'

'Save money!' He wept, tearing his hair in grief. 'I was going to dissolve the monasteries and seize their gold, but now my evil brother, Hangoth the Horrible, will get the crown!'

'Extreme happiness!' I said to his partner. 'Over-accept Hangoth the Horrible!'

She glowed with happiness: 'Hangoth the Horrible!' she cried, full of hope. 'But the coupons came from the Hangoth the Horrible Dry Cleaners. Don't you see? We can accuse him of plotting against you. You can become king after all . . .'

And so on. Such over-acceptances are often much longer, and an entire game might be composed of just a few of them.

Left to themselves, most players yo-yo between 'anger' and 'fear', so I yell 'Pride!' or 'Suspicion' or 'Joy!' or whatever, until they're used to applying a range of emotions.

It's usually better to use dull offers: 'Hello!' might precipitate the most amazing reactions:

'John! You spoke! You've regained your voice! You're out of the coma! Heaven be praised! I knew the doctors were wrong, I knew you'd come back to us.'

I'd allow this 'build' to take its course, and then I'd say 'Panic!'

'Back to you? Coma? Who are these people? Where am I? How did I get here? My face: I've got a beard? My hands – I'm so much older! What's happened to me?'

Had I shouted, 'Joy!', the dialogue might have been:

'Back to you? Coma? I'm alive. Hallelujah! I was in hell! I was burning! They were poking forks in me, but I had this asbestos lottery ticket and my number came up – they do it to tease the others. Daylight!

I can breathe the air! Flowers! Human beings! Saved! I'm saved!'

After which I might have shouted, 'Sadistic!'

'Saved, are you?' says his wife, spitefully. 'You think you can escape as easily as that? Do you think I'm really your wife?'

She mimes peeling away a false face and becomes demonic.

Some players are very fond of It's Tuesday, but I would only recommend it for occasional public use.

Other ways of making players extrovert include asking them to play scenes as lunatics or small children.

The Eyes

This is a no-blocking game, in which ideas are drawn instead of acted.

I experimented with many drawing games in the sixties (when I was developing Art-Sports), and this was one of the most successful.

Draw two dots on a piece of paper as 'eyes', and take turns adding a line each until the drawing reveals the owner of the eyes (and what's happening in the picture). The players don't speak, except to encourage each other. If you get stuck, just add two more eyes, and continue. When the drawing seems complete, create the title by adding a letter at a time.

I had often asked improvisers to make drawings together, but it wasn't until I said, 'Begin by drawing a pair of eyes,' that they created anything more than meaningless abstracts.

Play this game and you'll notice that your pen may begin a movement and then switch to some other area before it touches the paper. The replacement of one idea by another occurs in improvisation all the time, but this game makes it visible.

Some improvisers ('passengers') are afraid to take control – you draw an ear and they'll draw the other ear – while others ('directors' and 'bulldozers') will complete an entire face, or scribble huge lines that seize possession of the paper. If the players have less ego attached to their prowess at 'drawing' than to their 'improvising', they'll find it easier to laugh at such negative behaviour.

Children can be at least the equal of adults at this game.

A No-blocking Scene

Two improvisers crawled across the stage (from right to left), as if tackling the vertical face of a mountain. Our 'sound improviser' added some 'wind' and some 'Arctic' music, and one of them 'fell' into a section of audience and had to be 'hauled out'.

If this had just been an exhibition of mime skills, I wouldn't have remembered it, but they jabbed an 'ice-axe' into the stage and a player from outside the scene picked up the microphone and gave a moan. They jabbed again and the 'mountain' shook, and bellowed, and they clung on in terror. They reached a 'ledge' and stood upright (tiring of the 'sideways' effect) and the voice of the mountain befriended them, and guided them to a cave. The acoustics changed as they entered, and the lighting faded to a red circle. They felt their way cautiously around the edge of this, while the audience were agog – there was something very sinister about this soft-voiced mountain.

'Stretch your arm along the wall,' it said. 'Can you feel anything?'

The leading improviser groped about.

'Yes!'

'What is it?' said the mountain.

'It's a . . . it's a sort of crack.'

'Can you reach your arm inside?'

The audience gasped aloud at the eeriness of this suggestion, and the actor reached gingerly into the 'crack' up to his armpit.

'Can you feel anything?'

'Yes . . . Yessss . . . It's a sort of . . . knob.'

The mountain sighed. 'Could you scratch it?'

The audience cheered and applauded, ending the scene (because after such a gag no one would have taken the story seriously).

Being Negative

– *Will you take these cookies through the forest to Granny, please.*
– *But Granny nags all the time and she smells awful.*
– *Now, you know she can't help it.*
– *And it's raining!*

Being miserable minimizes the transitions the hero will have to make when something bad happens, whereas starting positively would maximize them.

If there's a choice, be positive. Eddie Murphy understood this: handcuffed and thrown into a police car, he beamed expansively and said, 'This is the nicest, cleanest police car I've ever been in!' Audiences were very responsive to this.

Positive interactions can make us laugh from sheer pleasure, but don't assume that improvisers are being positive just because they look positive.

Remove the Negativity
– Enjoying the party?
– Not much.
  [*'Be positive!' I yell.*]
– Oh, loving it!
– A real party animal are you?
– Yes. Grrr, grrr! You a friend of Simon?
– Sort of.
  [*'Be positive!' I say.*]
– Oh yes, we were at school together.'

The SAC group in Orlando, Florida, have a game that reverses the last sentence spoken when someone rings a bell.
'Let's take the car.' *Ding!* 'On second thoughts, why don't we walk?'
This can be used as a way to reverse 'negative' behaviour:

– You were in bed with my sister!
– No I wasn't.
  [*Ding!*]
– Well, you see, I'd been taken ill.
  [*Ding!*]
– I was mad with lust.

The terms 'positive' and 'negative' are misleading but they're the best I can come up with. Think of 'positive' as 'forward-seeking'. If the doctor finds something moving about inside the patient, that could be negative for the character, but positive for the scene.

Wimping

Little Red Riding Hood meets the wolf but doesn't tell him about Granny.
We wimp when we accept ideas but refuse to add to them; for example:

– Augh! What's that?
– Augh! I don't know!

Performers wimp in Word-at-a-Time games by postponing the noun;

for example: 'We *met* a *large*, hairy, *green*, angry, *three-legged* . . .'

Wimping typically occurs in situations where any answer would be correct (as when young writers call their characters 'the boy' or 'the woman', even though any name would do). Players wimp when they pretend to stare at the TV but neglect to establish what programme they're watching. Yet if it was a horror movie, they could be too frightened to go to bed, and if it was the local news, they could learn that they'd died in a road accident.

Wimping is sometimes defended on the grounds that it arouses the audience's curiosity, but if the players take something out of a box, and wipe their foreheads with it, and feed it, and admire its hinges, and stamp a passport with it, we'll never know what it is.

Some beginners wimp by constantly asking questions (rather than deciding something for themselves). Others wimp by beginning scenes with: 'Hello!' or 'I like your shoes.' Minutes may pass before we know who they are or what situation they're in. Coax such players to be specific; for example: 'Is this the doll's hospital?' or 'Take her up to periscope depth, Mr Christian!'

Wimping is a cousin of 'pimping', in which you force someone else to do the work (as when someone is handed a letter, but hands it back, saying, 'You read it! I'm illiterate').

Forcing Answers

In directed improvisations, the coach can force the players to be specific. If a beginner pretends to see a frog, say, 'What does its T-shirt say?' or 'Ask it why it's using a crutch.'

A player said that her dog was called 'Fudge', and added – stupidly using comic exaggeration – that she had nine more at home; the director told her to list their names. The audience always enjoys seeing an actor put 'on the spot' and it really doesn't matter what names she says so long as she replies confidently.

The Small Voice Game

This game emerged spontaneously, mid-scene. It is an excellent entertainment game, but beginners usually wimp shamelessly.

I ask Chris to walk through a forest and interact centre-stage with a small mimed creature, while Brenda supplies its squeaky voice from offstage. He enters, and slows down, expecting her to speak, so I say, 'You don't look as if you're going anywhere!'

'But I'd have been off the stage before she said anything!'

'If you help her, how will she learn? Keep walking. Maybe the "small voice" can catch you on your way home.'

I start the scene again and this time he's hardly onstage before Brenda says, 'Excuse me! Hello!'

Chris turns to her.

'Face the audience!' I say, and tell him to look at the ground for the owner of the small voice.

They continue:

'Hey, you! Yes, it's me!'

'What?'

'Down here!'

'Where are you?'

'Can't you see me? Here! In the puddle?'

Most beginners take a long time to see the voice (they 'bridge'), so I shout, 'See it!'

'Great heavens!'

'Surprised you, didn't I?'

'Yes you did, actually. Er . . . What do you want?'

'What do I want? I want to get out of the puddle! Good grief! Ah!'

'Sorry!'

'Don't squeeze me, I'm delicate!'

Chris will take it out of the puddle, and dry it, and chat with it, but typically neither player will establish what this 'it' is, and the longer they delay, the more difficult the act of definition will become.

I ask them to start again, but not to wimp. 'Definitions should come before problems. Say things like, "I bet you've never seen a talking beetle before!" or "Good Lord, Henry! So the experiment worked!" '

If the players define the voice as a beetle, they can agree to step on its evil brother. If it's an exhausted snail they can spit in its path. If it's a tiny naked man it can be a driving examiner who failed a witch. I once saw an interaction between a diabetic child and a 'chocolate' ('Hello, Vibeka – I'm here. Just a little nibble won't make any difference!'), but unless the small voice is defined, the improvisers are building on sand.

When you introduce this game, set it in some natural environment (forests are good), and make sure that the voice belongs to something alive. Trivia doesn't cost anything, so beginners will identify it as coming from a cotton-reel, or a chewing-gum wrapper, or a bottle-top (I must have seen fifty boring interactions with bottle-tops). Such inanimate objects are intended to display the students as original, and to minimize any emotional involvement, but it's better if the voice belongs to an admiring rat, or to a ninja mouse looking for your cat but prepared to take you on if necessary (I saw such a mouse hurl an athletic player about the stage with astounding violence).

The 'mountain with an itch' scene (see p. 113) was a 'big voice' version of this game, but teach 'small voice' first; little things are not as frightening as big things, and the mime is simpler – it's easier to pretend to put a beetle into your shirt pocket than it is to mime being dropped into the pocket of a giant. Later on the voice can be a sofa that's in love with you, or a part of your body, or whatever, but start with mimed frogs, or butterflies, or snakes, and so forth.

The 'rules' for this game are:

- See the creature.
- Add a resistance. Suspect that someone is playing a trick on you, or that you're going insane, or that your coffee was drugged. Be embarrassed by the possibility that you might be seen conversing with a toad, or with a lost chick, or whatever.
- Define the small voice *before* you establish its purpose. Either player can do this: 'Good lord! A mouse with a machine-gun!' or 'I don't suppose you've ever seen a frog holding an End-of-the World-Is Nigh sign.'
- Try to solve its problems. (And if you mime picking up the creature, don't just grab it – consider how you would pick up an earwig, or a worm, or an inch-high theatre critic or whatever.)
- If the problem doesn't lead anywhere, the creature should admit that it was lying, and present a new fantasy ('Actually, I'm not really a beetle, but you stepped on my space ship' or 'I know people don't think much of scorpions, so I wanted you to give me some rules to live by').
- (Optional) You can sometimes end the scene by introducing other small voices ('Peter! Stop talking to that big person and come into the hole!' Or the audience can be encouraged to join in, saying in squeaky voices, 'Come on everybody! Let's get him!').

If a small voice is just 'introduction' – if there's no tilt – end it quickly and cut to the next scene. For example, if you've refused to take a frog home, the next scene can show you waking up in the middle of the night to find it sitting on your chest (our snoggers can have you tucked up in bed in less than ten seconds).

Cancelling

Little Red sees the wolf and runs home – nothing is achieved.

Cancelling dismantles whatever has been established: you light a fire and a shower of rain extinguishes it; you feed a stray dog and it's flattened by a truck. Audiences enjoy seeing their heroes thwarted, but not at the expense of having nothing happen.

Constructive use as a way to end scenes; for example, Walt Disney's Pluto discards a small bone for a huge one that he sees in a lion's cage. After terrifying adventures he ends up with the bone that he started with. This cancels the action, and we know that the story is about to end.

Joining

- *What big teeth you have, Grandma!*
- *All the better to eat you with!*
- *Well, my teeth are as big as yours, so watch out!*

Having the same reaction as your partner is a way to avoid tilting the balance; for example, a player invited his partner in a scene to see 'his paintings':

'Wonderful!' she said. 'I'm a painter too and I paint in exactly your style. We could work on paintings together.'

This seems splendidly cooperative, but it's unlikely to lead anywhere.

A player who 'discovered a burglar' said, 'Excellent! I stole those jewels myself and I need someone to fence them for me.'

Such stupidity seems unfathomable until you realize that it absolves the improviser of the need to wrestle with the thief, or pursue the thief, or to be shot by the thief. It would be difficult not to be altered if you discovered a burglar in real life, but this player's 'wit' allowed him to continue unchanged (although it ruined the scene).

Never accept joining as proof that the players are working well together.

Constructive use – possibly to extend a platform.

Gossiping

- *Do you remember when the wolf gobbled us up, Granny?*
- *Oh, yes, it's lucky that the woodsman was there.*

Gossip avoids interaction by discussing things that are happening elsewhere, or at some other time. You can gossip with your neighbour for thirty years, and yet your relationship may never change.

Scenes often begin like this:

- Hello.
- [*Straight into gossip*] Great party last night.

We hear about the party, but we never get to see it.

Gossip can be entertaining, but at its worst it's just a mass of waffling that drags on until the improvisers find 'a laugh to end on'.

Joining often leads straight into gossip. Two students pretend to be strangers feeding birds: 'I call this one Tom,' says one, letting it eat out of her hand.

'That's amazing!' gasps the other. 'That's what I've always called it.'

Now they can name bird after bird, and minutes will pass with nothing happening.

Constructive use – excellent as a prelude to interaction – why search for 'good ideas' when you can use gossip to build a platform? Gossip can be valued for its own sake (especially if you add status transactions – Peter Cook and Dudley Moore were experts at this).

Gossip to Interaction

Two players begin a scene by gossiping, and after thirty seconds, a timekeeper says, 'Interact.'

'Gossip about last night's party,' I say, and two players start to chat.

- What were all those people doing in the bathroom?
- I hammered on the door.
- I heard you.
- People were having to go in the garden.
- And it was a wet night.
- It wasn't anyone I invited.

  [*'Thirty seconds,' says the timekeeper, and they start clearing up the remains of the party.*]

I interrupt to say that no one is being altered, and that 'clearing up the mess' is an 'agreed activity', yet another way to avoid interaction.

'But what can we do?'

'Find a dead guest!'

'The dead guest' shocks them equally, so I force a tilt by defining the dead guest as the friend of one of them and the enemy of the other.

Another example: Pandora has gossiped about the weather for thirty seconds. 'Interact,' I say, and she demonstrates the weather-machine that she's invented, leaving her partner in awe. 'Break the routine!' I say, and a hurricane blows them away so powerfully that they can't get back to switch it off.

Moving from gossip to interaction is easy (once you have the concept): players chatting about unfaithful lovers can take their revenge; a card-player can accuse his partner of cheating, and so on. (Teach Gossip to Interaction at the same time as Breaking Routines – see p. 84.)

Present Tense Only
(Not my game.) This restricts players to the present tense. They can't gossip about last night's party, but they can say, 'Great party, isn't it?' This places them at the party, rather than just reminiscing.

Agreed Activities

Little Red and the wolf play hide-and-seek and spin-the-turtle; then they practise ballroom dancing. The characters seem to be working well together, but no one is in trouble, and no one is being altered (except for the turtle).

Agreed Activities are kinds of physical gossip. Ask pairs of students to accept all ideas and many will pretend to dance, or play table-tennis, or study a homework assignment, or walk on a beach. This seems a safe way to improvise, but it's boring. Agreed Activities are fine as introduction but unless there's a 'tilt' it's as if nothing happened.

Constructive use – as a platform; for example, the card-players stop to investigate a sound in the attic; the joggers discover a wounded angel hiding in the bushes.

Bridging

Little Red keeps postponing the meeting with the wolf so as to have something to fall back on.

'Bridging' describes the building of bridges over streams that could be crossed in one stride. Asked to 'fire an employee', a boss might say, 'How long have you been driving buses for us, Jarvis?'

'Quite a while, sir,'

'Well, I've been looking through your file – it's far from satisfactory . . .'

The boss can now gossip about the file for minute after minute with the moment of 'firing' blinking away like landing-lights in the distance. It may be argued that he/she is building a platform to launch the scene from, but this platform is intended to last until the closing words. A more thrilling strategy would be to start the scene by saying, 'Jarvis! You're fired!'

This discards the ace up the sleeve, and the scene becomes riskier (and paradoxically much safer because it has less chance of boring the audience).

'Fired! Whatever for, sir!'

'It's the pilfering, Jarvis.'

'Oh, that!'

'Apparently you now own more buses than we do.'

An improviser asked the audience for 'an encounter with an animal', and a woman told him that she had thrown a rock at a bird and was horrified to see that she'd killed it. He relaxed visibly as he realized that he could reserve the killing until the last moment, but the result was worthless. He pretended to be at a picnic, and then his partner threw a stone at a bird and it dropped dead. 'The End' – yet it was her guilt that gave 'point' to the story. I'd have her arrive in heaven that's run by a bureaucracy of birds, or I'd ask the improvisers to be baby birds who are getting hungry and wondering what's happened to Mum.

When the audience is asked 'for a destination to end at', the scene will almost certainly lack vitality (because the bridging is 'built in'). I once asked an intelligent but dreary improviser to explain his technique and he told me that he felt nervous onstage until he'd thought up a possible ending. 'Don't do that!' I said, and he's now one of the best players.

Constructive uses – to help build a climax, and/or to create suspense; for instance, 'What big eyes you have, Grandma!'

Death in a Minute

My students at the Royal Court Theatre Studio never 'killed' each other, even though murder is the theme of many plays and movies. Death in a Minute was an attempt to correct this, but it proved to be an efficient way to teach students to avoid bridging.

I tell two players that they have one minute during which one of them is to be killed by the other, and that 'There'll be a five-second fade in fifty-five seconds.'

Beginners are likely to hear these instructions as: 'At the last split second you have to murder your partner.' Neither wants to be the one who dies (although this is like trying to win a mimed tug-o'-war), and they'll minimize the transition by starting as gun-fighters at high noon, or in the middle of a frenzied quarrel.

'Quarrelling, or "being murderers", would be an excellent way to begin a love scene,' I say. 'Because then you'd have somewhere to go. Why not begin as two sweet little old ladies having tea.'

'But if we're two sweet little old ladies, how can we justify the murder?'

'Act first, justify later!'

One 'sweet old lady' pours tea for another 'sweet old lady', and the minute is up before anything has happened. I tell them to start again and that I'll give them advice. One sips her tea:

'It's poisoned,' I shout. 'Clutch your throat! Die!'

'But we've only just started!'

'Just die!'

'But aren't I to kill her?'

'Just die!' shouts the rest of the class, cottoning on.

We start the 'clock' again and one of the 'old ladies' clutches her throat and writhes about, determined to synchronize her last spasm with the fifty-ninth second (it's almost as difficult to get beginners to 'die' as it is to get them to stay 'dead').

'Die now!' I say. 'Collapse to the floor and keep still!'

(We're fifteen seconds into the scene.)

'But what about me?' protests her partner.

'Time-out!' I say. 'Now you'll have forty-five seconds in which to justify the killing.'

'But I didn't kill her!'

'Stop defending yourself. Take the blame! Tell us why you poisoned the milk!'

We start the clock and the survivor turns to us. 'I couldn't stand her cat,' she says. 'It tears up my plants. And it stares at me all the time! It scratches at my door! It sets off my allergies! I hate it! I hate it!'

'Mime pouring some of the milk into a saucer,' I say, reincorporating the poison. The lights fade as she's saying, 'Pussy . . . Pussy . . . Nice pussy . . .'

The audience identify strongly with the plight of an improviser who is left alone on the stage, so even if your partner dies at the instant the scene starts, it should be easy to fill the remaining time by praying for forgiveness, or by killing yourself in a fit of remorse, or by phoning your lover to exult in your success, and so on. If your partner is a priest who drops dead while taking your confession, explain that your sins were so shocking that he had a heart attack, or that you shot him with a poisoned dart. Say, 'We were missionaries up the Amazon, but he got the natives to go to his church and burn down mine . . .'[1]

Hedging

– *What will you say to Granny, dear?*
– *I'll think about that as I walk through the forest, Mummy.*

Hedging is like bridging, except that instead of postponing a 'good idea', you 'waffle' in the hope that you might think of one. But you won't, because this is not a creative strategy.

The Expert Game
Set the scene in a TV studio. One player is an interviewer who asks impossible questions, and the other is an expert who tries to reply without hedging. (Preventing people from hedging is an important skill for professional interviewers.) We judge this game on the authenticity of the interviewer, and on the believability of the expert.[2]

Sidetracking

Little Red Riding Hood glimpsed a wolf through the trees, but at that moment she fell down a deep hole.

Let's say that two hunters are tracking a moose, and that they're getting close to it. They discover a fast-food restaurant, and go in for a coffee, but this restaurant was not in the mind of the spectators (who were expecting an interaction with a moose) so this 'arbitrary leap' wasn't needed. Perhaps the moose works there as a waitress, but the restaurant was introduced to avoid an interaction with the moose so I doubt that this will happen.

A servant is ordered to get into a coffin and he says, instantly, 'What's the other coffin for?'

This second coffin is a ploy to prevent (or delay) him from getting into the first coffin.

Some scenes are sidetracked by 'shiners' who rush in to share the glory, but others are sidetracked by players who enter a scene so that nothing will happen. Believe this, and you'll notice that the moment that the audience becomes really interested, an unnecessary character will intrude. 'Moses' is about to read the Ten Commandments when an angel arrives. This didn't happen in the Bible story, and there's seemingly no reason for it, yet it achieves its unconscious purpose (which is to prevent the reading). I saw a similar example in which archaeologists unearthed the Ten Commandments, and as they were about to read them aloud, someone entered and said, 'Telegram for you, sir!'

Sidetracking sometimes occurs because the players aren't paying attention. A team of dentists entered a giant's mouth to fix an abscess, but instead of draining the abscess they did a 'filling' (and the weak Judges didn't remind them).

Constructive use – as a way of shelving material that you can reincorporate later on. For example, if the owner of the restaurant in the moose scene had told the hunters about a curse that befalls anyone who shoots the Great Moose, we'd know that the moose had been shelved (good), rather than discarded (bad).

Being Original

Little Red Riding Hood is about to step out of the house when she's hit by a ton of spaghetti.

This is a form of sidetracking in which the improviser expects to be admired for dragging in 'clever' irrelevancies. If spaghetti is thought original, second-rate improvisers will mention it in scene after scene.

When you experience yourself as 'trying to get an idea', you're probably using 'being original' as a way to lock the brakes and skid sideways so that nothing will happen.

Looping

Little Red picked some primroses and some violets and some bluebells and then she picked some berries and some mushrooms and then . . .

If this continues she'll never meet the wolf.

'Loopers' will scratch their knee, and then their other knee, and then their ribs, and then their head. This may get laughs, but while they're 'spiralling' like this, nothing is happening. It would be better to scratch once, and say, 'Jeremy? Is that you?' and play a scene with your pet flea.

Gagging

Little Red peers into a glass that contains Granny's dentures, and says, 'What big teeth you have, Grandma!'

A gag is a laugh that you get by attacking the story; for example:
'Hail Caesar!'
'Copius! Why on earth are you wearing that bed-sheet?'
Perhaps we didn't need a story at this point, but laughter will reinforce gagging until it occurs in scene after scene, and then we're back to soup, followed by soup, followed by soup.

A hitch-hiker forced a young couple to drive to a desolate area and dig two graves. This was eerie, and the audience was enthralled, but instead of asking why, or pleading for their lives, they made gag after gag: 'This is a grave situation!' they said, and, 'What a funny time to do gardening!' and, 'Is there a skeleton service at this graveyard?' They did this to avoid being buried in that desolate place, and yet they weren't really going to end up in unmarked graves; they were going home after the show to their warm beds.

Comedians have always made gags, but not for two or three hours non-stop. Gags pall after about fifteen minutes (which is why music-hall comedians sang sentimental songs, and were sandwiched between the performing seals and the plate-spinners). Scheherazade wouldn't have lasted the weekend if she'd depended on one-liners.

The Gerbil
Tell a ludicrous story, and ask an improviser to enact it, throwing him/ her offstage at the first real laugh. Players 'compete' to see who can postpone the laugh for the longest time.

Begin by telling a distressing story, for example:

– Victor was cleaning house when he decided that Wilma's gerbil needed its cage to be 'refreshed'. He placed the creature in an empty saucepan but it jumped out, and ran into the street where it stuck to some freshly laid tar. Victor peeled it off the road with a spatula from the kitchen, and put it back in its cage on to fresh woodchips which stuck to it until it looked like an animated pine-cone. He found some solvent under the sink that cleaned off the tar, but the fumes sent the gerbil into spasm and then cardiac arrest. Victor tried blowing air into it, but it didn't revive, so he put the body in a shoe-box and waited for Wilma.

(If you don't like my story, invent your own, but remember that comedy treats painful things in a heartless manner.)

The players act out Wilma's return from work, and we time the game from the moment that Victor begins to explain the catastrophe. He includes all the absurd details, but struggles to delay the laughter until the moment when he chooses to release it. Then we replace him and restart the scene with two other players.

This game teaches you to suppress the laughter, and release it when you want it, but it's not really a game, since the players are failing deliberately. Play it when the spectators are already in a giggly mood, and the most innocuous remark can have the audience in hysterics, as when Wilma says, 'What's in the box?' or 'What have you been doing today?' Bad improvisers will try to avoid laughter by mumbling and being depressed, but I tell them that the scene has to be interesting or they'll be honked off for being boring:

'How was work?' says Victor as Wilma enters.

'Terrible!' she says. 'What an awful day!'

She knows that she is to receive bad news so her reply is a strategy to minimize the expected transition. I stop the scene and explain that it's pointless to go from 'unhappy' to 'unhappy'. The scene starts again:

– Hello, how was work?
– Wonderful! I got that raise!
– Great! Cup of tea?
– Love one.
  [*Victor makes tea.*]
– Your gerbil . . .
  [*We start the clock.*]
– Fluffy?
  [*The name 'Fluffy' is too much for the audience.*]

'Two seconds!' says the timekeeper.

We play another round, using two other players (or maybe we just replace the actor who is playing Victor). This time Wilma makes her own tea, and the new Victor is well into the story before he gets a laugh by referring to the 'deceased'.

The timekeeper says, 'Forty seconds.'

This game places the spectators in a curious position, since if they laugh, the scene will end instantly, so they try to suppress their laughter; yet if one of the first players were to reach the end of the story, they'd feel cheated. Ideally, we want the first few players to lose within fifteen or twenty seconds, so that other improvisers can leap on stage yelling, 'I can beat that!' When players are leaping gleefully onstage and failing catastrophically, everyone gets into a giggly and benevolent mood.

No Laugh Impro

This was a spin-off from the Gerbil Game. Start a scene with four or five people and eject anyone who gets a laugh. Have a timekeeper announce the number of seconds that each player managed to survive. Last person onstage wins the game. The scene must not be boring.

The skill of suppressing laughter until you need it is worth having, and the players are forced to be interesting without being funny.

Gag-Police

Gag-Police are seldom used, and always with the consent of the players. Anyone who makes a gag is dragged off and replaced by a gag-policeman for the rest of the scene. You can have Blocking Police, Originality Police and Stupidity Police, and so on. For example, a player who smiled non-stop agreed to be dragged off by the Smile Police.

Comic Exaggeration

– *Take these cookies to Granny, and these apples, and this haunch of beef. Oh, and you'd better take the refrigerator, and don't forget this set of encyclopedias . . .*

A player lies on the stage with his foot held in our fake bear-trap. Someone enters and says, 'Good lord! How long have you been lying here?'

'Three years!'

'What have you been eating?'

'Oh, I used to be very fat!'

He could have been a demon waylaying an unsuspecting mortal, but he was just trying to be 'funny'. His pointless exaggeration kills any interest in what will happen, so now the jokes will have to be really good.

His conscious intention was to be 'amusing', but his unconscious intention was to avoid an emotional transition (from despair to gratitude, perhaps?).

Conflict

— *Where are you off to, little girl?*
— *Go away, I don't talk to wolves.*
— *Come here!*
— *Ow! You're hurting my arm. Take that! And that!*
— *You little brat! I'll bite your head off! Ow! Ow! Stop kicking my shins!*

While this is going on the story is stalled (and it weakens the suspense if Little Red perceives the wolf as dangerous).

Students are taught that drama is conflict, but scenes based on conflict grind to a halt until the conflict is resolved, which it won't be — not if each improviser is determined to be the 'winner'.

The killing of a dragon is not narrative (it's just an episode) but the tracking of it and the aftermath could be.

Constructive uses — to increase the resistance; to sustain a climax.

Instant Trouble

Just as Mummy is preparing Little Red Riding Hood for the journey the wolf comes down the chimney and gobbles them up.

Beginners, especially teenagers, will leap onstage and start haranguing each other, or fighting. This harnesses their fear and negativity, but it creates boring scenes. Teach them to build positive platforms, and to delay chaos until later.

Constructive use — useful in street theatre when you need to attract a crowd.

Lowering the Stakes

Little Red makes no attempt to escape: 'Get on with it then,' she says, checking her lipstick in the mirror. 'I've been eaten lots of times, but the woodcutter always takes me home afterwards.'

One way to minimize trouble is to lower the stakes; for example, to challenge to 'a silly magic trick' when it could have been to 'an amazing magic trick'.

If a doctor says, 'What's the problem?' a beginner will offer a finger or a toe for examination. It takes courage to say, 'It's my abdomen, Doctor.'

A beginner 'interviewed for a job' will have a number of other jobs on offer, whereas a skilled player will be desperate for work and won't have eaten for three days. Graeme Davies understands this: asked to fire someone, he pressed an imaginary buzzer and said, 'Send in my daughter.'

The word 'again' is often a surreptitious way to lower the stakes. A statement like: 'My daughter tells me that you burst into her room last night, Perkins . . . again!' gets a laugh, but it weakens the crisis by implying that it's a regular event.

Consequences

Unless Theatresports is based on storytelling, the best players will get bored and drift away, and the spectators will say, 'Very amusing, dear; where shall we go next week?' – as though Theatresports was yet one more form of mindless entertainment.

NOTES

1 I should mention a really stupid game called Mega-Death which is a way of getting improvisers used to killing each other and which can be hysterically funny when played with elation. You're onstage for between five and ten seconds (or less) before someone else enters and kills you. Repeat this until the stage is filled with bodies.

2 For a fuller description, see my book, *Impro*.

7 Story Games

Creating Games

Creating an improvisation game from thin air is almost impossible (the best you can do is to adapt existing games). This is because games are an expression of theory.

If we assumed that improvisers kill their spontaneity by thinking ahead and that this thinking is verbal, we could screw up such 'planning' by saying, 'Invent a story by adding a word each,' or 'Every sentence has to be a question.' If we assume that drama is about one person being altered by another, this could lead to He Said/She Said games in which the players get their stage directions from their partners, or to the Box in the Pocket Game, in which a character who operates him/herself from a sort of TV zapper unwisely loans it to another person.

If such theories were correct, these would be useful games (and they are), yet I've met coaches who have no interest in theory, who just want 'new' games that they can exploit for their novelty value. I've even heard them say, 'All that matters is that you keep 'em laughing!' as if improvisation was just a branch of stand-up comedy.

Almost all of the games in this book were created by one or more of the following ideas:

- That improvisers defend themselves against imaginary dangers as if these dangers were real.
- That 'splitting the attention' allows some more creative part of the personality to operate.
- That drama is about dominance and submission.
- That stories achieve structure by referring back to earlier events.
- That the spectators want to see the actors in states of transition, and being altered by each other.
- That improvisers need 'permission' to explore extreme states.
- That when we think ahead, we miss most of what's happening (on the stage as in life).

Word-at-a-Time

The players construct a story by adding a word each. The sentences have to be grammatical, and they have to make sense.

William Gaskill's students had been telling stories by contributing a paragraph each, but I wanted to prevent anyone from thinking past the next word.

I asked two volunteers to sit beside me. Then I said, 'Let's invent a story by adding a word each: Sally . . .'

– Was . . .
– Going . . .
[*It's my turn again, and I stir things up:*] Mad . . .
– Because . . .
– Her . . .
– Father . . .
– Wanted . . .
– To . . .
– Put . . .
– His . . .
– Horse . . .
– Into . . .
– Her . . .
– Stable . . .

Some of these 'stories' fizzle out after one sentence, but some may complete themselves (although this would be unusual in the early stages).

Let's say that you're playing this game with three other people. If you start by saying, 'Henry . . .', you're likely to have a continuation in mind, perhaps 'Henry was late for school', but the next player may be thinking, 'Henry took a bath', and the next may be thinking, 'Henry took Betty to lunch' – so that by the time your turn comes round again Henry's 'lateness' will have gone for ever.

Word-at-a-Time (in a Circle)

A circle of from six to eight students invents 'stories' by adding a word each. Anyone who hesitates, or is ungrammatical, or who makes no sense, is ejected (ejectees becomes the Judges who say, 'Speed up!' and who enforce the rules).

Variant: have the group clap rhythmically, synchronizing the words with the beat.

Variant: each player says a word and then points to someone at random who must add the next word.

Variant: letters (and then stories) are written by groups of preferably four students.

Performance Word-at-a-Time

Two players stay close together and act out a Word-at-a-Time story as they are inventing it (beginners may have to be prompted or the adventure will degenerate into gossip).

- *We* are *walking* along *the* beach . . .
- [*I prompt*] Walk forwards!
- *When* we *see* a *cave* . . .
- Go in!
- *We enter* the *cave* and *explore* it . . .
- Have flashlights!
- *Taking* our *flashlights* we *go* along *a* dark *passage* . . .
- Hear something.
- We *hear* someone *singing* . . .
- See the person.

And so on. If you have difficulty 'prompting' this game, try asking the players to add the word 'suddenly'.

Once the players have the hang of it, stop prompting, and let them develop the story themselves.

This is an excellent challenge because it's so unlike most other games, and it can take the players on amazing adventures. A group from Loose Moose – The Three Canadians – have been playing it as street theatre in the centre of enthusiastic crowds.

Ask one of each pair of players to play the game with closed eyes and they are likely to be amazed at the vividness of the 'reality' that their mind creates.

Try asking both players to close their eyes while the rest of the class protects them from harm. If they're 'in a meadow', make bird sounds. If they 'meet little people', lie down and tug at their ankles. If they mention a storm, flick drops of water at them, and make the hiss of wind, and flap coats or boards to make the air move.

Be protective. If the story 'takes over', the players will forget where they are, and if they believe they're on a vast plain you may have to grab them as they run full tilt towards a brick wall.

Avoiding the Wolf

A hero must interact with a 'wolf' (a wolf being anything frightening), but beginners avoid such encounters.

- *We* go *to* the *store* where *we* buy *some* bread *and* now *we* go *home*!

A loaf of bread was the most 'unwolflike' thing that they could imagine, and then they were too timid to eat it or feed it to a duck.
Less frightened people will meet a 'wolf' and run away.

- *We* enter *an* old *house* where *we* see *stairs* leading *down* to *the* cellar. *Oh* no! *Suddenly* a *gigantic* suit *of* armour *walks* towards *us*. We *run* out *side* and *go* home!

An imaginary suit of armour can't hurt anyone, so why not fight it, or find out who's wearing it? Braver (or better-trained) students allow themselves more exciting adventures.

- The *monster* paralysed *us* with *its* sting, *and* wrapped *us* in *a* cocoon *of* threads *and* began *dragging* us *towards* its *lair* . . .

These improvisers will seem 'talented', but the difference lies in their willingness to accept the role of hero. If you meet something terrifying in a fantasy, tame it, or ride on it, or make love to it, or be torn to pieces – but interact. (The Senoi Indians, who specialize in 'controlling their dreams', give the same advice.)
Here's an efficient way to teach the game.

- Ask your students to meet a monster and escape from it.
- Dare them to interact with the monster and either destroy it or be destroyed. If destroyed, they continue in heaven or hell or inside the monster.

No Adjectives or Buts
- Players will wimp by using adjectives to delay the noun; for example:

- Cliff took Betty into his long, big, grey, enormous, vibrating, picturesque . . .

- When players are 'fluent', sometimes forbid adjectives or 'buts'.
- Ban clichés like 'finding treasure'.

What Comes Next?

The hero says, 'What comes next?' and is told what to do.

Improvisers should return to this game like body-builders to their weights. In its 'classical' form only one player is onstage.

'Make no decisions for yourself,' I say. 'Just ask, "What comes next?" and then do what we tell you. If the scene is boring, blame us.'

The class will probably make suggestions like:

'The phone rings.'

'You jump up and down!'

'You play the trombone.'

'You squeeze a zit.'

They soon get fed up with making a fool of the improviser.

'Stop sidetracking,' I say. 'Allow one action to lead to another!'

A struggle begins, with the story moving forward only to be thrust back. This will certainly happen when the suggestions are invited from a paying audience.

- What comes next?
- The phone rings.
- What comes next?
- You answer it.
- What comes next?
- It's a wrong number!
- What comes next?
- The phone rings again!
- What comes next?
- You answer it.
- What comes next?
- It's a wrong number!

The audience may be laughing every time, but nothing can develop. Even when someone breaks this log-jam the phone still won't be answered.

- What comes next?
- There's a knock at the door.

- What comes next?
- Answer the door!
- What comes next?
- There's no one there!
- What comes next?
- The phone rings!

Audiences want something to happen, but the individuals who are shouting the instructions are thinking like performers, and performers are afraid of the future.

I interrupt: 'How did the scene begin?'

'The phone rang.'

'Well, the knock at the door is a rejection of the phone.'

'So what do we do?'

'Answer the phone!'

They continue:

- What comes next?
- The phone's stuck to its cradle!

This is an example of the genius involved in being dull, because it's original in that it's not in the mind of anyone in the audience, and it's a block (because it kills the idea), and it's a wimp (because it refuses to add anything), and it's bridging, and it's instant trouble, and it cancels the action, and it's utterly negative, and it's a gag. (Getting stuck is a popular theme among beginners because it symbolizes not going anywhere.)

'The action is answering the phone!' I say. 'So answer it.'

- What comes next?
- You have a conversation.

This is another wimp, because no responsibility is taken for what's said. I remind them that it's our story, not the performers'.

'All right!' says a student. 'A man bursts in the door with a gun!'

'You dare!'

'But I'm taking the action forward!'

'You are not,' I say. 'The man with a gun is a different action, so it's an example of sidetracking, and of being original. Ask yourself what the spectators want.'

'They want someone to arrive?'

'No they don't!'

'They want him to go out.'
'No they do not.'
'Well, what then?'
'They want to know who's phoning!'
Someone says, 'Your mother-in-law is on the phone.'
This is intended to be negative, and the message will be bad news: they'll say, 'Her dog died!' or 'She's got cancer!' so I tell them that the next few suggestions have to be positive.

— What comes next?
— She's coming to see you.
— [*The actor looks pleased*] What comes next?
— Make yourself respectable!
— [*The actor tidies himself*] What comes next?
— You go to the cupboard.
— What comes next?
— Take out a rifle.
 [*This may seem negative, but it's not an attempt to kill the story.*]
— What comes next?
— You load it.

An audience would expect him to lie in wait for his mother-in-law and shoot her, but these students see obviousness as unoriginal so they sidetrack and bridge shamelessly.

— You shoot yourself in the foot!
— No he doesn't!
— The bullets are the wrong size!
— No they aren't!

They haven't a clue what will happen after they shoot her, so they're bridging desperately. I explain carefully that the loading of the rifle is a promise that needs to be fulfilled. (These students are intelligent and very successful professional actors – but 'future-funk' compels them to wreck the narrative.)
'Ninety-nine per cent of the audience expect him to shoot his mother-in-law. So shoot her. Stop trying to be creative!'
Our hero is told to crouch at the window.

— What comes next?
— You see your mother-in-law in the crowd.

– What comes next?
– There's a salesman at the door.
– No there isn't!
– The alarm clock rings.
– No it does not! [*They're panicking, because how can they guarantee the dullness of the story?*] Just shoot her!
– Bang! What comes next?
– She shoots back!

Everyone is laughing at the obviousness of this suggestion which takes the story forward without cancelling the mother-in-law.

What Comes Next reveals a struggle between positive and negative, with the negative winning (until the students have been retrained). The extent of the negativity is almost unbelievable – except to students of history. I taught this game in Lingen recently and it went like this:

– What comes next?
– You stand up.
– What comes next?
– You break your leg.
– What comes next?
– You try to stand up again and your other leg breaks.
– What comes next?
– You break your arm.

I stopped the game when the actor was being told to 'use his teeth to bite open a medicine box' (I'm sure that the next instruction would have snapped them off).

'Did you like that story?' I said.

'No!'

'But you laughed.'

'Yes, but it wasn't getting anywhere!'

'You feel untalented?'

'Of course.'

'Your failure is nothing to do with "talent". The story can't work because it's in a loop, and there's no platform, and it's insanely negative.'

Stories that are composed entirely of positive suggestions move effortlessly into the future, and they help us realize how aggressive and destructive we usually are. Try sequences of fifty positive suggestions, and you'll feel a huge wave of negativity mounting up, eager to sweep the hero into oblivion.

Try alternating positive with negative suggestions.

Negative: Tom falls out of the window.

Positive: a beautiful nurse takes him home to bandage him.

Negative: her boyfriend is enraged.

Positive: Tom is a better fighter.

And so on.

Two-person Version

Ask the men in the audience to control a man, and the women to control a woman. Someone is almost certain to shout a suggestion for the wrong sex, and if you've warned them against this, the error will be more entertaining.

Try sibling rivalries, or parent–child scenes, or 'strangers meeting' scenes, and so on.

Don't Spin Your Wheels

I divide a class into small groups and ask them to play What Comes Next, but when I check up on them I find no pleasure, no laughter, no enthusiasm.

'You're like wounded cyclists who are still pedalling even though they've crashed!'

'What do you mean?'

'No one's having any fun! The moment your story wipes-out, scrap it and start another.'

'But how will we ever learn if we don't persist?'

'Never persist if there's no joy! You're like those Theatresports players who drag out scenes in search of a laugh to end on.

'So what should we do?'

'If anyone feels that a story has screwed-up, kill it and start another!'

Maybe I ask them to play Word-at-a-Time so that they get used to abandoning their ideas.

Years of organized boredom have trained students to continue even when an activity doesn't interest them. Keep an eye on groups that are working on their own, and restart them if they aren't having a good time. When asked, 'Are you enjoying this?' players may say, 'No we're not!' but they'll sound astonished, as if they hadn't realized.

Using a Committee
This dramatizes the opposition between audience and performer.

Sit a 'committee' of three or four volunteers in front of the class, facing the acting area. Ask them to control the players while the rest of us applaud the suggestions that we like, and to say, 'Mmmmm' non-committally to suggestions that seem adequate, and go, 'Ugh' to suggestions that thwart us.

With luck, the class will stop thinking intellectually, will become a genuine audience and will start cheering and booing, whereas the 'committee' will be under increased stress to think like performers, and will be desperate to stop anything significant from happening.

– What comes next?
– There's a knock at the door.
   [*The audience go 'Mmmmmm . . .'.*]
– What comes next?
– There's no one there.
   [*The audience boo loudly.*]
– What comes next?
– There's a parcel on the welcome mat.
   [*Applause!*]
– It's another welcome mat.
   [*Boooooooooo!*]

I keep changing the committees, and the students are astonished at the difference between being a performer (working on a committee) and being in the 'audience'. It's weird to experience the reversal in your thinking as you move from audience member to committee member.

Committees soon become devious. One had a woman enter the reptile house and pretend to be looking at a crocodile.

– What comes next?
– You notice a coin on the end of its snout!

This is not an idea that could be in the mind of anyone in the audience, but (unable to bear a direct interaction between the girl and the crocodile) this committee member has reduced it to a hazard.

– What comes next?
– You reach out a hand to take the coin.
– What comes next?

– A door opens and the keeper enters.
[*Booooooo!*]
I'll improvise an interactive girl-and-crocodile sequence:
– The crocodile is watching you.
– It reminds you of your old dad.
– You throw it a sandwich.
– It thanks you and you're astonished.
– You look around for a loud-speaker, or a ventriloquist.
– The crocodile says, 'Yes, it's me, Jennifer!'
– Say, 'You can talk?'
– It says, 'Yes, but only you can hear me!'
– Be fascinated by its eyes.
– You climb over the railing.
– It asks you to lie down beside it.
– You feel really trusting and comfortable.
– Say, 'What do you want, Dad?'
– Say, 'It's about the will, Jennifer.'

Maybe it tells her where the will is hidden, or maybe it eats her so her brother will get the money. Who knows?

Prompt the committees when they get stuck, and keep reminding them that 'storytelling is difficult'. Create an atmosphere where 'failure' isn't punishing, so that everyone can laugh at the bizarre difference between watching and performing.

Keep Your Promises

Ultimately we want the committees to be at one with the audience so that they can meet its needs. This process speeds up if you interrupt after a few suggestions to focus their attention on to the 'promises' that are being made. For example:

– What comes next?
– You wake up in a tent.
– What comes next?
– You hear drums.
– What comes next?
– You're on safari.

I break in to ask the spectators what their expectations are. 'An attack by lions', they say, or 'nature-photography', or 'encounters with ivory-poachers', or 'a lost tribe ruled by She-Who-Must-Be-Obeyed', and so on. This information improves the chances that the committee will stay within the 'circle of probability', rather than flail about ineffectively outside it.

When the players are skilled, dare them to be 'committees of one'.

The Performer Becomes the Committee

I put someone centre-stage and say, 'Why don't you make the suggestions yourself?'

This so astounds everyone that they don't even laugh.

'Invent a bossy, parental, contemptuous voice,' I say. 'It has to be very officious and objectionable. Now ask yourself, "What Comes Next?" and have this bossy voice abuse you and order you about.'

I'll improvise the type of scene this generates:

- What comes next?
- Go to the fridge.
- What comes next?
- Open the door, stupid!
- What comes next?
- Take out the sliced bread.
- What comes next?
- Make some toast, of course!

Sometimes the player will struggle against the voice, but the voice must always win. For example:

- What comes next?
- Kiss him!
- Do I have to?
- Stop arguing and kiss him.

This game seems psychotic, but players who play it wholeheartedly report that it diminishes their self-censorship, since they feel as if the 'voice' is taking the responsibility for what they do.

Variant: try sweet voices, loving voices, coaxing voices, uncertain voices, frightened voices, and so on.

Variant: play scenes in which two characters each give themselves instructions.

Paradoxical What Comes Next?
Playing What Comes Next as badly as possible gives insight into how stories are destroyed.

- [*INSTANT TROUBLE*] The house explodes.
- [*CANCELLING*] The house assembles itself again.
- [*CANCELLING*] Wake up – it was all a dream!
- [*BEING ORIGINAL*] Your head disappears.
- [*CANCELLING*] You grow a new one!
- [*SIDETRACKING*] A woman rushes in the door!
- [*CANCELLING*] She falls out of the window.
- [*BEING NEGATIVE*] She breaks her leg.
- [*GAGGING*] She makes no bones about it!
- [*JOINING*] You break your leg.

Variants
● The heroes add some of their own ideas to the audience's ideas (don't let beginners do this).
● As well as asking, 'What Comes Next?' the hero asks questions like: 'What do I feel?' or 'What's ahead of me?' or 'What's that over there?'
● A 'presenter' questions the audience about the hero; for example: 'What emotion does he have?' 'Why does she want revenge?', 'What secret is he hiding from her?'

Coda
When you introduce What Comes Next there'll be suggestions like: 'You're stuck to the chair!' or 'Run around the chair!' or 'Stand on the chair!' These activities are refusals to take the hero anywhere and they won't be justified: if you're told to run around the chair, this won't be to annoy the tenant downstairs: if you're told to stand on it, this won't be to change a light bulb.

What Comes Next allows us to analyse such defensive strategies and to correct them. Without analysis, it teaches relatively little.

Non-sequential Lists

If I ask you to list nouns, as quickly as possible, each will suggest the next; for example:
'Cat, Dog, Kennel, House, Table, Chair, Sofa . . .' and so on.

This feels 'natural', whereas naming disconnected objects feels very unnatural, and threatens your automatic self-censorship. I'll type out a list of disconnected words as fast as I can:

'House, Waterfall, Mandrake-root, Grinling Gibbons, Wellington Boot, Forest Fire, Grandfather Clock, One Parsec, Margarine, Shirley Temple . . .'

This makes me sweat, and skids my mind to a halt. I'm not worried by Grinling Gibbons (an eighteenth-century wood-carver) or Wellington Boot, but what has Margarine got to do with Shirley Temple?

Performance Non-sequential Lists
− We challenge you to see how many disconnected objects a player can name in twenty seconds.
− We accept!
  [*The spectators count each noun in unison.*]
− Cabbage!
− ONE!
− The North Wall of the Eiger!
− TWO!
− A twenty-dollar bill!
− THREE!
− A sleeping princess!
− FOUR!
− A . . . a . . . a . . . a castle!

Everyone boos − because of the perceived link between 'princess' and 'castle'. The timekeeper (usually the Commentator) says, 'Twelve seconds' − or whatever − and another player comes centre-stage. After six or seven items, most players contort as if wrestling with invisible opponents (in a way that could give us clues about brain organization) and give up. Our inability to censor non-sequential lists makes such games feel enticingly risky, but make sure that there's enough laughter to dispel the anxiety.

This is really a warm-up game for Link the Items.

Variant: improvisers from both teams play the game together, shouting words alternately and trying to avoid any connections.

Link the Items

One player suggests disconnected events, and a second player connects them. Play Non-sequential Lists first.
  For example:

– John woke up one morning to find that the sky was filled with black clouds. He looked at the bookshelf and saw that his Bible was missing.
– Remembering the prophecy that a black cloud would annihilate wrong-doers, John ran to get his New Testament, but every Bible in the city had turned to ash and the smoke was blotting out the sun.
  Another example:
– Father Christmas was angry because the elves were on strike. A whale was seen with two heads.
– 'No more toys for earth-children, until they do something about the pollution!' said the Chief Elf.
  I'll try the game with three unrelated items.
– Susan was having trouble finishing her homework. Charley was battering a slot machine with his fist. A band of bagpipers began marching along the avenue.
– Susan couldn't finish her homework because Charley had forgotten his ear-plugs and she was worried what might happen. Charley was battering his fist against the ear-plug machine which had swallowed his money and had given him nothing in return. The bagpipers drew closer and the savage sound began having its usual effect. Charley staggered away but already he was snarling in a Scottish accent and wolf-hair was beginning to push out from under his clothes.

Verbal Chase

One person asks 'non-sequential' questions and another links them together; for example:

– Why did you open the umbrella in the living room?
– To bring bad luck!
– And the egg whisk?
– Suicide weapon!
  Another attempt:
– Where were you at ten minutes after midnight?
– In bed.

- With what fruit?
- A ugli-fruit.
- And the bananas?
- They were for the chimp?
- What's its T-shirt say?
- Africa for the Africans.
- And the space-ship?
- He left it double-parked.

A common fault is for the questioner to do all the work:

- Double-parked in front of the Mayor's office?
- Yes!
- And the pig was in the back seat?
- That's right!
- Eating the new tax regulations?
- So it was!

Verbal Chase leads naturally to the Expert Game (see p. 123) and to the Boris Game.

The Boris Game

An interrogator asks disconnected questions and a victim connects them. Boris inflicts punishment if the answers are not forthcoming or are deemed unacceptable.

This game was so popular in the sixties that our audiences would chant, 'Borrris! Borrris!' until we played one, but it's been brought into disrepute by people who imitated it but had no idea of how it worked.

The Boris Game is a packaging for Verbal Chase in that 'arbitrary leaps' are made that have to be immediately justified. The skills it trains are important, although the game itself is rather limited.

Introduce the game as 'advanced'. This will put the students on their mettle and absolve them from any screw-ups.

Get an interrogator to ask disconnected questions, and insist that the prisoner makes sense of them.

- Ms Ferguson, is it?
- Look, I just came in here to use the toilet facilities.
- It's an official matter, madam. May I ask why you were washing that money?

– I . . . I . . . er . . . I was counting the notes and some fell in the washbasin.

The answer was designed to avoid trouble, so the interrogator strikes the victim viciously with an 'airship' balloon. Both players yell loudly when a strike is made. (Airship balloons are between two and two and a half feet long and several inches in diameter – they are not the floppy balloons used to make balloon-animals. See p. 254.)

– Auuughh! All right! I'll tell! I'll tell! I was trying to wash the blue dye off!
– And the scorpions?
– Er . . . they . . . er . . . Auuughh!
[*The balloon attacks again (yelling and writhing as if in pain makes it easier to spew ideas out of your unconscious – perhaps it was what Proust was doing in his cork-lined room).*]
– I threw them into the ticket-seller's booth so that I could snatch the money!

The forcing of incriminating answers means that bizarre material emerges. The interrogator can shape this into a narrative by rejecting answers that sidetrack or cancel, or seem too gaggy.

This much understood, it's time to remove the balloon and add Boris. From now on the interrogator never touches the prisoner. Let's have Katrina start the game by saying:

'Bring him in, Boris!'

Howls of terror and pain are heard and Boris, who is about eight feet tall, forces Gunnar onstage and thumps him into a chair. Katrina begins courteously. Perhaps the first question is:

'Perhaps you can tell us where you were on Thursday the 16th, sir?'
If the response seems unsatisfactory she says: 'Help him, Boris!'

Boris twists Gunnar's nose, or arm, or hurls him at the ceiling, or applies whatever other penalty seems appropriate. At the University of Waterloo (Ontario) an over-enthusiastic Boris broke his victim's collar-bone – they had to stop the show and call an ambulance – but in general, screams of pain are more effective than gymnastics, and there have been excellent Boris scenes from which the victim emerged unscathed.

– Well?
– I was – I was at home!
– With a dead horse?

– It was a surprise for the wife!

This answer pleases Katrina so she restrains Boris, and continues the interrogation.

– And the broken accordion?
– It was to . . . to . . . to . . .
– Help him, Boris!

And so on, with Gunnar struggling desperately to drag some sort of coherence out of the chaos, and to incriminate himself so that Boris won't abuse him.

What gives this game its peculiar charm (and allows the audience to laugh unreservedly) is that although 'Boris' is a gigantic thug, of horrifying aspect, he's also quite invisible, i.e., the 'cruelty' is self-inflicted. Both interrogator and victim should be aware of exactly where this imaginary 'Boris' is at all times; we don't want them staring in different directions, but if they do, the interrogator should introduce Igor, Boris's ill-natured twin (I hope you're following this).

This is one of the few games in which beginners will choose to be Heroes, resisting torture stubbornly – because until they confess, nothing will happen. Boris must therefore be so terrifying that the victims will admit to absolutely anything.

Interrogators who are afraid to share control will say 'Pull his nose, Boris!', or 'Rip off his leg!', but it's better to make a blind-offer like 'Help him, Boris!' and let the victims choose their own torments.

The Classic Boris
The game as I first devised it had these formal rules:

- Ask Boris to bring in the victim – or just shout, 'Next!' The victim then hurls him/herself on to the stage, or pretends to be frog-marched, or whatever (as if propelled by the eight-foot-tall Boris).
- Start politely, but if the answers aren't incriminating, say, 'Help him, Boris!' or 'Jog her memory, Boris!' The victim can then howl in fake agony (try to reserve any gymnastics until later in the scene).
- At unpredictable intervals (perhaps just once) the interrogator should say, 'Let's recapitulate,' and review the material, adding additional information, and trying to make sense out of the rigmarole.
- At some point the interrogator presents the victim with an object – for example, a handkerchief or a shoe, or perhaps even an audience member

– and says something like, 'Perhaps this will jog your memory!'

The victim expresses appalled and guilty recognition, and weaves the object into the story.

● Force some sort of resolution, and/or call in the next victim.

Emphasis must be on story, rather than on 'acrobatics', or the game has little sustaining power. The game can be very exhilarating – like skiing in total darkness. I'll improvise a Boris and see what emerges:

– Bring him in Boris.
– Auggghhhhh! No . . . Augh! Ooof!
– Just sit him in the chair! Gently, Boris! I'm sorry, sir, but the batteries have run out on his punishment collar.
   [*Both are looking at the same point which is some eight feet above the stage.*]
– Keep him off me!
– Boris! Back! Back! Now then, sir – perhaps you would be so good as to tell me how long you have been a member of this club.
– Club? I came in here to use the telephone!
– Help him, Boris!
– Augh! All right! I'm lying!
– Boris!
– Aughhhhhh! I'm . . . I'm a new member!
– Weren't you black-balled?
– No! Yes, I was! I was!
– You don't know what being black-balled means, do you?
– Don't I? No, no I don't! You're right!
– Every member of this club dropped a black ball into the vase when you were proposed for election! And that means that they do not want you to set foot in here, ever!
– True!
– So how did you get a letter of invitation?
– I forged it!
   [*A good answer because it's incriminating.*]
– And who taught you this technique?
– I er . . . I . . .
– Help him Boris!
– Augghh . . . No . . . Augh . . .
– Steady, Boris! Easy on the neck. Drop him! Drop him! You were saying, sir.

– What . . . what was the question?

– You know the question!

– Yes! Yes I do! I . . . I . . . was given a Flexie-Boy Printing Set when I was a child.

– And what has this to do with Sammy the Goldfish!

– Oh, noooo!

– Boris!

– Auuugh! I was going to steal him!

– Rubbish!

– Not steal, but reclaim him as my own! I educated him. I stood books against the bowl so he could read but it gave him migraine, so I took him to the vet and unbeknownst to me they flushed him down the toilet and substituted a run-of-the-mill goldfish and claimed it to be a miracle cure!

[*If the interrogator is enjoying these flights of fancy, they are allowed to continue.*]

– And the knitting needles?

– And? Augh! Well, I thought the anaesthetic had made him lose his memory. He couldn't read. He couldn't finish the scarf he was knitting . . .

– You're lying! Help him, Boris!

– Augh! Augh! No! I swear! The real Sammy tried to find his way through the sewage system, and he emerged into this club, in the visitor's toilet, and recognizing him as an amazingly talented goldfish, they gave him the place of honour in the fish tank in the billiard hall.

– How did they know he was special?

– I'd taught him to yodel.

[*A pause while the interrogator decides whether to accept this.*]

– Very well! Let's recapitulate. You say that Sammy the Goldfish was rightfully yours, and that you tried to become a member of this club in order to reclaim him. Then, after being rejected on grounds of moral turpitude, you used your Flexie-Boy Printing Set to forge a letter of invitation to the secret ritual!

– I admit it!

– And do you recognize this?

– Augh! Oh, no! Auggghhh! Where did you get that? Put it away, please. You know everything, I'm finished, I'm finished!

– And what is it?

- [*Weeping*] It's a handbill advertising Marvo the Magician's performance at the Town Hall tomorrow.
- Read on! What does it say here?
- Marvo the Magician . . .
- And what else? Boris!
- Augggh! And his yodelling goldfish! Auggghhh!
- Boris, stop it, you can play with him afterwards! Now then, sir – just who is this Marvo?
- Me! It's me! What use denying it?
- All right then, stop weeping! Tell us about the chest of drawers.
- It's where I keep the underwear that I steal from launderettes.
- And what's that to do with Sammy the Goldfish?
- I dress up in it as part of our act.

And so on to reach some kind of conclusion.

I've located this Boris scene in a gentlemen's club, and once the form has been mastered it's quite usual to set the game in bowling alleys, or royal bedrooms, or dungeons below Swiss finishing schools, or wherever.

The audience enjoy seeing the improvisers working at the end of their tether, and occasionally something astounding will emerge (which is why our fans used to chant until we played the game). Young male victims, in particular, enjoy having Boris throw them around, but a good scream is worth any amount of gymnastics.

A Boris Game has to generate some sort of story if it's to be more than gags and acrobatics. The free-association and justification skills that it trains are more important than the game itself.

Escape Hatches

We hope that Boris stories can achieve some sort of consummation, but in case of need the victim can implicate the interrogator.

- I . . . I gave the money to you!
- Me?
- You think I didn't recognize you behind that moustache?
  Or the victim can implicate Boris:
- And how did you get up to the second-floor window?
- Boris tossed me up!
- Boris tossed you up!
- I'm sorry Boris, I had to tell him.

Or the victim can attack Boris, and hurl him about the stage (perhaps another player can grab the mike and supply Boris's screams).

Or you could use the 'Androcles' escape hatch in which you realize that you once removed a thorn from Boris's foot.

Keyboard Game

Type a story at an imaginary keyboard, speaking it aloud while other players act it out (and sometimes add ideas of their own).

This was an attempt to create a split-attention game, like the Hat-Game (see p. 156).

Sit upstage and to the side (angled towards the audience but with a good view of the action). Speak the story as you 'type'. At first the keyboard should take up most of your attention, but soon you'll only need to indicate it occasionally.

It's usual to ask the audience for a title, but why not just type whatever title occurs to you? And if you don't like it, 'delete' it and type another. If you must ask for a title, insist on one that inspires you. 'Originalities' like *The Hind-leg of the Drunk Porcupine* are a form of sabotage.

At first the players who enact the story just repeat, or mouth, the dialogue the typist gives them, but once they get the hang of the game they should start adding their own ideas (but don't let them take over entirely).

Some simple rules are:

- Place the hero in a stable environment.
- Establish a purpose and/or a tragic flaw.
- (Optional) Change the scene: go from home, to work, or to a movie.
- Have the hero interact in a way that involves suffering and chaos.
- Achieve an ending by reincorporating material that was shelved earlier in the story, and either trash the hero or create a new stability.

Let's say that the title is *Harold's Adventure*. 'Type' that 'Harold woke up one morning feeling particularly well. The sunlight was streaming into his room . . .'

A player becomes Harold waking up. Perhaps he opens the window and hears birdsong, and says, 'What a great day! I think I'll phone in sick!'

What 'promises' are implicit? Only that Harold has decided to take the day off and that he'll have an adventure (or why would we be telling his story), so let's have him phone his boss and say that he's ill.

Now what? How about giving him a tragic flaw? This will add suspense because the audience will expect it to become relevant later on. Let's type: 'Harold's overriding fear was his dread of losing control. He checked his appearance in the mirror. All was as it should be: his clothes were neat, his buttons were sewn on tightly, and his hair was the correct length. He sighed happily. Today was going to be a good day . . .'

We've stressed the good weather, so the audience will be expecting some outdoor activity – walking the dog, painting the fence, visiting the zoo – so let's type: 'Harold decided to visit the zoo.'

The spectators will be eager for the zoo to alter Harold (or why take him there?), but a typist who is afraid of the future will cancel the zoo by sending him home to see if he left the stove on, or will bridge the zoo by having him miss the bus, or will sidetrack it by having him remember an appointment somewhere else.

Get Harold to the zoo, and type: 'Harold found himself all alone in . . .'

Choose any area: '. . . in the Ape House.'

He needs to interact with something, so let's have him become fascinated by Guy the Gorilla: 'Harold stared at Guy, and Guy stared back.'

An improviser leaps onstage to become the gorilla. And if Harold moves on to another cage, the spectators will feel disappointment (denied the 'promised' interaction with the gorilla), so let's break the routine of staring at a gorilla. Type that 'Harold noticed a gleam of metal in the gorilla's fur.'

Perhaps the actors can take over the story for a while and Harold can realize that he's looking at a zip-fastener. An 'acrobat' can then unzip herself from the gorilla suit, and they can fall in love and both be employed at the zoo as gorilla impersonators. The spectators will be interested in this, but they'd like more chaos (especially as Harold's 'tragic flaw' is that he hates chaos), so let's 'delete' the zip-fastener and take the story in some other direction. Type that the gorilla extends a finger, and that Harold touches it and discovers that he's inside the cage, covered in fur, and that he can see his own body beating its chest outside the bars (obviously inhabited by the mind of the gorilla). This keeps the implied promise that his orderly world will become disorderly.

But what if you feel the need for more structure? Reincorporate something from earlier in the story. Harold lied about being ill and the spectators will be remembering this, so if his boss arrives at the zoo, the story will be seen as having a point, especially if he abuses the gorilla/ Harold which can then throw him about.

Now that Harold has had an adventure, and has lost control, you can type that the gorilla got a job as a lumberjack, and that Harold became famous as the gorilla who made paper aeroplanes; or we could regain the platform by having Harold wake up in his apartment and realize that it was all a dream, and then have the gorilla enter with a breakfast tray.

If none of these ideas pleases you, it may be because we gave Harold a flaw, but neglected to give him a strong purpose. Let's go back to Harold being fascinated by the gorilla and have him decide to rescue it and return it to Africa: 'Next day Harold dressed himself in the zoo-keeper uniform he had stolen, and parcelled-up the much fuller version that he'd tailored the previous evening. Today was the day when he would return Guy the Gorilla to the wild!'

And proceed from there.

Escape Hatches

But what if inspiration fails? This possibility can turn the game into an ordeal. (I overheard an improviser say, 'I'll be ready to improvise my first keyboard story in about a year.') Such players have seen the game in performance, and imitated it, without knowing that it comes with a set of escape hatches.

Let's say your mind blanks out as Harold sees his body (inhabited by the gorilla) beating up his boss. Just type something that will bring the gorilla into the same frame as you; for example: 'Suddenly Harold heard typing. There was a small door low in the wall. He opened it and saw another gorilla typing away . . .'

Harold/Gorilla is now looking directly at you (the creator of the story), so type: 'Harold stepped through the door and . . .'

Harold can complain about the story, or recognize you as an old friend; he can criticize the story; or he can 'read' it aloud from the computer screen: 'Harold woke up one morning, and saw that the sun was shining into his room . . .'

Another player can rush onstage to wake up in the morning, and the lights can fade, leaving the audience with the illusion that something had been achieved, because stories are circular, and starting and ending with the typist achieves an ersatz circularity.

If your hero is in a forest, he could discover you typing away furiously behind a rock, or in a hut, or inside a hollow tree, or you could be very small and sheltered under a leaf.

It sometimes helps if you characterize yourself; for example: 'A drunken degenerate was drooling over a keyboard . . .' or 'She peered into the kennel and saw Fido typing away . . .' or 'There was a beetle in his shirt pocket. It was typing a story on a miniature computer.'

Some other escape hatches include:

- Type 'Something unexpected happened!' and let Harold solve the problem.
- Ask the audience, 'What comes next?'
- Give a 'substitution' sign by placing one horizontal flat hand on your other vertical hand to make a 'T' shape. Someone will replace you, and you're free!
- Pretend to delete the last few sentences. (The audience love to see characters in the story 'deleting' themselves.)
- Have your hero read a letter, or a diary, or a book, or a newspaper aloud. Then creep silently away, so the hero becomes the story-teller and creates a new story that will be acted out; or the lights could fade, since handing on to a new typist gives an illusion of 'circularity'.
- Enter the scene as a character – as Harold's boss, perhaps – and let Harold rush to the keyboard and continue the story. Keep alternating.
- Remember something that was shelved earlier in the story, and feed it back in.

Variant: the story is typed by Captain Ahab, or by the wolf that ate Red Riding Hood, or by a vengeful God, or whatever.

Variant: ask for a genre: 'film noir', 'science fiction', 'Western', and so on (genres don't wreck keyboard stories, but never accept a genre unless it inspires you).

Variant: 'Dear Diary' – the storyteller is writing in his/her diary, or is composing a suicide note, or Captain Kirk is updating the *Enterprise* log.

8 Being There

When I interrupted my first students mid-scene to ask what they were doing, they'd say, 'I'm about to sit on the sofa,' or 'I just came in the door.'

But they'd never say, 'I'm wondering where to sit.'

So I tried to find ways to keep the students' attention on what was actually happening, rather than on what had already happened or was about to.

Three-word Sentences

If every sentence has to be three words long, then the players must attend to what they're saying. Instead of 'Come in!' they'll have to say, 'Come in please,' or 'That you, honey?'

This prevents beginners from leaving their mouths on 'automatic' while their minds gallop off into the future. Rapport is noticeably improved (and it becomes almost impossible to make 'gags'). This game has a calming effect on panicky improvisers.

The game imposes a slowness which can be read as emotional involvement.

Players must speak in complete sentences: no trailing-off is allowed.

One-word Sentences

This game forces non-verbal solutions which will need to be coached until the players cotton on. Let's say that Eric and Renee have greeted each other and are now 'stuck'. I need to suggest an activity; for example: 'Open a cupboard!'

Eric opens a cupboard and mimes taking a tray from it; he sets it on the table, and says, 'Brandy?'

'Please!'

He pours two brandies: 'Cheers!'

They drink, but now they're stuck again, so I tell Renee to mime taking something out of her pocket and show it to Eric. Eric 'takes' it, treating it gingerly. He 'sights' along the barrel and it's obvious that it's a gun.

'Fired?' he asks, sniffing it.

'Recently,' says Renee.

He places the mimed gun on the table. 'Husband?'

She wants to say, 'I shot him between the eyes,' but is restricted to one word. 'Dead,' she says, taking back the mimed gun.

And so on.

Most improvisers look for verbal solutions. This game forces them to find physical ones. The resistance to speech makes them seem 'emotional'.

Coached Word Length

Instead of shouting an emotion the trainer shouts the number of words; for example: 'FOUR!'

'Can I help you?'

'TEN!'

'Perhaps you can assist me with a small problem . . . sir.'

And so on. The audience will laugh and applaud, but the chance of anything happening is minimal, so this game is not recommended.

The Hat-Game

They call him *El Sombrero* because he makes at grabbing people's hats and running – William Burroughs, *Junkie*

Play a scene with the secret intention of seizing your partner's hat. If you succeed, you win, but if your attempt fails, or if your own hat gets taken, you lose. Challenges are usually to the 'best out of three' Hat-Games.

William Gaskill asked some drama-school students to try to snatch each other's hats during written scenes (and not to get their own snatched). They became very witty and amusing and he arrived back at the theatre, still elated, saying that he'd 'found the secret of clowning'.

Teaching the Hat-Game

The hats should be easily removable – not jammed down over the ears, and they should be worn fairly level, although they mustn't shade the eyes.

Trilby or fedora hats are good (keep a dent in the top of them or someone might lose some hair). Don't use hats that are large and floppy.

Avoid peaked caps – students grab at the peak and this brings their fingers close to the wearer's eyes.

I ask a student to take a hat slowly and carefully from the head of someone who makes no attempt to protect it.

'Take it from the side, or from above,' I say. 'But not from the front; you don't want to get your little finger stuck up a nostril.'

Once they've 'got the distance', I let them speed up. Some students understand this as 'knock the hat off with as much strength as possible!', and they prepare to give a savage clout in the direction of their partner's head.

'Knocking a hat off doesn't count!' I say. 'Hats are to be *taken*, not batted into the air! Unless you grab ends with the hat in your hand, you lose!'

Once they've learned to take a hat deftly, I stand two students close together, and let one try to take a hat while its wearer tries to protect it by grabbing it first or by dodging.

'Look after your partner!' I shout. 'Be gentle! Don't hurt people! It's only a game!'

Anxiety makes students inept.

'Keep the arm relaxed. Think quick and light, not heavy and strong, and your hand will move faster.'

I give both students a hat and tell each to take the other's the moment that they see an opportunity (while protecting their own). I encourage them to add dialogue, and to move about: that is, to play scenes. Everyone laughs, when a hat is taken, or is grabbed for and missed (if the onlookers don't laugh, something is wrong).

'Hats' are all that some players will talk about.

'I like your hat.'

'Yes. It's a very nice hat. Yours is a nice hat too!'

'Where did you get it?'

'Same place you got your hat.'

I insist that the hat should not be mentioned (no encounters in hat shops, no discussions about 'I had a hat like that once'). Then I liven up the scene by asking them to 'take hats' while they're being nuns, or brain surgeons, or cans of baked beans, or mice, or politicians at an apathy conference, or whatever; and I encourage them to accept ideas, and to be brimming over with health and good nature.

Sometimes I let a winning hat-taker continue for round after round, and perhaps I'll add a Commentator: 'That's the third hat Karen has won. The Lions are now leading by fifteen points. Karen spends hours each day manipulating her hands in rice-pudding to strengthen her fingers. Oh and it's a grab – unsuccessful I'm afraid – that's Karen's fourth consecutive hat . . .'

Most students attach their 'ego' to winning (which turns play into work) so I say, 'What's it matter? It's not even your hat! Are you supposed to be an expert? Of course not! Take risks! Win or lose, either way we'll be entertained!'

If losers display indifference, I'll ask them to look astonished, or confused, or to laugh at themselves, otherwise the interaction will be less pleasing (we always long to see one person 'lowered' by another).

Holding Your Ground

I had assumed that 'taking the hat' was an athletic skill, but some 'slow' people could almost always take a hat, while some fit and agile people failed utterly. Only one student in ten seemed to have a talent for the game; these were all male, and they were all among the better improvisers.

What had the Hat-Game to do with gender? And with the ability to improvise? It was true that most women had a shorter reach than the men, and yet I knew a dwarf who would swarm up people and seize their hats with his teeth.

I noticed that the 'untalented' players (almost all women) stepped backward, even if only for a few inches, whereas the successful players held their ground, or moved forward, tempting their opponent into making an ill-advised grab.

'Better to lose the hat then to retreat,' I said. 'If you must move, move forward. Walk into your opponent – be aggressive!'

I stood the retreaters against a wall but they jerked their heads back and cracked the plaster, so I placed heavy chairs behind their knees, and sometimes I'd walk into the scene and push them forward. Women were soon as successful as the men, but there was still a baffling connection between skill at improvisation and skill at taking a hat.

Let Your Hand Make the Decisions

A Japanese swordsman wrote that if you fight someone who has no plan, you'll be thinking, I'll do such and such! as your severed head bounces down the temple steps! (Well, he didn't put it exactly like that.)

'Planners' in the Hat-Game are at a similar disadvantage. They'll say, 'There's something on your shoe!'; hoping that you'll look down and forget about your hat, but this just reminds you. Or they'll say, 'I've got a terrible migraine,' clutching their heads as an excuse for keeping their hands adjacent to their hats, but this keeps experienced players alert.

Hat-Games demand a split in the players' consciousness: part of the mind plays the scene, while another part watches attentively. Until players can make this split, their hats are vulnerable.

'How old are you, Grandma?'

'A hundred and sixty-three,' she replies, using comic exaggeration (which I wish she wouldn't).

'Goodness! What year were you born?'

While she retreats 'inside herself' to subtract 163 from the current year, her hat can be wafted gently away.

The worst players plan so far into the future that they may not realize that their hat has been taken until the laughter brings them back to reality.

A Zen monk told me: 'When I learned The Hat-Game I was told that the point was to be as funny as possible. I'm amazed to hear you telling me that the game is about "mindfulness"!'

(Playing Hat-Games with Zen monks is fun because they roll about on the floor, laughing prodigiously.)

Risk the Hat

If you move beyond arm's length, I'll say, 'Risk the hat!', but if a barber mimes putting a sheet over you as a preliminary to cutting your hair, I'll say, 'Take your hat off! Fan yourself with it! Scratch your head! Don't put your hat back on until your partner moves away.' It's exciting when there's a 50 per cent chance that the hat can be taken, but totally boring when the chance is 100 per cent. Players should never manoeuvre into a position where the hat can be taken at will.

If players remove their hats unnecessarily, the Judges should wait a moment, and then say, 'Keep the hat in play!'

Take it When You Can

Hugo has his hand on Christian's shoulder, but they are enjoying the scene so much that he makes no attempt to take the hat. This is a form of bridging, and the value of the Hat-Game as something unique is lost.

Some players believe (quite wrongly) that every scene should be about six minutes long, but we need contrast, and a Hat-Game that is over in a few seconds can provide this.

Safety

Stages are not the safest of places – as Peg-Leg Bates discovered (the one-legged tap-dancer who had trouble with knot-holes) – but Hat-Games became a lot safer after we said that the aggressor will lose unless a hat is taken cleanly. This made it possible to win by luring your partner into launching a failed attempt, and prevented savage clouts to the head and damaged fingers. Once a grab has been attempted, the round is over (the Judges determine what is or is not a grab).

I've only heard of one mishap (a player got a poke in the eye that made it water a little), but coaches must stop 'planners' from looking away when they grab or there'll be carnage.

Blindfold Hat-Games

These are fun but potentially dangerous. Blindfolded players play a scene while trying to take each other's hats (their colleagues preventing them from crashing into walls or falling off the stage). Audiences love this game, but sooner or later someone is going to be injured. If you insist on playing it, at least wear goggles to protect the eyes. Never let beginners play this game.

The Three Canadians showed me a street-theatre version played barefoot among dozens of mouse-traps.

Scoring the Hat-Game

The usual challenge is to a 'best out of three, one-on-one Hat-Game', with each hat earning three points.

In 'one-off, one-on-one' Hat-Games, the Judges point at the winner, who earns five points.

Take Out the 'Improvements'

• *Deciding when the hat can be taken.* Most beginners start grabbing for the hat immediately, even when they've no hope of success. This has led some groups to say that the hat can only be taken after a whistle is blown, yet the moment the whistle sounds, the grabbing starts again – so this achieves nothing. It's best to let unskilled players make their grab and get it over with. Once they have mastered the art of 'attending', there'll be no problem.

• *Forbidding people to grab their own hats.* Hat-Games can be very funny, and the humour is intensified by the close proximity of the players who duck, weave and grab their own hats first – relying on 'awareness', not distance, for protection – but a 'West Coast' game-sheet says, 'Players may not protect the hats with anything other than their wits.'

This misconception arose after a course in Vancouver at which I demonstrated the game rather briefly, and the error travelled to San Francisco, and from there to Australia, New Zealand and Samoa.

Players stayed out of arm's length, only moving in for the kill, and Hat-Games soon fell out of use.

• *Justifying the 'grab'*. One Theatresports group insisted that the hat should be taken as part of the scene; that is, the hat should be taken for a reason. This trained the players to plan, and to ignore the moment-by-moment availability, or non-availability, of the hat. Then they said that Hat-Games were boring, and stopped playing them.

Variant – giving the hat: the players are bare-headed, but each holds a hat, waiting for an opportunity to place it on to their partner. This adds variety, but the original Hat-Game is funnier because the loser's status is visibly lowered.

Variant – Bum Tag: not a Hat-Game at all, but a similar idea. The player who touches the other's behind first wins. If a player sits down, or backs against a wall, the Judges must say, 'Keep the buttocks in play!'

I sometimes set this game *en masse* as a warm-up.

Gaskill's Samurai Game
Recommended as a training game.

William Gaskill invented this in about 1960 as a way to discourage 'planning' (I suspect that he was inspired by the duel with the virtuoso swordsmen in Kurosawa's *Seven Samurai* movie).

Lucy and Tony face each other. Neither moves a muscle until Lucy, giving no signal, reaches out and touches Tony – and wins. Had Tony leapt back so that the contact wasn't made, she'd have lost.

Players are to be motionless until one makes a move (either defensively or aggressively), and then the game restarts.

For the arm to move efficiently, the torso must clamp up or the arm will move the shoulder (action and reaction being equal and opposite). If this tension precedes the motion of the arm, it alerts your partner, who will either retreat or touch you first (like the boxer who told me that he watched for his opponent's 'decision' to punch and then punched him first).

Play Samurai and you'll feel the tension gathering seconds before you make your move, but if you can let your 'body' make the decision, there'll be no visible preparation, and you'll just feel calm. Such 'body-thinking' occurs in sport all the time; good table-tennis players can't think 'The ball's going to bounce there so I'll extend my bat eighteen-inches at an angle of thirty-five degrees . . .' because they'd be too slow.

Now ask two players to wear hats and face each other, a couple of feet apart. Either can win by taking the other's hat. No dodging is allowed, and no feints. When you're staring into the eyes of your partner from a distance of twenty-four inches, this kind of interior dialogue is likely to occur:

'Shall I take it now? Not yet! How about now? Yes, I'll take it!'

I interrupt this by shouting instructions like: 'Step back! Relax! Calm down!' and I might suggest that they try repeating 'I want nothing!'[1]

Beginners seem hypnotized by the hat. It's as if their eyes are flashing: 'HAT! HAT! HAT! HAT!'

I tell them that if they feel themselves tensing up, they should say, 'Pax,' and step back before starting the round again.

Some students will still be deciding to take the hat seconds before they make their move.

'Why not just raise your hand and take it.'

'That's not going to work!'

'Why not? The hat is always available!'

'No it isn't!'

'How long does it take your hand to touch your partner's hat? A third of a second? Perhaps less? Your partner's eye has to register the movement, the message has to travel to the back of the brain to be processed, and a message has to be sent to activate the muscles. If you acted spontaneously you could take a hat before the wearer knew it was gone.'

Hat-Games encourage you to be 'present', and to wait patiently until your partner is 'absent'.

Making Faces

Servants make faces secretly at their masters, who try to catch them.

Many of my first students paid no attention to each other. Baffled by this, I consulted my 'Things My Teachers Had Forbidden' list. *Making Faces* was at the top, and I realized that it could be used as a 'see the other person' game.

Grandmother's Footsteps

I sometimes use Grandmother's Footsteps as a warm-up for Making Faces. It's a game from my childhood that is sometimes known as Red Light, Green Light or Statues.

Alan faces the wall and the class creep towards him. He looks round suddenly, and anyone that he sees moving returns to the starting line to begin again. When someone gets close enough to touch him (or the wall) the game is over.

Making Faces – Party Version

I ask the group to spread out and pretend to be at a party: 'Recognize old friends,' I say. 'Exchange gossip, circulate, find the refreshments.'

Then I say, 'Try to make faces at each other without being caught. Point your fingers and say "bang" to "shoot" anyone you catch making a face at you!' If you're shot, you have to leave the game. (I've always wanted to play this on a lawn with water-pistols.)

Making Faces in Threes

This is the only version that most groups know, but I invented it as a training game.

I had divided a class into master–servant pairs, and had asked the servants to make faces at their masters without getting caught, but to my amazement the masters refused to look away, believing that they could 'win' by preventing any faces from being made at all.

To correct this, I placed three plain chairs facing the audience with their edges touching (it helps the comedy if the players' 'space' overlaps a little). I sat a player on each chair, and asked the one in the middle to be the master, but I said nothing about making faces.

'What are you boss of?' I said.

The master interpreted this question as 'choose an idea that will win you admiration', so she scanned through twenty ideas to select the 'best'. Even if this were a good strategy (which it isn't), how could she make an informed choice before she knew what the game would be?

'Pick anything,' I say. 'A hospital, a shop, an atomic-power station, a bakery, a school for detectives: take anything!'

'All right – I'm in charge of a zoo!'

'Good. Now interact with your two zoo-keepers, but don't send them away.'

She 'retreats' into some inner space where she tries to dredge up good ideas. This makes her feel quite desperate, so I say, 'Why search for ideas when you have servants to think for you? Just start a sentence with "What about . . ." and then add the name of an animal. Say, "What about the wolves? What about the otters?" Or make them tell you what you were going to say next, and hit them if they don't know!'

'Hit them?'

I hand her a two-foot-long airship balloon to hit them with. This is a fine arrangement, because if the servants fail to have an idea, the audience will enjoy seeing them punished (see p. 254).

– Torben! What was I about to say?
– You were about to ask about the snakes, madam!
– Have they been stretched?
– Extensively, madam.
– And the elephants?
– We've emptied them, madam!
– And those boys who were climbing over the fence?
– Eaten, madam.
   [*I interrupt to say that she should include the other zoo-keeper.*]
– Are you in charge of the camels, Pamela?
– No, madam!
   [*Pamela is blocking to stay out of trouble, but we want her in trouble so I interrupt and tell her to say, 'Yes!'*]
– Yes. They're my responsibility, madam.
– And what's the problem?
– They've lost their enthusiasm, madam.
– The vampire bats?
– Full, madam.

Naming animals frees the master from the need to seek 'good ideas'. (Until this is understood, most students try to avoid the middle chair.)

Now I ask whether the servants look like good servants.

'Torben is slouching a bit.'

'Make him sit up! Your servants must be a credit to you. Pull him about. Hit him with the balloon!'

I tell the servants to look respectful: 'Convince the master that you are good servants! Look obedient.'

The spectators love to see the masters exercising their power, but masters have to be prodded into exercising it.

'Pamela's smiling!' I say. 'Please do something!'

'Is that true, Pamela?'
'It's the sheer pleasure of being near you, madam!'
'Pay attention to Torben as well,' I say.
'Torben! Stop fiddling with your hands! What was I about to say?'
'You were about to raise our salaries, madam!'
'So I was!' She turns and beats Pamela.
'Augh! What was I doing, madam?'
'You were sprawling about! Sit up and pay attention! Now then, what about the penguins?'
'On vacation, madam!'

I play this Keep the Servant on the Hop Game with other students, and then I divide the class into groups and let them try the game *en masse*.

Once the masters have practised dragging ideas from their servants' minds, and are willing to discipline them, I say, 'Fire any servants you catch making faces at you!' (Or I might give the instruction by passing notes to the servants secretly. Then the master only cottons-on when the audience starts howling with laughter.)

The servants will be eager to make faces, having been so abused, but some masters may fail to notice that their servants' faces are screwed up, or that their tongues are poking out, even though they're confronting them nose to nose. Some servants keep being 'fired' because they make faces, not realizing that the master is looking right at them. This game encourages the players to start 'seeing' instead of 'planning', and it's salutary for actors (because most actors try to impress the audience with their face-making skills, and get caught at once).

I shout advice to the masters like: 'Look at the other servant! Share the scene with both of them!' or 'Don't you hear that sucking noise behind you? Find out what's causing it!' or 'Does Klaus seem odd to you?'
'Odd?'
'His position. And why does his mouth look "frozen"?'
Klaus was caught 'mid-face' and he's still holding the expression.

– Klaus! What's wrong with your face?
– I'm trying to look intelligent, madam.
– Well, it's not working!

Or I might say, 'Did you see Yuri make a face at you?'
'No.'
'But you saw she was smiling – she's still smiling. Even if you don't see

the face-making, you should enforce respectful behaviour. Let's have some discipline! Tell her to behave like Klaus!' (Klaus is looking profoundly bored whenever the master looks away.)

Masters who are failing to catch their servants are probably deciding on a complete sentence before they speak and completing it before they look. If so, I say, 'Catch your servants unawares! Turn your head mid-phrase!' But I wouldn't tell the students this before it was necessary.

Some masters stare straight ahead, trying to glimpse the servants with their peripheral vision.

'Look at one or the other!' I shout. 'If they can't transgress, how will you catch them?'

Beginners who play the role of master 'know' that their servants are making faces, and they snap their heads from side to side from the very first moment. I explain that the truth should dawn on them gradually, that they should find it almost incredible that any servant would be so disrespectful.

Some servants make a one-second face and then revert to normal. 'Take risks!' I say. 'The master has to know that however innocent you look, you were making a face a split second earlier!'

'But we'll get caught!'

'What does it matter? If you were Hamlet, would you refuse to die? You're not really a servant. Don't you realize that we're longing for you to get caught so that we can laugh at you?'

A servant gets caught deliberately.

'Don't try to get caught!'

'You said that was what the audience wanted!'

'Yes, but they don't want you to make a face while the master's looking straight at you! Increase the risk, but fight desperately to survive, and then we'll love you for your courage and indomitable spirit.'

When servants are caught I tell them to protest their innocence (but that they must leave if the master insists).

Some actors choose to be so grotesque that they're caught immediately. Sticking out your tongue is enough, but they'll compete to see who can make the most interesting or ugliest face and this makes them forget that the boss is trying to catch them.

Played elegantly, the servant will remain on the very verge of being caught, but surviving by a hair's breadth, perhaps for many minutes.

Relating to the Spectators

Once the basic skills have been practised, I tell the servants that they should wave to people in the audience, letting them know what a fool their master is. The master doesn't know that the audience exists, but if the servants are its mischievous friends, this will open the scene up and will increase the likelihood that they'll be caught.

'The game doesn't end when a servant is fired,' I say. 'We have many unemployed servants ready to replace them!'

A servant is ejected and half a dozen volunteers offer themselves as replacements. Given permission, most students have an enormous desire to make faces, and even the shyest will join in (if you've picked the right moment).

Let everyone try the role of master.

Stop before the laughter has exhausted itself.

'Social Space' Shrinks to Zero

Make a face at someone and you'll feel a force wanting to draw you towards their neck, as if you wanted to bite or nuzzle it. Servants who give way to this urge are caught instantly, or are discovered leaning at all sorts of odd angles. I've never seen any reference to this in the psychological literature, but try poking your tongue out as you draw your head back and discover how unnatural that feels as compared to doing it as you move your head forward (almost as weird as smiling while you hold your breath).

'Respect the master's space!' I shout. 'Make no distortions that you can't reverse instantly! Resist the impulse to lean in!'

Even if the students sit upright, they'll still want to put their hands close to the boss's head. Discourage this.

'Making Faces' in Fives

Speed up the training (involve more people) by adding a chair to each end of the row. The master (M) is in the middle, the servants (S) are to either side and the under-servants (U) are at the ends; so they're arranged like this: U-S-M-S-U.

The servants make faces at the master as in the previous game, but they now have under-servants who are making faces at them. The master fires the servants (as before), but the servants can now fire the under-servants. Masters can report the under-servants' misbehaviour to the servants (if they see it), but they seldom fire them.

When a servant is fired, the under-servant moves up a place. Replacements always begin at the 'U' positions.

Pecking Orders

Remove a servant and an under-servant from one side so that you are left with a one–two–three pecking order (U-S-M). Get them to rob a bank, or to arrive at the beach for a picnic, while still playing the Making Faces Game.[2]

'Making Faces' in Master–Servant Pairs

In two-player scenes, the master will be reluctant to let the servant make faces (not wanting to be the straight man) but I thwart this by shouting instructions:

'Look away to see the time! Go to the cupboard. Look in a drawer. Drop something and bend down to pick it up. Throw a dart at a dartboard and walk past the servant to retrieve it. Turn away and address a remark to someone in the audience. Go to the phone . . .'

They'd prefer to look away about once every minute and a half, but I force them to look away at least every ten seconds.

The game should continue to the point of total insanity. If the master kills the servant, and looks away, the corpse should still make faces, and if the master meets the servant in hell, the game continues.

Variant to avoid: 'We challenge you to a one-on-one Making Faces Game in which each actor makes faces at the other without being caught.' Yet the point of the Making Faces Game is that one person makes fun of another, so this is a form of joining, and gives minimum results.

The Vampire

Become a vampire: contort your face, writhe and hiss and show your teeth, but return to normal when your partner glances at you.

The force that sucks you towards the master's neck is magnified when your whole body 'makes a face', but if you succumb, you'll be leaping on your partner right away. Imagine that you are a vegetarian and that the act of biting someone would utterly disgust you. Or be a teacher, frantic to keep your job, and being interrogated by a suspicious headmaster.

Let's imagine that you're a vampire who desperately needs to rent a basement apartment:

- Do come in.
- Thank-you!
  [*The landlord turns away, and you become totally vampire. The landlord turns back.*]
- Were you hissing?
- Was I?
- I thought I heard something.
- My . . . my asthma.
  [*The landlord turns away again.*]
- There's lots of cupboard space.
  [*You reel away, desperate to resist the temptation to bite, and the landlord turns to see you clutching the door-frame.*]
- Very solidly built, this house.

Start with a determination not to bite anyone, and gradually allow your 'good resolution' to crumble. Perhaps you jump on the landlord, only to stagger away, hot with embarrassment:

- Oh, God, I'm sorry!
  [*You weep passionately.*]
- Er . . . I say . . .
- All right! I'll lie down and you can drive a stake through me! What else is there to do? Go on, see if I care!
- You do seem to be in a bad way.
- Put a scarf around your neck or something. Keep away from me, you fang-teaser!
  [*Perhaps you 'bite' the victim, while apologizing profusely.*]
- I'm bleeding! You bit me! You . . . you're mad!
- Yes, and now there are two of us!

The Vampire is not a game to use often in performance (once a year, perhaps), but use it in class to teach the importance of 'having a resistance'.

Leave for the Same Reason

This is not a performance game. Three beginners are asked to leave for the same reason, but without using dialogue.

My first students would never leave before a scene was over, so I invented this game as a corrective, but it proved to be an excellent way to coax beginners to avoid original ideas, and to cooperate.

I sit three students side by side and ask them all to leave for the same reason.

One says, 'It's hot here!' and then they leave because it's hot.

We try again. One says, 'There are too many ants here!' and they exit to avoid the ants.

But now I say, 'Again – but don't talk.'

This throws them into confusion. Perhaps I go into my 'have you played this game before' routine:

'Have you played this game before?'

'No.'

'So why should anyone expect you to be good at it? Just try it and see what happens.' They stare straight ahead, each determined to be in control. Perhaps one extends a hand and leaves because it's raining, one starts itching and leaves to escape the fleas, and the third applauds and leaves because the performance is over. They seem quite pleased with themselves.

'Did you all leave for the same reason?' I ask, and they have no idea.

'It's no use staring straight ahead; you'll have to see what the others are doing!'

'But what if we don't have any ideas?'

'See what's happening, and do what the others do.'

I've sat them in a straight line to magnify the problem, but they don't realize this.

'Start again,' I say, and then, after a few moments: 'Do what your partners are doing.'

'They aren't doing anything!'

'Maria just wrinkled her nose, so why not wrinkle your nose. Maybe you can leave to investigate some delicious smell. Larry is blinking, so you should all blink, and leave because the light it too bright, or because the pollution is irritating your eyes. If Nathan sighs, you could all sigh and mime throwing earth into a grave and leave because the funeral's over.'

I make several groups play the game, but one player will scratch, and others will pay no attention; one will sniff but the others will ignore it.

'Take any idea!' I say. 'Ideas are an ocean to splash about in. Don't be selective. Just do what the others do!'

This advice seems simple enough, but 'offers' are still being ignored, and I have to keep shouting instructions: 'He's moving his neck, so you should move your neck. Now Maria's rubbing her neck and groaning, so you should also groan. Leave because you're in terrible agony and need medical treatment!'

They play the game again. This time they manage to leave because they were fishing when a large fish pulled them offstage.

'Again,' I say, but this time they protest that they can't think of anything.

'How about having a huge fish pull you away?'

'We just did that!'

'No one said you have to be original. If you leave for the same reason every time, we'll admire your good nature.'

They start again; one adjusts her hair but the others ignore this.

'Notice that she's adjusting her hair! So adjust your hair.'

'Now what?'

'Mime that your hair's coming out in shreds! Leave for that reason.'

We repeat this game until it seems nothing special. Larry moves his foot, and his partners move their feet and increase the movement until they tap-dance away. Maria coughs, and they put on gas-masks and leave because the air is poisoned. Nathan feeds a bird, and they scatter bread until hundreds of birds attack them. Perhaps I get students to play the game speaking in gibberish (see p. 214) or have them add dialogue that has no connection with their reasons for leaving.

'Great game last night!' says Nathan, holding his palm out as if testing for rain.

'Wasn't it,' says Marie, putting on a raincoat.

'That last goal was spectacular', says Larry, opening an umbrella.

As their skills increase, less and less offers will be allowed to float by, and with luck this game can alter their attitudes to all improvisation. Perhaps they'll understand that the player who is searching for 'good ideas' can't respond to what's already happening.

Dubbing

One Voice

Dialogue is improvised in unison. This is one of the great beginners' games and it delights both players and audience.

This was a spin-off from Word-at-a-Time games. Some students became so skilled that I said, 'Why don't you both say all the words?'

They laughed at the seeming absurdity, but I explained that if they started by saying, 'Err', or by making the very first sound of a word, it ought to be possible to improvise dialogue *en masse*. To our amazement we found that this ability is innate (why would such a skill have evolved?). The greater the number of players, the easier this game becomes (because players who try to be original are drowned out by those who are being obvious). At a conference in Svenborg, each 'character' was composed of two hundred and fifty people, and the game worked flawlessly.

Teaching 'One Voice'

'Can you say what I say, as I say it?' I ask, kneeling in front of the group to diminish their anxiety. Then I say, 'Gooood mooorning' very slowly, exaggerating my lip movements.

'Gooood mooorning,' they repeat after me.

'Don't say it after I say it. Say it as I say it: Goooood moooorning!'

This time they synchronize their 'Gooood moooorning' to mine.

'It's a . . .' I add.

'Itt'sss . . . aaaa . . . veeery . . . niiiiceee . . . daaaaay . . .'

I'm now following them, but I doubt they realize this. By emphasizing the movements of my lips, and by saying obvious things, I make it easy for them to 'speak as I speak'.

I let other people take over my role, and I encourage the group to talk faster. It's soon possible to remove the 'leaders' and yet have the group improvise dialogue at almost conversational speed.

I stand some men along one wall and some women along the opposite wall.

'Be close to the other people in your group,' I say. 'And keep looking at them. Don't get isolated. Keep checking up to make sure that you're all on the same wavelength!'

I ask the women, 'Can you be one teenage girl?'

'Yesss weee caaan!'

Then I ask if the men can become one teenage boy. Perhaps I also ask them a simple question, like what day it is.

'Toodaay iiisss Friiidaaay!'

I turn to the women.

'Can you tell us where we are?'

'At the Looose Mooose Theeeatre!'

Now I ask them to play a scene in which they meet as strangers and agree to have coffee together. If an answer is unintelligible, I tell the other group to say, 'Whaaaat?'

It's easy for them to invent such a dialogue:

- Haallooo therrrre!
- Haallooo!
- Hooow arrre yoouuuu?
- I'mmm fiiiineee!

I prompt them with obvious sentences, and tease them by making them ask things like, 'What's your name?' The answer to this question is not predictable, and arouses a lot of laughter:

- My name is Ssuusshharrlleen!
- Whaaaaat?
- Charrrrrlene!
- Hi, Charrrleeeene!

Afterwards I point out that although almost every line evoked laughter, nothing clever or witty was being said. I explain that people love the obvious – which is all you get in this game – and that because none of them felt responsible for any failure, they were undefended. Undefended people look so beautiful, and so filled with light, that we want to laugh from the sheer pleasure of being in their company.

I'll also remind them that the audience was especially delighted when a sentence was so messed up that it couldn't be completed. 'They don't want you to be experts who never fail. They're longing for a sentence to degenerate into unintelligibility so that they can laugh at you. If you never made an error, they might as well be watching a rehearsed text.'

A player who speaks loudly and firmly can dominate an entire group. Some people argue that this makes it easier but I intended the game to encourage cooperation, not obedience.

'Don't lead!' I say. 'If you contribute half a syllable, wait to see where the group want the sentence to go. If nothing's happening, just make a tentative sound and wait to see where the others take it.'

I ask ten people to be a father, and ten to be a mother, and ten to be a son or daughter who has borrowed the Mercedes until midnight, but it's now four in the morning. I prompt lines of dialogue like 'It's your fault!', 'You're too soft with that boy!' and 'He doesn't take after my side of the family!'

The son or daughter arrives, and a quarrel starts. Masses of people swirl around the stage in tight groups and hurl abuse at each other. I keep the scene going (if I need to) by yelling things like 'Notice that he's drunk!' or 'Tell your parents you've decided to be an actor!' or 'Walk over and hit him!' or 'Notice she has bits of straw all over her.'

One Voice Parties (in Pairs)

I ask many pairs of students to link arms, or put their arms round each other's shoulders, and 'speak in one voice'.

'Be guests at a party,' I say. 'Meet old friends, find out where the food is . . .' and so on.

Then I let them play doctor–patient scenes, or parent–child scenes, or 'strangers meeting' scenes – each character being composed of two or more people.

The Professor

A group becomes a professor who answers questions put by the audience.

I'm embarrassed to have invented this game because it's played so self-indulgently, and because weak Judges allow it to dribble on. The audience is almost always asked what subject the professor should specialize in, which is crazy, because people speaking *en masse* have a mental age of about three: 'Ichthyology' was accepted on one occasion, and 'quantum physics' on another. These suggestions got laughs, but they ruined the game (as they were intended to).

Introduce a tightly packed group of players as a professor who has a few moments to answer questions from the audience on any topic.

Someone asks: 'Why is the sky blue?'

'Becaaauuse it's the colour of God's pyyyjaaaamas!' they reply, *en masse*, and if the game is a novelty, the audience will react as if it were the wittiest answer imaginable.

More questions are dealt with.

'Keep looking at each other!' I say. 'Don't lead. Don't say anything clever. Be obvious. Keep making eye contact with each other. Don't get isolated. Remember that you're all in the same boat!'

This 'keep making eye contact' instruction applies only when the game is being learned, but I've taught so many beginners' courses that players all over the world stare at each other when they play One Voice games. Glance at each other occasionally, to spread good vibes, but don't stare at each other unless you're in trouble.

This game can put people in a good mood, but keep it short, and end it while the spectators are hungry for more (after all, nothing of consequence is likely to emerge).

This chairman who introduces the professor should ask only one or two questions (if any) before turning the scene over to the audience.

The Audience Speak

I was at the Gothenburg Folk Theatre when I realized that an entire audience should be able to speak in one voice. I was told that this would be impossible with the 'reserved' Swedes, but I'd seen Swedes at ice-hockey, so I tried it, and it worked wonderfully. We were thrilled (it seemed an entirely new form of theatre), but it needs a big enough audience to drown out the intellectuals (because intellectuals feel obliged to say 'clever' things).

The Gothenburg playwright Kent Anderson wrote a play that included this idea. It worked well on the main stage where I had invented the game, but not when they transferred the production to their smaller space – confirming my belief that the game needs a 'critical mass' of audience to guarantee success.

I introduce the game after the improvisers have played a short One Voice Game. Then I say, 'Do you think the audience could do this?'

'Yeessss,' say the improvisers.

Then I ask the audience, 'Can you speak in one voice?', and if I've chosen the right moment, they'll probably say, 'Yyesssss weeee cannnn!'

But even if they were to say, 'Noooo weeee caaaan't!' this would be an admission that they could.

Either way, they'll laugh for at least thirty seconds at their own 'cleverness'.

Perhaps I'll ask the players to be the audience's 'blind date'. They cluster together and mime knocking on the 'fourth wall':

'Aaaanyboooody hoooome?'

'Whoooo's there?' roars the audience.

'It's yooour bliiinnd daaaattee!'

Almost for sure the audience will say, 'Goooo awaaaayyyyy!'

'Weee've brought whiiskyy!' chant the actors.

'Cooommmmee innnn!' roars the audience, shrieking with laughter, and applauding itself wildly.

In Copenhagen recently, the 'blind date' mimed bringing a very large 'present'.

'Do you know what it is?' chorused the actors.

'It's aaaa biiiccyyyccclleee!' screamed the audience, without hesitation, although how such agreement was achieved baffled us.

You could set up a scene between a parent and their naughty child:

'Daddy, Mummy, I've been naughty!'

'Whhaaat haavveee yoouu doonnee thiiiis tiimmee?'

Or the audience could be God interviewing new arrivals in heaven, or the players could try to give the audience a speeding ticket.

One Voice games demonstrate the value of being obvious because the audience laugh so much and yet nothing clever is being said.

Lip-Sync

A player in a two-person scene provides both the voices.

Lip-Sync probably goes back to Ig and Og in the caves, but I discovered it when I was teaching students to be ventriloquists (using each other as dummies) and realized that the dummy might just as well get up and walk about.

Stage One I ask a master to choose a voice for herself (perhaps her own voice) and to invent a quite different voice for her servant.

'Who should lead?'

'No one leads. If the servant opens his mouth and no voice comes, then he must pretend to yawn, or gulp down a passing fly, or whatever.'

I ask the master to call the servant.

'Angus!' she shouts. 'Get in here!'

'Aye, ma'am, what'ivers t'matter?' she says in a Scottish accent, while Angus gesticulates but forgets to move his lips.

She switches to her own voice and reminds him, saying, 'Angus! How many times do I have to tell you not to talk without moving your lips?'

She becomes Angus's voice and says, 'I didn't want you to see my teeth, madam!'

She switches back and says, 'Are you wearing my dentures? Return them at once!'

And so on.

I prompt beginners so that the servant knows what the master will say. For example (my words are in italics):

– *Call your servant in.*
– James!
– *Say in his accent: 'You wanted to see me, sir?'*
– You wanted to see me, sir?

- *Say, 'I did indeed'.*
- I did indeed.
- *Say, 'Didn't I forbid you ever to be taller than me?'*
- Didn't I forbid you ever to be taller than me?
- I'm my brother, sir.

Repeating my words is not much fun, so they'll soon start adding phrases of their own and I'll drop out.

If the servants are having trouble synchronizing their lips, I'll tell the masters to add an 'err' before the servants' sentences.

After the game has been demonstrated successfully, I'll let the class play it in pairs, and quite soon I'll ask them to change partners and play it again.

It's easier to develop scenes using this game than it is when both players contribute the dialogue.

Stage Two So far the servant has been controlled by the master, but if the servant makes physical blind offers (see page 192) the control is shared. Seized by the throat, the master will have to gasp something like, 'Pay me the money you owe me!' or 'I'm not going to jail for you this time, sir!' Clutch the master's feet, and he/she will have to give you phrases like 'Forgive me, sir! I can't get the dog out of the lawnmower!' or whatever. But exercise some restraint: don't swamp the master.

Most servants underdo the movement of their lips, hoping to conceal any errors. Encourage them to overdo the lips, so that they seem to be talking in an exaggerated manner (audiences enjoy seeing mistakes if they are made wholeheartedly).

If the voice always leads the lips (or vice versa), correct this. Control must be shared.

Two-way Lip-Sync

Each player dubs someone else's voice, but please don't do this! I invented it as a gag for ending Lip-Sync, but I've seen groups of five or six players spend ten minutes, each speaking for one of the others, even though no one could follow what was happening. It was a regular feature of their show, but when I asked if this version had ever 'worked', they said, 'Oh, it did once,' but couldn't remember when.

Challenged to this game, be merciful: keep it short, and ask for the challenge to be a one-on-one.

Lip-Sync from Offstage[3]

Onstage characters are dubbed by players sitting offstage (use a mike). Start by asking the 'voices' to weep, or laugh, or sigh, or scream, while the onstage players lip-sync to the sounds. Then add dialogue. Encourage the 'actors' to make blind offers that the 'voices' can justify. Point out that these blind offers make it easier to construct stories (because the shared responsibility halves the players' anxiety). This is a good voice exercise since the speakers are imagining their sounds as coming from way ahead of them. And it's excellent for developing funny voices.

Try this game with the voices as 'shadows' – each voice stands next to its 'body' and moves with it. The proximity encourages bolder scenes, although it may be a nuisance in public performance.

Lip-Sync with Audience Volunteers

The actors provide the voices (because they're the ones who are skilled at developing interactions).

Coach the volunteers to overdo the lips.

The 'voices' must force activity by saying things like 'I'll get you a juice from the refrigerator,' or 'Shall I lie on the bed so you can examine me, Doctor?'

If the volunteers are treated discourteously, a Judge should haul the 'voices' on to the stage and make them apologize. Don't make the 'voices' of audience volunteers embarrassingly stupid.

Variant: two players work onstage together with an audience volunteer. One of the two players does all three voices.

Invisibility

Endow your partner (or partners) with invisibility, and act out the consequences.

Fear is still as much a part of us as our ribs (which overlap to deflect claws) so I ask the players to remember being alone in a house at night when something in the next room crashed to the linoleum. And then I ask them to imagine how eerie it would be if a coffee mug floated into the air, or if a book began reading itself. If the players can conjure up such anxieties, they'll stop being 'intellectual' and will react spontaneously.

This game is entertaining, even when it's badly played. If your invisible partner is reading a newspaper, it should be perceived as 'floating in mid-air', yet you may not realize this immediately. And beginners will react when there's no reason to. For example, if an invisible person enters a room, the effect may be exactly the same as if the door had been opened and closed from the outside by someone who didn't enter. Leaping off the sofa, and screaming, 'Augh! What's happening?' would be inappropriate.

If two players are endowing each other with invisibility and pretending to be terrified, it's likely that neither will leave the stage, and nor will they make physical contact. If one is lying on the sofa he/she will stand up as soon as the other approaches (not wanting to be sat on). Afterwards they argue that it's more entertaining to keep just missing each other, but it's a refusal to be altered.

The best way to teach the game is by side-coaching the instant that errors occur.

I set up a scene in which Deborah will act normally, while Tom will endow her with invisibility (so Deborah is to be the straight man).

She sits on the sofa reading, and Tom enters, ignoring the book that's 'floating in mid-air'. I start the scene again. This time he stares at the book in alarm.

'Tom! Are you all right?' she says.

He stares in all directions.

I interrupt to tell him that that's fine, but his ears must be telling him where she's speaking from.

'Is that you Deborah?' he says. 'Oh, no! You're invisible again.'

He's establishing that this often happens, so that he'll need to change only minimally. I stop the scene and remind him that in this world there are no invisible people, that his character must be insane, or drugged, or haunted, or the victim of some trick.

'If an invisible hand grasped your arm you wouldn't think, Oh! An invisible arm has grasped my arm. You'd think that your arm had gone stiff, and when you saw white indentations on your wrist you wouldn't think, Oh! Of course! Invisible fingers are pressing into me, because there are no invisible fingers. If an invisible man collided with you in the street and knocked you down, you'd think you'd slipped, or were having a heart attack, because colliding with an invisible person couldn't be a valid explanation. Sit on an invisible person who is sleeping on a sofa and you'd feel an inexplicable warmth and softness as you found yourself suspended in mid-air, and the sleeping person might wake up to find that they were paralysed.'

We start the scene again.

'How was work, darling?'

'You can hear where the voice is coming from!' I shout, and he stares at where her head was when she stopped speaking. 'Help him!' I shout. 'He's behaving weirdly.'

'Are you all right, Tom? You look as if you've seen a ghost!' She drops the book and walks over to him.

'Don't look at Deborah. Look at the book!'

He plays terror, but he still won't leave.

'Don't stay if you are afraid,' I shout. 'Run out of the door!'

'But then the scene will be over.'

'It's your house! You live here! You'd come back eventually.'

Deborah touches him, and he screams and scrambles backwards to the door.

'Tom! It's me!'

His eyes follow her.

'Look at the point in space where you last heard the voice.'

It's good to have a door that can be opened, and shut, and slammed, and bolted – yet all over the world improvisers are performing with no door, no bed, no desk, no sofa: is it any wonder that their improvisations are so verbal?

Each Partner Endows the Other

Neither player can see the other. I coach them to blunder into each other – taking care not to hurt each other – and to gasp and scream so that they can startle each other even more.

Tom picks up a chair to defend himself against the invisible terror, and Deborah strikes at it to see what's holding it up. Tom gasps, and Deborah screams but he doesn't react.

'Scream when she screams! The sound was right beside you! Be terrified!'

As we see example after example, the students begin to understand the need to react intuitively, rather than to think thoughts like, The book is floating in mid-air – perhaps I'd better look surprised! Such 'intellectual' thinking is always too slow.

Don't mime objects in this game, and don't wear a hat or we won't know whether it's invisible or floating about in mid-air.

The Ghost Game

Recommended for very occasional use.

Three or four characters enter some deserted interior – a haunted house or an old temple, or whatever. If anyone leaves, they must play the Invisibility Game when they re-enter. When (and if) all the players are back onstage none of them will be able to see any of the others. Only skilled players should attempt this in public.

I invent a situation where the characters will be isolated; for example:

'You're all travelling to a summer house when your car breaks down, far from anywhere. It's at night or at dusk. You see a house in the trees and you walk over to ask if you can use the phone. But it seems derelict. When you enter you discover that the electricity is still on (but there's no phone), and you decide to spend the night there. When anyone leaves the stage they play the Invisibility Game next time that they enter.'

The instructions are simple, but I may have to explain them several times.

'You mean that the first time I come in, I can see everything.'

'That's right.'

'But the second time I enter, I can't?'

'Exactly.'

We start the game and they'll still get it wrong.

'So we can't see the people who haven't left the room.'

'Correct.'

'But what if we leave and return together?'

'Anyone who leaves plays the Invisibility Game when they re-enter.'

'But can we see each other.'

'No, because you'll be endowing invisibility when you re-enter.'

Even after all this someone will leave and come back pretending to be invisible.

'Oh, you mean I can't see the others. I think I get it.'

Eventually we get the rules clear.

They enter, and look for a phone and check if the place is inhabited. They decide to bed down for the night.

– Ron: Get the cases, Olly.
– Peggy: Why should Olly get the cases?
– Ron: Perhaps we should all get them.
– Olly: I'm checking the house.
– Peggy: I'll get them!

[*Peggy gets the cases from the car, and endows the others with invisibility when she re-enters. They try to calm her but she drops the cases and runs out shrieking.*]

— Ron: I'll get her. [*He returns almost instantly, and stares around, wondering where the others have gone.*] She ran round to the back of the house . . . Olly?
— Olly: I can't get this case unlocked. It's got her medication.
— Ron: [*Staring at the case but not seeing Olly*] Augh!
— Olly: Sorry, I thought . . . Just trying to be helpful.
— Ron: Olly! Stop playing tricks.
— Olly: What are you on about? Are you feeling okay? [*Touching him*] Ron?
— Ron: Augh! Someone touched me!
[*Peggy is heard calling them from outside the house.*]

Perhaps the game ends with the characters all screaming with terror and hiding under the cushions, or thrashing at imaginary spirits, or huddled into corners. Or maybe they're all back at the car, which is now a total wreck, and they peer inside and see their dead bodies.

Try a visit to a haunted house by a cub reporter, a sceptical scientist, the chairman of a society for Paranormal Research, and a medium.

NOTES

1 I found this mantra in Joanna Field's *A Life of One's Own*. I mentioned it to a Zen monk who met me a couple of years later and said that it was the best mantra he'd ever used.
2 Pecking orders are described in my book *Impro*. All I'll add here is that members of 'clown' pecking orders should stay close together, whenever possible, so that we see them as one organism.
3 Described by Viola Spolin in her book *Improvisation for the Theatre*.

9 Some Filler Games

When I directed the Theatre Machine I divided games into narrative and anti-narrative. Anti-narrative proved rather a mouthful, and we were soon referring to such games as 'filler games' (because I used them to fill in the gaps between stories):

'How was the tournament?'

'Nothing but filler games!'

Anyone familiar with public improvisation will be relieved to have missed that event, not because filler games are 'bad', but because sequences of them soon become tedious. The best filler games add variety, and inspire the players. If you've made the audience weep, it can be wonderful to 'cut' to a filler game like a Questions Only Game, or even a Freeze Game, but sequences like the Alphabet Game, followed by Hitch-hiker, followed by Strange Bedfellows, followed by Chain Endowments are like soup followed by soup followed by soup.

If you're bored by players who seem 'talented' and 'bright', they're probably using too much 'filler'.

(See Appendix Three for more filler games.)

The Die Game

An improviser from San Francisco showed us this game in 1979. It's used for warming-up the spectators.

Four, five or six players face the audience, and a title is agreed on. A conductor explains that any player who is pointed at will begin a story (or continue it), and that if he/she hesitates, or is ungrammatical, or makes some other error, the audience should shout, 'Die', forcing the miscreant to 'commit suicide'. The last one left 'alive' will be the winner.

The audience is rehearsed in shouting 'Die' until they agree to be really loud – shouting makes them more responsive – and then the story begins with the conductor trying to throw the players by pointing at them unexpectedly, and by lingering on any individual who seems about to crack up.

Players who are to 'die' will often ask for an object to 'die' with. For example:

'Can you name an implement you might find in a kitchen?'

Someone shouts, 'Cheese grater!'

The players then cheese-grates himself or herself to death (and the audience laugh at the stupidity), but it's best to find your own way of dying. If you're stuck, perhaps the sound imp will provide a rapidly approaching train, or whatever.

Variant: each player is given a genre: sci-fi, religion, romance, Western, and so on. I'll improvise a sample:

Sci-Fi: 'As the spaceship approached Beta Four there was no sign of life from the colonists. Captain Skoog would be glad to be rid of the cargo of . . .'

Religious: '. . . monks who had come to set up a branch of their order. His . . .'

Romance: '. . . handsome profile assumed a masterful severity, as Communications Officer Ulla-Karin failed to detect any answering transmission . . .'

Western: '. . . from the Crossed Tentacle ranch far below where Tex had just wrestled one of the local Xangs into submission. The branding-iron was hissing into its body armour as it stared skywards. Following its gaze, Tex saw the bright star hovering over the foothills and . . .'

Religious: '. . . all over the prairie the rough soma-chewing Xang-boys knelt in awe, believing the atomic fire in the sky to be the sign they had been . . .'

Romance: '. . . Er . . . er . . .'

The player dithers and the audience yells 'DIE!' with relish. Any game that gets the audience to yell loudly is useful, but I'd hate to see the Die Game in show after show. Use it as a warm-up game, not as a 'closer'.

Variant: no genres are agreed on beforehand. The conductor shouts out a genre as he points. I wouldn't recommend this.

Emotional Goals[1]

The players start with one emotion (or 'condition') and modulate to another: for example, from sad to happy, proud to ashamed, silly to intelligent.

Start by asking a group to move from, say, 'interest' to 'panic'. Perhaps they're so engrossed watching creatures trapped in a rock pool that they become marooned by the incoming tide. Try various emotions, and stress the need to make gradual transitions.

Then have pairs play the game.

Then have each player choose his/her own emotions: one may be heading from terror to lust, while another goes from panic to calm. This game works best with two players, or two players and a 'passenger' – add more and it's difficult to follow.

Teaching Emotional Goals

Asked to change from 'anger' to 'affection', most students will start mildly peeved and take fifteen seconds to get totally enraged, yet they're supposed to be heading towards affection, not away from it. My advice is to begin with whatever intensity you can muster and start diminishing it immediately.

I encourage the players to make transitions by tiny steps, telling them that if I photographed them at fifteen-second intervals I'd like to be able to shuffle the prints and then lay them out in the order in which they were taken. This concept of 'gradualism' is easier to grasp if they've already played the Tempo Game (see p. 207). Changing violently is dramatic, but changing slowly and continuously can also grip the attention (study Garbo, Vanessa Redgrave, Brando, and similar great actors).

Endowments

These were useful in the early days while we were still flailing about. For example, we'd send an improviser out of earshot, and then get a 'profession and two physical qualities' from the audience – perhaps they'd suggest a 'teacher' who is 'blind' and has 'a huge nose'. Then we'd fetch the improviser back in, and play a scene in which his/her partners endowed him with these items, using gibberish (see p. 214). Sometimes we'd play the scene in English, while giving the information indirectly; for example:

- Come in. Careful! Keep your head straight! I suppose you find the door a bit narrow!
- It's always nice to visit you little people!
  [*Instead of 'a huge nose', they've conveyed 'gigantism', and the spectators will laugh at the misunderstanding.*]

– I'll drop a peanut. Perhaps you'd like to pick it up? No need to bend down!
– I'm an elephant!
  [*Boos and laughter from the audience.*]
– I've got a big nose!
  [*Applause.*]
– I'm afraid I forgot my homework.
– Do you want to copy mine?
  [*Laughter at the error.*]
– I'm a teacher with big nose!
  [*Applause.*]
– Careful! There's a desk to your right.
– I'm blind!

I prefer the gibberish version. Endowments guarantee a laugh but it's like shooting fish in a barrel.

Variant to avoid: some players will become 'crippled' to communicate a limp, or get hiccups to convey that their partner has indigestion. Do this and endowments aren't worth playing. It's reasonable to reach for something on the ground and say, 'You dropped your white stick,' but it's moronic to signal the need for your partner to become 'blind' by becoming 'blind' yourself.

Variant – Chain Endowments: (not a game to see more than once) – several players are sent out of earshot while the endowments are being decided. Then 'A' endows 'qualities' on to 'B' who conveys his understanding (misunderstanding) to 'C', and so on. The information becomes increasingly garbled and the audience laugh.

Freeze Games

The players start an activity – directing traffic, perhaps – and then someone shouts, 'Freeze!' and runs into the scene to change 'directing traffic' into some unrelated but visually similar activity.

These visual puns are among the most popular of all improvisation games because they almost always get a laugh, and there's no risk that anything might happen. They are claimed to develop the players' imaginations (and I saw excellent examples when I gave workshops at Chicago's Second City) but so do many less destructive games. They teach the players to be original, and to sidetrack and cancel. They were never played in my classes at the Studio (and never by the Theatre Machine), but you might get challenged to one, and any game can be a straw to grab at when you're desperate.

Perhaps we see two people who are pushing a boulder, but someone else shouts freeze and rushes in to change the activity into three sailors tossing about in a storm. Perhaps the next freeze changes them into four downhill skiers. People laugh, because they like transformations, but why train students to kill stories? Morph from 'playing the accordion' to 'stretching chest-expanders', to 'firing an arrow', to being 'nailed on a cross' and you'll be admired, but it's like warming yourself by burning the floorboards. We need coherent sequences like 'firing an arrow', and 'killing an animal', and 'discovering a collar around its neck that says "Property of the Emperor"'.

Guess the Phrase

I saw this game at Chicago's Second City Theatre and told Bernie Sahlins that we'd 'steal' it (and, anyway, it's probably a development of my Guess the Situation Game: see p. 217).

Martin is sent out of earshot while we get the audience to agree on a well-known phrase, song title, or whatever. He returns and takes part in scenes that attempt to convey the phrase to him (his partners are not allowed to mention any of the keywords in the title).

Let's say that the phrase to be communicated is 'birds of a feather, flock together'. A few players flap imaginary wings and start discussing migration. Martin becomes a bird and they start billing and cooing together.

'The early bird gets the worm?' he says, and everyone laughs or groans.

A new scene begins instantly, with Martin being shown around a baronial hall by the owner.

'Shot and mounted most of these birds myself. I've got a complete set of Darwin's finches in the conservatory . . .'

Martin makes a guess: 'You've feathered your own nest?'

A duck-hunting scene begins:

'Look at that! They're packed so close that I can shoot them all in one burst!'

'The early worm gets the bird?' says Martin hopefully.

A new scene establishes him as the newest member of an ornithology club. The players hand him some binoculars: 'Amazing!' they say. 'Look how the grebes are avoiding the loons!'

Martin says, 'Birds of a feather flock together,' and everyone cheers. Typical phrases might be:

- Let sleeping dogs lie
- Love thy neighbour
- Don't bite off more than you can chew
- Don't judge a book by its cover
- The gods help those who help themselves
  Typical song titles might be:
- 'Like a Virgin'
- 'Que sera sera'

Obscure proverbs or song titles are useless, but a well-known title like 'Like a Virgin' can suggest scenes in the back seat of a car, or human sacrifices.

Guess the Phrase improves communication skills.

The No 'S' Game

Excellent for beginners. The players must avoid words that use an agreed letter. Don't select letters that are rarely used (and don't let beginners select vowels).

I invented this game mid-lecture when I was extemporizing ways to interfere with verbalization.

Some players are so used to leaving their mouths on automatic that they'll begin a no 'S' scene by saying 'Please, sir . . .' or 'Sit down, Susan . . .' and lose instantly, to the delight of the spectators. This game forces the players to attend to what they're saying, and it can also convince them of the value of failure, since the spectators are longing for a player to screw-up so that they can laugh, and feel superior. If the players are making no errors, tell them to speed up (because there's no point in playing this game unless someone loses).

Variant: replace anyone who uses a word with 'S' in it and let the scene continue.

Destructive Variant: each player is asked to avoid a different letter, even though the spectators have enough trouble listening for just one forbidden letter. This is an excellent example of the way simple games can be ruined by adding complexity.

A Scene without . . .

The audience is asked to complete the phrase 'a scene without . . .'; for example: 'a scene without scruples', or 'without air', or 'without guilt', or 'without a friend', or 'without a brain', or 'without hope', or 'without talent'. It's okay to ask for suggestions, because even the most malevolent audience member finds it difficult to be destructive in this context.

Sideways Scenes

Excellent for very occasional use. The rear of the stage is treated as the floor, and the 'fourth wall' between actors and audience is treated as the ceiling, so we pretend that gravity is pulling the players away from the audience instead of towards the centre of the earth.

This game dates from the class in which I set out to find every possible way that we could play a scene (backward scenes were invented at the same time).

Set a desk and two chairs on their sides, with their 'feet' against the back wall (or rear curtain) as though the audience was looking down through the ceiling of an office. Perhaps the boss lies on the floor with the top of his head towards the audience, and with his feet against the rear wall. Perhaps he struggles out of his coat and 'hangs' it on an imaginary hook (on the floor some five feet away from the rear wall). Now he can lever himself towards the desk, 'rowing' himself along with his lower arm, while moving his feet backward and forward along the wall. This gives the illusion that he's walking. He can 'sit' at the desk, pressing his bottom against its sideways seat. Perhaps he takes some papers out of the sideways drawer and 'rests' his feet on the sideways desk.

Any doors in the back wall are treated as trap-doors. Perhaps one opens, and Perkins emerges, wriggling on to the stage as if climbing up a ladder. He holds the boss's coffee mug sideways and 'walks' along the back wall to place the mug on the vertical surface of the sideways desk. Maybe we've rigged it with Velcro so that it stays in position, or perhaps the boss berates Perkins when it crashes to the 'wall' (i.e. on to the stage floor): 'How dare you throw my favourite mug at the wall just because I halved your salary!'

Many pleasing effects are possible. For example, if the boss is shot, he becomes dead by standing in some crooked position against the rear wall (perhaps the police will tape around his outline).

I remember a scene in which Dennis Cahill 'buzzed about' wearing a fly costume, and 'landed' on the 'ceiling' (i.e. on the fourth wall'):

'It's that confounded fly again.'

'I'll get the spray from the cupboard, sir.'

They sprayed him, and he 'fell' away from the audience and crash-landed on to his attacker in terminal agony. Try a levitation scene in which a guru edges towards the audience as if floating to the ceiling; or a spiderman scene; or present an interview with an acrobat; or stand a bed upright against the rear wall and have the players stand against it and hold the bedding up in front of them. I've seen a love scene on a sofa that was stood on its end and with the lovers being held in position. It took about ten 'handlers' to achieve this, most of whom had rushed out from the audience, but it was worth the effort.

Sideways scenes can be hysterically funny, but I've never seen other groups use them. Dirty floors may be one reason. We wash our stage before each performance, but I remember a space in New York's Bowery district where anything that touched the floor was soiled by an oily black paste.

Yes-But

We were told about this game by a spectator at a Theatre Machine performance who had learned it from Viola Spolin's *Improvisation for the Theatre* (a book which describes work in the Compass Players and Second City tradition).

Kurt asks questions that can receive a 'yes' answer, and Gloria responds with sentences that begin with 'Yes, but . . .'. For example:

– Are you closed?
– Yes, but do come in!
– Are you the animal doctor?
– Yes, but I don't do snakes!
– I'm afraid this is an emergency – that lump is the professor.
– Yes, but . . .

And so on. One common way to end the game is by having both players use 'Yes, but . . .' sentences.

– You'll have to go in after him!
– Yes, but then I might be digested!

- Yes, but I'll get a rope to tie around you.
- Yes, but I'm no good at knots.
- Yes, but I was a boy scout!

You can usually fade the lights somewhere about here. Keep such scenes short.

I use Yes-But to demonstrate the difference between intellectual and intuitive thinking. I might begin by answering 'yes questions' that are put to me by the students.

'How old are you?'

'I'm sorry, I have to be able to give a "yes" answer.'

'Are you a hundred years old?'

'Yes, but I'm quite fit for my age.'

'Do you read much?'

'Yes, but mostly about current events.'

'Are you interested in politics?'

'Yes, but I'm not sure who to vote for.'

Then I tell them that I've been 'staying safe' by thinking up the answers before I open my mouth. Would they like me to be braver? Yes, they would.

This time I say, 'Yes! But!' vigorously and loudly, and with no idea what will follow.

'Are you a hundred years old?'

'Yes! But I feel like ninety-eight!'

'Did you vote in the election.'

'Yes! But if it made any difference they wouldn't let me!'

'Have you ever run for parliament?'

'Yes! But I kept running.'

Deciding what to say before you speak leads to planned answers, but shouting, 'Yes! But . . .' with a blank mind drags out 'unchosen' answers which are almost always more entertaining.

After Yes-But try the more positive Yes-And. If you use this game in performance, to add variety (why else?), keep it short.

NOTES

1 Emotional Goals are described by Viola Spolin in *Improvisation for the Theatre*.

10 Procedures

I might unlock a student's folded arms by saying, 'Alternate between wanting to hit your partner and wanting to caress your partner!' If I want more aggression, I might say, 'Flash your lower teeth when you talk!' If I need someone to look 'at home', I might say, 'Sit on the sofa wrongly, but comfortably'. If I wanted someone to be powerful, I might say, 'Keep your head still when you speak.' If someone was gabbling, I might say, 'Talk! . . . Don't Talk! . . . Develop the interaction . . . Talk . . .'

These instructions are procedures that can be applied irrespective of the game you're playing. They are 'buttons' that can be pressed to achieve a particular effect. Some actors are 'good', no matter what movie you see them in – these are the ones who can press their own buttons.

Blind Offers

When I introduced the term 'offer' it was thought to be so all-embracing as to be quite useless (an 'offer' being anything that you say or do), but the term allows us to discuss interesting offers, dull offers, controlling offers, blind offers, and so on.

If you present a mimed object, saying, 'You left your hat here,' this is a controlling offer, whereas if you'd said, 'You forgot this yesterday,' it would have been a blind offer (because you'd be allowing your partner to make the definition). For example:

– Good morning, Perkins!
– [*Blind offer*] We're ready for you now, sir.
– [*Blindish offer*] And the frog?
– It's had the injection, sir.
   [*Sir snaps his fingers* (blind offer) *and Perkins mimes dressing him in heavy protective clothing. Sir splutters and Perkins mimes opening the face-plate.*]
– There's no air in here, Perkins.

– I'm sorry, sir. I'll go behind the protective wall and start pumping.
– Very well!
[*Sir clumps towards the imaginary frog*]

The use of such blind offers led the *Stage* newspaper to accuse us of presenting rehearsed scenes under the guise of improvisations (big headlines on the front page), because how could Sir have known that Perkins was a lab assistant? And how could Perkins have understood that the frog needed to be injected? But the truth is that Perkins decided on the spur of the moment to become an assistant, and Sir accepted him as such.

'But the frog?'

'There was no frog until Sir said, "And the frog?" He could have said any other noun.'

A blind offer like, 'We are ready for you now, sir,' has infinite possibilities. Perkins could have mimed sealing the frog into a flask, and Sir could have said, 'We've got you now, Hillary, and we're going to throw you in the sea, and God help any poor soul who rescues you!'

Or he could have said, 'Thank you, Perkins. Are the candles lit?'

'Yes, sir, and the congregation has sung the first hymn.'

'You know, this is the first time I've ever anointed anyone!'

Never to know the next step, but to have the courage to take it, is an exhilarating way to improvise, but beginners (and frightened improvisers) prefer to make controlling offers. One said, 'I've a present for you! It's for your birthday! It's a bottle of whisky! It's your favourite!'

This alienated her partner who retaliated by blocking furiously: 'It's not my birthday! And I never drink alcohol! Who are you, anyway? How dare you burst in here!'

Perhaps saying that 'the first person to make a controlling offer loses' could be a new game.

Justify the Gesture

I apologize to my students for the 'stupidity' of this, and ask them to humour me:

'Ann, raise your arm. Brian, look at her for one second. Brian, return her "to neutral". Ann, shower him with gratitude.'

Now I ask Brian to make a gesture – perhaps he puts his hand on the top of his head. Ann looks at him for a moment, returns him to neutral and is thanked profusely.

I let all the students try this procedure, alternating between making an 'abstract' gesture and having their partners cancel it. They know that I never suggest a game unless it has a purpose, but this one makes no sense.

'Stage two!' I say, and explain that they can either play the game as before, or they can justify the gesture: 'If a finger is being pointed, you could pretend to manicure it; if someone covers their ears, you could mime "turning down the stereo", but don't force ideas – just be mildly interested as to whether an idea presents itself or not.'

It's difficult to accept this advice if 'not being inventive' is experienced as a defeat.

'You need the same attitude as the spectators,' I say. 'They're under no pressure to be "right" or to be praised for their "good ideas", so their imaginations work automatically. Extend your palm and they'll see you as about to catch a ball, or testing for rain, or wanting your palm read. They don't think up these ideas, and your minds can work in the same ordinary way.'

'But we're under more stress.'

'Not if you keep reminding yourself that it's a stupid game and that it doesn't matter whether you win or lose. Just be mildly interested in whether the Great Moose will give you an idea.'

'And if we don't get an idea?'

'Return your partner to neutral – you get thanked anyway.'

'But that's boring.'

'I didn't ask you to be entertaining. This is an exercise in seeing whether you can allow the mind to work by itself.'

They try again.

Ann extends a hand. Brian kisses it. Ann says, 'Thank-you!' Brian raises his arm, and Ann raises her arm and pretends to be 'strap-hanging' (on a train). Brian thanks her.

'Thank each other more!' I say. 'We need enthusiasm!'

Ann extends her arms and Brian pretends to photograph her – she becomes a model and thanks him.

I interrupt: 'I didn't ask you to get an idea every time. It's better to return your partners to neutral than to scour your mind for "good ideas" (and we'll praise you for being honest). Believe that your ideas are nothing to do with "you", treat then as gifts that are showered on you, and you'll be as effortlessly creative as when you're listening to a story.'

I explain that if a book mentions a child on a beach I'll 'know' that it's a boy, and I'll 'see' the colour of the sand, the height of the waves, the size and proliferation of the clouds – not to mention Mum and Aunt Florrie sitting on a blanket and eating cucumber sandwiches; but if the next sentence tells me, 'It was a cloudless day and the girl was alone on the desolate shore . . .' the first *mise en scène* will be replaced by another, and this process will continue for page after page, inexhaustibly.

If students have shared this experience, they may suddenly realize that creativity is a matter of 'attending' rather than 'thinking', and that reading a book might be as creative an act as writing one (although less arduous).

The game continues and previous solutions begin to interfere with current ones.

'Why are you hesitating?'

'I can't get an idea.'

'I think that you had an impulse to lift a small bird from her finger but then you remembered that someone had done that earlier, and you wanted to be original!'

'True!'

'Accept the idea that presents itself. After all, we've only got two arms and two legs, and if we keep on playing this game, we'll soon have provided justifications for every conceivable position. Besides, it's not the same bird.'

Master this game, and working together will become effortless. You sit down, and someone starts to examine your eyes. You point, and your servant 'shoots the bird' that you had no idea you were pointing at.

He Said/She Said

Tell your partner what to do, and then add a line of dialogue.

This game was suggested by actors at Tournus (Denmark) when we were exploring ways to control each other. They named it He Said – Removing His Trousers, which has more of a lilt to it in Danish.

My three-year-old son learned it instantly, and without error, but most adults find it baffling. This is because toddlers are used to being yanked about and having their faces and bottoms wiped, and they're eager for revenge, whereas most adults erect walls against intrusion. I only once met an adult who wasn't confused by this game, and he was still living with his mum.

An example:

– I'm home!
– He said, throwing his satchel on to the table. 'How was school?'
– She said, picking it up and looking inside it. 'Mum! That's mine!'
– He said, trying to pull it away from me but failing miserably. 'I just want to see what you have for your homework.'
– She said, emptying it out on to the table. 'I finished my homework at school, Mum.'
– He said, giving me a phoney smile and edging towards the door. 'I talked to your teacher today.'
– She said, grabbing me by the neck. 'Whatever for?'
– He said, turning pale and refusing to look at me. 'You haven't been to school for a month. You told your teacher we had moved to another city!'

This game may sound coercive, but your partner can't really control you against your will. For example:

– 'There are no more patients, Doctor.'
– She said, unbuttoning her blouse. 'Nurse Kimble, stop it at once!'
– He said, buttoning it up for me . . .

I introduce He Said/She Said when the students are in a good mood, and I explain that although it's easy for small children, it's difficult for adults – this arouses their curiosity, and gives them less need to punish themselves when they fail.

I explain the game and lead a couple of volunteers through it, telling them that I'll feed them the dialogue:

'Say: "Hallo! Max!"'

'Hallo, Max!' says Linda.

I tell Max to say: 'She said!'

Max is confused.

'Just say, "She said . . ."'

'She said . . .'

'Embracing me.'

'What?' he says.

'Say, "She said, embracing me."'

'I don't get it.'

'She just said, "Hallo," so now you say, "She said, embracing me." Just say the words.'

He does.

'So now she embraces you.'

Linda embraces him, saying, 'Nice to see you.'

'Not yet,' I say. *'First he has a line of dialogue, then you tell him what to do.'*

'Let me get this straight,' she says. 'I can't say, "Nice to see you"?'

With any luck the onlookers will be laughing at the obtuseness of these performers, but I turn to them and say, 'It looks easy, but it's like being trapped in glue.'

I let other students attempt the game, and again we have total confusion, so I spell out the rules once more:

'Tell your partner what to do, and then add a line of dialogue. Is that clear?'

'Yes!'

'Does that sound difficult?'

'No!'

'So the confusion lies in us, not in the instructions. Don't get disheartened – it takes about forty minutes to master this game.'

Defences

The students' inability to remember the rules vanishes as soon as they discover more subtle defences; for example, it feels safer to be controlled from a distance (which is why sergeant-majors prefer to scream into your face from an inch away), so players soon learn to say, 'He said, going to the door,' or 'She said, climbing on a chair and flapping her arms.'

I point out that they're trying to minimize interaction, but that it's more fun to work closely together. For example:

– 'You swine!'
– She said, throwing me to the floor and kneeling on my chest. 'Augh! You're hurting me!'
– He said, loving it. 'It's your turn to wash the dishes!'
– She said, dragging me to the sink . . .

Many improvisers describe what their partner is already doing; for example: 'He said, breathlessly,' or 'He said, entering the room.'

Other players give themselves the stage directions: 'He said, cowering away from me as I kicked the door shut and produced my amazing weapon,' or 'She said, astonished at the way I burst into tears and ran from the room.'

Dialogue will soon expand into whole paragraphs (because while you are continuing to talk your partner can't control you). For example:

– He said, sitting in the chair. 'This may be quite serious, John. I've got your tests back and there's a large hole where your brain ought to be. There has been a rash of brain-snatchings recently, Nobel prize-winners, famous celebrities, so I suppose you should take it as a compliment.'

You can prevent this by adding the Three Word Sentence Game (see p. 155); for example:

– He said, shining a light through one of my ears and out of the other ear. 'My brain's stolen?'
– He said, turning pale. 'I must operate!'
– He said, turning to the cupboard and taking out drills and scalpels. 'Not now, Doctor!'
– He said, backing to the door, but unable to find it because he has no brain. 'Please calm yourself!'
– He said, removing the brain of a hamster, slicing the top of my head off with a chain-saw, placing the rodent brain into position and gluing the top of my head back on. 'Eek! Eek! Eek!'
– He squeaked, twitching his whiskers . . .

And so on (the comical is often identical to the horrific).

Some players will take only minimal control; for example: 'She said, sipping her tea,' or 'He said, looking bored.'

I correct this by shouting additional instructions; for example: 'She said, sipping her tea, *and realizing that it tasted strange*,' or 'He said looking bored *and starting to undress*.'

Variant – gibberish version: if your students are experts at gibberish, make them use gibberish dialogue (see p. 214) while continuing to give the instructions in English. Bizarrely, they'll find this less confusing.

– 'Enyam regor?'
– He said, sitting on the sofa, and taking my hand. 'Ocil lej?'
– She said, blushing and lowering her eyes. 'Akni yo selow?'
– He said, slipping an engagement ring on to my finger . . .

Variant: two players supply the dialogue, while two other 'shadows' stay very close to them and supply the stage directions. (Good as a training game and it can encourage bolder scenes, perhaps because the players feel less alone.)

Variant – with audience volunteers: the players give stage directions to a volunteer from the audience, as well as to each other.

Variant – 'pimping' version: this is the preferred form when working in front of a raucous audience. For example: 'He said, bursting into song,' or 'He said, reading The Fall of the Roman Empire . . . aloud.'

This can get laughs, but it turns the game into pure 'filler' (a game in which no story is likely to emerge).

Variant: supply adjectives instead of stage directions; for example:

- Sorry I'm late – SUSPICION.
- You're late rather a lot these days, what's going on? – PRIDE.
- They had a little celebration for me at work – ACCUSATORY.
- I know where you've been. I followed you – CONTEMPT.
- Yes, I've been going to night-school. I'm trying to improve myself which is more than you ever do.

And so on.

Substitution Impro

This presents an exact opposite to the ever popular (and destructive) Freeze Game (see p. 186) in that the situation continues even though the actors keep changing.

I wanted beginners to signal for someone to take over when they felt at a loss for an idea, or experienced themselves 'planning', but they were too proud.

So I tried asking players to 'substitute in' (always try the opposite), and I achieved this by shoving onlookers into the scene forcibly. This created a new way of improvising and made beginners wonderfully confident, because why should they plan, or worry about 'doing well', when they know that they're about to be replaced?

Set up a master–servant scene, or boy–girl scene, and get the class to agree that the players will keep being substituted. At first, few substitutions will occur, but this 'agreement' allows you to shout 'replace them' and even to push students physically into the scene. With luck, once the substitutions reach a certain frequency, everyone, including absolute beginners, will be eager to leap in (it's a bit like starting a cold motor). Sometimes the players will be substituted every few seconds, and there's a visual overload. If two characters are about to kiss, they may get changed so many times that the action goes into extreme slow-motion. A character who is shot may keep being 'recast' as he/she falls to the floor, and even the corpse may keep 'morphing' while the murderer tries to cover up the crime.

If someone is on their knees you should kneel as you replace them (a tap on the shoulder lets them know they have to leave). If they're in mid-sentence they should let you complete it. If their arms are outspread, your arms should be outspread.

If one character speaks in a foreign accent, while another speaks upper-class English – these dialects should be sustained through the scene.

This is an excellent performance game. It can occur spontaneously as a way of ending a scene, but it's really more suitable for Free-Impro – because the game is less exhausting when there are more players.

Variant – Battle of the Sexes: this presents a dispute between a man and a woman (men substitute the man, and women substitute the woman). Ask the women to cheer for the woman and ask the men to cheer for the man. This can create so much enthusiasm that spectators will run on to the stage and take over from the players. I remember my delight when this first happened. A 'husband' said cuttingly, 'Oh, it's you!' and a woman rushed out of the audience, to replace the 'wife', and said, 'Did you think it was your mistress?'

Then a male spectator leapt onstage to say, 'Married to you, who can afford a mistress?'

Don't let men substitute for women (or vice versa). It's a gag, and once you use it we can't take the game 'seriously' any more.

Battle of the Sexes provokes cheers, boos and roars of laughter. A lot of hostility is discharged harmlessly, but there are quieter versions; for example, you can start with someone sitting alone in the park who is approached by a stranger. Perhaps they leave together and the scene continues in a café, or in someone's house.

How often have you watched improvisers and wished they'd done or said such-and-such? Tag-team impro lets you leap onstage and satisfy this desire.

Moving Bodies

The characters invent their own dialogue, but their bodies are operated like puppets by other people.

When Roddy Maude Roxby saw this game at Jerome Robbin's studio (in the early sixties), the 'puppeteers' were telling their puppets what to say, but I wanted the control to be shared, so I said, 'Let the puppets invent their own dialogue.'

Movements should be justified. For example, if your puppeteer points your finger, then you'll need to say something like 'What's that over there?' or 'Look at this ladybird on my finger!'

Conversely, if you say, 'Look at that!' you can hope that your puppeteer will point your finger for you.

Only the part of the body that's being moved should move (don't 'help' your puppeteer).

Sit two 'puppets' on chairs a few feet apart (to allow the puppeteers easy access), and start them off as strangers in some public place – in a park, or on a cruise ship, perhaps. Warn the operators not to yank them about, or put them in painful positions.

Explain that a puppeteer who wants a puppet to tap its foot will have to keep on tapping it – that the puppet won't take over the movement.

If you move a puppet's arm, its head may move as well, and if you lift the chin, the neck may shift forward, so I shout reminders like 'Just the arm,' or 'Not the neck!' or 'Only move the part that's being moved!' Puppets must isolate parts of the body that habitually function as a unit.

Puppeteers are likely to 'forget' parts of their puppet; an arm will be left sticking out, or a puppet will be walked to the door (leg by leg) with its head twisted sideways. I might allow this to happen in performance, unless I thought that the puppet was in pain, but I don't want puppeteers to be stupid deliberately (the accidents are funny enough).

Errors should be justified. If your head has been left facing down you might say, 'Footprints!' or 'I'm too ashamed to look you in the eye!' If you are toppling over, you should say things like 'Quick! My heart medication!' or 'I think we need a mural on that ceiling.'

If your head is turned in some inappropriate direction, you can drop hints.

'A lovely view,' says your partner.

'Yes, I only wish I could see it.'

Moving Bodies scenes are not suitable for bare stages. If the players forget this, the Judges should say, 'Some furniture please!' (Sofas offer more possibilities than chairs.) Try starting with one puppet on a sofa and a second puppet entering.

The game is so entertaining that some players want to use it at the end of every performance. Discourage them, or the shows will become too predictable, and the laughs too easy.

Variant – Moving Bodies with audience volunteers: you can create enormous benevolence by letting audience volunteers be the puppeteers. Ask them to be gentle, and express your hope that some sort of story will emerge. Remind them that elbows do not bend backward, and that fingers should be kept away from orifices. We tell them to step back sometimes from the puppets rather than move them non-stop. When my six-year-old son volunteered, he just lifted his puppet's little finger up and down so that its owner seemed to be getting more and more impatient. The other volunteer was a teacher who kept hissing to him that he was 'doing it wrong' while she jerked her puppet savagely about.

If a puppet is being reduced to a 'talking head', it should say things like 'I'll just stand up and walk over to the stereo,' or 'Shall we dance?'

Beginner puppeteers often forget that when we stand, our legs have to be beneath us, and one of the pleasures of Moving Bodies is watching a small puppeteer handling a large puppet that's threatening to over-balance.

Explore the Possibilities

When a Moving Bodies scene turned into a flying lesson, six people ran out of the audience to help 'fly' the student around the auditorium.

Why not create a version in which a puppet becomes tormented by questions of free will?

How about a puppet who is aware of the puppeteers and is diagnosed as insane?

Variant to avoid: some cowardly impro groups cast audience volunteers as the puppets. This is not what the audience want to see, and few volunteers have the skill to isolate the part of the body that's being moved.

The Arms

I saw The Arms in a Laurel and Hardy film. It's an excellent impro game because it involves instant cooperation (it's now one of the most popular improvisation games in the world).

Party Version

'Find a partner,' I say. 'Call yourselves A and B. Bs stand behind As with your arms thrust under their arms. The As should put their hands behind the Bs' backs. Each pair is to become one person with A supplying the voice and B doing the gestures.

Then I coach them to break a few taboos:

'Can the Bs touch the As' hair? And could the As move their heads a little as if they were doing the touching themselves?'

And then: 'Could the Bs touch the As' faces?'

And then: 'Could they adjust the As' clothing?'

Asking them to 'adjust the clothing' evokes the most laughter. Sweaters are tugged about, necklines adjusted, and so on.

'Be at a party,' I say. 'Meet old friends! Find out where the drinks are! Shuffle about and introduce yourselves to strangers! Mingle!'

I gaze out of the window so that no one feels under scrutiny, and after twenty seconds or so I get them to change partners. Each change of partner makes the students more alert.

The Arms can be seen as a 'sensitivity' game which allows people to invade each other's space without feeling threatened (they'll be laughing too much to get uptight about this odd way of hugging each other). If players ignore their partners, and start 'planning', encourage them to respond to what's actually happening.

Arms Teacher

I select one pair of arms and ask them to address us.

'Be a teacher,' I say. 'But establish that the class is about to end so that the moment you feel the need to be "clever" or "original" you can just say, "Class dismissed," or "For homework tonight I want you to . . ." – and we'll fade the lights.'

I encourage the arms to point at members of the audience, and the body to say things like

'Tutti! Are you cheating?' or 'Suzanne! Put your hands on the desk where I can see them!' or 'Etienne? Did you throw that paper aeroplane?'

Once the group is comfortable with this, I ask a set of arms to imagine that there's a table in front of them, and I tell B to mime picking up an item that A can describe. Perhaps B mimes lifting some smallish object, and perhaps A says something like 'The sex life of snails is a closed book to many people, but I have here a male snail, called Nat.' The left hand displays Nat to the spectators. 'And I have here a female snail, called Betsy.' The right hand mimes lifting Betsy. 'Calm down, Nat! Stop it, Betsy! Just a moment – I'd better tie on the little blindfolds.' And so on.

Common sense says that The Arms Game would be easier if either A or

B were in charge, but the control should be shared. If A says, 'I have here a stick of gelignite!' the arms should pick up a 'stick of gelignite'. If B's hand covers A's mouth, A should yawn. Some of the best moments in improvisation occur when no one is sure who's leading and who's following.

In the days when we were addicted to tobacco, we'd have the arms light a cigarette for the body to smoke (this was excellent for gigs where the audience spoke no English). Shaving the face with foam and an empty razor might be fun.

Two Sets of Arms

Take two pairs of arms and ask them to face the audience. Explain that if they want to approach each other, they'll have to move crab-wise (because the illusion works best when seen from the front). Ask for:

- An interaction between strangers
- A problem
- A possible tilt
- A solution

Perhaps they'll become two strangers at a late-night bus stop who discover that the last bus has gone. Then one will realize that the other was the school bully (and can be bullied into sharing a taxi?)

Loading the Pockets

This is a corrupt version in which the pockets are crammed with objects. The arms produce these one by one and the body comments on them, but the game is reduced to pure 'filler' (no narrative). Especially unpleasant is seeing the improvisers cram their pockets before playing a scene. It can be charming if an object is discovered in a pocket accidentally, but 'unloading objects' has become built into the game as a way to minimize risk. One object would be enough, but at the moment when the improviser might 'move into the future' – being inspired by a rubber knife to commit suicide, or by a peanut to expound the problems of living with an elephant – the arms will sidetrack by presenting a new object.

The Dwarf

This was a trick played at parties in my youth but we've used it in improvisations and in plays. B's arms protrude under A's arms, and A's hands are thrust into boots. Cover A's chest with cloth so that we just see the boots projecting underneath (build a special costume?) and stand this 'dwarf' just behind a table or a sofa. The effect will be of a misshapen creature about three feet high. Let it 'walk' about on the table (or sofa-back), have it clamber up after 'falling' over the edge, have it dance about, and do the splits, and lie on its side (resting on one elbow), and flaps its arms to rise into the air. Have it sit with a bump, and twist its foot (or let someone else twist its foot) three hundred and sixty degrees. Dwarves work well when they're cheeky, extrovert characters.

The Giant

B is lying on a bench with bare legs dangling over the end, feet towards the audience. A faces 'front' and stands astride B. A's legs are hidden in cloth bags and the costume covers both bodies to give the effect of an eight-foot-high person who happens to be sitting down. Sometimes this giant should lean one way while its legs point the other way, so it should seem inherently unstable. You can add instability by having the body lean back and wave its arms for balance while the feet lift into the air.

It can force people to do exercises – it can touch its own toes by letting them swing up to meet its hands. It can bully its servants. It can be a terrible coward who gloats over the misfortunes of others. Make sure that it's always loud and exuberant. (I used two giants for the High Priests when I directed the *Wakefield Cycle*.)

Adjective

Apply an adjective to a scene, for example, the slow-family, the fit-family, the evil-family, the suspicious-family, the religious-family, the silly-family, the right-wing-family. Or have a pecking order of bigots, or start a suspicious master–servant scene. (Stanislavsky said, 'Never play adjectives,' but it's okay if you justify them.)

Wide Eyes

Improvise a scene with your eyes as wide open as possible. Keep the lids raised even when you glance down.

Unless we were being brutalized, we all had wide eyes in early childhood, and when we wanted something they became so enormous that it was difficult to refuse us. Since then, many of us have closed our lids defensively; it follows that if we can be persuaded to relax our eyes, we are likely to become more open, and vulnerable, and uninhibited, and to arouse protective feelings in other people.

Ask students to notice Harpo's eyes, or Goldie Hawn's, or Benny Hill's, or Nina Hagen's. Explain that tight eyes may be okay for 'baddies' but that they don't encourage us to feel positive and outgoing.

Wide Eyes en Masse

Set up a thirty-second 'party' at which everyone has tight eyes. Discuss the sensations. Then have a 'party' in which all the guests have wide-open 'innocent' eyes. Notice how in both cases the students' self-consciousness is diminished (because they're concentrating on what they're doing rather than on our opinion of them). Then have a party with a mix of narrow-eyed people and wide-eyed people.

Wide Eyes – Friends Meet

Before you mention eyes, play a twenty-second scene in which two great friends meet after a long separation. Get them to repeat this with eyes wide open, and the difference may be astounding – there'll be more enthusiasm, larger gestures, less fear of the space. Tell them that if they glance 'out front' occasionally, they'll notice that most of the onlookers also have wide eyes (it's infectious).

Warning

Some professional actors open the eyes unnaturally wide. This 'blob on a boiled egg' effect may occasionally be useful, but it's the equivalent of shouting all the time. The eye that is 'open', trusting and friendly is the eye with the pupil fully exposed but with no white above or below it.

Learn to open your eyes by relaxing them, rather than by pitting one set of muscles against another. Try lying down, and 'letting go', while trying to sense the exact weight of your eyeballs (this can be emotional).

Wide Mouth

My airline magazine interviewed the man who auditioned the dancers for the Crazy Horse nightclub in Paris. He said that when in doubt he opted for the ones with 'big mouths'. I thought about this and realized that many models and 'dynamic' people seem to have extra teeth.

I asked students to project their voices very loudly while making their mouths smaller (narrower) than usual. This released a lot of laughter and they became extremely bossy. There are mouths in everyday life that are so contracted that one wonders what they are refusing.

Then I tried for the rebound effect by asking them to make their mouths slightly wider than usual. Positive behaviour was released (a sort of Mel Gibson in *Lethal Weapon* dogginess). Widen your mouth just a little (perhaps parting your lips slightly). Look at the objects and people around you and you'll probably feel bolder (Some people feel as if they could 'eat the world'). Fear of the audience lessens, just as in the Wide Eye procedure.

I'm not referring to grinning or smiling, but to the widening of the mouth a quarter of an inch or so. It's the intention to widen that creates the effect.

High-status people expose the bottom teeth (people like ex-President Jimmy Carter can do this even when looking friendly and good natured) whereas low-status people expose the top teeth. Try biting the bottom lip, raising the upper lip and giving a stupid giggle (notice how the back of the neck wants to shorten).

If you expose both sets of teeth and breathe audibly you may want to smash things (don't), and the space to the sides may become more important. Elbows tend to move sideways and the body tends to rotate left and right a little. Use the effect for thugs, or executioners. An executioner's black hood that hides the head and face except for the mouth and chin intensifies the effect.

Tempo

This game came from the class in which I tried to discover fifty ways to play a scene. We tried 'slow' scenes and 'fast' scenes, and I realized that dramatic speed was related to the pace at which ideas are changing; a marathon runner might be 'slow' (dramatically), whereas a sentry, standing at attention, who is approached by a dog that cocks its leg, might be 'fast', although you might only know it by the sweat breaking out on his forehead.

Beginners get 'security' by 'joining' each other, so if one is fast, they'll all tend to be fast (you've probably seen productions like that). I asked them to maintain different speeds, but the results were poor until I asked a 'slow' player to have a new thought every thirty seconds, and a 'fast' player to have a new thought every five seconds. For example:

- I like flying . . .
- Where's my ticket? I left it in my . . . No! It's up in the bathroom. Did I pack my razor?
- I like to get a window seat.
- Perhaps it's in the suitcase! But which suitcase?
- If you're going to be cooped up . . .
- Did I pack the alarm-clock?
- You might as well have a good view.
- No time to shave! Do I look respectable?
- Of course, if it's cloudy . . .
- Passport! Where is it?
- Your passport? Isn't that it?
- That's the old one. Ah! It's in my pocket!
- Passport . . .
- Shampoo! I'll get some from the bathroom.
- When they look at the photo in my passport . . .
- Did you phone the airline?
- They usually ask me to make the face . . .
- Oh, God, I'll do it myself. The phone book!

And so on. It's always a pleasure seeing actors who do *not* take the same tempo.

Ask groups of people to change ideas at the same pace. Perhaps try a slow picnic that gradually accelerates to become a fast picnic (the changes of pace need to be justified). Try pairs in which one player changes from slow to fast, and the other from fast to slow – ask them to control the rate of change so that they 'pass' each other midway. Try threesomes in which A maintains a neutral tempo, B moves from fast to slow and C moves from slow to fast (leaving the stage just before he/she explodes).

Sound Scape

A player offstage makes sound effects for the onstage players.

This dates back to one of the first classes at the Studio when I clanked tin-cans while someone moved about wearing a mimed suit of armour. It led to scenes with improvisers and jazz musicians.[1] Use a microphone.

Typical sounds include:

- Doors creaking and slamming
- Taps or showers running
- Footsteps
- Voices
- Cars revving
- Beds creaking
- Animals barking, howling, whining, etc.
- Chalk screeching on blackboards
- Bones or muscles cracking as the players stretch
- Metal vibrating ('doooinggg!')
- Things being inflated/deflating
- Fists smashing
- Yawns, sneezes, 'tuts', etc.
- Emotional sounds like panting, gulping, sighing, weeping, laughing, etc.

This can also involve dubbing the dialogue (although it would be unusual). For example, Jasmine mimes opening a door (creak). She closes it (slam). She walks to the shelf (footsteps). She mimes removing a huge tin (scrape). She mimes opening it (wrenching sounds, plus the whining of a huge hungry animal). She pours the contents on to the floor (slurping sounds). She pats the huge thing that's making the slurping and panting noises (patting sounds) and says, 'Did you have fun today, darling?' and a huge voice on the mike says, 'Yes, I chased the postman!'

Sounds can be accepted physically (every joint can creak, and your digestion system can make strange noises), or placed in the environment (the undertakers' sign is creaking in the wind) or used to establish mood – although music is better at this.

Collect 'noise-makers'.

You're Interesting

This is a way of marking time on the stage while seeming alive and interested.

When beginners are trying to think of clever things to say, they'll pay scant attention to anyone else. They're also likely to look feeble and unsure as a way of lowering our expectations. 'Being interested' reverses these tactics. The rules are:

- Feel fit and awake

- Be interested in everything that the others say or do
- Say nothing interesting, and don't be so uninteresting that you become interesting (by talking about nothing but cabbages, for example)

Players who say dull things are likely to look bored. If so, remind them to be healthy and alert, and make sure that they respond with interest to whatever is said. For example, if 'Good morning!' creates no effect, I'll interrupt: 'She said, "Good morning," so be interested! Look surprised! Let it have some effect on you.'

I start the scene again, and they react with interest to the 'Good morning,' saying, 'So it is!', but now this 'So it is!' is ignored, so I interrupt to explain that if you say, 'Good morning,' to someone who says, 'So it is!', the rules oblige you to make the 'So it is!' interesting as well.

'So it is' gets the sheepish response: 'Sorry I'm a bit late!'

It's very likely that this line will create no effect. If so, I'll tell them to say, 'I'm glad you managed to get here,' or 'Yes, we kept some cake for you,' but if someone says, 'Did you have an accident?' I'll 'delete' that remark as 'too interesting'.

Once the students agree to obey the instructions they look wonderfully alive and fearless. Their interest makes us interested. The coach should develop the story by throwing in the occasional interesting idea; for example: 'Say, "I've been promoted,"' or 'Say, "I've joined the police force."'

I'll apply the rules to this last suggestion:

- A policeman! That must be so interesting.
- [*Brightly*] Really? Well, I suppose it must look glamorous from the outside, but it's all run of the mill. Parking tickets . . . interrogations . . .
- Interrogations? Goodness!
- You're interested? Well, that's encouraging. But it's mostly just chatting to citizens who don't quite know their place.
- Oh! Not people like me, then? Hah! Hah!
- No, no, just social misfits. I look on it as further education.
- Further education? Really! The teacher is always right, eh?
- What did you say?
- [*Alarmed*] Er . . . what did you think I said?
- [*Suave*] I thought you said something very interesting. Drink up!
- Drink up? Er – are we going anywhere?

- We're having a party at Headquarters.
- [*Suppressed panic*] But I couldn't er . . .
- Of course you can. It's just round the corner.
- Um . . . er . . . [*Gulp*]
- Drinks are on us. And you'll get a 'Help Your Local Police – Beat Yourself Up' T-shirt.

I'd reject this last remark as too interesting.

Struggling to say 'dull things' while being 'interested' diminishes future-funk, and is more entertaining than the usual 'I'm the wittiest' interaction.

Boring the Audience

This harks back to the times when I shouted, 'Be more boring!' to the students at the Studio (most of whom were dreary when they did their 'best', but became fascinating when they were content to be just average).

Let's imagine that an acting scene has been admired by everyone. I might take the players aside and whisper something to them before asking them to play the scene again. This second presentation will almost certainly seem noticeably improved, and sometimes the actors will seem wonderfully talented, revealing a truth and absorption that we've never seen in them before.

'So what did I tell them?'

'To be interesting? To be expressive? To be more relaxed? To pay attention to each other? To be truthful? To have a subtext? To have a purpose?'

I'd told the players that they should bore the audience without being bored themselves. This removed the pressure to 'do their best' and allowed something other than the social personality to operate. It's fun to watch their amazement and sometimes total disbelief that their attempt to bore us had made them more interesting (especially if they're famous).

William Wyler stopped Olivier from emoting by reading the newspaper while making him do the same shot as many as fifty times. Looking back on it Olivier was grateful, but telling him to 'bore the camera' might have wasted less film.

Wallpaper Drama

Recommended as a training game. This was a spin-off from work on 'transitions' (it's useful for improvised soap operas).

Morph between positive and negative, always going through neutral and always giving all three states the same value.

For example:

Positive
— Hey, great to see you.
— Isn't it your birthday?
— You remembered!
— I bought this for you.
— Oh, you shouldn't have!
Moving towards neutral
— You'll like it. It's an egg-whisk.
— Ah well, I can always use another one. It's the thought that counts.
— Yes, well, I was thinking of you.
Moving towards negative
— It's my twenty-first birthday. And what do you bring me? A bloody egg-whisk.
— If you don't want it, I'll have it back.
— I want it!
— Show some gratitude then!
Moving toward neutral
— Yes, well, I'm sorry.
— The thing is, I didn't have any money. Actually, I took the egg-whisk out of the kitchen drawer.
— Stole it from your mum?
— I wanted to give you something.
Moving towards positive
— We could make some egg-nog.
— Great!

And so on. I called this game Wallpaper Drama because if you do it well, you can burble on for ever and yet sustain some sort of interest. It's a way of marking time on stage, but the coach may need to prod the scene occasionally; for example: 'Tell him you're pregnant,' and then, 'Tell him it's not his.'

Left to themselves, beginners move between negative and neutral, and will avoid being positive. Don't let this happen.

More tricks (not mine) for soap operas. Enter a circle of light at one side of the stage (and/or touch the proscenium) to explain privately to the audience how you feel. Go to the opposite side of the stage to supply narrative and/or explanations. Have an object that you touch when you want the audience to tell you the next line.

Straight Men

When two comedians work together it's usually as a straight man (a long-suffering 'parental' figure) and a comic (a pesky 'child' who annoys the straight man) – think of Burt and Ernie on *Sesame Street*, or ventriloquists and their dummies. But in public improvisation there are very few straight men.

Why not have the scenographers stick a Velcroed 'S' (for 'Straight man') on to any improviser who is compulsively gagging, and tell the audience that this player is to be serious, and will be dragged away by the gag-police if he/she makes any jokes?

We need a strong contrast between the straight man and the comic. Jerry Lewis and Dean Martin were an example of this, as were Margaret Dupont and Groucho Marx. Here's the British comedian Bernie Winters describing the moment when he and Mike Winters emerged from obscurity:

> Mike pleaded with a tailor in a little back street near the theatre to work through the night to make a special suit for me. It was a crazy Teddy boy outfit, with drainpipe trousers, heavily padded shoulders, and a velvet collar. Mike designed it to make me look like a sack of potatoes moving across the stage . . .
>
> I stumbled on-stage with my suit and big hat. I ran up and down a couple of times and looked around. The audience howled with laughter, and neither of us had opened our mouths yet. This really threw us. We weren't used to reactions like that. I was very nervous, and this made me do my 'ee' giggle. They roared at that. After this, we could not go wrong . . .
>
> Mike had pinpointed our problem very well. We were trying to be funny man and straight man but there was not enough contrast

between us to carry that over. That bulky suit made the perfect contrast to his immaculate suit.[2]

Being a straight man is a skill worth acquiring – teach it at the same time as 'being a passenger'.

Gibberish

Sounds replace words so that the players appear to be speaking a foreign language (many impro games can be played in a gibberish version).
When students are skilled at gibberish:

- They become 'better listeners' (gibberish dialogue feels pointless unless you're being altered by what's said to you)
- They are less afraid of the space around them, and 'phone-box' acting – in which gestures stay close to the body or snap back as if pulled by rubber bands – disappears
- They learn to interact and develop stories non-verbally
- Their resonance and articulation improve
- They bring great insight and 'physicality' to the playing of text

Gibberish Cards

The students who hate gibberish will think up an expression like 'Iruy d'nat ruk!' and check it mentally to see if it sounds right; it won't, and this 'failure' inhibits them. And even students who like gibberish tend to use very few sounds; for example: 'Oggy Bog? Soggy Doggie Yoggy!'
There is no way that this can sound like a language.[3]
How could I prevent students from prejudging the sounds that they made, and ensure that their gibberish was fluent and had the full range of vowels and consonants?
I wrote gibberish sentences along the narrow ends of playing cards, so that the players could use them as a 'gibberish script', but months passed before I dared to introduce such a bizarre idea (many things that seem normal now seemed lunatic forty years ago). Finally I plucked up my courage and said, 'Use these cards as your script.'
Students who had suffered agonies of embarrassment became instantly proficient (how could they be 'wrong' if they were reading from a card?), and since the cards contained all the sounds in the language, there was no more 'Oggy Woggy Boggying'.
If players become over-fluent (sounding like tobacco auctioneers, or

those worshippers who 'speak in tongues') – if they try to impress us
by speaking as quickly as possible – I ask them to repeat some of the
gibberish phrases that their partner says to them, and sometimes to be
at a 'loss for words'. I ask them to adapt their gibberish to their
partner's gibberish, so that they both seem to be speaking the same
language.

Lee Strasberg urged his students to make their gibberish understood,
but I'd ask you to watch your partner to discover if you're giving them a
compliment, or an insult, or a proposal of marriage. When the meaning
is established by the recipient, the emphasis is on 'reacting', rather than
'acting' (see Giving Presents, p. 58).

Toddlers love 'speaking in tongues', and you can practise your
gibberish with them without feeling embarrassed.

A Class in Gibberish
One improviser sits waiting and another enters. Each holds one
gibberish card. They meet, speak their sentence, and leave together. As
there's no need to be inventive, there'll be minimal stress, and they'll be
'ingesting' a gibberish vocabulary which they can elaborate on for the
rest of their lives.

Various students try this, and then I allow each player two cards each,
for example:

– [*Entering*] Mahkram Artep?
– [*Standing up*] Ena hej!
  [*They're leaving together.*]
– Resarf nok!
– [*Nodding head*] Reksew!

I encourage them to add a slight foreign accent.

Some of these interactions are amusing and some aren't, but no one
can guess why.

'Because the sounds are so silly?'

'Then why aren't all these interactions funny?'

Some students adopt stupid walks and comical gestures, but they
evoke minimal response, whereas we are laughing at players who
seem quite normal. The class is baffled until I take pity on them.

'If you say, "Eid leakim!" to a dull improviser, this will have no effect,
whereas a "brilliant" improviser will look surprised, or interested, or
angry, or shocked, or embarrassed, or whatever. This makes us laugh

because of our delight in seeing things happen, especially if a drop in status is involved.'

They try again, but most of them alter themselves as they speak, and this has little effect.

'We want at least one of you to be altered by the other!' I say. 'It's the illusion that someone is forcing a change in you that gives us pleasure!'

I get them to play longer scenes in gibberish and they are soon complaining that the cards are a nuisance. I wean them by suggesting that they should begin to add some gibberish sentences of their own.

When they are skilled, I let them try Italian gibberish, or German gibberish, or English gibberish, or Canadian gibberish, or Deep South gibberish, and so on. They'll enjoy this so much that they will lose any residual inhibition about making the 'wrong sounds'.

Alternating Gibberish and English

Version One: the players switch from Gibberish to English and back on command (try this with Party Endowments, p. 233).

Version Two: A starts speaking gibberish while B speaks English, but any player can switch at any time, forcing his partner also to switch; for example:

- Nots ruh tyr rej?
- He's with a patient.
- Onito tenileh!
- [*Switch*] Tenileh?
- Yes, it's going to be twins.
- Adaran!
- [*Switch*] Renk luaf semaj!
- Oh dear! Should I call the nurse?

Some of the changes from English to gibberish (and back) should occur mid-sentence. This encourages the transfer of the spatial and vocal confidence that are characteristic of good gibberish to the normal improvisations.

Gibberish Shadows

Have two beginners play a scene, but give each an experienced 'shadow' who stays close and feeds them gibberish sentences, so that the students who play the scene aren't responsible for the sounds that they're making.

Jokes in Gibberish

A friend was woken in the dead of night by such strange sounds that he went to the window and saw a group of deaf–mutes telling dirty stories. This inspired me to divide the students into groups of four or five, and to ask them to swap jokes in gibberish.

Beginners start by translating existing jokes, but the build-up to the climax can only be done by observing the reactions of the listeners. I tell them to forget about translating existing jokes:

'Watch the onlookers for clues as to when to hold back, and when to release' I say. Most joke-tellers continue past the point where the listeners expect the punchline, but this can be corrected.

Introduce gibberish jokes as 'advanced' or your students may get discouraged.

Reality Testing

My RADA students dined out while pretending that they spoke no English, and this made their 'gibberish' very authentic (because they were desperate not to be 'rumbled'). Sometimes I sent them out into Gower Street clutching a dirty piece of paper with a fake address on it. They'd spout gibberish to passers-by, who always sent them off in some definite direction. (I apologize to Dillon's bookshop, which was pestered by unintelligible young 'foreigners'.)

Guess the Situation (Gibberish)

This keeps the actors in the 'present moment', and removes any lingering anxieties about using gibberish.

Roger is sent out of earshot while we agree on a situation. We decide that he's a brain surgeon, and that Sarah has brought her son, Tony, to his clinic.

Roger returns and is told that Sarah and Tony will play a scene with him, and that afterwards he'll be asked who he was, who the other players were, where the scene took place, and so on.

'So where's the difficulty?'

'The catch is that you'll be speaking in English, while Sarah and Tony will be speaking gibberish.'

'Am I a foreigner in another country?'

'No, no: treat them as if you understand everything.'

The scene starts with Sarah imploring him on her knees. He's baffled but I tell him to make a guess.

'I'm sorry!' he says. 'I've made up my mind! You're to be executed in the morning!'

Tony points at his head.

'Yes! We're going to chop off your heads!'

Tony and Sarah try again.

'Ah!' says Roger. 'Well . . . on second thoughts, I'll just condemn you to the galleys . . .'

There's no way that he can understand them, so they ease off a bit. Sarah mimes chipping a hole in Tony's head.

'Well, I suppose you can execute him yourself, if you want to!'

Sarah clutches Tony and covers him in kisses.

'I'm sorry, but the law says that we have to execute adulterers!'

It's delightful to see Sarah and Tony making blunder after blunder. Any qualms that they may still have about using gibberish are swept aside by their need to communicate. I stop the scene and ask Roger, 'Whose place is this?'

'Mine.'

Applause. I congratulate Sarah and Tony on getting that fact across.

'And where were you?'

'In my palace? In Italy?'

'Why Italy?'

'They seemed so excitable.'

'And who were you?'

'Some sort of judge?'

'That's not completely wrong. And who are these people?'

'Guilty lovers? Incestuous lovers?'

We tell him the situation and everyone laughs again (we've been laughing most of the time) but Sarah and Tony have learned how misleading they were, and will do better next time.

Another example: Olive goes out of earshot and we decide that the scene will take place in David's apartment. Pat is David's sister, and her dog has messed all over the new white carpet. Olive is to be the dog.

They greet her as if she were human, and she tries to shake hands. They step back and point at the floor. She mimes picking up the things they are pointing at . . .

I stop the scene and forbid anyone to give the secret away. Then I ask her what she's understood (absolutely nothing).

'Would you mind trying this scene again?'

She agrees and two more students act out the situation with her, profiting from the errors they've just seen: for example, they whistle her in, and press her down on to all-fours. Suddenly she barks, and we cheer.

Divide the class into threes and let them play Guess the Situation *en masse*. This is excellent for increasing the confidence of beginners. Encourage them to choose situations that will be fun. Perhaps the family has just returned from Mum's funeral, and the 'guesser' is Mum (i.e. Mum is a ghost).

Guess the Situation is so entertaining that even beginners don't mind 'failing' at it.[4]

Status[5]

Status Games involve the conscious manipulation of our level of dominance.

I adapted Konrad Lorentz's observations of dominance behaviour among jackdaws to the training of improvisers, and I used the word 'status' because I was too shy to shout, 'Dominate!' and 'Submit!' like some Krafft-Ebing character.

Status is not confusing so long as we understand it as something we do, rather than our social position; for example, a king can play low status to a servant, while a servant can play high status to a king.

– I wonder if you'd mind adjusting my crown, Tonken.
– I've only got one pair of hands!
– But, Tonken! I own you!
– You're not fit to own anyone! Spreading me with jam at that picnic!
– But how else were we to keep the flies off the guests?

Our behaviour (reinforced by our appearance) signals our importance, or lack of importance, otherwise we wouldn't be able to pass someone in a corridor without trading punches. Instead of fighting, we scan each other for status information, and whoever accepts lower status moves aside. Sometimes this automatic system screws-up, and then it can be awkward even to get through the same door.

Status can't be avoided (since every movement is likely to claim or yield more space and this tips the balance) so friends make it into a game by hurling mock insults, or giving fake respect. Hence, we can interact with acquaintances for years, and yet stay remote, whereas some playful people become our friends almost immediately. If you can raise and lower audiences' status for fun they become friendlier and more benevolent.

Students can be transformed instantly by Status Games, not because they're learning new skills, but because they're being encouraged to exploit the skills that they already use when they're teasing their friends.

The discovery of status transactions was thrilling, amazing and even frightening. We understood that no behaviour is 'insignificant', that when we interact together our brains are counting the blink-rate, and measuring changes in pupil size, and examining sentence structure, and observing left/right synchronization, and registering even the tiniest head movement, and gauging the distance between hand and head, and so on.

Establishing Status

We hold eye contact when we want to dominate someone (or when we look at someone we adore), but we break eye contact and take a quick glance back when we're feeling submissive.

Another important signal is given by the distance of our hands from our heads. Touch your mouth as you look at someone and you'll probably feel 'hesitant', but we'll perceive you as 'lowering your status'. Smoking is 'cool' because a cigarette moved towards the mouth conceals a gesture of submission. Conversely, if you touch someone's face or head (and the gesture is accepted), this raises our status, which is why we do it to children, and may account for the curious behaviour of barbers.[6]

Other things being equal, the person playing the highest status uses the most space, and is the most relaxed (except when being challenged). Someone whose arms are tightly folded and whose body is stiff and symmetrical will seem eager to be high status, but fails compared to someone lying on a sofa, legs lolling apart, fearless of attack.

We placate higher-status people by ruining our posture, and by constricting our voices. Otherwise we'd all look poised and at ease, and our necks would be long, our movements would seem effortless and we'd resonate when we spoke.

Teaching a Range of Status

Most of us are better at playing 'high', or better at playing 'low', but both attitudes are defensive. One says, 'Keep away, I bite!' and the other says, 'I'm not worth biting.'

Clint Eastwood is a high-status expert, and his best-known movie line is 'Make my day' (i.e. 'Make a move and I'll shoot you'). Try saying it as you wag your head about and you'll notice how ineffective this is.

Woody Allen is a low-status expert. Here's an example of him raising his status in order to demolish it: displaying a gold watch, he said, 'This speaks for breeding and it's mine. It's an antique gold heirloom – actually my grandfather on his deathbed sold me this watch.'

Bad drama schools exploit the preferred status by giving high-status roles to aristocratic students and subservient roles to low-status students, but Hugh Crutwell (my boss at RADA) did the opposite.

A friend who played in B-movies became fascinated by status transactions: he played high to agents and directors (and they hated him); he played low and they loved him (but they didn't give him work); he matched status with them and they gave him leads in A-movies: 'Keith,' he said, 'they thought I was one of them!' And now he is.

In a 'natural' state status determines who will breed, so teenagers are fascinated by it, and long to improve their skills.

Circular Status
John is higher status than Ron, who is higher status than Terra, who is higher status than John. You can achieve this by standing them in a circle and saying, 'The player to your left will dominate you, and the player on your right will submit to you.'

Such scenes seldom get anywhere, but it's good to practise playing high status to one person, while playing low to another. (The dialogue in the Ghost Game (p. 181) was an example of this.)

Status Parties
I ask a class to be guests at a party: 'Mingle!' I say. 'Meet old friends. Ask where the food is. Exchange gossip. Find the hostess. You know how to behave at parties!'

Anxiety will make them adopt each other's tempo and use of space (I've seen many theatre productions where this has happened), so I stop them after perhaps thirty seconds and divide them into Group A and Group B.

'We'll try another party,' I say. 'But this time the As will blink more often than usual, whereas the Bs will hardly ever blink (although, if they have to, they can open and close their eyes slowly). Start the party again! Mingle!'

This splits the group into high-status players and low-status players;

the blinkers (low status) are shortening the backs of their necks and becoming isolated, just as in real life, whereas the others are loud and confident, and are trying to dominate each other. Apply one status technique and others will 'lock on' automatically. Many things will be happening that I have not requested: for example, the non-blinkers will tend to hold eye contact, while the blinkers will keep looking away and glancing back as if the power streaming from the Bs is too powerful to confront.[7] Few of the students will enjoy both experiences equally (because they have a preferred status), but I get them to try both.

I might set up several status parties, using various techniques; for example, the As could use long and grammatically complete sentences, while the Bs use fragmented sentences and are out of breath whenever they speak:

– Ah, Jeremy, I thought I might meet you here.
– [Gasp] Mary . . . er . . . Well, I . . . yes, what a surprise . . .
– Rather a good party, don't you think? At least it would be if that confounded dog of yours didn't keep pestering everybody!
– [Gasp] Fido? Er . . . is he . . . er . . . [Gasp] misbehaving?

Or imagine the opposite:

– [Gasp] Rather a . . . er . . . [Gasp] good party, don't you think? [Gasping laugh] At least it would be if [Gasp] that [Gasp] confounded . . . er . . . [Gulp] dog of yours didn't keep [Gasp] pestering everybody!
– Fido? Is he misbehaving?

For another party I might ask the As to keep their heads absolutely still during each phrase that they utter, and never touch their heads; and I might tell the Bs to move their heads normally when they speak, and to touch their own heads and faces.

Or I might get the As to move more slowly and smoothly than usual, and to delay before replying (inserting a physical delay as well; that is, don't flinch), while the Bs would make small and unnecessary movements, and respond instantly.[8]

Or I could ask the As to use a long thoughtful 'errrrr' at the beginning of each sentence and to tend to rotate one foot slightly outwards, while the Bs respond with an immediate and tiny 'er' and tend to turn one foot inwards (one way to drop instantly in status is to stand with toes together and with heels out – try it).

Status Challenges

Status challenges in Theatresports tend to be disappointing because the players milk it as a way to 'be funny'. They'll try to be low status by crawling onstage, or by pretending to pick their noses (as if 'low status' was the same as being disgusting), while others will try to be high status by claiming to be millionaires, or rock stars.

Ideally, status should permeate all scenes, a good 'situation' being one that makes the status very clear (and perhaps reverses it), but unless the players are experts, challenges to status transactions create inferior work.

Two-person Games
Both play low

– [*Nervous laugh*] I was so . . . er . . . grateful for your . . . er . . . invitation.
– Oh, please . . . I never thought . . . I mean . . . I'm so . . . so proud that you came.
– Er . . . no one invites me anywhere, actually.
– They don't?

Low-status players are hesitant to contradict people; they're like the editor in Evelyn Waugh's *Scoop* who always said, 'Up to a point, Lord Cooper . . .' when he meant 'No'.

One plays high, and one plays low

– So this is where you live, Cedric! Rather squalid!
– I'll clear a space on the bed for you, sir. I'm so sorry!
– Bit dark in here! If you could wash the windows, we might be able to see the view.
– That . . . er . . . that is the view. It's a cement wall.
– Well, I'd have that torn down for starters . . .

Both play high

– Shoes off, Paul. Can't have you trampling dog-shit everywhere.
– So this is where you live? It can't be pleasant sharing that toilet on the landing.
– It's just a *pied-à-terre*. I spend most of my time abroad, actually.
– Come hunting on the estate this weekend. We've a deer park full of animals all trained to stand sideways so you can get a good shot at them.

– Oh, I can't stand the country. Mud everywhere. Yokels gelding things.
– My dear fellow, we don't allow mud on the estate.

Start with one high and one low, and reverse status gradually during the scene

– Thank-you for being so quiet. I'm trying to avoid the landlord.
– Behind with the rent, old chap? Perhaps it would help if I bought one of your paintings.
– Would you? Would you really?
– Rather an interesting view you have here . . .
– That's not the view, it's a picture.
– My goodness! But these clouds are so real I could reach out and touch them! Oh!
– You've . . . You've smeared it!
– I, I'm so sorry.
– Idiot!

Status Transitions

When students are skilled at the conscious manipulation of status, I might get them to play status parties again, but this time I'll ask each group to change gradually to the other group's behaviour, so those who start high will end low (and vice versa).

I ask a student to sit on a chair, feet flat on the floor with toes touching and heels apart, and with one hand touching her mouth. Then I place her partner towering over her, perhaps with one foot on an adjacent chair. Most students resist the dominant position, perhaps even leaning back from their cringing partner, but if I tell them to point at their partners and to yell something like 'Why did you do it?' or 'Don't you ever disobey me again,' this almost always shifts the body forward into an aggressive pose, and allows the aggressor's space to 'pour over' the submissive victim.

Then I ask them to play a scene that will end when each has achieved the other's starting position (it's not important which chair they end up on). Most students will try to maintain their status, unchanged, for at least a minute, but I shout, 'Keep altering! Don't get stuck! Janet, open your legs a little! Bill, touch your nose for a split second!' and so on.

After your students have played this game in pairs, get one to sprawl on the sofa in a high-status way, legs apart, while the other kneels with head towards him/her and with forehead touching the floor. Have them play scenes which end when they have swapped positions.

The players must find justifications for the changes.

The Rejection Game

Groups of improvisors who are 'pretending to be friends' often look weirdly isolated: their postures are too formal, there's extra tension in their muscles, their space doesn't flow into other people. This secret 'caution' is one reason why the actors in movies often look so unreal – especially in the average Hollywood movie from the 1930s (and I presume in the average stage production of that time).

The Rejection Game is one of my ways to toughen up improvisers, and make them genuinely friendly, even though it may seem cruel and even terrifying when you first encounter it (it's especially scary to anyone pubescent – because that's when rejection is at its fiercest).

Take a group of four of five players, put them in a scene and say, 'When the scene ends one of you has to be rejected by the other three – it must absolutely not be you!'

This can cause instant panic, because the person who is rejected really loses. However, since we can kill people, and rape people, and torture in theatre, and in movies, why shouldn't we reject each other for fun? Why should being thrown out of a group be worse than being caught at tag?

'No one will be forced to play this game,' I say. 'But if you're ejected, we can tell you why, and this will improve your ability to stay in a group.' If I still can't get volunteers, I might say 'It's really a friendship game, since if you have a friend in the group, you're safe, and the two of you can eject someone else.'

Maybe I'll set up a scene in which the couple who have moved in upstairs have been invited down for coffee, or I'll have four friends come into a lounge bar. It's a great help to have a sofa, chairs and a low coffee table. People feel safer on the sofa than they do at the edge of the group.

If I've chosen my time right, I'll get four volunteers, but the scene will continue for minute after minute with no one being rejected. The moment anyone becomes vulnerable, the others will rescue him/her by making eye contact or by giving their attention. I might have to show them how to reject someone, and how to become stronger in the group. For example, I might tell a player who feels vulnerable to take his chair and move to the other side of the group to say something to another player. This can tie him to one person, and isolate someone else. Or I might try turning someone into a ghost: 'Keep talking together, but when John says something pay not the slightest attention, so that he feels as if he doesn't exist!'

Even then someone may look at John, and rescue him with eye contact. If so, I'll intervene.

Three can exit, leaving one onstage.

One can be driven away.

One can be clearly isolated and 'out of the group' even though he or she's still there physically.

You can strengthen your position in the group by using the following techniques:

- Talk to an individual. Those who make general remarks weaken their position.
- Don't control the group. Taking charge and bossing people around will isolate you.
- Never cross your legs away from the group.
- Don't fold your arms, or clutch the furniture or yourself.
- Don't pull your feet under the chair.
- Open the body so that your space flows into other people's.
- Find the person most sympathetic to you and try to make a link with them.

You aren't rejected until you accept rejection. If you stay calm, and unperturbed, you can bide your time until you see a chance to link to somebody.

Once the players have played the game a few times, all anxiety is swept away by roars of laughter. The style of improvisation alters – it becomes obvious that the players were only pretending to be friendly, whereas now they genuinely are.

An Example of Status Reversal

Here's a scene improvised at Loose Moose (the players were challenged to a status reversal).

Platform: Ron was sitting on our sand-coloured carpet, and it wasn't at all clear what he was intending to do.

'Build a sandcastle,' I said.

Ron became a child building a sandcastle. The audience watched this platform for at least thirty seconds as waves and seagulls were added (by Vanessa Valdes, our sound imp) and then Dave entered and added some 'chaos' by kicking Ron's castle to pieces.

'This is my part of the beach,' said Dave. 'So take off!'

If Ron had obeyed, the sandcastle would have been 'cancelled', and the routine of driving Ron away would have been completed. This could have been an introduction to another scene; perhaps Dave and his girlfriend could have spread out towels and settled down (shelving Ron to recapitulate him later); or the routine of 'being nasty' to Ron could have been broken – Ron could have wept and said, 'Dad you're so mean to me!' but Ron broke the routine by making the moral choice of 'refusing to be bullied'.

'We'll fight a duel for this part of the beach then!' he said. 'You! Fight with me! Choose your weapons.'

'Sandcastles,' said Dave, brilliantly reincorporating the sandcastle.

Someone added a sports-type commentary as the competition began. Dave's sandcastle was small, but Shawn Kinley, our scenographer, entered and crouched under a sand-covered cloth. Ron moulded this and Shawn gradually stood up. Dave looked aghast to see how big Ron's castle was getting. When Shawn reached his full height he pulled the cloth away, and posed as a statue. The main routine of this scene (the competition) seemed to have been completed without being broken, and if Dave had said, 'All right you win!' the audience would have felt disappointed. Dave could have offered to buy this amazing statue, or he could have recognized it as his father (and Ron as his long-lost brother), but I remembered that Shawn had been a 'mechanical man' in a department-store window, so I told Ron to 'operate' him with a TV remote control, and Shawn came to life, jerking mechanically, and reachieving the platform by kicking Dave's sandcastle to pieces while Vanessa added inspiring music. Dave slunk away in awe as the lights faded.

Being the Same Status

People are hardly ever of equal status, except when they're forced into uniform and made to perform identical and restricted movements (chorus lines, troops being drilled, etc.), but trying to make the status gap as small as possible is an excellent training.

Two players attempt this, while the coach interrupts occasionally to ask the class, 'Who is higher?' or 'Who is lower?'

If opinions are divided, I congratulate the players and ask them to continue, but if the class tells me that Frank is higher than Tony, I'll say, 'Which of them is wrong?', hoping to be told that this is a silly question (since either of them can restore the balance).

Players soon learn that they can solve the problem by mirroring each other. When this happens I place them in positions that don't allow mirroring; for example, I might ask one to sit on the floor and lean back against the sofa that the other is sitting on (you often see people in such positions at informal gatherings).

Being the Same Status forces the players to observe each other moment by moment, and is probably the most important Status Game.

Fight for Your Number
I ask three students each to choose a number from one to three but to tell no one. Then I say that Ones should be the most dominant person in a scene, that Twos should be less dominant and that Threes will be the least dominant.

I invented this game as a model for interactions between strangers, but it proved to be an excellent model for interactions in families, so I'll cast the players as Dad, Mum and Mum's sister, or as two teenagers and Gran (or whatever), and let them play scenes in which each player tries to achieve his/her secret 'number'.

This usually results in some sort of status battle; perhaps a son is being elevated unwillingly to Number One by Mum; or perhaps three sisters will all be trying to out-submit each other. Some Threes will be so submissive that they look as if they've wandered in from some other pecking order, so I tell them not to behave like Eights.

Ones should dominate everyone, but they should prefer to dominate a Two, and they'll have to 'do battle' with any other Ones who might exist. Twos will need Threes to lord it over, and Ones to look up to. Threes will look up to everybody, but they will long for a Two to relate to.

To increase the tension, ask a four-person group to choose a number from one to three, or a three-person group to choose either one or two, because then there'll always be at least two players fighting for the same number.

Self Up/Partner Down
Left to themselves, students prefer to work either on their own status or on their partner's status, but you can add variety by asking them to alternate these strategies. For example, here's an example of Self Up/ Partner Down.

'You're not handing in written homework are you? Why don't you use a computer. Look at my essay! You'd swear it was printed professionally. I shouldn't think your grubby little paragraph is going to impress anybody . . .'

Or try Self Down/Partner Up:

'You've got such a wonderful memory. I'll forget my own name one of these days. I'm boring you, aren't I? I don't have the gift of the gab like you!'

Alternating in this way adds transitions, and you'll seem more 'creative'.

Playing the Wrong Status

Choose a relationship that implies a large status gap: a teacher and a child, perhaps, or a mugger and a victim, or a brain surgeon and a patient; and then play the opposite status. Let's imagine a low-status mugger, and a high-status victim:

- Excuse me, miss. Er . . . Miss! Er . . .
- What are you muttering about?
- I'm a mugger! I . . . er . . . I mug people!
- I've read about this sort of thing . . .
- Give me your money! Er . . . hand it over!
- It's Ryan, isn't it? So this is how you show your gratitude for all those hours when I tried to teach you geography! Ungrateful boy!
- Auggghh!! My arm! It's broken!
- Just dislocated! Lie still – I'll fix it for you!
- Auuugghh!

And so on.

Or you could pit a low-status hijacker against a high-status pilot.

- You want me to fly where?
- I'm sorry it . . . it's either Ohio or Iowa, I get them confused.
- You've no idea how to fire that gun, have you?
- Yes I do! And I'm prepared to use it!
- If you pull the trigger a flag will pop out. They sell them in the airport shop.
- They do?

Peter Cook played a high-status beginner to Dudley Moore's low-status Welsh piano teacher. I haven't seen this sketch for thirty years but I remember that part of it went something like this:

- This note is 'A', and this is 'B' and so on, up to 'G', and then we start again with 'A'.
- Oh, I don't think that will do at all. We'll refer to this note on the far left as Number One . . .
- [*Gulp*] Ah, well, perhaps you'd be so good as to press number twenty-two then . . .

Passengers
Try adding a passenger to status scenes. For example, if a high-status sister is to harangue her low-status brother for not cleaning the apartment (or whatever), add a woman he picked up in a bar (who stays neutral and tries to be uninvolved).

Low-status Trick Presentation
Out of hundreds of jugglers, I remembered only two. One was a cheerful man who refused to work with any object that he'd dropped (and he dropped many); the other was W. C. Fields who had manipulated cigar-boxes while his face expressed, 'Is this really a fit occupation for a grown man?'

This made me realize that the trick is less important than the presentation, so I began to train the presentation without the trick.

I stood a 'flat' either side of the acting area, and asked Tony to enter from behind one, run centre-stage and say, 'Trick,' and then leave as Petra was entering from the other side to do the same thing.

'Time it so that there's no dead stage! Overlap!'

Then I said, 'Try again, but bow before and after you say, "Trick!" '

I urged the rest of the class to cheer and applaud and shout, 'Bravo!' as Tony and Petra keep entering alternately to say, 'Trick!'

'Run on with small steps to demonstrate your eagerness, and be so happy that it's obvious that you'd never dream of challenging their superiority. *See* them and bow, *see* them and say, "Trick," *see* them and bow again, and *see* them before leaving.'

This improved things, but although they looked at us, we had no sensation that we were seen, so I made them play the Beep-Beep Game for a while (see p. 260).

'But why is it so important that we *see* the audience?'

'Because it allows you to give us friendship signals, and to be yet more pumped up with inner delight each time you realize how wonderful we are.'

I added a pianist to play loud circus music, and said, 'After the first bow, raise a hand to stop the music. The pianist will give a "drum roll" and you'll prepare for the trick, perhaps by rolling up your sleeves, or by exercising your fingers, or by taking a few deep breaths. Convey that you're about to attempt something very special and difficult. Look slightly worried about your chances of success.'

'But that means we have to keep them waiting.'

'Absolutely. But not because you're high status. You're making them wait because the trick is so difficult, and because you want to do it well for them. Then say, "Trick," and make a happy gesture of release and smile, so that we know that the trick is over. The pianist can help by glissandoing into more circus music.'

When this has been achieved I might give them a simple trick to perform; for example: 'Clasp your fist with the thumb inside. Keep it still, and hit it from underneath with your other fist, letting the thumb shoot upright, as if the blow with the second fist had created that effect.'[9]

I ask them to wait until the split second *after* the 'drum-roll' before deciding whether to do 'my' trick, or something spontaneous. They can stand on one leg, or put their tongue out as they twist their ear, or whatever. Any 'trick' will do, as long as the build-up is well done. The first time we tried this game in public Richardson Morgan mimed unsheathing a sword each time that he entered and did 'tricks' like cutting his hand off (vanishing it into his sleeve), slicing a fly into eight pieces, knighting an audience member, swallowing the sword and extracting it from below, and so on. Minutes passed with the audience getting more and more ecstatic, not because the tricks were wonderful (although they seemed wonderful at the time), but because of his enthusiasm, and his understanding that the actual trick was of no importance.

Many students will do small tricks, my 'thumb' trick, for example, in front of their face, which confuses the image. Get them to do it in front of their chest (or to the side if their costume is too jangly).

If students achieve the correct presentation, our cheering will be effortless, but when they're screwing up, we'll be having to force ourselves to shout, 'Bravo' and applaud.

'Presentation minus trick' is now taught in clown schools, and the rules are exactly the same as those I devised in the sixties. The child in me is very pleased about that.

The Kinetic Dance

Let's say I touch my face for a moment. This will diminish my 'power' and you will almost certainly move to restore whatever 'agreed status' we have unconsciously achieved. Perhaps you'll rotate your foot inwards, or move your thumb closer to your fingers, or touch your own face. Such adaptations become very obvious whenever someone enters or leaves a group, but they're occurring all the time. If they weren't, the levels of dominance and submission would be altered accidentally, and that would be intolerable.

These 'connectivities' are referred to as the kinetic dance (which means the dance of movement), and they are suppressed when people are in grief, or when they're hostile, or when they're 'acting'.

I wrote in *Impro* about the 'threads' that seemed to link the actors when they arrived at rehearsal, and which 'snapped' when they began acting. I was describing the appearance and disappearance of the kinetic dance.

In life, we establish status relationships automatically, but when we are on a stage the relationship is more likely to be between actor and audience (and then every word and gesture will be artificial, no matter how cleverly this is concealed, and there'll be no kinetic dance). Conversely, if a status relationship between the characters is achieved, the kinetic dance will kick in and the actors will respond intuitively to each other, and will no longer experience the spectators as stern judges.

One paradoxical way to demonstrate the synchronization of people's movements (through their posture) is to ask the class to freeze and maintain the direction that their eyes are looking in. Then ask two students who are sitting next to each other to remain frozen while the rest of us walk to the opposite wall. This couple will almost certainly look 'emotional', as if they are reluctant to make-up after a quarrel, or as if they are very lonely. This is because they had shared out their space to include people who have now moved away. This has added an unintended message. Often one will seem angry, and the other repentant. We can reverse the message by lifting one of them (complete with chair) and placing him/her on the opposite side. If they seemed a little hostile before, they'll now seem friendlier.

'Okay, you can move,' I say, thanking them as I turn away. Then I say, 'What's happening now?' and the group laugh because the students that we froze will be making instant adjustments until they find a 'correct' relation to each other, and to us, and they will have done this quite effortlessly and unconsciously.

By this, and similar tricks, a conscious awareness of the dance can be developed so that it's not just a blind-sight phenomenon any more. The absence of the dance can tell the impro coach (and the players) that something needs fixing.

Party Endowments

Four players secretly endow each other with qualities. Then they interrelate while pretending to be at a party. This focuses their attention on the other players, and creates transitions.

I invented this party version as a way of encouraging players to be discreet. 'Parties' suggests slightly formal behaviour, and allows me to shout things like 'Don't let him know he's detestable – after all, you invited him!'

I choose four volunteers, preferably two men and two women: 'There are three people on the stage with you,' I say. 'Decide that one is stupid, and that one is smelly, and that one is attractive.'

Some students (especially professional actors) will misunderstand, thinking I'll be the sexy one, or I'll be the stupid one, and so on.

I explain once again, and they start discussing the qualities that they will endow.

'Keep it secret!' I say.

'But how can we get it right if we don't know what the other players are doing?'

'You're assuming that the person that you find smelly has to know this fact.'

'Exactly!'

'But if I treat you as deaf, that doesn't mean you have to become deaf!'

'But I might be treating someone as attractive, and someone else might be treating them as smelly!'

'Happens all the time! We can't even agree about flavours of ice-cream, or what kind of dog to own, so we certainly won't agree about people.'

I cast one player to be the host, and tell the three guests to enter at fifteen-second intervals (it's easier for us to see what's happening if they arrive separately). Then I say, 'The door is locked – why?'

'They live in a dangerous neighbourhood!'

'Not necessarily, but improvisers are often reluctant to move, and if the door is locked the host will have to answer it instead of shouting, "Come in!" And why is it a party?'

'Because you want a four-person scene?'

'It's a party because there's an obligation to be polite. I don't want you saying, "You smell like a fish!" when you meet the smelly person. You'll have to find some more civilized way to solve the problem.'

Beginners are likely to demonstrate their attitudes. For example, the host who opens the door to greet a smelly guest will recoil, gasping for air. When that happens, I'll shout, 'Don't let him know that he's smelly! Be courteous!'

'But how will the audience know what I'm doing?'

'They don't have to know. If you're doing something that they can't fathom, you'll be a lot more interesting than if you held up a sign that said, "Look! I'm treating him as if he was smelly!"'

Comprehension dawns: 'You mean I don't have to show the audience?'

'Just worry about how to handle your smelly guest, but be courteous. The most you can do is open a window, or say casually, "Came straight from work, did you?" Be tactful. Leave to answer the phone, or make some introductions so that you can make your escape.'

If a guest is being contemptuous, I might say, 'You're endowing your host with being an idiot, but you accepted the invitation. Can't you deal with stupid people without offending them?'

A player might certainly display interest in a sexy guest, but if the admiration was too blatant I'd say, 'Be afraid of being rejected!' or 'Don't be thought a slut!'

I keep reminding them to be truthful. If someone is pushing their chair very obviously away from an obnoxious person, I'll say, 'Conceal your feelings! Move your chair just half an inch!' or 'A smelly person who endows you with attractiveness may be hard to shake off, but that's no reason to spoil the party. Find something interesting on the bookcase, or go to the window and admire the view. Only be rude if someone is an out-and-out pest!'

Once the students have familiarized themselves with the game, I replace 'stupidity' with 'being amusing' (i.e. the game becomes 'sexy', 'smelly', 'funny'). This makes everyone feel good-natured, but their laughter is likely to be too cautious. If so, I interrupt and ask the players to point at the person they find amusing, and then I say, 'Next time this person speaks, please laugh, even if they're just saying, "It's a nice day."'

Restrain players who demonstrate their laughter to the audience.

To keep things moving I give advice like 'introduce people', or 'offer drinks', or I might force someone to exit by saying, 'Remember the present you left in the car!' If the scene still isn't developing, I'll shout something like 'Have a heart-attack!' or 'Start a quarrel' or 'Hold a seance!'

Each player is likely to forget at least one of the three attitudes, so I jog their memories by saying, 'The funny one is getting funnier!' or 'Find a way to get the attractive one to a bedroom!' or 'Avoid the smelly one!'

Left to themselves, beginners would just chat, but my side-coaching turns attitudes into purposes: 'Offer your guests refreshments,' I say. 'Pour them drinks.'

Then I might say, 'Who is the attractive one?' and if players point at the host who is leaving to make hot drinks, I'll say, 'Offer to help! Offer to grind the coffee! Remember something important that you need to tell them!'

When the scene is over, I ask the players to point to the sexy one, and the smelly one, and so on. This makes them laugh vigorously to affirm that it was 'just a game'.

Experiment with different endowments; for example:

- A reputation for hitting people at parties
- Easily shocked
- Tactless
- Nosy
- Rather delicate, in need of cosseting
- Physically fit, active, muscular, energetic, etc.
- Rich and desirable
- Makes snide remarks (is tactless)
- Unimportant and irritating
- Deeply religious
- Hypnotic personality
- Compulsive liar

The kinetic dance locks in when the players are endowing each other with qualities, whereas if they're thinking, I'll be the sexy one, or whatever, it vanishes instantly.

Endow Everything
Let's say that four improvisers have endowed each other with humour,

smelliness and attractiveness. If they've enjoyed this, I might get them to repeat the scene with the same endowments, plus having an attitude to whatever else they happen to be relating to.

'If you want to be dull,' I say, 'have a similar attitude to everything: it's a dirty sofa, the carpet has holes, the view is depressing, the wallpaper needs replacing, the biscuits are stale.

'But if you prefer to be interesting, choose contrasting endowments: the sofa is old but comfy, the wallpaper is tasteful, the coffee-table is like the one you have at home, the area is rather squalid but the view is magnificent. Then there'll be a transition every time you switch attention, and you'll seem more alive, more responsive.'

If someone mentions a movie, or ice-hockey, or pets, or whatever, I'll shout, 'Praise the movie! Change expression when ice-hockey is mentioned! Have an attitude to dogs!'

After practice, you should be able to change your attitudes to each person mid-scene: let the smelly one gradually become attractive, and the boring one saintly, and so on. Use three players (four is too complex).

Variant: move the party to a new locale: to a cinema queue, up to the park, and so on.

Sandwiches

If the players of a Party Endowments scene are skilled at status transactions, I'll ask them to stand in a circle.

'Point to the person on your left,' I say. 'This person is higher status than you. Now point to the person on your right: this person is lower status than you. The remaining person is the same status as you.'

Now I ask them to play a scene, using the same endowments as before, but adding these status endowments (this gives each of them six qualities to endow, but they'll already have practised three of them). This makes for some interesting combinations; you may be endowing your unusually attractive partner with low status, a smelly player with high status, and so on.

I've just described a 'sandwich' in which status was spread over the bread of the party endowments. We can add more layers. A player who is endowing everyone with a quality and a status may also be having an attitude to every topic brought up in conversation, plus moving from one emotional state to another, plus sustaining a new body-image by being 'heavy, sustained and indirect', plus pursuing a 'Stanislavskian objective'.

Such sandwiches may sound insanely complicated, yet we achieve them effortlessly in life. Try adding Fast-Food Stanislavsky to Fast-Food Laban (see pp. 283–301), or to the Fight for Your Number Status Game (see p. 228).

The King Game

If the master is not happy, he snaps his fingers and his servant commits suicide (to be instantly replaced by another servant, ad infinitum). The game is a competition to see which servant can survive the longest, and it makes the players exquisitely attentive to each other.

I was experimenting with minimum-gap status transactions (in which two players compete to be just a shade higher or lower than their partner), and as I always try the reverse of whatever I'm experimenting with, I explored maximum-gap status transactions.

I place a master on a throne, or arrange him/her comfortably on a sofa with lots of cushions and grapes and other comforts. Then I say, 'If anything irritates you, no matter how minor, snap your fingers and your servant will commit suicide and we'll send in a replacement.'

I appoint a timekeeper to time how long the servants survive.

'We'll call fifteen seconds good! And twenty seconds excellent! Anyone like to try for twenty-five?'

This gives the masters permission to be severe, but even so, some will frown and allow their servants to make blunder after blunder. I interrupt such scenes and point out the moments when the master became irritated:

'You wanted to kill him after three seconds because his demeanour challenged you, but you thought that wouldn't be fair. Then you wanted to kill him because he cringed. Then you wanted to kill him because he asked you what you wanted. Then you wanted to kill him because he passed right in front of you on the way to the drinks cabinet. Then you wanted to kill him because he took a position behind you that made you feel uncomfortable. How will our servants learn if you're so forgiving?'

Often the masters have no idea that the servant is annoying them.

'Are you biting your lip and frowning?' I say.

'Er . . . yes.'

'Well, that's a sign that you're not happy, so kill your servant!'

Or I'll say, 'You're shifting about on your throne. Snap your fingers if you feel restless and we'll try a new servant!'

'But he hasn't done anything wrong!'

'The servants have to make being onstage a pleasure, and yet you're visibly unhappy. The sooner you kill a bad servant, the sooner we'll find one that it's a pleasure to work with!'

Or 'You didn't like it when she shoved her elbow into your face.'

'I wanted to give her a chance.'

'Don't give her a chance. She's been pestering you from the moment she stepped onstage, isn't that right?'

'Yes.'

'Well, if you don't kill her, she won't improve.'

'What did I do?' she says, astonished, because she'd thought she was succeeding.

'Well, for a start, you took big steps and waved your arms about. No servant is allowed to do that. It looked as if the regular servant was ill and they'd brought in a scullery-maid.'

I turn to the master: 'Then she stood over you and made you feel so uncomfortable that you crossed your leg away from her (an unsuccessful James Bond did that when the baddie approached him), and then she held eye contact, forcing you to look away. And then she asked if there was anything you wanted and you didn't like having to make a decision.'

'True!'

I'll often ask the servants if they know why they were killed.

'No idea!'

'Perhaps the master can tell you.'

The master may not know either – masters are told to kill on impulse, but sometimes they'll say things like 'You weren't respectful!' or 'You were too servile!'

If masters kill on impulse, I can usually tell them why they were irritated, and this gives them insight:

'The servant asked you if you wanted anything – that's why you killed her.'

The servant protests: 'But I'm a servant! Isn't that what I'm supposed to do?'

'Servants are paid to take the weight of trivial decisions away from the masters.'

'That's right!' interrupts the master. 'You were supposed to know what I wanted!'

The servant still looks baffled.

'You were a nuisance,' I say. 'Your job is not just to "serve" her. Offering a mimed drink or a foot-massage may help, but the real secret is to involve the master in an interesting situation.'

Each master presents a slightly different problem, and before the class can get discouraged I ask them, 'If you got a job working as a servant in a royal palace, how long would it take before you were allowed to serve the king at a banquet?'

'Months!' says someone.

'Years!' guesses someone else.

'Well, then – this game is easy compared to that – it'll only take an hour or so to master it.' (It takes rather longer but I don't tell them that.)

Servants who stand around waiting for orders are killed right away, but those who have a purpose (like opening the curtains or telling the master about an assassination plot) tend to survive. Some discover the jester role, and become entertainers or confidants, like the clown in *King Lear*, or like John Brown (Queen Victoria's gillie who 'tippled' with her during the long Balmoral afternoons).

After the students have floundered for a while I advise them to:

- Enter with a purpose
- Never say, 'Is there anything you need, ma'am?'
- Be physically and vocally discreet
- Convey that the space belongs to the master and that you intrude into it only when necessary
- Don't look servile – or as if waiting to be punished
- Don't out-stare (out-status) the master
- Don't leave awkward pauses
- Giving the master a newspaper, or serving coffee or breakfast may help, but you're unlikely to survive for long unless something of dramatic interest is happening.

Variant: the servant dies at the second finger-snap (or at the third). Save this variant until you feel the need to increase the interest. It's entertaining to see servants, shocked by the first finger-snap, continue in exactly the same suicidal way.

Pecking-order Version

Once you have a servant who is skilled enough to survive indefinitely, build a pecking-order by calling in an under-servant who can be killed by either the servant or by the master. (Time the lives of the under-servants as well.)

Degenerate Version: The master tells the servants what to do and how to do it, and kills them if they don't perform well (pointless).

Passenger Version: Add a passenger – the master's lover, or masseur, or language teacher.

Master–Servant[10]

Parent–child material is expressed in a disguised form. Players can work out personal traumas without realizing it (excellent for working with children).

It's a mistake to assume that the master is high status and the servant low; that is, to confuse the social status with the interactive status. For example, the servant can beat the master while still looking like the servant; the secret is that whatever status you play, you should always treat the space (the territory) as belonging to the master.

Create a platform by having the servant serve the master in a formal way – and then break the formality (i.e. break the routine of 'serving the master'). For example, let's say that the servant has just served tea and cucumber sandwiches:

– Thank-you, Perkins.
– Might I have a word with you, sir?
– Fire away!
– I left Sammy's bowl on the record-player at speed thirty-three and a third, and when I came back you had him on forty-five.
– I was just trying to build up his muscle.
– Build up his muscle? The water was practically boiling.
– You exaggerate, Perkins!
– You just wait till I run your bath for you!

And so on.

When we present a Master–Servant scene, the spectators are hoping that personal material will make cracks in the formality. For example: 'Was that my daughter I heard in your room last evening, Perkins?' or 'Have you been reading my private diary, sir? or 'Why didn't you tell me I was your son?'

Blind Offer Version

If the master snaps his/her fingers the servant knows what to do. Build a scene while you do this. The master gives no verbal orders. The servant's response is always right.

Piggy-Back

Have the masters use their servants as horses, entering and leaving while riding piggy-back on them – take care not to injure anyone. An example:

• A good master and a good servant play a scene that ends when they gallop off to the park.
• A bad master and a bad servant do the same thing.
• Both pairs meet at the park and quarrel. One master challenges the other to a joust using boxing gloves on poles . . .

Perhaps one is injured? Perhaps they fall in love? Perhaps they quarrel without jousting, and there are two more separate Master–Servant scenes before they meet again and fight the duel.

Give the masters balloons to beat their servants with (see p. 259).

Slow-motion Commentary

Roddy Maude-Roxby (of the Theatre Machine) whipped Antony Trent in slow-motion, using a real whip, which, of course, merely stroked the victim who was howling as slowly as possible while Richardson ('Rick') Morgan supplied a sports-type commentary. Afterwards Rick suggested that we could turn this into a game.

Beginners believe that extreme slow-motion is boring, but experienced players know otherwise. I remember Ben Benison and Rick miming a table-setting at the Mercury Theatre, Notting Hill, in 1969. They mimed unfolding a tablecloth with incredible slowness, billowing it out so that it would settle on a mimed table. I timed this as lasting eight minutes, yet the audience were enthralled, although there was no music and no commentary.

Slow-motion adds variety and hinders players from searching ahead for 'good ideas' because they have to attend to their bodies, and bodies are in the present.

Even if only one finger is moving, and at a speed of less than an inch every five seconds, there needs to be some connection with the centre of the body. In all slow-motion work the body's centre of gravity must be in motion, no matter how minutely. Achieve this, and your movements will be 'integrated' – you won't look like a robot that moves one part at a time.

I put one player onstage (moving in extreme slow-motion) and I ask another to commentate on this spectacle, sometimes adding trivia, sometimes going mad with excitement, sometimes deploring imaginary infractions, sometimes being silent as if nothing could be added to this astounding performance. One of the pleasures of this game is that when hardly anything is happening the commentator may be allowing the event to 'speak for itself'.

Almost for sure, I'll have to ask players to 'Slow down! Do less! Move imperceptibly!', and each time that the commentator suggests that something is about to happen 'Oh, I think he's heading for the chair!' – they are likely to speed up (unless restrained). But no matter how excited the commentator becomes, the 'elegant' performer maintains exactly the same pace. This refusal to accelerate can be quite magical.

A New Zealand game-sheet describes this Slow-motion Commentary Game as: 'The improvisers move as slowly as possible, while the commentator talks as quickly as possible.'

The writer must have seen a performance in which the commentator never stopped gabbling, but real-life commentators would be fired if they were so intrusive.

I ask commentators to imagine that they have cards that supply trivia for each competitor; for example: 'Ron Harris is wearing the red jock-strap that has become his most famous distinguishing mark,' or 'Plucky little Audrey Swinburne's father took time off from the local glue factory to supervise her training . . . her swimsuit was knitted by her eighty-two-year-old grandmother,' and so on.

Here's an example of a commentator whipping up excitement together with a 'colour-person' (a colour-person is usually an 'expert' of some kind, or perhaps the trainer of the athlete onstage (the activity was 'entering a room'):

– Oh . . . and I think something's happening. I can see a slit of light around the edge of the door – I thought I saw the knob starting to rotate. Difficult to be sure as the knob is entirely circular. What do you think, Kevin?
– I think it must be turning, Monty, otherwise the Judges would have counted this competitor out by now.

– Number Fifteen, Burt Kropotkin from Ompsk – disqualified last year after a fifteen-minute poke in the eye at Madison Square Garden. Oh, and yes! Something is definitely starting to happen, I can see the tips of two fingers edging into view. Oh and he's absolutely sweeping on to the stage.

[*Pause during which the door opens two more inches.*]

Sometimes the commentary can 'direct' the player, for example:

– Burt Kropotkin, making a flawless entry. I can see his trainer shouting advice. Great concentration, this boy. A strong supporting section here in the crowd. Oh and I think there's an error. I don't think he's set himself up properly for this move . . . What do you think Kevin?

– Definitely a tactical error, Monty. I think he may be going to cannon into the door jamb.

– It seems inevitable, Kevin. Too late for him to alter the trajectory. This will lose him his chance at second place! Oh, yes, he's about to give himself a most tremendous crack on the head in about three minutes' time . . .

And so on. Perhaps concluding with something like 'Rather a slow start at the International Entering A Room competition here at Chutney. And now it's time for these important messages . . .'

I encourage commentators to:

• Allow the event to speak for itself
• Get excited, and build 'climaxes' (even though no climax exists)
• Explain the finer points of the game, infractions of rules, and so on.
• Supply background information on the characters, or on things peripheral to the event.

A good commentator will keep switching modes; for example:

'A gathering excitement at the Barnsley Toad-Swallowing. Frank Quimby sizing up this specimen – Frank Quimby who threw in the towel at toad number seventeen in the quarter-finals in Vladivostok, but holding his own among the leaders here today. A time limit of five minutes for each toad, as always . . .' [*Long pause*] '. . . a blank expression on Frank's face as the seconds tick by. Frank's suit with the extendible gussets was made by Mr Fish. Frank told me earlier that . . . Oh, and some dispute among the Judges as to whether Frank is moving, or whether he's really frozen with terror as it appears from the press-box

. . . Frank Quimby, one of the all-time greats, seemingly overawed by this prodigious toad. The Judges in conclave. Some fighting in the crowd, I'm afraid. A lot of money wagered on this event. The clock still ticking on this call. A London policeman in trouble over by the Royal Box. I can see his helmet being tossed about by the crowd . . .' [*Pause*] '. . . Frank's trainer is asking for a time-out, but the Judges are overruling him . . . Oh yes! I think he's heading for a baulk. Frank Quimby about to baulk. A toadal disaster for the Manx Wizard. Definitely a mistake to have spent so much time in preparation. Always one last toad in the future of every competitor. What a disappointment for this . . .' [*Wild excitement*] '. . . Oh and he's going for it. He's leaning forward. He's going for an engulfment. Frank Quimby's jaws are beginning to gape. Frank, rumoured to have had his jaws altered so that he can dislocate them at will . . .'

During this commentary all Frank has done is incline his head about one inch towards the table while baring his teeth a little.

Variant: two (or more) players move in slow-motion.

Variant: have the commentator supply his own colour-person and so on, using different voices.

Wider Applications

I've classified this game under 'Procedures' because a commentary can be added to any scene. Here are a commentator and a colour-person laying some voice-over on to two players who are not in slow-motion, but who are trying to keep their status as close as possible.

– She's flashing her top teeth at him, Tom.
– Yes, she's definitely lowering her status by that move. He'll have to respond to that if he wants to keep the balance. Yes, he's putting his hand to his face.
– Her blink-rate has increased, Tom, and she's a little breathless when she speaks. He'll have to compensate.
– Oh, there goes his hand to his chin . . .
– Always a popular move.

And so on.

Such a commentary can side-coach players in a way that would otherwise to too intrusive.

'Oh, and that's the third idea he's killed. This scene is becoming weighed down by a relentless negativity. What do you think, Nigel?'

Nigel whispers into the mike, saying, 'I think he may be about to accept this new offer . . .'

The players must allow gaps so that comments can be inserted. This can calm beginners who are rattled, but the commentators have to be experts. Practise the skills in class rather than in public.

Verse

This was yet another of my attempts to force my students to abandon control of the future.

The rule is to say any line that comes to you, and trust that either you or your partner will be able to find a second line (or that someone will prompt you with one). The spectators will laugh when a rhyme is bad, and they'll applaud an apt rhyme. If you can accept whatever your mind dredges up, you'll be sucked into adventures that are beyond your conscious control.

For example, suppose you say, 'Well, here I am on holiday.'

This needs to be rhymed, so add any line that fits; for example: 'I think I'll row across the bay!'

Rowing may have been the last thing in your mind, but go with it.

'Here's what I need, a little boat.'

The next line eludes you while you mentally run through 'stoat', 'cantaloupe' and 'grope', but someone shouts, 'Float', and you say, 'I think I'll see if it will float!'

The spectators can see that you're allowing the verse to control you, and they admire your courage in launching out on to a sea of couplets.

'Oh dear, it seems the boat is sinking,
I cannot swim . . .'

A rhyme totally escapes you, but someone saves you by calling out, 'And I've been drinking!'

'A mermaid sees my horrid plight,
And keeps me in her bed all night.'

You've been launched, quite unintentionally, into a version of *The Little Mermaid*.

Popular verse challenges (and forfeits in Micetro and Gorilla Theatre) include 'to the best scene in verse' or 'to a limerick based on an audience member's name', or 'to the best epic poem that lasts until the audience begs for mercy'.

Verse, spoken or sung, is now likely to be part of any impro show, and yet the players may never have read any. We live in a verseless culture (compared with Elizabethan England or Sei Shonahan's Japan) so I ask my students to learn limericks (so that they at least know the form – this is Canada) – and I offer them travesties of verse, before confronting them with the original:

'Forgive me please, you corpse with bleeding wounds
That I am courteous to your murderers'

And then I'll present them with Mark Antony's lines from *Julius Caesar*:

'Oh pardon me thou bleeding piece of earth,
That I am meek and gentle with these butchers.'

It's likely that they feel the difference quite strongly. Or I'll have them say:

'Heavenly powers, come and keep us safe!'

And then give them Hamlet's actual line:

'Angels and Ministers of Grace, defend us!'

Even the dullest student is likely to feel the increase of power, and some will get hooked.

The Klutz

Pretend to hurt yourself, recover gradually, and then hurt yourself again.

Knock-about comedians say, 'Look at this big laugh I got,' as they compare bruises, but the comedy lies not in the pain but what happens after it. W. C. Fields said, 'I never saw anything funny that wasn't terrible. If it causes pain, it's funny; if it doesn't, it isn't. I try to hide the pain with embarrassment, and the more I do that, the better they like it.'

Physicality is less important than sound. If you scream and say, 'I can't move!' we'll see you as 'having cramp' or 'a slipped disc', even though you've done nothing physical.

Distinguish between fast-pain and slow-pain. A jab with a pin is fast-pain; a crushed foot is slow-pain.

If people believe that you're really hurt, the laughter will stop immediately – unless they hate you – so pain has to be exaggerated to demonstrate that it's not real.

The Theatre Machine, when travelling, would play The Klutz Game with an audience volunteer: the improviser ending up crippled, but still eager to interact. The taller you are, the greater the strain on the body, but if you're short, you can learn to do spectacular falls. Study tumbling with a good trainer. Meanwhile, here are some suggestions that are unlikely to involve you in serious injury:

- Bite tongue
- Be stung by an insect
- Slap leg harder than you intended
- Get electric shock
- Poke self in eye
- Have elbow slip off the table, so that the head your hand was supporting falls to table (make the bang with your other hand)
- Catch one foot behind the heel of the other as you walk and then try not to trip
- Get hand stuck in jug, vase, and so on
- Hurt a tooth as you bite into something
- Bump into the furniture

Derek Flores played a park bench scene with an audience volunteer who was asked to use the 'bad things happen to everyone I make friends with' tilt. He injured himself again and again, while trying to persuade her she was wrong, that 'it's a coincidence', thus giving the impression of a man so driven by carnal desire that he'd walk through fire if necessary.

Being Concussed
When I was a child I saw three clowns bouncing on a trampoline, but only two of them were funny. The third copied everything the others did – I guess they were training him – but he wasn't funny. I thought about this quite often, but I was an adult before I realized that he was the one who'd never looked confused.

Let's say that a servant takes the master's hand and then throws himself into a forward roll. The intention is to make it look as if the master has thrown him, but unless the servant pretends to be disorientated, it will seem like a gymnastic trick. If you're hit by a balloon, and fall over as if hit by an iron bar, you should look in the wrong direction as you scramble to your feet. The bafflement and double-takes release the laughter, more than the blow or the crash to the floor.

Ben Benison once hit an audience volunteer with a balloon, and the stranger jerked into the air, rotated until he was horizontal and crashed in that position on to the concrete (he was a gymnast). We were horrified – but had he clambered up, staring in all directions, it would have been hysterically funny.

When clowns fall, or are biffed on the head, we may be laughing at their changed attitude to the space.

Advancing (And Not Advancing)

Chaplin stressed the need to have an 'attitude', and Laurel and Hardy spoke of the importance of pain, but how did Keaton imagine trapping himself in that paddle-wheel like a mouse in an exercise-wheel? And how did Chaplin think of that cabin poised over the abyss in *The Gold Rush*? (Someone claimed to have given Chaplin that idea, but the cabin teetering on the edge of a cliff is not so special – what's amazing is the sheet of ice that runs between the two doors and traps the characters in a repetitive nightmare.)

These silent comedians gave great attention to 'insignificant' details. Chaplin, as a waiter, blew his nose on a napkin, before tucking it into a customer's shirt and patting it smooth. He 'washed dishes' by letting a dog lick the plates clean, and then running them through a mangle to 'dry' them. Playing a barber, he'd mix the shaving soap to music, and taste it to see if it was 'done', or he'd put the brush into the customer's mouth while he sharpened the razor, and perhaps he'd find a fly in the shaving cream and shave that as well.

An eerie 'persistence' was added to this preoccupation with detail. Keaton decides to keep awake by playing patience and continues to shuffle and place the cards even though they're so wet that they're turning into papier mâché. Stan and Olly are holding up a grand piano (after one of its legs has fallen off) when the horse that happens to be standing on the piano knocks Stan's hat off. Stan bends to retrieve it, leaving Olly bearing the weight of piano plus horse. Does this happen once? No, it happens over and over again with Olly getting increasingly frantic.

In one movie Stan and Olly stop their car at an intersection and are waved on by a traffic cop. Misunderstanding his gesture, they walk over to him.

'Get back in the car!' he snarls, and they obey him. Then he waves them on as before.

Baffled, they leave the car a second time (meanwhile, the traffic starts to back-up). This action of 'misunderstanding the traffic cop' comprises most of the film. And yet, if repetition or persistence was the secret, someone who stuffs envelopes or guts fish for a living would have us howling with laughter.

Staying with It

In one of the very first classes at the Studio I asked a volunteer to 'start an action' and he mimed feeding a dog.

'Make the activity more interesting,' I said, and he mimed that the animal was running away.

'What are you doing now?' I asked.

'Shouting to my dog.'

It was as if I'd said, '*Change* to something more interesting!', and yet no one noticed the evasion.

I asked another actor to describe what he was doing in words ('so we'll know if you've changed it').

'Reading a newspaper.'

'Make the action of reading the newspaper more interesting,' I said, and he 'dialled a telephone'.

'What are you doing?'

'Cancelling the picnic because the forecast is rain,' he said, being negative so that nothing would happen.

'But that's a different activity. Can't you stay with the activity of "reading the paper".'

'You mean I can't finish what I'm doing?'

'Exactly!'

'But what should I do?'

'Can't you get interested in some news item?'

He stared at the paper and tried to look surprised. 'How was that?'

'Fine, now make it even more interesting?'

'More interesting?'

'Find the item difficult to read and take out a magnifying glass.'

'Isn't that a different action?'

'I don't think so, not if you're still reading the newspaper.'

He obeyed: 'Now what?'

'Gasp with horror!'

He did this.

'Why were you gasping with horror?'

'You told me to.'

'Yes, but how would you justify it?'

'It could say that my friend has been murdered!'

'Good. Make the action even more interesting.'

'But how?'

'Add disgusted or interested sounds. Read the news item aloud. Mime showing it to the audience.'

His usual technique might have involved 'pouring himself a drink' or 'phoning his mum'.

'You keep getting ideas that you don't need?'

'Yes.'

'That shows how creative you are, but let ideas float in one ear and out of the other. Attend to what you're actually doing and stop worrying about the future.'

Let's say that you are asked to make 'taking the top off a boiled egg' more interesting, and that you intend to 'find a live chick' in it. 'Finding the chick' would be a new activity, so you'll have to find some other way to hold the attention. For example:

- Mime tapping the egg with your spoon and hear it tap back
- Mime attacking it with a bread-knife
- Mime picking up the egg and bashing it on the table
- Mime attacking it with the bread-knife and succeed! Lever the flap of the egg up very slowly and suspiciously and receive a squirt in the eye as the egg 'seals' itself up again
- Wrestle with the 'lid' of the egg against something that's trying to keep it closed from the inside

Such ideas are in the tradition of silent movies (and cartoon films) and they present themselves automatically when the mind is held to one activity.

One way to introduce this procedure of 'not advancing' is to select a detail from a scene already in progress. For example, two students in Tampura were about to start 'fishing', and were paying very little attention to the preparations (because they were wondering what they'd do after they'd begun to fish).

'Wait!' I said. 'What are you doing at this exact moment?'

'We're going to put a worm on the hook!'

'That's what you are intending to do, but what are you actually doing?'

'Getting the worm out of the tin.'

'See how long you can keep us interested in that activity.'

They tried shaking the tin.

'Poke your finger in and get bitten!' I said. 'That'll make it more interesting.'

This began a long 'excursion' about the bleeding being impossible to stop.

'Don't change the activity,' I said. 'Just stick a Band-Aid on your finger and stay with the worm.'

I suggested that they could order the worm to leave the tin, or tempt it out with a voluptuous finger, or hypnotize it (and get hypnotized instead) or threaten it with a revolver. The audience saw me as very 'imaginative' until I explained that I was just using an alternative way of thinking. The players were eager to learn this 'procedure', so it became the perfect time to teach the discipline of 'staying with it'.

The trick is to extemporize on whatever you're doing at the split second that the command is given, irrespective of any plans that you may have. Told to 'stay with it' at the moment that you drop an egg could lead to Max Sennet-type ideas: you grab at it, but it slips out of your hand; you dive for it just before it hits the floor and accidentally knock it out of the window; a bird flies off with it and you pursue the bird on a motorbike; a truck slams into you and you try to grab the egg as you hurtle through the air. Yet none of these ideas was in your mind when the command was given.

An exact description of the activity is needed. If you agree to 'brush your hair' this will limit you to brushing your own hair, but 'brushing hair' could include 'brushing other people's hair', or 'brushing the hair of a giant'. An activity defined as 'scratching my back' can include scratching with a chair-leg, or rubbing against a tree, but scratching someone else's back would be forbidden. 'Swimming' can involve the breast-stroke, the back-stroke, being swept over a waterfall, drowning, emerging in heaven in an ocean of champagne – but still swimming.

Let's say that you're 'waiting for a friend at a bus stop'. Can you mime using a phone? Yes, if this is an attempt to find out what happened, because it will still be part of the action of 'waiting for a friend'. Can you give up and phone a taxi? Yes, if your action was defined as 'waiting' (because now you'll be waiting for a taxi).

What if you're 'brushing your teeth' when 'a tooth drops out?' Has the action been changed? Not if you start brushing the tooth.

An elegant way to choose an action is to notice what is already happening: for example, 'breathing', or 'growing older', or 'touching your nose', or whatever else is occurring. (I saw the Belgian clown Charlie Rivel extend the action of 'preparing to sit on a chair' for minutes, and he never managed to get his behind on to the seat.)

I ask a student, 'What are you doing now?'

They tell me, 'Waiting for instructions.'

I say 'Stay with that activity. Make "waiting for instructions" more interesting.'

This could involve phoning someone; asking the audience for advice; praying to God; consulting encyclopedias; shouting, 'What am I supposed to do?'; looking through scraps of paper; trying activities at random to see if they might be the right ones; weeping in despair; slashing your wrists and having God say, 'That's right, Sidney!' while you scream, 'But I'm not Sidney! I'm Philip! What are Philip's instructions?' You could be like a character out of Beckett or Kafka.

I speed up the training by asking the students to work in pairs, one as a performer who defines and then elaborates an action, and the other as a trainer who gives encouragement and stops any digressions. When the performer runs out of ideas, the trainer should suggest some, and if neither knows what to do, then at least their trouble is shared.

Let's say that you define your action as 'breathing' and that you start breathing more fully – this will hold the interest for a while – but then your trainer says, 'Make it more interesting!' and you add a contented 'ahhhhhh' sound as you breathe out.

'Make it even more interesting.'

You mime opening the window and exult in the fresh air, but now your mind goes blank.

'Add a resistance. Make it difficult to breathe.'

You start to pant a little; you take little gasps.

'Make it more interesting!'

'How?'

'Start to suffocate!'

You push your ribs in and out manually. You start to die. You crawl over to a 'table' and open a 'drawer'. You seize a 'knife' and pretend to perform a tracheotomy on yourself. Your imaginative powers astonish the audience, but you're just fulfilling the requirement.

You can always make actions more interesting by adding dialogue or changing emotion.

Let's say you're 'stroking a cat': if your mind goes blank, just explain to the audience how it soothes you to do this, and how sensual it is, how the cat really loves it, and so on. Or begin to change from sensuality to some other emotion – rage, perhaps: 'This cat is so spoiled. Who strokes me? Who gets my meals? Who lets me sleep in a patch of sunlight all day!'

Make one small activity more interesting and you'll be thinking like Chaplin or Keaton – not with their genius, perhaps, but we'll begin to see you as a 'natural' comedian.[11]

Advancing the Activity

Players who are trying to 'stay with the action' can't help taking little excursions. For example, if you're trying to stop your finger from bleeding, you might run to get a first-aid box, but this excursion must be kept short or it'll be seen as 'advancing to a new action'.

Advancing forces the students to expand a 'small excursion' into an unanticipated new activity.

Let's imagine that a student is 'not advancing' the action of 'taking the top off a boiled egg'. Perhaps the egg is impervious to everything, including chain-saws and pneumatic drills (you can see this sort of thing in cartoon films all the time). She can't help her mind suggesting 'advances' for the action. Perhaps she's planning to find a chick inside it, and to make friends with it, and have it fly away so that she can be sad and show what a sensitive person she is; but she sighs, and her trainer shouts, 'What are you doing now?'

'Trying to open the egg.'

'Weren't you sighing?'

'Was I?'

'Make "sighing" more interesting.'

She has now 'advanced' from 'failing to open the egg' to 'sighing'. This new action must also be made more interesting. 'Sighing' could lead to suicidal despair accompanied by tearful verbalization about her life being a series of fiascos, and now she can't even open an egg. Perhaps she's planning a really 'interesting' suicide (some stupidity like battering herself to death with the egg?), but her trainer says, 'Advance!' as she glances at it.

'What are you doing?'

'Looking at the egg,' she says, reluctantly.

'Make "looking at the egg" more interesting.'

Perhaps she hides behind the furniture and watches the egg through binoculars, or perhaps she mimes examining it with a magnifying glass and discovers that the egg has a little door marked NASA. Her suicide has now vanished into the same limbo as 'finding the chick'.

The instructions to advance are intended to take her on a zigzag course into an unanticipated future.

As players become confident, they wean themselves from the trainer and learn to press their own buttons. It's then easier for them to do solo 'advancing scenes'.

Think up sequences of advancing while you're waiting for the bus. Choose snippets of activity. 'Playing golf' is too general, but 'setting the ball on the tee' is perfect, and can involve irate gophers, and thieving magpies, and earthquakes, and so on.

Variant: have several students (or the rest of the class) combine to be the 'trainer'.

Variant: let two players take turns advancing their scene; for example:

Pat makes 'looking at the last snowy owl' more interesting.

Melissa makes 'discovering that it's a wooden decoy' more interesting.

Pat makes 'realizing that loggers are trying to lure the last snowy owl so that they can shoot it' more interesting.

And so on.

Advancing should not be confused with bridging; players who bridge are trying to delay their arrival at a known destination, whereas advancing forces the player to travel to unknown destinations.

Hitting with Balloons

You strike someone with a long balloon and he/she reacts as if struck by an iron bar (but recovers a lot sooner).

Balloons invigorate us: they're brightly coloured, they move strangely, they're 'safe' and 'dangerous' at the same time (exploding loudly but harmlessly), the long ones are subliminally erotic, symbolizing both penis and breast and they have the smoothness of youth. I'm referring to the long 'airship' balloons which inflate to a couple of feet long and are inches in diameter (not the long thin balloons that are used for making balloon animals). The airship balloons that we used in the sixties were solidly coloured, about a yard long and three or four inches in diameter. I've found some in Berlin (for fifty pfennigs each), but the largest that I can purchase in England or North America are shorter (twenty-four inches long) and most are semi-transparent.[12]

Balloons as Slap-sticks

Slap-sticks were two thin strips of slightly separated board that made a loud slap when you struck someone with them (some had explosive caps to make them sound louder). The victim needed to be padded, and there was still a chance that you might hit them with the edge.

Airship balloons are an excellent replacement; no padding is needed, and if the balloon bursts, you can be handed another one. The Theatre Machine used to have a hundred (or more) balloons at the sides of the stage and backstage (or stuck to the walls by static electricity), and sometimes we'd have destroyed most of them by the end of the performance.

If a student has a fear of balloons, take the class outside where there are no walls to reflect the sound (but so much laughter is released by balloon-hitting that it should be easy to desensitize nervous students).

Hitting with Entry

Entry involves hitting through the object, as in those martial arts demonstrations where the head is accelerated to a point beyond a concrete block, trusting that it's the concrete that will shatter. Human beings instinctively strike at the surface of other people as a way to assert status without doing serious damage – so entry has to be taught, or the balloons will be just tapped against the other person.

'Hit your forearms with the balloon,' I say. 'Try to burst it with the force of the blow!'

The intention to burst the balloon forces the master to grip the balloon firmly (instead of just letting it waggle), and it becomes obvious that however hard you strike, the balloon isn't going to hurt anyone.

'Now strike your partner with the intention of smashing the balloon right through them.'

Hitting with balloons gave our Master–Servant scenes a new vitality. Masters who seem 'mediocre' become demonic, and inspired, if they hit with entry.

Restraint

Beginners hit their servants as if they were beating carpets. This may be suitable for ending a Benny Hill sketch, but it has very little dramatic value.

'Give each hit a separate build-up!' I shout.

Masters will find this unnatural, and I may have to grab their arms to stop them giving a shower of follow-on blows.

'That's enough!' I yell. 'One hit only. Now beg your servant's forgiveness!'

Masters can easily make themselves enraged (they love negative emotions), but their balloons will seem quite 'dead'. Played correctly, the balloon seems to be getting enraged while the master seems to be trying to calm it down. I explain that if the masters are struggling *not* to hit their servants, the balloon will become a gauge that exquisitely records the master's feelings. Perhaps it's held behind the master's back, as if to keep it out of the argument, but it begins to vibrate, taking little swipes at the air as it works its way round to the front again. Sometimes the master will raise the balloon to strike, but will then force it down again with both hands as if trying to press it under water. Some masters beat themselves in their rage, or destroy their balloon, only to be instantly handed another.

The moment to hit is when the balloon can no longer contain its violence. A good hit is like a sneeze: something that comes after a 'build'. Sometimes the hit is delayed too long and 'misses the wave'. If so, let the tension subside so that you can start building to a fresh climax.

Once you've hit your servant (against your better judgment) apologize, make amends, but start to build the balloon's rage again until it is impelled to lash out once more.

The Wheel of Tension

We have an inner rhythm that most of us are unaware of, but if you clap your hands, and wait (without counting) for perhaps twenty or thirty seconds, there comes a moment when you know that it's time to clap again. (This could probably be used for medical diagnosis: 'How am I, Doctor?' 'Well, your temperature's normal but your clap's all over the place.')

It's as if a huge wheel is revolving slowly at the edge of your consciousness, and prompting you to clap once at each rotation.

Trainers should interfere with this regularity, insisting that the moment of hitting should be unpredictable. Teach this skill by having the moment of release decided by the trainer.

'Not yet. Get angrier. Don't hit him. HIT NOW! Once! ONLY ONCE! Back, back. Help her up, dust her down, tidy her clothing. Now remember why you hit her and vibrate the balloon a bit. Calm the balloon down. Pour her a brandy – notice that half the brandy is missing! Get enraged but try not to show it. Ask where the brandy has gone. Realize that your servant has been stealing your brandy. Let the balloon go berserk. DON'T HIT HER! IT'S TOO LATE. Let the emotion subside a little. HIT HER AGAIN! NOW HIT HER AGAIN . . . Ask her to get you your tranquillizers. Make her swallow a handful . . .' and so on (see Spasms, p. 314).

Balloon Fights

I might desensitize balloon-shy performers by setting up 'sword-fights' with the balloons, *en masse*, until only one person is left standing – all those who are stabbed by a balloon being 'dead'.

I might also try 'sword-fights' in slow-motion, and it's likely that I'll hear a 'tap' as a balloon hits someone. This means that the balloon was speeding up to tap the surface.

'Slow-motion!' I say. 'Think of pressing the balloon into the body! Keep the centre of the body in motion, not just the arm that you intend to strike with, or you'll look like a railway signal. If you're slain, be smashed to the floor in slow-motion and bounce a few times – but don't speed up – there shouldn't be a sound as you hit the floor.'

Moving and falling in slow-motion is excellent for balance and physical control.

The placing of the blows is important: 'The hit has to be "received",' I say. 'Don't strike the knees from in front, strike from the rear so that the legs can buckle.'

I demonstrate this, moving the balloon in slow-motion and continuing to move it after I've made contact, exerting an increasing pressure.

I make a slow-motion thrust to the stomach and the servant grasps the balloon and bends over as I continue the motion. Then he grips the balloon so that it either bursts or makes a horrid wrenching noise as I pull it away from his fingers.

'Strike at one shoulder so that your servant can spin around,' I say. 'Or hit straight down so that your servant either staggers about clutching her head or falls straight down to the floor. But avoid hitting the side of the head because we don't want a balloon to explode beside someone's ear.'

Some servants speed up to evade the slow-motion balloon. This is silly, so I teach them to grimace with increasing horror as a balloon comes towards their face. If necessary, I'll hold their heads still as the balloon moves inexorably towards them.

I get the students to play scenes or to 'fence' in slow-motion, using slow-dialogue:

'Taaaake thaaaaaaat yooouuuuu swiiinnnnne!'

'Ooooohhh, noooooooo. Auuuuuggghhhhh!'

This is excellent for breath control.

Once slow-motion hitting has been mastered I ask the students to begin speeding up their interactions, and for the servants who are hit to fall over. Mats or carpet will now be useful. Fit and healthy students can do spectacular falls, but they won't stay fit and healthy unless you employ a really good tumbling instructor. And remember, it's not the actual fall that matters as much as the cries of pain and the disorientation.

Most servants prefer to stand just beyond hitting range (as if the balloons really were iron bars). I tell the masters, 'Make the servants come to you! Don't go to them!'

And I tell the servants, 'Stand close. Try to be within three feet of the master. You're allowed to duck when you're swiped at, but you're not to avoid the blow by increasing the distance.'

There's something comical (and perhaps political) about the servant who tries to avoid being hit, and yet who always stands in the line of fire.

A Master–Servant Balloon-hitting Scene

– Perkins!

– Sir?

– Didn't I forbid you ever to be taller than me?

– Well, it's so stupid, all the servants going about on their hands and knees and the maids not being able to make the beds unless you go upstairs with them . . .
[*The balloon is extremely agitated.*]

– . . . I mean, just because you're short!

– Short! [*Sir strikes Perkins to the floor and is overcome with remorse.*] Good God! What a brute I am. [*He helps Perkins up.*]

– No harm done, sir!

– I've such a terrible temper.

– Oh, no, sir.

– [*Sir's balloon begins to vibrate.*] Are you contradicting me?

– No, I wasn't, sir. You do have a temper.
[*The balloon becomes more alive, and Sir sits suddenly on the floor. Perkins dives to the carpet. Sir stands up.*]

– Just testing you, Perkins! [*The balloon is calm.*] I wonder if you could get me that *Increase Your Height* book from the top shelf.

– The top shelf, sir?

[*The balloon starts to tremble again.*]
– Certainly.
– Perhaps you'd like to climb up with me, sir?
  [*The balloon takes little swipes in the air. Sir appears to be restraining it forcibly.*]
– I don't keep a dog and bark myself. Fetch me the book.
– There, sir!
  [*Perkins hands Sir a book.*]
– What?
  [*The balloon is enraged.*]
– Your books, sir.
– Did you just climb up and get it?
– Like a flash, sir.
– Don't lie to me! You got this from the bottom shelf. *Ballroom Dancing for Midgets*! Auuugghh! [*Master smashes Perkins down, mad with rage, and is horrified by his own violence.*] Are you all right, old chap?
– Augh! Oh yes, sir, just startled me a bit.

And so on.
It helps to roar or shriek or scream when hitting or being hit.
Even if the master always manages to restrain the balloon, the threat keeps the scene alive, and holds both master and servant to the present moment.

The Spontaneous Balloon

Balloons were rare in my childhood and I wanted to be able to deflate them and save them for another day. If I tied them by looping the neck – as usual – but inserted their mouths just a third of the way through the loop, the pressure of the air and the friction of the rubber would make a tight seal, and yet I could deflate these balloons at will.

If I pushed the mouth less than a millimetre or so into the loop, I created a spontaneous balloon that might discharge at any moment (my parents never understood why balloons in our house would suddenly whoosh about).

If the 'gimmicked' knot is at the end that hits the servant, it's quite likely to deflate, and it gives the audience great pleasure to see the master reduced to flapping a little strip of rubber impotently in the air.

A Need for Caution

Some balloons contain a pinch of talcum powder to stop the rubber from sticking to itself. Deposits of talc are usually contaminated with asbestos – one commercial sample of baby powder was found to be 38 per cent asbestos – so if you find talc in your mouth or on your lips after inflating a balloon, you should wash your mouth out. (Buy a balloon pump?)

Beep-Beep

I apologize for the seemingly infantile nature of this game, but it trains improvisers to relate comfortably and good-naturedly to audiences faster than anything else that I've dreamed up.

The first play I directed had speeches where the audience were addressed directly, and yet the actors preferred to talk to the side walls or focus their attention on the gap between the stalls and the dress-circle. Even at the Studio (where we were all on the same level) the improvisers would talk to an imaginary audience who floated two or more feet above our heads, and if we stood up, this imaginary audience would float a few feet higher.

I attended a performance of an avant-garde play where an actor sat on my knee and spoke a few lines of dialogue. She looked into my face but glass eyes would have been more expressive. How can an actor sit on your lap and seem to talk to you, and yet be utterly remote? And conversely, how is it that great talk-show hosts seem to see us when they stare into the lens of a TV camera?

The Elizabethans took pleasure in speaking directly to the audience, and our contemporary reticence has been attributed to the withdrawal of our stages behind the proscenium arch. And yet Ken Dodd or Dame Edna aren't inhibited by the architecture, so the problem must lie elsewhere.

Let's imagine that a stranger is approaching us along a corridor. Human beings are programmed to make eye contact, but breaking this eye contact would involve a status transaction, so if we want to stay 'unconnected', we'll freeze our eyes so that our gaze will slide away as we continue to move forward. This eye-slide was what the actor who sat on my lap was giving me (she was naked at the time).

But what if you realize that the 'stranger' approaching along the corridor is a friend. Your behaviour changes. You express interest by raising your eyebrows, by widening your eyes, by smiling, and so on (even the pupils of your eyes will get bigger). The Beep-Beep Game was my way to replace eye-slides with 'recognition behaviour'. You may be among thousands of people, and in darkness, but if the great rock star is flashing recognition signals into the audience, you'll experience yourself as 'seen'.

My actors understood that eye-slides were alienating so they had been directing their attention to wherever the spectators weren't.

Teaching Beep-Beep

A speaker addresses a group of from six to eight seated people, each of whom raises a hand and then begins to lower it slowly until the speaker makes genuine eye contact. The hand then returns to its first position and starts descending again. If a hand should descend low enough to touch the thigh, its owner says, 'Beep! Beep!' until genuine eye contact is made. The speaker's task is to prevent or minimize these interruptions.

'It's impossible to win this game,' I say, 'because the "audience" has such a great desire to say, "Beep! Beep!" that they'll speed up!'

Everyone laughs, and the spectators get 'permission' to accelerate, and the speaker realizes that he/she won't be singled out as a 'loser'.

I turn to the group and say, 'If you feel "seen", please return your hands to their starting position and begin lowering them again.'

Some nervous speakers can't talk coherently when they first play this game. If so, I might say, 'Just concentrate on the eye contacts!' or 'Count to a hundred out loud,' or 'Describe our physical appearance.'

I try several speakers, and then I say, 'Did you feel that people were cheating?

'Yes!'

'Why?'

'Because even though I made eye contact, some of them kept lowering their hands.'

'You may have looked into their eyes, but they had no experience of "being seen". You have to let them know that you "saw" them. Why do you think Groucho Marx gave himself big, thick eyebrows and learned to waggle them up and down so quickly?'

Many speakers make themselves look 'dead', as if a formal photograph was being taken, but suppressing the beep-beeps makes them more expressive: they have to smile, or tilt their heads, or waggle their eyebrows. This makes them seem 'nicer' and friendlier and more alive. Groups who teach impro to managers of oil companies and so on say that the Beep-Beep Game is one of the quickest ways to turn corporate 'zombies' into human beings. Seemingly dried up, cerebral and defensive people come alive second by second as they realize that it's nicer to give friendships signals. A few minutes' training can give permanent results.

Addressing an Audience

Let's say that you're addressing an audience in a theatre like the Royal Court in Sloane Square, London. It has stalls, a dress-circle and an upper-circle, and in my day the lights were dazzling, so that you only saw the first few rows.

Divide the front stalls into sections one, two, three and four, and the rear stalls into sections five, six and seven. Slice the dress-circle into sections eight, nine and ten, and the upper-circle into sections eleven, twelve and thirteen. Stand downstage, and as you speak to the audience, let your attention switch unpredictably from section to section, and give a recognition signal each time. Run through sequences like One, Three, Eight, Thirteen, Nine, Four, Ten, Two, Eleven, Five, Twelve, Six and Seven so that no one can ever guess which part of the house you will address next. Then the whole audience will experience themselves as 'being seen', and will warm to you, and feel in 'safe hands'.

NOTES

1 See my article 'Improvisation and all that Jazz,' in *Plays and Players*, August 1964.

2 *Shake a Pagoda Tree*: Mike and Bernie Winters (London: W. H. Allen, 1975).

3 Jay Ingram, writing about 'speaking in tongues', says that, 'Some people are never able to do it, and given that they are usually active in a church in which tongue-speaking is not only accepted, but welcomed as a sign of encountering the Holy Spirit, this failure can be depressing' (*Talk Talk Talk* (Harmondsworth: Penguin, 1993)).

4 I was teaching Stat Oil's Gas Station Attendants in Sweden recently, and they were the best ever at this game.

5 If you want more detailed information on Status games, see my book, *Impro*.

6 'The head of a chief was . . . hedged around with the most terrifying taboos . . . the hands of a person who had cut a chief's hair were for some time useless for important activities, particularly for eating. Such a person had to be fed. This often happened to chief's wives or to the chiefs themselves, and among the Maori these feeding difficulties were more than anything else indicative of exalted position' (Cohen and West, *Taboo*, 1956).

7 He who blinks less is higher in status (see the confrontations between gangsters in

Scarface (starring Al Pacino) and yet we're seldom conscious of this. Takashi Shimura's performance as the doomed bureaucrat in Kurosawa's *Living* has haunted me for forty years, but it wasn't until after a dozen viewings that I realized that he had suppressed blinking until his eyes brimmed with unshed tears. Some secret part of my brain had responded powerfully to that. Great movie 'stars' seldom blink in close-up, and one Japanese theatre troupe forbids its performers to blink onstage (tears run down their faces throughout the performance).

8 If there's someone with you, get them to ask your name. Gasp it out instantly and notice how submissive this makes you feel. Have them ask you again, but this time make no response for at least a second (don't move a muscle), and then look at them for half a second before saying your name with your head absolutely still. There'll be a difference in the way you experience yourself, and in the sound of your voice.

9 I invented this 'trick' when I was a child: it doesn't sound much, but one of our improvisers showed it to master comedian Ken Dodd, who leapt about the stage doing it while being insanely gleeful.

10 For more information, see my book, *Impro*.

11 'Not advancing' can be seen in tragedy. Does the blinded Oedipus stagger across the stage and exit again like the sodomized Lawrence of Arabia in Terence Rattigan's *Ross*? No, he doesn't: the chorus express their horror, then he complains about his misery, then he talks with the chorus, then he curses the peasant who rescued him as a baby, then he launches into a massive speech of woe, and after all that he plays a long scene with Creon.

Advancing can occur in serious plays. Another example: in Suzanne Osten's production of *Hitler's Childhood*, Hitler's mum scrubbed him clean, and this action was made more interesting by scrubbing the stool he stood on, and the floor, and the furniture, and so on, reducing him to a possession.

12 I've discovered some reasonable airship balloons (524 Airship, standard assortment) manufactured by the Pioneer Balloon Company, Wichita, Kansas, 67220; also at Pioneer Europe Limited, Bishop's Stortford, Herts, CM23 5PP, England; also at Pioneer Balloon Canada Limited, Hamilton, Ontario, L8E 2W3; also at Qualatex, Balloon Pty. Ltd, New South Wales, 2100, Australia; also at Globos Qualatex de Pioneer, S.A. de C.V. Puebla, Pue, Mexico.

11 Serious Scenes

Fun I love, but too much fun is of all things the most loathsome – William Blake, *Second letter to Dr Trustler*

Public improvisation is usually a comic form, partly because comedy is often better when it's improvised, but also because watching tragic scene after tragic scene would be like attending a series of road accidents. Perhaps if we sobbed and keened with the same abandon that we laugh, we'd feel 'cleansed', but we don't, and it's as if large lumps of ice are forming inside of us.

Most comic improvisers regard 'being emotional' as 'losing control', but as George Devine pointed out, no matter how berserk you are, some part of your brain is still aware of the edge of the stage and stops you from falling into the audience.

If Theatresports is presented as a riot of organized stupidity when the audience are invited to throw wet sponges at the player, the audience will expect more stupidity, but an emphasis on storytelling means that 'serious scenes', and scenes with pathos, can be accepted as part of the show. Scenes that follow serious scenes are likely to be a lot funnier.

Substituting Phrases

If you've quarrelled on the phone, and been hung up on, you'll have noticed a surge of emotion. Anything that thwarts speech can magnify emotion.

Try opening your mouth to say one thing, and at the last split second substitute something else (or say nothing). Perhaps you decide to say, 'The storm's over,' but then, as your lips part, you say, 'Weather's clearing up!'

Master this trick and we'll see you as a deeply serious and/or tormented person. A variant of this involves opening your mouth to say either 'I love you' or 'I hate you', before making your substitution.

Speech Plus Physical Contact

Another method is only to speak when your partner makes physical contact with you.[1] If the contact is broken mid-sentence, stop speaking instantly.

If the problem is solved – for example, if your partner puts an arm around you or holds your hand – break the contact, or it'll be like being out of arm's reach in Taking the Hat.

Do you have to talk in a scene? Of course not. No one should have to rely on words to push a scene forward, so try 'not telling' your partner that you're playing this game. For example:

'You're very quiet today.'

You nod and sigh, so your partner tries again:

'Something wrong?'

Perhaps you could sob, hoping to lure your partner over to touch you or hug you, so that you can say something like, 'I'm in love with you and it's driving me crazy!' If this doesn't work, you could stride over to seize him/her, and scream your love aloud, but it's usually best to be patient. Glower! Laugh hysterically! Lock the door! Rip the phone out of the wall! Slash your wrists! Have a heart attack!

Even when your partner touches you, there's still no need to speak. Your silence may rip your partner out of a cocoon of would-be-clever chat, and reveal a truthful and expressive actor (because your non-verbal behaviour will be presenting both a mystery and a resistance).

Try the game in real life with friends who have no idea that you're improvising with them – then you can't argue that their reactions aren't 'real'.

Love and Hate

Love scenes do not have to be sexual: two brothers at odds over a woman can confess their love for each other; Job can love God; a dog can love its master; a child can love its teddy-bear. Love scenes can offer relief from unrelenting comedy, but uptight improvisers treat them as just another opportunity to get laughs.

Asked to play a love scene, beginners will hold hands while the snoggers supply a 'moon', and the sound imp adds 'smoochy' music.

'Great beginning for a murder!' I say.

They're baffled.

'Or for a break-up of a marriage scene.'

'But you wanted a love scene!'

'If you begin as lovers, you'll have nowhere to go except bed.'

Love scenes should establish a platform that has nothing to do with love; for example, with a doctor examining a patient, or with a neurologist learning to scuba dive, or with a girl changing the water in the school aquarium:

- I've known you ever since you were a tadpole, Freddie.
- Ribbit!
- Do you like the way I make sure that the fresh water is always at room temperature?
- Ribbit!
- You're a good listener, Freddie. You're my best friend in the whole world.
- Ribbit!
- Sometimes I wish you could talk, though.
- I love you, Rita!
- Did . . . did someone speak?
- Ribbit!
- Was it . . . was that you, Freddie?'

Maybe they kiss and she becomes a frog – who knows? – but even a loving interaction with a frog can bring a tear to the eye, and release a bucket of laughter in the scene that follows.

To add a resistance, set up a situation in which it would be untruthful for two people to say, 'I love you,' to each other and then make them struggle desperately say it. They win, not by saying it, but by their persistent and continuous desire to say it. For example, I might tell them:

'You both work in the same organization, or you're students at the same college. You've been introduced to each other, but have never had a chance to exchange any personal information, even though you think that the other person is wonderfully attractive. You enter the a common room to get coffee, and see the other person. You sit together and for the first time you get a chance to "know" them.'

I explain that in life they wouldn't know the other person's intention, and that they'd be afraid to be too forward for fear of spoiling things. I want them wriggling on the hook of this need to confess their love, and if I see they've escaped from the hook for a moment, I'll say, 'Try to say it!' – but this might apply to their partner not to them. Then I forbid them to use substitutes like 'I think you're great!' or 'I really like you.'

I watch the scene to see the moments when the future seems clear – when they know what they're going to say – and I intervene to disrupt their plans.

– Hi, er . . . can I sit here?
– Er . . . sure. You're in sales aren't you?
– That's right. I . . .
– *Try to say it.*
– I, um . . . some sugar?
– Oh, yes.
– *Get personal information.*
– You . . . er . . . live near here?
– *Try to say it!*
– I . . . take the bus.
– Ah . . . I have a car, but the parking's so . . .
– *Try to say it!*
– Difficult everywhere . . . Parking . . .
– Yes.

With luck, the players will learn to stay 'on the hook' and I'll have to intervene less and less. When the scene becomes 'real' to them, they lower their voices. Don't tell them to speak up, not until they've played the game a few times.

Saying 'I love you' used to be an ordeal for the actors at the Studio, they used to sweat and shake, but these days it doesn't seem like such a violation.

'If you aren't embarrassed, you're missing the point. If you're glib, or if you know what the next few sentences will be, concentrate so much on the need to say, "I love you" that you can't think straight.'

Then I put players on the hook of saying 'I hate you!', asking them to make their choice secretly, so that neither knows the other's intention. If you're struggling to say, 'I hate you,' to someone who is struggling to say, 'I love you,' to you, this can be very upsetting. But why shouldn't you be upset? You're an actor.

This game has been popularized into 'Two people desperately in love can't use the word love.'

Emotional Sounds

Make emotional sounds while you are playing a scene, but in such a way that no one will notice.

Emotional sounds integrate the mind with the body (which is why they're used in martial arts, and why the *Karma Sutra* recommends them), but they're suppressed when we think intellectually. For example, if I were telling you my ideas in person, I'd make no sounds (apart from 'errs' and 'ums'). And if sounds did begin to intrude, you'd know . . . *ummm* . . . that I was moving . . . (*slight 'tut'*) . . . from the world of the intellect . . . (*sniff*) . . . into the world of the senses, for example . . . (*phoof*) . . . er . . . thinking of . . . (*barely audible intake of breath through the lips*) . . . taking a coffee-break, or that I was . . . (*slight moan, smack of lips and intake of breath*) . . . being attracted by one of the students.

Right Down to the Toes

Watch people who are flirting and you'll see that their feet are as expressive as any other part of them, but ask them to flirt on a stage, and it's likely that no feeling will get through to their legs at all. The 'dominant' leg may vibrate with tension, but whatever was flooding through their bodies is now blocked as if some valve in the neck, or chest, or hips has cut off the flow.

I might take such students out of earshot and ask them to play the scene again, adding emotional sounds, '. . . but in such a way that no one can guess what you're doing'.

If they succeed, their entire bodies will be expressive, and the rest of the class will be eager to know what I told them.

'Guess!'

'To respond to each other more? To relax? To concentrate? To be truthful? To be more imaginative? To be filled with emotion?'

I set up similar scenes, but no one can identify the 'magic dust'. This is because our verbal intellect dismisses emotional sounds as 'irrelevant'. When I explain, the class is amazed that such a seemingly unimportant button can create such instant improvement.

Perhaps I ask some students to sit on a sofa, and then ask them to sit a second time, while adding a satisfied 'ahh' sound, or a discontented 'ooof' sound so that the onlookers can see the difference.

If beginners find it difficult to think up sounds, I'll appoint 'shadows' who stick close to them and say, 'Sigh', or 'Groan', or 'Choke back a sob', and so on. (It's easier to think up the sounds if you don't have to make them yourself.) Or I might write a list of sounds that the players can hold like scripts; for example:

- Push the air through the lips to make them vibrate
- Growl
- Roar
- Weep
- Scream
- Sniff audibly
- Groan (especially when you sit or stretch)
- Sigh (an ahhhh sigh)
- Sigh (an mmmmm sigh)
- Hiss
- Cry, 'Hah!'
- 'Ooooooo!'
- 'Tut'

I advise improvisers to use 'emotional sounds' when they are challenged to a 'serious' scene, or to a scene with 'emotional truth', or to a scene with 'pathos'. The spectators won't notice the sounds consciously, but they'll experience the players as 'actors' rather than as 'just comedians'.

If physicality minus sounds is desired, make sounds in rehearsal but suppress them in performance.

People have thought about adding emotional sounds long before I did. I asked an elderly European actor to become expressive by adding such sounds – working with him through an interpreter – and suddenly light seemed to dawn. He repeated the scene making bizarre and very loud 'harrrrummmmpt!' and 'aurrrroughh' sounds between each sentence, sounds that weren't integrated with the text and that made not the slightest difference to his 'use of himself'. I asked my interpreter what was happening and was told, 'Oh, we call that the grunting/snorting school of acting. It used to be quite popular.'

Perhaps a hundred years ago someone taught actors to make emotional sounds as a way to unlock spontaneous behaviour, but the purpose of this system has been forgotten, and the intellect has taken over the making of the sounds. Hence the importance of saying 'Add emotional sounds *but in such a way that no one notices*.'

Why Do Emotional Sounds Work?

If the part of the brain that defends us against other people is verbal, and if emotional sounds are controlled by the less verbal hemisphere, then we might predict that when the intellect seizes control our left and right sides will synchronize (or one half would be suppressed) and that there'll be no emotional sounds. Such behaviour is typical of stage-fright. Conversely, we might predict that adding emotional sounds would trigger both sides of the body into working independently (which is what happens). I can't find any research to substantiate this, only hints that suggest the opposite, but I admire the physicist who preferred a beautiful theory to one that fits the facts, because 'after all, the facts are always changing'.

Used truthfully, emotional sounds keep the actor in the present moment, instead of allowing his/her mind to gallop ahead.

Variant: write emotional sounds on strips of paper and scatter them over the scenography so that the players can pick them up at random.

Mantras

I tried to regain the incandescent world of my childhood by screwing up my 'intellectual' thinking. I did mental arithmetic while reading aloud, and I repeated the alphabet backwards while playing the piano (and so forth). Chanting the first line of nursery rhymes silently while I interacted with people ('Georgie Porgy . . . Georgie Porgy . . .') was helpful. I tended to become monosyllabic, but people preferred me that way, and they never complained that I seemed inattentive. Nowadays I don't need such 'techniques'; I just 'attend' to the world instead of evaluating it and it blazes up in a way that can be a real pest if I'm trying to get on with things.

Being onstage threw my students into the state of 'high alert' that had insulated me from the world. Wanting to 'succeed' forced them to be as intelligent as possible. They seldom looked cute, or bewildered, or vulnerable, or tender – why should they when they were busy protecting themselves against failure?

I asked them to repeat nursery rhymes silently to themselves.

'Notice that you can still see everything,' I said. 'And hear everything.'

If students expressed the rhythm of the phrase by letting their bodies 'beat time', I said, 'Don't throb in time with the phrase! No one must know that you're using a repetition! Speaking may be difficult, but keep your attention on the repetition even as you answer my questions.'

I homed in on a student: 'Tell me your name.'

'Rachel.'

'Did you stop the repetition in order to speak?'

'No.'

Her voice had sounded quite different, so I believed her. I turned to someone else: 'Where are we?'

'The Royal Court Theatre Studio.'

'But you stopped the nursery rhyme when you spoke.'

'I had to.'

'Describe the furniture in your bedroom.'

His eyes moved as he scanned a mental image, so I knew that he was a visualizer (most actors are).

'Try picturing the words as they trundle through your mind, and make sure that you always know exactly where the sentence has got to, even as you speak. Now tell me again – where are we?'

'H . . . Here . . .' he said, successfully, but then he snapped out of it: 'It's too difficult.'

'But you succeeded! And soon you'll be able to say whole sentences. If you spoke fluently, we'd know that the verbal part of your brain had seized control and had snapped you out of it.'

I asked the students to interact, and to improvise dialogue, even though their 'personalities' were entirely preoccupied with 'Three blind mice . . . Three blind mice . . . Three blind mice . . .', and there was a startling improvement. 'Guarded' performers who were used to being 'in the head' were suddenly 'in the body'; and emotional situations that would force the average player to make jokes out of sheer embarrassment were carried through with absolute seriousness. Every word that broke through the obstacle to speech seemed to have vast emotion and 'history' to support it. It was as if we were spying on scenes that were really happening. Sometimes we wept.

If students talked in paragraphs (not allowing their 'intellect' to be hamstrung), I started them again, and gave them some minimal dialogue: 'Hi . . . How are you? . . . I've a problem . . .'

To students who kept losing concentration, I said, 'Just ask yourself "What am I doing here? Oh, yes, Keith told me to repeat the phrase . . ."' (Meditation teachers give similar advice.)

It took me a while to realize that I had reinvented the mantra – a sacred phrase or word that spiritual trainees repeat to themselves as a way to be 'in the world' rather than 'evaluating the world'.

One might imagine that mantras would make students inattentive, but the opposite is true. Mantras in life or on the stage confront us with what's happening, rather than with our verbalizations about what's happening; they distract us from the need to defend our status, and they stop the social personality from scampering into the future in pursuit of safety or adulation.

I Love You – I Hate You

Repeating phrases like 'I love you' or 'I hate you' is easier, but unless I begin with nursery rhymes, actors misinterpret the mantra as 'a purpose to be achieved'. So I wait until they've succeeded with 'Baa Baa, Black Sheep' or whatever, and then I'll say, 'Repeating "Baa, Baa, Black Sheep" has nothing to so with a desire for a sheep, has it?'

'Of course not.'

'So a nursery rhyme is not a purpose. It's not a Stanislavskian objective.'

Then I might sit a couple of actors in front of the class and tell them to repeat 'I love you'. They become 'stiller' and their breathing improves. I say, 'Stay exactly as you are, but switch the mantra to "I hate you".'

It's as if a cloud is passing over them. They appear to be harder and colder, and yet they seemingly haven't moved a muscle. I ask them to change back to 'I love you' and it's as if the sun is shining on them again.

'But how is that possible?'

'I don't know, but think of mantras as a way of changing your "substance" rather than as supplying a purpose.'

I ask the entire class to say, 'I love you, I love you, I love you,' to themselves.

'Notice each other!' I say. 'Sustain the mantra and manage to say, "Hi!" or "Hallo!" to somebody.'

While they're doing this they look gentler, softer and more loving. They don't look seductive, but they seem nicer people. I switch them to 'I hate you' and it's as if they are slightly contemptuous and 'meaner'. Start an inner chanting of 'I love you' and look up from this book, letting your eyes settle on people or objects; then change the mantra to 'I hate you' and you'll probably experience a mild form of the states that I'm writing about. Notice alterations in your breathing.

Melissa begins a non-mantra scene in which she arrives, intent on accusing her best friend of seducing her boyfriend. She seems unaware of the 'space', having decided to walk to the sofa and sit down first. I ask her to start again using a mantra, and this time she slides one of her feet along the floor as she enters, expressing her character's reluctance to go through with this painful business. She looks ravaged. She looks as if she's sat up all night weeping. She looks as if she has no idea where to go in the space. She doesn't seem like an actor at all.

Other examples: a man plays a scene in which he tries to seduce someone. When he repeats the scene using a mantra, his knees open or close according to how well he's doing.

A woman tells her partner that she's pregnant, but when she repeats this using a mantra, she strokes her thighs.

The mantra can allow the complexity of human interaction to be reproduced on the stage – if you need it.

Contradicting the Mantra

Repeat 'I hate you! I hate you!' to yourself as you seduce someone, and you'll look like one of Hollywood's 'Great Lovers' (Joan Crawford, Valentino, Charles Boyer, and so on), whereas if you use an 'I love you' mantra while trying to reject someone gently, it'll be like watching *Brief Encounter*, or one of those Soviet movies where lovers agonize as they have to leave each other.

It took years for me to discover the value of purpose against mood, but this would have been discovered naturally by movie stars who were filled with hatred after climbing the 'ladder to stardom' and were then asked to play love scenes.[2]

Side-coach with insulting dialogue, like:

- 'Why are you so nervous?'
- 'You've no idea how to dress.'
- 'What makes you think I'd be interested in you?'
- 'Everyone in the office despises you.'
- 'Come into the light and let's have a good look at you.'
- 'You're a loser – hasn't anyone ever told you that?'
- 'You play your cards right, you could have me!'

Jesus is a character in one of my plays, and if he repeats an 'I love you' mantra, he always seems to be better lit than the other actors. This may seem impossible, but I used to eat with an Indian dance company and if I wanted to describe the lead musician, I would say, 'You know, the one who always seems to be pumping out light,' and people would say, 'Oh, him.'

Alfred Lunt

I've found a reference to 'repetitions' in a book about the Lunts (Alfred Lunt and Joan Fontaine). This was in the Theatre of Taxidermy where it can be bad manners to help each other, but during a coffee-break Alfred sidled over to a young actor who was floundering.

'You seem to be having a bit of trouble,' he said.

'Yes, I'm sure they'll fire me.'

'I couldn't give you a little advice?'

'Oh, please, Alfred, anything.'

'Just start repeating, "You son of a bitch! You son of a bitch!" to yourself before your scene starts, and keep doing it until you're offstage again.'

'Are you serious?'

'Try it. It'll solve everything.'

He tried it, and the director shouted, 'Thank God! At last you've understood!'

Lunt was admired by other actors for his mysterious ability to be truthful in practically any circumstances.[3]

NOTES

1 Recorded in Viola Spolin, *Improvisation for the Theatre* (1964).

2 Olivier writes that he and Merle Oberon were being directed by William Wyler and were loathing each other '. . . spitting at each other all day, in real hate, and he [Wyler] suddenly made us do a love scene, which went beautifully in one take' (Laurence Olivier, *On Acting*, 1966).

3 People are always rediscovering the mantra. Joanna Field, an art professor, was sad that paintings had become objects to 'think' about, rather than to experience, but cured herself by repeating, 'I want nothing . . . I want nothing' as she looked at them.

12 Character

Who Are We?

We're taught that we're each one 'creature', just as we learn that we're in our heads (or wherever else our culture wants us to be). This goes back at least as far as Plato, who defined the 'mature citizen' as someone whose 'reason' has subdued the conflicting parts of his personality, but I see the 'mature adult' as someone who has learned to present the appropriate personality. Con-men and 'great communicators' have always done this.

When Pierre Janet, in the last century, told his patients that other personalities were 'inhabiting' them, these popped into existence. This recently became a therapeutic 'fad', and a risky one. The *Scientific American* reports that Nadean Cool 'split' into over a hundred personalities (including a duck) before settling out of court for 2.4 million US dollars.

Theatre exploits such 'personalities' and they often intrude into everyday life (as when Valentino was filming *The Sheik* and his table manners became so disgusting that his wife refused to eat with him). If we regarded the emergence of these 'other selves' as a sign of mental illness, our students would panic, but theatre praises them, and casts them as characters in plays. Every actor hopes to 'become' the character, rather than having to go onstage night after night 'pretending'.[1]

When the state wants to depersonalize us, it dresses us identically, and refers to us by a number, and makes us repeat identical postures and movements, and makes us maintain blank expressions (no 'dumb insolence'). So to release other personalities, we should probably take the opposite approach. Alter our face, or our body image, or paint ourselves green, or dress-up as riot cops, or as brides, or wear tutus, or business suits, and we may suddenly experience ourselves quite differently. Plato's 'mature citizen' would 'pull himself together' and 'snap out of it', but if we had the courage and the incentive to 'go with it', other creatures might emerge, and in the right circumstances this could be construed as exhilarating and liberating (and a skilled acting teacher will create the right circumstances).

Changing the Body Image

- Make your mouth as small as possible and speak very loudly, and notice what a tyrant you become.
- Expose the top teeth and grin, biting your bottom lip. Now push your head forward and giggle – who is this submissive creature? (Notice how the back of the neck wants to shorten and how the shoulders want to rise.)

  Bare both rows of teeth and let the breath hiss audibly through them and your eyes probably open wider, and you become aware of the space to either side of you, as though there might be something at the periphery of your vision that you could rend, or crucify.
- Michael Chekov, in *To the Actor*, suggests altering the body image by placing your mind in different parts of the body (or outside the body). Imagining the mind as a 'silver ball' in your chest that radiates a wonderful light into the universe can turn you into a Seigfried-type hero. 'Become' a small, hard, black, steely ball located in one of your eyes, and move about while you sustain this sensation, and your whole 'self' may be transformed.
- Viola Spolin suggests writing adjectives on paper strips, and writing body parts on strips of a different colour (the colours are useful when you have to sort them out). Pair these arbitrarily and walk onstage with happy feet, or with a silly bottom, or with a proud chest, or a nasty nose. Try two body parts at a time, adding crazy fingers to lustful lips, or embarrassed knees to a sensual mouth. Have scenes in which entire 'families' have angry chins and slow thighs, or happy hips and nervous hands. Let the onlookers have fun guessing the qualities that are embodied.
- Change your appearance by wearing a mask while sustaining whatever sound the mask suggests to you.
- Paint your face white, and see someone else looking back from the mirror.
- Try make-up, wigs, fake moustaches, false cheeks.
- Make inarticulate sounds and gradually turn them into a voice that is not yours.
- Ape your pet.

- Imitate your parents – you're experts on how they move and sound.
- Go disguised into the real world. Play scenes in public disguised as other characters (don't be discovered; don't get arrested; leave people in a better state than before you arrived).

Machines

Not recommended for public use. Machine Games were around in the sixties and my guess is that they came from educational drama.

A player repeats one gesture and one sound in a mechanical way. Then another player stands next to the first and does the same. More players arrive until a 'machine' is assembled: a mass of people are on stage, wheezing, hissing and chugging away in synchronization.

This may be useful as therapy for shy people, but it hardly bears watching as a performance game. I saw it used as a challenge and both teams created similar 'machines' which was doubly tedious.

The Theatre Machine would sometimes 'build' a machine for a 'new employee' to operate (perhaps it would ingest someone, Chaplin-wise), or they might assemble an 'oracle machine' that would give answers a word at a time, but just to 'build a machine' as an effect is cowardly (because where's the risk?).

People Machines

When students know each other well, I might teach them the Machine Game described above, and then ask them to construct a 'Keith' machine (each component making one of my characteristic gestures and sounds). They'll so like this idea that half a dozen students will run out to 'represent' me on the stage.

'One at a time!' I say.

I might suggest that they go on to base machines on other people (on other teachers or on celebrities). Then I might let them volunteer themselves as subjects (never let them volunteer each other). With luck, everyone will soon be eager to see themselves spread across the stage like a cubist painting. It's easy to take offence when one person imitates you, but not when a whole group does it.

Audiences love mimicry, yet very few students have the patience to imitate other people. Mel Gibson told a talk-show host that he'd been working on his Sean Connery voice for three months. Only one student in a hundred would persist in such a venture without encouragement. People Machines provide the encouragement. The players become better observers of other people, and the group becomes friendlier.

Study celebrities on video-tapes.

Being Animals

A procedure of ancient lineage: Anthony Hopkins added some 'snake' to his cannibal Dr Lector in *Silence of the Lambs*; Olivier incorporated some of Disney's *Big Bad Wolf* to his *Richard the Third*; Eartha Kitt adopted the persona of a cat; Toshiro Mifuni based his *Rashomon* bandit on a lion.

Stage One
Diminish shyness by asking the entire group to be the same animal. Give parties for identical animals: mice squeak and groom their whiskers and nibble cheese; pigs grunt, roll in the mud and fight for the swill; snakes hiss and use lots of sibilants (but they walk upright, albeit 'slitheringly'). Taboos about bodily contact are diminished: snakes slide over each other, cats rub against each other.

Students will ask, 'What mixture of human and animal should we be?'

'Be so like the animal that we'd lock you up if you behaved like that in everyday life. Wolves should wolf their food, and kittens should romp. Lizards should stare, and flick tongues.'

Stage Two (Covert) Animals
This much achieved, I'll point out real-life examples of grunty people, squeaky people, snorty people, elephantine people, goose people and rodents-in-a-hole-in-a-river-bank people. Then I'll ask the students to be human beings with the spirit of animals, but to avoid any behaviour that would get a human being classified as insane.

Once the students have laughed a lot, and become confident, I might set up a party with snakes and mice, or dogs and cats – on their best behaviour and obliged to be courteous to each other. After a few of these parties the class can vote on the best snake or the best bear (or whatever). Then we'll play scenes in which the winning bear is a teacher who is interviewing a really slithery parent, or in which a chicken responds to an advertisement for 'companionship' and arrives at the home of Mr Wolf.

All physical transformation games (Moving Bodies, The Arms, Fast-Food Laban, etc.) put attention on to the body, and as bodies only exist in the present, the students usually have a good rapport with their partners.

The Mouse Police

I was teaching stage one mice to become covert mice, when I realized I could accelerate the process by sending in the Mouse Police to arrest any mouse that went beyond the limits of being human. It can be a great pleasure to see a mouse become totally mouse when its cover is blown.

The Mouse Police (who, of course, are *not* mice) ask questions, find clues, look for suspicious behaviour, and so on. Played as an entertainment game, a mouse *must* be caught (or there's no pay-off for the audience).

Here are the Snake Police (who are not snakes) entering a household:

- We've had a report that some snakes have moved into this area!
- Ssssnakes Offisssser?
- Mind if we look around?
- Ssssertainly. Be our guessst.
- You don't blink much, do you?
- I have exssselent eyesssssssight, Offisssser!
- What are all these mouse patties doing in the fridge?
- My ssson's sssscience project.
- Where are the stairs to the basement?
- Sssstairs? . . . Well . . . there's a hole.
- A hole!
- Well, we only moved in ressssently. Sssssylvia, have you sssseen the ladder?
 [*One of the snakes becomes hysterical and tries to wriggle under the sofa.*]
- Hold him, Joe! Pin him with your forked stick! Don't let him get his tail around that piano-leg!   .
 [*And then the aftermath:*]
- Oh dear, how ssssshocking. Sssstanley was just our lodger. Why, we could have been sssssswallowed alive in our bedssssss!

Obsessions

The players sustain emotional sounds while regarding the space behind as more 'interesting' than the space in front.

This was a spin-off from my attempts to make actors explore phobias.

Let's say that I ask an actor to play a scene in which she is convinced that death will arrive in the next few seconds.

'Everything seemed normal when you left for work,' I say, 'but a hand tried to drag you into the toilet; a sales clerk threw knives at you; dwarves with pepper-spray dropped from the chestnut trees; and now you're home, after escaping a thousand deaths, and it's all still happening.'

I cast a student to be her boyfriend, and tell him that she's never behaved like this before, and that he'll have to calm her down. They play the scene but it's not very interesting.

'You're acting as if you're about to die in the next few minutes, and this allows you to plan ahead, but you should believe that you're about to die in the next second. Keep hallucinating fresh dangers. Let your attention leap to the gigantic razor-blade that is about to thrust up from between the floorboards, and then to the strange smile on your significant other's face, and then to the weird feeling in your stomach from the doughnut that you ate, and then notice that the carpet is eating through the sole of your shoes, and so on.'

I start the scene again, and pressure the girlfriend into changing focus: 'Detect poison gas! You touched the chair and now chemicals are burning into the skin. The ceiling is a foot lower than when you entered the room! The green wallpaper is impregnated with arsenic! The pigeon on the window-sill is from the bacterial warfare lab! Someone is aiming a rifle from the roof opposite! Did that vase just move six inches? Is that really your boyfriend? What's he holding in his fist?'

The students begin to understand that they can use images to trigger leaps of attention, but they're still working intellectually, and their minds are too slow. It doesn't make us jumpy to look at them, and their focus will be almost entirely forward (which is not how people who have no idea where the next threat is coming from would behave).

I tell them to attend to the space behind them where a hand may be about to snatch them into another universe, or where a psychotic gymnast is shadowing them. I ask them to believe that their worst terrors are lurking just outside of their peripheral vision.

We start the scene again, and the homecomer enters, unaware that I've stood someone behind the door to leap out at her.

'Auugghh!'

'You're terrified you're about to be killed, so how come you didn't even look behind the door?'

She continues, but now someone grabs her legs from under the table.

'You're supposed to be scanning for danger!' I say. 'But you're thinking instead of seeing.'

I stop the scene and a student steps out of the wardrobe, and one emerges from behind the armchair. The class agree that obsessions are really difficult.

'I'll tell you the secret. Gasp with horror.'

'What?'

'Gasp! Pant! Scream!'

We all make terrified sounds.

'You notice that the sounds jerk the body about – it's utterly unnatural for the body to be still while it's shrieking and gasping with terror. Keep the sounds going throughout the scene and intersperse them with dialogue.'

Mike is lying on the sofa, reading a newspaper, when Jean enters, slams the door and leans against it, only to leap away as if bayonets were about to come thrusting through the wood. Her moans, gasps and shudders of terror make her seem genuinely obsessed, and she keeps spinning round, convinced that something terrible is about to seize her. Mike is confused:

– What the . . .
– They're after me. Close the curtains.
– What?
– Look out the window. Is there a man across the street?
– He's putting a coin in a parking meter.
– That's him. [*She spins around*] Augh! Who's in the cupboard?
– No one.
– Smoke? You smell smoke?
– I don't think so.
– Who's been going through my things? [*Spasms and grabs her neck*] Augh! Poison dart!
– Darling – calm down.
– Let me go! Augh! You're not Mike! Who are you?

[*They wrestle as she tries to remove his face.*]
- Get that mask off!
- It's my face. [*He tears loose and backs off.*]
- Can't trust anyone!
[*She spins round and attacks a teddy-bear, and then presses it to her throat as if trying to tear it away from her. Mike removes it.*]
- What's happened to you?

And so on.

By this time the onlookers should be feeling very jumpy and exhilarated.

'But why didn't you tell us about making sounds earlier?'

'Because then you wouldn't have understood their value.'

Once Instant Death has been mastered, other obsessions become easier. You could be obsessed with a 'horror of physical contact', sustaining disgusted sounds while being nauseated by the feel of your clothes or by skin, and always wary lest a tub of mucus slurp over you from behind.

An example: two students elbow through the door, arms held slightly away from the body (because armpits are disgusting). Their fingers tremble with disgust, and they sustain, 'Augh! Ugh! Eugh! Urg! Yuk!' sounds. Politeness obliges them to shake hands, but only with fingers that are compressed into a tight wedge. A shudder goes through their bodies as the contact is made, and all the while their obsessed eyes flicker about the room in the anticipation of even greater vileness.

Or you could be obsessed with a desire for physical contact, sustaining the scene by erotic moanings and groanings: your hair could be wonderful to touch or suck, skin could be enthralling, the pressure of your clothes against you could be ecstatic. You could adore the feel of your shoulder against your neck. You could yearn to press your face into anything soft or sensual, and you could always be scanning for anything deliciously touchable that might be gathering just behind you.

Perhaps the spectators hear sensual moans as the door opens and a student enters, fondling the doorknob. He/she leans against the door to close it, and slowly slides down to the floor, purring with pleasure . . .

'Had a nice day?'

'Mmmmmmmmmmmmarvellous!'

'Look around,' I shout. 'Don't get focused in one direction. A great fleshy wonderness is about to solidify just outside your range of vision.'

And so on.

I might set up a scene with a teacher who has a horror of touch and a student who has an insane longing for contact. I'll have to provide a resistance, or the student will be crawling all over the teacher. Perhaps the student should be afraid of being expelled, or in awe of the teacher.

Any feeling can be played as an obsession if you can discover a sound to base it on.

Grade your responses. If you had a phobia of dogs, even a dog-leash, or a kennel, or a drawing of a dog, or a toy dog might alarm you, but not with the intensity of being leapt at by a drooling Rottweiler. If you love physical contact, caressing a smooth doorknob might be enjoyable, but hair, skin, or a warm coffee-pot might almost drive you mad with desire.

As with characters based on animals, obsessions come in a 'psychotic' version and a 'normal' version. A psychotic obsession of lust will delight the audience (who see their secret feelings personified) but a 'normal' obsession of lust would be more useful to an actor, and is achieved by staying just this side of anything that would get you categorized as insane.

Fast-Food Laban

Laban was a movement theorist (among other things), and his best-known student in England was Yat Malmgren, who taught for me and William Gaskill at the Royal Court Theatre Studio.

Pin this chart on the wall (Laban would have had twenty-four items).

WEIGHT	SPACE	TIME
Heavy	Direct	Sudden
Light	Indirect	Sustained

Selecting one quality from each column gives you eight choices:

- Heavy-Direct-Sudden describes *punching*.
- Heavy-Direct-Sustained describes *pushing*.
- Heavy-Indirect-Sudden describes *slashing*.
- Heavy-Indirect-Sustained describes *wringing*, as in wringing out a cloth.
- Light-Indirect-Sustained describes *stroking*.
- Light-Indirect-Sudden describes *flitting* about.
- Light-Direct-Sudden describes *dabbing*.
- Light-Direct-Sustained describes *smoothing*.

These qualities refer to body use, but not to the actual bodies. For example, Fatty Arbuckle and Oliver Hardy were heavy physically, but light when they were performing. Don't miss Olly and Stan dancing in *Sons of the Desert* and *Way Out West*.

I ask four or five players to agree on one quality from each column. Let's say that they choose 'punching' (Heavy-Direct-Sudden).

'You are the Punch family,' I say, 'and everything you do or say has to be punchy. Decide your relationships (quickly), and show us the Punch family coming down to breakfast.'

Perhaps Father enters briskly with a newspaper. He opens it so suddenly that it rips in half. Then the daughter slams her way into the house.

- Where were you last night, Jan?
- Out with Mike!
- And what are those grass stains on your back?
- We were watching meteors.
- [*Mum slams the breakfast dishes on to the table*] Stop it the two of you! It's our anniversary. [*Punching him in the shoulder*] Don't spoil it!

Groups of students act out the Stroke family and the Slash family, and so on. When they've become skilled, I let them play scenes in twos, and I increase the difficulty by making them choose opposing qualities: we might have a punchy landlord interact with a stroking tenant, or a dabbing doctor interact with a wringing patient. It becomes especially pleasing when they switch types: a scene between a slashing teacher and a smoothing pupil might be replayed with a slashing pupil and a smoothing teacher.

Ask the players to choose their movement qualities in private, so that we can guess what they intended, but the important thing is not that the guesses are accurate, but that the players are transformed. Sometimes I'll interrupt a scene, warning the players not to say anything – not even to nod or shake their heads – while I ask the audience to guess the qualities. Then I'll let the scene continue and ask again (until the guesses are correct). If people believe that you're punching, when you intended to be smoothing, this tells you what you need to eliminate.

Students who are naturally 'light' should practise being 'heavy' and vice versa. Ideally, improvisers should be able to assume any way of moving.

Any game that asks you to sustain a different body image is likely to fix your attention on what's actually happening, rather than on the past or the future.[2]

Fast-Food Stanislavsky

Lists are ways of giving the players permission to create characters that may be alien to them.

Long ago I directed a play at the Danish State Theatre School and discovered that the students knew hardly anything about the ideas of Stanislavsky (the great Russian director and acting teacher). He believed that if an actor is absorbed in trying to achieve a purpose, automatic systems will kick in (as happened to Tony Curtis, who was screwing up his debut as a messenger-boy until an older actor murmured, 'Try to get a tip').

Fast-Food Stanislavsky was my attempt to speed up the learning, and to my astonishment it made the players seem boundlessly imaginative.

Having a Purpose is not Enough

A student is playing a character whose aim is 'to get money':

'What are you doing?' I say.

'Trying to get money,' he says, a bit miffed.

'And what have you done to achieve this?'

'I was about to ask for a loan.'

'But what have you done to get a loan?'

'Nothing yet. I was working up to it when you interrupted me!'

'But you've already had five minutes!'

I make him play the scene again, without the bridging, but this time I shout instructions:

'Offer your labour! Steal something! Steal something else! Try blackmail! Offer violence! Beg! Weep! Flatter him! Offer to prostitute yourself!' and so on.

The scene is packed with incident, and the student seems very 'talented' (which he hadn't seemed before). My instructions give him massive 'permission' to act wholeheartedly because I'm the one shouting things like 'use blackmail' and 'prostitute yourself', so if anyone is to be thought badly of, it's me.

I might introduce Fast-Food Stanislavsky by setting up a death-bed scene in which Father is dying, Mother is nursing him and the son is arriving home with his new wife. For example:

- Father: Don't cry, my dear.
- Mother: Oh, John, John . . .
- Father: There, there . . .
  [*Doorbell.*]
- Mother: That must be them. [*Goes to the door.*]
- Son: Hallo. [*Gives Mum a hug and introduces his wife.*] This is
  Georgina.
- Wife: Pleased to meet you.
- Son: How is he?
- Father: Not long for this world, Tom.

The players are so solemn and miserable that onlookers are howling
with laughter. I apologize, and say that the exercise was a trap.

'But what was so funny?'

'You were trying to show us how sad you were!'

'But it's a death-bed scene!'

'But how do the characters know?'

'But he's ill! You said he was dying!'

'But will he die in the next five minutes? In half an hour? Next week?
For all you know, he may drag on for months!'

Light dawns. I ask them to suggest a purpose for their characters and
they say, 'To make my husband comfortable,' 'To express my love,' and
so on.

They try this but the scene is very boring (predictably).

'Too monotonous,' I say, 'and too sentimental. Forget about making a
good impression on the audience: let's have Mum get sympathy, the son
give everyone a bad time, and the daughter-in-law make them think
she's intelligent.'

'What about Dad?'

'He can try to cheer everybody up.'

'But he's dying!'

'People don't necessarily change character just because they're ill.
Beethoven made jokes when they operated on him without anaesthetic!'
(Litres of fluid had spurted out of him and he said it was like Moses
striking the rock.) 'Cheering people up might be part of Dad's nature.'

They play the scene again: Father speaks in a cheerful voice and offers
them a drink, Mother sighs and looks pained, the son calls the daughter-
in-law clumsy, and the daughter-in-law tries to look 'intelligent'.

'Well,' I say, 'that's not much!'

Lists

I tear paper into long strips, and write a purpose at the top of each:

The father's strip says: 'to give people a good time'.

The mother's strip says: 'to get sympathy from other people'.

The son's strip says: 'to give people a bad time'.

The daughter-in-law's strip says: 'to be thought intelligent'.

This fails to delight them (because at some subliminal level they understand that knowing your purpose doesn't help), but then I divide the class into husbands, wives, sons and daughters and ask each group to write a list of things that their 'characters' might do to achieve their purposes.

They laugh happily as they write their ideas, but some of them soon get stuck, even though I'm only requesting six items.

'Don't search for good ideas,' I say. 'The purposes don't have to work.'

'Why not?'

'You've seen a lion-tamer removing his head from the lion's mouth and towelling off the saliva? Well, it would have been a lot more memorable if he'd failed.'

Here are four typical lists:

Father
To Give People a Good Time

- Smile – be friendly
- Give presents
- Ask advice
- Respond promptly
- Introduce people
- Offer food, drinks, drugs, etc.

Mother
To Get Sympathy from Other People

- Have a brave smile
- Be clumsy
- Have a handicap
- Be a martyr
- Wear a pained expression
- Whimper

Son
To Give People a Bad Time
- Criticize
- Speak roughly
- Be sarcastic
- Insult people
- Correct people
- Complain

Wife
To be Thought Intelligent
- Use long words
- Invent statistics
- Use foreign phrases
- Name drop
- Make sensible suggestions
- Whistle Bach

I ask them to hold the lists like scripts, and to play the death-bed scene again.

'These purposes are not in any particular order,' I say. 'So choose any item that you can make truthful. If ideas of your own occur to you, use them; if we like them, we can add them to the lists later on.'

This time the scene starts with the mother adjusting the father's pillows:

— Father: [*Smiling*] Thank-you, my dear.
— Mother: [*Whimpering*] Oh, my back. You're too heavy for me.
— Father: [*Asking advice*] About the will. Do you think . . .
    [*Doorbell.*]
— Mother: [*Being a martyr*] Oh, no! They're here already, and I haven't cleaned up! [*Spills medicine – being clumsy*] Oh!
— Son: [*Offstage – speaking roughly*] Answer the bloody door.
    [*Exit Mother with brave smile. Father writes a name on a present that he has wrapped. Enter Son and Son's Wife followed by Mother.*]
— Father: [*Responding promptly*] Hallo, Son!
— Son: [*Complaining*] I thought you'd be worse than this from the telegram!
— Mother: [*Limping – having handicap*] They'll be the death of me, those stairs.
— Father: [*Introducing people*] And this must be Enid!
— Son: [*Correcting*] It's Ingrid, you daft fool! [*To Wife, insulting*] Don't hang back like part of the wallpaper!
— Wife: [*Offering chair to Mother*] You should be sitting down.
— Mother: [*Pained expression*] Oh, I don't mind standing.
— Father: [*Offering drink*] I hope you like Icelandic sherry.
— Wife: [*Foreign phrase*] Dei gustibus . . .
— Son: [*Criticizing*] It was the bloody drink that got him into this state in the first place! His liver's like cardboard!

And so on. This is far more interesting than watching them trying to look miserable.

A purpose needs a resistance, and the best resistance is the truth, but beginners will apply an instruction that pleases them even if the behaviour is quite false. Given an instruction like 'tickle' on a Give-a-Good-Time list, they'll stride right into Dad's sick-room and start tickling him, even though he's desperately ill or fast asleep. Once the novelty wears off they realize that 'being stupid' is less fun than 'being truthful', and at this point the lists will begin to create character.

I let groups of students write out more lists – To be Thought a Saint, To Ruin Someone's Life, and so on. Their instructions will be 'safe' but I salt them with bold suggestions like 'hit', or 'tickle', or 'find a zit and panic', or 'tie to bed'.

I'll improvise an interaction between a 'good-time' list and a 'bad-time' list.

To Give a Good Time
- Respond promptly
- Agree and praise
- Talk about others
- Offer food, drink, nice experiences, etc.
- Ask advice

To Give a Bad Time
- Shout
- Criticize
- Talk about self
- Be controlling
- Ignore
- Give advice

– Gerald: [*shouting*] Helen!
– Helen: [*responding promptly*] Yes, Gerald?
– Gerald: [*criticizing*] Why do you always let the fire go out? Just imagine if a ship had sailed by without seeing the smoke of our signal fire?
– Helen: [*agreeing and praising*] Yes, and you always set me such a good example. You're so masterly, the way you rub two dry sticks together.
– Gerald: [*talking about self*] All those years in the military taught me self-discipline.
– Helen: [*offering food*] Would you like an oyster, Gerald?
  [*He ignores her.*]
– [*offering nice experience*] How about a back-rub?
  [*He still ignores her.*]
– Why don't I squeeze a coconut for you?
– Gerald: [*controlling her*] There's only one thing for it, Helen, you'll have to swim to the mainland.
– Helen: [*asking advice*] Which direction would that be, Gerald?

Perhaps a ship could pass by and they could scramble to the top of the island to wave the Union Jack. Perhaps Gerald could plunge into a crevasse, and Helen could rescue him while he's complaining at how incompetent the rescue is. Without the lists, it's unlikely that Gerald would be so piggish, and Helen so accommodating – although therein lies the humour. The scene would be more competitive, and nothing would happen.

Beginners prefer to stay with their first choice (transitions make them feel insecure), so I shout, 'Something else from the list!' at intervals of from five to fifteen seconds.

You can get the students used to the lists very quickly by handing one to each student and asking them to be at a party. Place a pile of spare lists at the side so that the guests can change their lists and join in again as 'someone else'.

Improvise family scenes in which all the relatives play the same list. Then, even if the instructions make the students do weird things, they'll feel secure because everyone will be expressing the same weirdness.

Students can experiment with roles that seem quite alien to them. Someone who would never choose to explore his/her femininity could play a To-be-Thought-Beautiful list. A timid person could experiment with a Give-a-Bad-Time list, or a Life-of-the-Party list. Any anxiety about self-revelation would be greatly diminished because players could always say, 'But it was on the list!'

There's no limit to the lists that can be used; for example: To be Stan Laurel, To be Mae West, To be a Gorilla, To be a Mad Scientist, To be a WASP, To be John Wayne, To Relate Well to the Audience, and so on. Virginia Satir, the family therapist, asked her students to play four roles that occur in disturbed families; these can be adapted as lists. They are: To be a Computer, To be a Confuser, To Accept Guilt and To Make Guilty.

Students soon interiorize a repertoire of contrasting lists, and may not even realize that they are incorporating parts of them into their scenes.

Lists don't have to be naturalistic. For example, the To-be-Thought-a-Hero list:

- Start a fight
- Be prepared to draw a weapon
- Be on a quest
- Be athletic
- Have an enemy
- Be high-status
- Display strength
- Detect dangers
- Display resistance to pain
- Have a firm and resonant voice
- Keep head still when you speak

- Imagine a silver ball about an inch inside your chest that radiates an amazing light[3]
- Show scars or a wound
- Take chances
- Tell stories about your amazing adventures
- Kill something
- Rescue someone

Let's say that Henry holds this list as his 'script' and leaps through the door (being athletic) and bolts it shut (having an enemy), surprising Irene:

– Can I help you?
– [*Showing a wound*] If you could just pull this knife out of my back.
– Oh dear.
– [*Resistant to pain*] Just a scratch.
– There's a first-aid box somewhere . . .
– [*Detecting danger*] Look out! [*He pulls her to the floor and lies on top of her*] Cover your ears. It's a grenade.
  [*A pause: they pant*]
– Our luck's in. It's a dud! [*Firm and resonant voice*] Is this the interview for the assistant librarian?
– [*Irene is a little shaken*] That's right.
– I had no idea there was such competition for the job. [*On a quest*] But no on will stop me! I intend to be the best assistant librarian in the entire universe.

And so on.
Some lists seem made for each other, for example:

To be the Life and Soul of the Party
- Joke, tell jokes
- Laugh; be loud
- Be flamboyant
- Agree
- Remember names and use them
- Introduce people
- Be fit, athletic
- Suggest dancing
- Tease

To be Thought Normal by Other People
- Have quiet and/or nervous voice
- Be formal
- Have a dog
- Fear the unfamiliar
- Sit symmetrically
- Be easily shocked
- Laugh moderately
- Be a churchgoer

- Break taboos
- Tickle people
- Make people perform

- Seek reassurance
- Join in with caution
- Try to avoid bodily contact

Such a Life-and-Soul-of-the-Party list might create a character who was an out-and-out pest, and a To-be-Thought-Normal list will surely create a character who is 'neurotic', but what matters is that the players reveal different aspects of themselves.

- [*Being loud*] I say, are we the first?
- [*Formal*] How do you do?
- [*Laughs*] Where's Celia? [*Being loud, joking*] Hump the Hostess! Hunt, not hump – still, you know, Celia!
- [*Easily shocked*] Celia is my sister!
- [*Remembering name*] Norm, isn't it! Good old Norm! [*Introduces himself*] Lief! My name! Swedish!
- [*Fearing the unfamiliar*] Ah . . . Oh . . .
- [*Teasing – feeling Norm's biceps*] Weightlifter, are you?
- [*Disliking physical contact*] No, don't! Don't! [*Being churchgoer*] It must be from moving the pews on club night.
- [*Stretching athletically*] Can't beat healthy exercise. [*Suggests activity*] Nice thick carpet! Why don't we wrestle?
- [*Seeking reassurance*] You really think . . .
- Celia won't mind! [*Tickles him*] Tickle, tickle, tickle.
- Augh! [*Trying to laugh moderately and having dog*] You'll start the dog barking. Sit Basil! Sit! Down boy!

'To-Seduce' Lists

I separate the men from the women, and ask each group to write out a To-Seduce-a-Person-of-the-Opposite-Sex list. They sit in huddles at opposite sides of the room and keep exploding into laughter. Here are two such lists:

To Seduce a Man
- Smile
- Be vulnerable
- Be breathless
- Move sensually
- Say 'yes' a lot
- Be mysterious

To Seduce a Woman
- Make her laugh
- Be athletic
- Get her drunk
- Be rich
- Hold eye contact
- Give personal info

- Move close to him
- Candlelit dinner
- Admire his taste
- Flatter his ego
- Pose sexually
- Sit close, with legs tucked away from him
- Undulate subtly
- Be happy
- Rapt attention
- Tease
- Ask him to dance
- Loosen clothing

- Beg, plead, weep, grovel
- Touch her breasts (accidentally)
- Be boyish
- Be worried you might be gay
- Lock door
- Apologize for being aroused
- Play with her hair
- Offer money
- Tie to bed
- Strip
- Moan and rub against the furniture

Even 'joky' instructions (from me), like 'lock door' and 'offer money', can create strong situations.

Each group chooses its own 'champion' to try out these lists. Establish a strong resistance or you'll have to throw buckets of water over them. It helps to tell the woman that she mustn't be thought a whore, and the man that he should be afraid of 'putting her off'. Remind them that in real life the person we are trying to seduce may be someone programmed to give us a 'bad time'.

Any Purpose for any Scene
Some people believe that a close study of the text can reveal the actor's purpose – this certainly seems to be the 'university view' – but I remember a scene in which a student had to murder her professor, and afterwards I asked her if murdering her professor was really the best purpose.

She looked baffled: 'But I have to murder him!'

'Not necessarily. Let's say you are burgling a house; burgling a house is what you're doing, but you might really be trying to impress your friends or annoy your parents.'

I asked her to choose a list at random: 'What does it say?'

'To be thought clean and tidy.'

'Couldn't that be your purpose?'

'But being tidy has nothing to do with killing someone!'

'Killing him is the "text", it's what happens, but the text is not the purpose. Can't you imagine characters who are so obsessed with being neat and orderly that they murder someone as if getting rid of a piece of dirt?'

She tried again using this To-be-Thought-Tidy list and became a 'character' instead of an 'abstraction'. She dabbed at a spot of blood on her dress while her victim writhed in agony. She closed the corpse's eyes and polished its spectacles. She chilled our blood, and was revealed as someone with an excellent dramatic imagination; yet the first time she'd played the scene we'd seen a clichéd murderer whom she'd learned from TV or the movies.

Someone chooses a list at random that says, 'To Give Someone a Good Time.'

'How about basing a murder scene on that?'

The class are sure this is an absurdity, but I tell them that any list can function with any scene:

'You could enter an office by sticking your head round the door and giving a cheerful greeting. You could bring the boss a cup of coffee, and endow him with a sense of humour. You could take an instant photograph of him. You could make him close his eyes as if to pop a sweet into his mouth, and then you could stick a gun in it, pull the trigger, and place a cushion under his head as he falls to the carpet.'

Almost every student wants to try playing the scene this way.

'Okay,' I say. 'How about a purpose like "Not-to-Commit-a-Murder"?'

They laugh at the seeming impossibility.

'But think – if I were to burst into the dean's office with a revolver, determined to kill him, I'd experience a huge resistance. I'm not a murderer by nature, so until I shot him I'd be trying *not* to squeeze the trigger, even though the text would force me to do it!'

We write out a Not-To-Murder-Someone list: 'enter reluctantly . . . show him the gun . . . give him a chance to escape . . .' and so on.

We try the scene, and the effect is startling. The actor speaks as if the words are being torn out of him. At one point he sweeps things off the desk in rage and then starts to pick them up apologetically. He weeps and hands his victim the gun, but the scenario has to be completed so he wrestles it back and fires. He clutches his dying victim as if to keep him in this universe by brute force. He staggers back in horror and disbelief. He pretends to throw up into the waste-basket. It's like a scene imagined by Dostoevsky.

I've known actors to roll on the floor with elation when they realize that any scene can be played with any purpose. It thrills them that an actor can be more than 'just a puppet', that a performance can bring things to the play that the writer and director had never imagined. Some say it's changed their lives.

List and Written Text

Lists can be applied to written text, but many of the suggestions will be impossible or difficult to use. Consider this list:

To be Thought Beautiful by Others

- **Smile a lot**
- **Have expressive eyes**
- **Pose**
- **Walk tall**
- **Sit elegantly**
- **Look in mirror**
- **Check appearance**
- **Be languid, sensual**
- Criticize others' looks
- Be a model
- Ask opinions of your attractiveness
- Have a rich or glamorous lover
- Panic when you find a zit
- Name drop celebrities
- Fish for compliments
- Be interviewed
- Glide about, dance
- Show photos of yourself
- Worry about flab, wrinkles, etc.
- Exercise
- One of your features is ugly

The first eight instructions (in bold type) could be applied to almost any text, but the others might or might not be usable. For example:

- *Criticize others' looks* It's difficult to convey this without dialogue, but if you treated people as if they disgusted you, it might help establish your character.
- *Be a model* Perhaps the scene might be set in a studio where a 'passenger' is photographing you.
- *Have rich or glamorous lover* We could add a body-builder who massages you, or Warren Beatty could be feeding you grapes.
- *Panic when you find a zit* You could deal with a zit during a scene, while making no reference to it.
- *Name drop*, *Fish for compliments*, *Ask opinions of your attractiveness* and *Be interviewed* These are impractical if we respect the text; but *Glide about, dance*, *Show photos of yourself* All these seem possible.
- *Worry about flab, wrinkles, etc.* Perhaps you could be using a mirror to

examine your deterioration, or you could be poking at the fat under your upper arms.

● *Exercise* You could pump iron or use a rowing machine while you quarrel, or give orders, or do whatever else the scene demands.

● *One of your features is ugly* You might need dialogue to establish this, but maybe you could keep hoisting one side of your bra, or rubbing cream into your bald head, or whatever.

Come in, Nielsen
Here's a fragment of text to which two Danish students applied lists that were chosen at random (circa 1973):

— Come in, Nielsen. Sit down. I suppose you know why I've sent for you?
— No, sir.
  [*Klaus slides a newspaper over to Nielsen.*]
— You know we can't employ anyone with a criminal record.
— Won't you think it over?
— Good-bye, Nielsen.
— I didn't want your stupid job, anyway.

Here's this text with Klaus using a To-Give-Someone-a-Bad-Time list, and Nielsen using a To-Show-People-You-are-Happy-About-Everything list.

> [*A rhythmical knock on the door. Klaus works at his desk, paying no attention. Nielsen's smiling face appears around the edge of the door. She gives a whistle. Klaus looks up, amazed that any employee could be so disrespectful. She strolls in, swaying as if she has a pop tune inside her head.*]
> — [*Sarcastically*] Come in, Nielsen!
> [*He starts to write again. Nielsen tries out a few dance steps and starts to sing.*]
> — [*Angrily*] Sit down!
> — [*She sits down and looks around, admiringly. She shifts her bottom on the chair, enjoying the sensation. Pleasure*] Ummm . . .
> — [*Without looking up*] I suppose you know why I sent for you?
> — [*Friendly laugh*] No.
> [*He pushes the paper across the desk, using the back of his hand. She picks it up, casually.*]

– [*Interested*] Ahhhhhhh.

[*She settles down to read the wrong item. Klaus takes the paper back roughly, folds it over and over, and thrusts the news item at her as if he'd like to rub her nose in it. He laughs coarsely but she reads it with approval, as if she likes the way they've written up her escapade. She touches her hair as if the photo has suggested a change in hairstyle.*]

– [*With satisfaction*] You know we can't employ anyone with a criminal record!

[*He claps his hands obliquely against each other as if to smack dirt off of them. Nielsen 'sings' her next line lightly, influenced by the pop tune that's continuing inside her head.*]

– Won't you reconsider?

[*Klaus cuts the news item out with scissors and places it in a file where it will remain for ever as a black mark against her. Meanwhile, she offers him a cigarette which he ignores. She keeps on offering it as if his refusal were a game. She makes coaxing movements with her head as if to a child. She lights a cigarette and sucks the smoke deep.*]

– [*Bored with her antics*] Good-bye, Nielsen.

[*He puts the file in the drawer and starts writing again. She blows smoke over him.*]

– I don't want your stupid job, anyway. [*She snaps her fingers to her inner rhythm.*]

'Take new lists at random, and play the scene again,' I said. This time Klaus used a To-Give-Someone-a-Good-Time list and Nielsen used a To-Seduce list.

[*There is a discreet knock on the door. Klaus hurries to open it. He smiles, and then hesitates and looks down, regretting the task imposed on him.*]

– Ah . . . er . . . Come in, Nielsen.

[*Nielsen stands smiling at him. Klaus is taken aback and confused. He makes an awkward gesture towards the chair.*]

– Er . . . Sit down.

[*He gives a nervous laugh as she looks at his body. He sighs and clicks his tongue, shrugging his regret for the necessity of this interview. She stands a little away from the chair and looks as if she might sit in his chair (invading his space). Klaus gestures again and she sits, pouring her body into the chair. She adjusts her dress, not by pulling at the hem but by smoothing her thighs. She leans back and puts her arms behind her head*]

to emphasize her breasts. Klaus raises his eyebrows and shrugs helplessly.]
— I suppose you know why I sent for you?
[*She smiles as if he were hinting at seduction. Then she lowers her head and flutters her eyelids. She looks up and holds eye contact and Klaus gulps.*]
— [*Suggestively*] Noooo . . .
[*Klaus indicates the newspaper with his eyes as if he wants nothing to do with it. He touches it with his fingernails as if to push it over to her, but then he picks it up, goes round the desk and squats beside her to show her the item. He lowers his voice.*]
— You know we can't employ anyone with a . . . [*Gulp*] . . . crim . . . criminal . . . re . . . re . . . record.
[*Nielsen presses his hand to her body.*]
— Won't you reconsider?
[*He moves as if to return to his chair, but throws the newspaper angrily into the waste-basket and veers away towards the window. He speaks emotionally, as if forcing the words out against his will.*]
— Good-bye, Nielsen.
[*Nielsen walks over to him and kisses him on the mouth.*]
— I didn't want your stupid job, anyway. [*She lowers her head and rests her cheek on his chest.*]

They were completely absorbed during the scene, and seemed quite different from their usual selves.

Using Combined Lists
Once the students are proficient, I set up three-character scenes in which each person plays two lists. Not all lists work in pairs, but seducing one person while giving someone else a bad time can be just like life.

I'll improvise such a scene. Liz will give her boyfriend Brian a bad time and play a To-Seduce list to Charlie; Brian will try to give Liz a good time while playing a To-be-Thought-Intelligent list to Charlie; Charlie will try to convince Liz that he's normal while getting sympathy from Brian.

— Liz: [*Hurling insult*] Idiot!
— Brian: Er . . . sorry.
— Liz: All over the floor.
— Brian: [*Offering help*] I'll clean it up. [*Being positive*] Floor needed scrubbing.

– Liz: Let me! [*To Charlie*] He can't do anything right.
[*She bends down to clean up the spill, giving Charlie a panorama of her behind.*]
– Brian: [*To impress Charlie*] I was thinking about my short story.
– Liz: You, a writer! He can't even spell.
– Brian: [*Agreeing with Liz and 'being intelligent' for Charlie*] True. It's because I'm left-handed. The non-verbal hemisphere, you know.
– Liz: [*Giving tasks*] Brian! Why don't you go in the kitchen and start the washing up?
– Charlie: [*Being normal*] Oh, should I help?
– Liz: No, you're the guest. Besides, Brian likes any task that's repetitive.
– Brian: [*To Charlie*] No problem, washing up. You just need time for the fats to dissolve . . .
– Liz: You're so full of it, Brian.
– Charlie: [*Being normal*] Really, shouldn't I help? Augh! [*He's banged his shin on the coffee-table to get sympathy from Brian.*]
– Liz: Oh, you poor thing.
– Brian: [*Knowing things*] Ice! [*Rummages in freezer*] Ice to prevent the haemorrhaging.
– Liz: [*Seducing Charlie*] Come and lie on the bed. You did make the bed, Brian?
– Brian: I put clean sheets on, dear.
– Liz: [*Complaining*] They were like a biscuit this morning!

An advanced student could start off playing one list and then gradually 'dissolve' to a second list. This may sound complicated but we achieve it effortlessly in real life when we are introduced to strangers and gradually revise our opinion of them.

Problems
Some students scan to find the best choice, rather than taking the first that they can make believable. If this continues, give them lists with only six activities.

Others choose incongruous activities as a way of getting laughs – persuade them only to accept 'items' that they can make truthful.

Some stay with one item (this minimizes transitions). Solve this by giving their lists to students who stay outside the scene and shout appropriate activities.

Lists as Performance Games

Lists aren't really suitable for public performance, but here are two games that I've used:

Announce each instruction loudly, in a detached way, before you obey it. The audience like to see you being controlled by some outside force, and if you've said that you will 'invade his space' or 'kill something', this introduces a pleasurable anticipation.

Enlist volunteers from the audience to read out the instructions. Tell them that we'd like some sort of story to emerge.

Coda

Lists are yet another device to stop the student from thinking ahead (because the moment you wonder, What now?, a glance at the list will give you the answer).

Lists 'give permission' for improvisers to be a bit rough with each other. Most professional actors treat each other rather like prisoners in high-security prisons (with politeness and extreme caution: 'I'm so sorry, did I nudge your elbow?' 'Oh, think nothing of it'). Sometimes these attitudes are imported into Theatresports but it's destructive when players have to treat each other as if made of glass (there is often practical joking between star actors on film sets in an attempt to break these barriers down). Rough-and-tumble, tickling and mock insults are all part of the game of friendship. Lists give permission for this. They also encourage players to abuse themselves, to weep, to confess that they are terrible in bed, that they're the one who forgot to close the air-lock, and so on.

When the students are truthful, it looks as if a genius is directing them – such accurate observations, such a profusion of transitions. The actor I mentioned earlier (p. 221) who moved up from B-movies to major roles in A-movies owned a set of Fast-Food lists. He consulted them whenever he read through a new script. Then he would say to a director, 'Would you like it like this?' and then 'Or like this?' or 'How about this way?', and they thought him infinitely flexible and imaginative.

In the absence of a great teacher (and how often will you find one of those?) students will at least learn that:

• Knowing the characters' purpose isn't enough – what really matters is how your character tries to achieve this purpose.
• A purpose can be valuable and transforming, even if you fail to achieve it.

• There is no 'best' purpose, and even if there was, it certainly couldn't be arrived at by an analysis of the text.

Lists work well with status transactions, and with Fast-Food Laban. Playwrights have found them useful. See Appendix One for a selection of Fast-Food Stanislavsky Lists.

The sooner you realize that you are playing a list in everyday life, the sooner you will be able to modify it (if necessary), or exchange it for a more agreeable one.

NOTES

1 Actors have noticed that when they have a cold, their character doesn't, and it's been clinically observed that although one multiple personality may have a severe allergy, another, sharing the same body, may not.
2 I often teach Fast-Food Laban together with Fast-Food Stanislavsky.
3 See p. 276.

13 Miscellaneous Games

Bell and Buzzer

This game reached us from Orlando. A volunteer is invited to cast the players as his family, and to ring a bell when they are on the right track, and to press a buzzer when their guesses are wrong.

- Oh, what a day! Is the tea on?
  [*BZZZZZ!*]
- I think I'll have a beer!
  [*RING!*]

It's proved an excellent addition to the Life Game. Some groups use it as a way to get laughs by thwarting the actors; for example:

- I think I'll get in the car.
  [*BZZZZZ!*]
- I won't get in the car.

I'd prefer to use it to remove pointless blocking; for example:

- I won't get in the car.
  [*BZZZZZ!*]
- I'll get in the car.
  [*RING!*]

Scenes with Fingers

Jim Curry (a Calgary improviser and playwright) invented this game when he landed a Frisbee on the stage, while making flying-saucer noises. Then he walked his middle and index fingers about the stage as if they were astronauts exploring a strange planet. He spoke dialogue for them using squeaky voices, and they interacted for a while. Then one said; 'According to my responder, there's an alien life form in that direction, Bill.'

Another player scrabbled his gloved hand towards Jim's hands which 'squeaked' in alarm, crying, 'Phasers on kill!'

The gloved hand leapt on to 'Bill', but Joe 'fired', and it flopped over on to its 'back' and lay motionless.

– What a remarkable creature.
– Yes. A sort of mammalian spider. The pelt may be valuable.

While they were 'skinning' the glove away from the hand they heard a tiny scream, and turned to see a nude Barbie-doll (walked on by a third improviser): 'You've killed my poor Glorp! Father will punish you!'

Improvisers from both teams crept onstage, each operating a pair of finger creatures: 'Seize the earthlings, and take them to the palace . . .'

Suddenly a gigantic hand – that just happened to be backstage – thrust through the curtains, and the 'attackers' all 'knelt' as if it were God . . .

And so on.

No one ever gets self-conscious about the acting ability of their middle and index fingers, so the 'operators' become absorbed almost instantly (i.e. undefended against the eyes of the onlookers), and they become fascinating to watch. Don't hide them.

'Finger characters' should be happy and perky and speak in tiny voices. This is not an important game, and it's only suitable for smallish theatres with good sight-lines, but it's unlikely to resemble anything else that the audience has seen.

In a recent unconnected game an improviser 'drank a potion' that turned her into a giant. Her companions fell to the ground, screamed in squeaky voices, and ran their fingers across the stage as the giant pursued them in slow-motion. This delighted the spectators.

People as Objects

Improvisers become chairs, tables, telephones (or whatever else is needed) for the players in a scene.

This is a traditional mime game.

Most players enjoy being a bench for someone to sit on, or a polar-bear rug, or a shower, and no one worries whether their mime is 'good'. There's a generosity about offering yourself in this way that puts everyone in good mood. One of our players caused a sensation at an 'away' tournament by spending an entire scene as an armchair. His hosts, used to seeing even their 'corpses' leap back to life after a few seconds, were astonished.

People can be waxworks, or statues, or mirrors, or chairs, or sofas, or foot-stools, or projections in a slide-show, or horses carrying their riders piggy-back.

People as Objects is seldom used as a challenge (it's too repetitive), but it's always available as a way to spice up other games, and it will sometimes appear in the guise of: 'We challenge you to the best use of the other team!'

Dennis's Puppet Show

Dennis Cahill (Artistic Director of Loose Moose) invents a story for glove-puppets that are operated by two audience volunteers.

You need a puppet theatre. Ours is made of three folding sections with an oblong hole in the centre, but you could improvise one – over the back of a sofa, perhaps. The important thing is that the puppeteers are hidden (because it's more fun to imagine their difficulties).

Someone 'backstage' hands puppets to the volunteers, whispers advice, and hold a microphone for them.

Dennis's 'showman' character is so jaded and disillusioned that it doesn't matter if the puppets are inept or stiff with fright, but most volunteers soon become uninhibited, and the spectators are eager to reward them.

Changing the Object

This was a mime exercise from France: students sat in a circle and passed a mimed object from one to another, altering it each time. For example, if you accepted a mimed ice-cream, you licked it, and then changed it to something else – an envelope, perhaps. Anyone who 'couldn't get an idea' was exposed as 'unimaginative' and the game became a training exercise in 'not being spontaneous'.

Taught with kindness, it can become an excellent way to teach the students to relax, and to ease up on their intellectual control.

Asked how they feel when the object is approaching them, the players describe their anxiety as rising to a peak, and then falling almost to zero as the object moves on around the circle. Discussing their fear releases some laughter – they hadn't realized that everyone was under the same pressure.

'Has anyone studied mime?'

Two students identify themselves (not joyously).

'The game will be especially unnerving for you,' I say, 'because you'll be demanding more of yourselves. And you'll be tempted to fall back on old material.'

This amazes the absolute beginners who were sure that the more experienced students would feel the least stress.

'How can you succeed at this game?' I ask, and they explain the trick of thinking ahead.

'But what if you intend to change into a mouse, and it's handed to you as a mouse?'

They laugh again – students always laugh when I discuss their anxieties.

'Improvisation is about spontaneity,' I say. 'So keep a blank mind, and if ideas occur to you, let them float in one ear and out of the other.'

'But what if our minds are blank when our turn comes?'

'Handle the object. If it's a piece of gum, don't just mime chewing it: roll in into a ball, pull it into pieces, stretch it. Observe it in a disinterested way. If you stretch it, you may suddenly be taking off a surgical glove, but don't force anything. If it doesn't want to alter, pass it on "as is". Then the rest of us won't feel so bad when we can't get an idea.'

This makes them laugh again.

Someone is handed the mimed object and starts to panic (inwardly).

'Don't think! Shake it, and press it, and feel its weight, and rotate it, and stroke it. See what happens.'

I point out that their imperfect mime makes any mimed object seem to be altering: that their alarm-clock is getting smaller as they wind it up, and that their yo-yo resembles a bouncing ball.

'The only people that we'll be sure have the right attitude are those who don't change the object – because the rest of us may be pre-planning.'

They laugh at my definition of 'failure' as 'success', and most of their anxiety disappears.

'But what if we're bad at mime?'

'Tell us what the object has become and we'll be impressed by your good nature and humility – no one says you have to be wonderful mimes.'

If I can detach their egos from success and failure, ideas will come in profusion: a fisherman casting a line will become a cowboy lassoing a horse; a weightlifter will be transformed into an acrobat hanging from a trapeze.

Someone claims to be stumped by this exercise, so I ask him to handle a mimed stick and it looks as if it'll turn into a bow. He moves it to the side and it looks as if he's waving a flag. He gives up and makes a hopeless gesture and it looks as if he's releasing a bird. I draw his attention to this, and make him laugh, and suddenly the game presents no problems for him.

Changing Real Objects

Tom Osborn (who was a reader at the Royal Court Theatre and is a playwright) introduced real objects into the game. A walking-stick can become an umbrella, a harpoon, or an ear-cleaner. Remove a pin from a shoe and it can become a grenade. Clutch a chair to your chest and it can be used as a set of bagpipes.

I like to work with a heap of props at the side of the stage, and their transformations can be magical. A bench can become a canoe; a sofa can become a pool to dive in to; a boat can be up-ended and used as a shrine. Handle the objects, instead of thinking what to change them into, and they'll change of their own accord.

Invite the audience to donate props for the players to transform.

Mimes usually baffle me: I see them as rubbing their eyes when they're actually miming binoculars; when they do 'the wall', I'm likely to think they're cavemen making handprints. But I'm never confused when someone uses a brick as a camera, or a shoe as a telephone.

14 Entertainment Games

I'm not saying that other games aren't entertaining, but these were 'pot-boilers' for when we were in trouble. You can play Master–Servant games for ever without boring people, but these games are so specific that they soon outstay their welcome.

Stealing

This is a spin-off of the Making Faces Game. The master looks away so that the servant can steal. Give the servant a huge coat (with extra pockets sewn into the lining?) or an over-large boiler-suit. This game was important to us when we travelled from city to city, playing to audiences who knew no English.

[*A table is piled high with 'junk' (nothing breakable).*]
– Next patient, please.
[*Pat enters, very happy and 'positive'. He could be wearing a 'man-mask' or a fright-wig plus false nose.*]
– Take a chair.
[*Pat picks up a chair.*]
– What are you doing?
– You said take a chair.
– No, no! Sit down! [*Turning away*] I'll just get your file.
[*Pat very deftly takes a doll, a hot-water bottle, and a length of red tubing, and stuffs them into his clothing. The Doctor turns back.*]
– [*Pat is holding a kettle*] Do you use this for sterilizing things? [*Puts kettle back on table and hides the tubing that was protruding from his coat.*]
– Yes. Germs, you know. Pesky little . . .
[*Doctor just misses seeing the stealing of a large airship balloon and a book.*]
– Where's my mutator? [*Pressing buzzer*] Nurse!
[*Someone replies from the team-bench.*]

– Yes, Doctor?

– Have you seen my mutator?

[*A pen and a whistle are palmed from under the Doctor's nose.*]

– It should be on the shelf, Doctor.

[*More items are stolen and the boiler-suit is beginning to look like a 'fat-suit'.*]

– Where did I put the confounded thing?

[*Looks under desk for his mutator allowing Pat to steal more props, one of which falls on the Doctor's head.*]

– Will you keep your hands off my desk!

[*An explosion as the balloon pops.*]

– What was that?

– Explosions, Doctor. It's what I've come to see you about! They wake me up at night! They frighten people in elevators.

[*The Doctor turns to the cupboard to consult a book about this rare affliction. Pat stuffs more objects away but now some are re-emerging and having to be pushed back in – an umbrella is sticking out of a trouser leg and a flag is poking out of his neck.*]

– Just as I thought – it's the digestive system.

[*He turns and sees Pat stealing something.*]

– Put that back!

– [*Innocently*] Doctor?

– I'll turn around and when I turn back I'd like to see it on my desk where it belongs.

[*He turns away. The item is replaced but four more things are taken.*]

– [*Turning back*] Thank-you.

If something bulges visibly from Pat's clothing, the Doctor must protest, and retrieve it. One of the pleasures of the game is seeing the irate Doctor reclaiming items from a patient who is apologizing sincerely while managing to steal yet more (by picking the Doctor's pockets, and so on). A particular delight is seeing the Doctor shaking Pat (perhaps holding him upside down) while dozens of objects clatter to the stage.

John Breem at our International Summer School ended the scene by cramming the Doctor into his boiler-suit.

The Knife Game

The improvisers remove their skins and emerge as 'new' creatures. This game is seldom used, but it's useful as a symbol for the 'concealed self', or for sex, or as a way to become aliens in sci-fi scenes.

I was teaching Face Wipe, a children's game that involves passing your hand in front of your face and altering each feature as it's obscured (the effect is of replacing one mask with another), when I thought, Why not the entire body?

Handle a mimed knife as if it's very sharp. Perhaps mime throwing it at the wall. Hold it with both hands, blade facing upwards. Pretend to be under mental stress. Delay for a moment and then ram the blade deep into your forehead. Scream as if you're in terrible agony, and recover. Seize the hilt and pull the knife blade down your face and torso, keeping it at right-angles to the flesh (careful at the groin) and on down one leg, screaming or groaning. Pull the knife out and place it on an imaginary surface. Breathe easier. The onlookers will be baffled, but very attentive (they want this mystery to be solved).

Mime pressing your fingers into the start of the slit and rip the edges apart with lots of birthy gasping and groaning. Cry, scream, howl (such sounds release emotion in the onlookers) as you slip a new and distorted face out of your skin, each feature grotesque as it emerges. Use one arm to drag the other out of its sleeve. Now use this deformed arm to extract its twin. Roll your skin down your body, making excited sounds, as if the experience were intensely pleasurable. Peel off the skin like a pair of tights. Hang it on a hook or fold it up. Stroke your new body. Be delighted with it. Gloat at yourself in a mirror. Leap about gleefully and with enormous energy.

Examples from Performance

The parents leave and the sweet teenage babysitter admits her boyfriend stealthily, saying, 'Did you bring the knives?'

The audience are gripped by the mystery of this, and when the teenagers remove their skins the effect is shocking.

Perhaps the child wakes up. Perhaps the parents are heard returning. Perhaps there's a mix-up with the skins as they climb into them again.

Another example: Peter carries his bride over the threshold of the motel room. They are rather shy. They check the bed, the view, the bathroom, the Gideon Bible, and so on. Finally she says:

– Did you bring the . . . you know . . . Peter?
– [*He mimes opening a box of knives, and hands her one.*] Chrome steel!

- Inlaid with mother of pearl. How beautiful.
- It's been in the family.
- An heirloom!

Perhaps they delay a little. Perhaps one weeps and is consoled by the other. And then:

- Shall we start?
- Do me first, Peter.
- Oh, God, how it excites me when you say that.
- Yes, dearest, but you will be gentle?
- You know I'd never hurt my precious darling.
- Do it then! Do it now.
  [*She screams as he stabs her in the forehead with terrible violence, and removes her skin.*]

'More sounds,' I shout. 'Be more reptilian!'
She becomes a terrible hissing lizard-thing who throws him down and slits open his body, and tears him out of *his* skin.

The effect is eerie, psychotic and intensely sexual. Do it well and it's an image of astounding violence. Save it for special occasions.

Perhaps the lizards smoke a cigarette. Or perhaps room-service arrives and they skin him as well – there are lots of permutations.

Variant: a student discovers that his room-mate is an alien. Someone discovers that their lover is a snake person who is sloughing a skin. One partner refuses to do it and gets skinned forcibly.

Hand on Knee

Roddy Maude-Roxby (of the Theatre Machine) discovered that if he placed his hand on the knee of a woman sitting to one side of him, while talking to someone sitting to his other side, this hand would be allowed to remain there, as if it had become dissociated from its owner.

'We can get a game out of that,' I said.

Martin, Neil and Stephanie sit side-by-side on plain chairs that have the edges touching. They pretend to be on a train. Neil sits on the middle chair and whenever he speaks to one of his partners he places a hand on the other's knee, seeming to have no awareness of this.

I make him do the action of talking to one partner while placing his hand on the other's knee fifteen to twenty times, getting faster each time. This seems silly, yet without this drill he would either place his hand on the knee of the person he was talking to or would forget to place it anywhere.

Then I say, 'I want a scene in which Neil disconcerts the others with his hand-on-knee trick. Start low-key, but build up to paroxysms of rage and embarrassment. Neil's character has no awareness of what he's doing, so he sees himself as being tormented by you.'

Stephanie and Martin have had time to plan their response so she cries, 'How dare you!' and Martin pretends to enjoy the sensation.

I tell them that 'normal people' are reluctant to create a scene, and that when TV programmes play jokes on people the victims are usually inexpressive, that it's only when they believe themselves to be alone that they respond uninhibitedly.

'That's true!' said a student when I was inventing the game. 'That's why I was late this morning.'

She told us that a seat on the train had felt rather uncomfortable, but that it had taken her a while to realize that she was sitting on the hand of the man next to her.

'What did you do?'

'I behaved as if it wasn't happening and then I got out at the next station.'

I ask them to pretend that they're quite unprepared for this hand-on-knee outrage.

'Be baffled,' I say. 'Ask yourself, "Is Neil mad? Or just eccentric? Have the other passengers noticed?" Try to behave like normal people.'

They start again and Neil puts his hand on Stephanie's knee.

'Not yet!' I say. 'Take your time. Establish being on a train. Look at the adverts. Look out of the window. Read the paper. Be a little shy. Let the spectators wonder why we're showing them this tableau.'

Now they seem like ordinary, slightly bored passengers. We have time to look at them before Neil says something to Stephanie and rests his hand on Martin's knee.

'Have we passed Birmingham?'

'Er . . . er . . . I don't think so . . .'

Neil continues this conversation, hoping that Martin will do something but I interrupt.

'Don't get stuck talking to Stephanie,' I say. 'Confuse them by saying just a few words before looking out front again. This removes the problem before the abused person can decide what to do about it. Stare straight ahead while they wonder if it really happened.'

They start again:

'Are those local cows?' says Neil to Stephanie, resting his hand on Martin's knee.

'I really have no idea.'

Martin hasn't moved a muscle except to lower his eyes to look at Neil's hand. Neil removes it and looks straight ahead. Martin stares out of the window, slightly ruffled. Neil turns to him, placing a hand on Stephanie's knee: 'Do know if we've passed Birmingham?'

'It's three more stations!' says Martin, tersely, while Stephanie pretends that no violation is occurring.

'Plonk your hand down more firmly,' I say.

Neil plonks his hand on Martin's knee and talks to Stephanie. 'We haven't passed Birmingham, after all. That's a relief.'

His victims are looking enraged so I tell him to stare straight ahead.

'Let them simmer for a while,' I say. 'Tease us with the delay.'

Martin crosses his legs away from Neil.

'Don't do that,' I say. 'Don't make it harder for Neil to place his hand on you. Pretend that there's a wall beside you so that if you crossed your legs like that, they'd be sticking through the side of the train.'

Stephanie looks blank, but she gulps once, and pulls her skirt down about half an inch. Everyone jogs up and down with the motion of the train.

'I suppose we are stopping at Birmingham,' says Neil to Stephanie, as he clasps Martin's knee.

'Excuse me!' says Martin, and Neil turns to him and grips Stephanie's knee.

'Yes?'

'Oh . . . nothing,' says Martin, being British.

'How wonderful the trees look in the autumn,' says Neil, addressing Martin. Stephanie decides to ignore his hand.

'Squeeze her knee!' I say. 'Make her jump!'

He obeys and she gives a squeal. He swivels towards her.

'Yes' he says, clamping on to Martin's knee.

'Look! Just stop that!' says Martin.

'Stop what?' says Neil, clamping on to Stephanie.

'Behave yourself!' she screeches.

'That's right!' adds Martin.

I shout to Neil to become neutral again. Now there are three ruffled people for us to study. This pause can be sustained for quite a while.

'What do you mean, "behave myself"?' says Neil, clasping Stephanie but addressing Martin. She lifts Neil's hand and places it on his own knee, but he doesn't react (he's too busy planning what to say), so I interrupt.

'Go back to where she touches your hand. If a stranger touched your hand on a train you'd certainly notice!'

We return the scene to that moment.

'Yes?' says Neil.

'Keep your hands to yourself!'

'You touched me!' says Neil.

'Oh, leave me alone!' she says.

Martin glares angrily at the back of Neil's head.

'Squeeze Martin's knee harder!' I say. 'Force him to do something!'

'Stop it!' growls Martin, grabbing the offending hand and plonking it on Neil's own knee.

'Are you mad?' says Neil, clamping on to Stephanie who bursts into tears.

'I've had enough of this!' says Martin. 'And stop pestering this young lady!'

'What are you on about?' gasps Neil, glancing front for a moment as if he believed he were sitting between two mad people. Then he turns to Martin.

'Look I don't know what . . .'

Stephanie screams and tries to pry his fingers away.

'Augh!' cries Neil, outraged that she's bending his fingers, but hanging on to Martin's leg for dear life as Martin stands up and shouts, 'Sir!'

'Yes?' says Neil, turning to Martin and grabbing Stephanie, who screams and hits him with her purse.

'Hey!' protests Neil, turning to her and grabbing Martin.

'Will you leave her alone!'

'What?' says Neil, turning to Martin.

Stephanie starts shrieking: 'Stop it! Stop it!'

'Stop what?'

Martin grabs both of Neil's hands: 'Pack it in or I'll throw you off the train!'

All three sit fuming, with Neil staring straight ahead. He glances at Martin but says nothing. He looks front.

Perhaps a ticket collector could arrive, or Neil could become terrified as he understands that it really is all his fault (I've never seen that).

Perhaps Martin could insist on changing places with Neil (for Stephanie's protection). He could then turn to Neil and say something like 'You really must learn to control yourself!', clasping Stephanie's knee as the lights fade – but don't build this ending into the game.

Played for laughs, Hand on Knee is pure filler and we'll have no sympathy for the characters, and yet, if the players attend to what's happening moment by moment, their struggle to be normal can be memorable (as well as very funny).

It's not a game that you'd want to see more than once a year.

Spasms

One player spasms at irregular intervals, while giving a loud shriek. He/she has no awareness of doing this. The pay-off lies in the effect on his/her partner.

We saw this game when it was used as a 'front-curtain' scene to cover a set-change at a Christmas pantomime. I imagine that it's an ancient lazzi (comedians' trick) that never went out of favour.

Tom and Deborah enter from opposite sides of the stage, pass each other as strangers, and double-take as they realize that they know each other. They greet each other effusively and swap information, but suddenly Tom shrieks and spasms. He continues to do this at irregular intervals, unaware that he's behaving strangely, but baffled by Deborah's reactions to him. He accuses her of acting strangely, and she tries to explain what he's doing by demonstrating the spasms. Soon they are both spasming, and getting angrier (or happier) until they exit, perhaps one pursued by the other, and accompanied by gales of laughter from the spectators (we hope).

How to Spasm
The sound must be elated, and the spasm should open the body, rather than contracting it. It should really convey a moment of manic happiness, because if the effect is grotesque it may excite horror rather than laughter.

If the mood takes you, line up the players and have them spasm for the onlookers who can choose the preferred spasm by acclamation (hold your hand over each player's head in turn and say, 'Applaud').

Left to themselves, beginners will gradually subdue the spasms and shrieks (losing confidence), but the effect should be identical each time.

Timing the Spasms

We have a slow and regular inner rhythm that most of us are quite unaware of. I encourage independence from this rhythm by telling trainees only to spasm when I clap, and then I deliberately clap at moments when they'd prefer me not to. For example, two players are whispering as they break into a house:

- Careful.
- It's so dark in here.
- Where's the flashlight?
  [*Clap!*]
- Yagggurrrach!
- Ssssh!
- What?
  [*Clap!*]
- Yagggurrrach!
- Will you shut up!
- Shut up What?
- The noise. Pack it in!
- What are you talking about?
  [*They are both expecting me to clap but I ignore them.*]
- Where does he keep the photographs?
- In the desk. It's . . . [*Clap!*] Yagggurrrach! . . . over there!
- Will you shut up? Idiot!
- I'm not doing anything . . . [*Clap!*] Yagggurrrach!
- There! That 'Yagggurrrach' stuff!
- What 'Yagggurrrach' stuff? [*Clap!*] Yagggurrrach!
- There! You did it again!
- Get your hand off my mouth, I can't breathe.
- Well stop going 'Yagggurrrach!'
- Who's going 'Yagggurrrach'?
- You are! You're flapping your arms and going 'Yaggurrrach!'
- Yagggurrrach?
- Yes, yagggurrrach. Will you stop yelling? [*Clap!*]
- Yagggurrrach! You're the one that's doing the . . . [*Clap!*]
  Yagggurrrach . . . yelling.
  And so on.

Variant: the spasmer starts to believe his/her partner. I've never seen this, and I won't unless I force it to happen (improvisers hate 'losing control').

Paper-Flicking

A high-status interviewer offers the earth to a job applicant, while unconsciously abusing him/her.

This was inspired by the Spasm Game.

Stephen – let's make him a destitute actor – is interviewed by an enthusiastic agent who promises him fame and fortune. He seems about to escape from poverty, misery and endless rejection. The agent writes information down about him – phone number, address, and so on – oozing approval, but rips out the pages as soon as he's written on them, screwing then into tight little paper balls and hurling them violently at Stephen's face (at unpredictable intervals).

Not only is Stephen being abused, but the information about him is being destroyed. He leaps up in rage, but I interrupt.

'You need this job!' I say. 'You can't pay the rent. You've got children to feed. Maybe this is some sort of test.'

I start the scene again, and perhaps the next few hits are ignored, but then we get interactions like:

– Ow!
– I'm sorry?
– You hit me in the eye!
– I what?
– You threw a piece of paper and hit me in the eye!
– My dear Mr . . . [*He looks at his notes.*]
– Southwold. My name. You won't find it there.
– But I just wrote it down.
– That was before you tore it off and threw it at me.
– Impossible!
  [*The agent writes the name again.*]
– South . . . wold . . . Have you been under a lot of stress lately?
– No, no . . . Not at all . . .
– Because until now everything about you has suggested that you are exactly the sort of person we need. In fact, with your qualifications we should certainly raise your starting salary. [*He hurls another paper ball savagely and accurately.*]

- Augh! Look! Look!
- Something the matter?
- Er . . . No . . . Nothing . . . Perhaps I could give you my phone number again?
- Fire away!
  [*Southwold unwraps a paper ball and pushes it gently across the desk.*]
- Why would I want this?
- It's my phone number.
- But I just wrote down your phone number.
- [*Weeping*] Please take it!
- There's no need to get hysterical.
- You said I was perfect for this job!
- So you were.
- Well, then, for God's sake . . .
- So it seemed!

Encourage the agent to screw the balls of paper tightly, and to throw them so that they sting (hurled with a cry of violent rage, perhaps). They must be thrown at unpredictable intervals. He/she should switch between insane violence as he throws and total approval. The audience want many paper balls to be thrown, so why not prepare some ahead of time and hide them under the papers on the desk?

The victim could try to join in with the joke.

- Ha! Ha!
- I beg your pardon?
- Very funny!
- I don't follow?
  [*The victim hurls one of the paper balls back.*]
- My dear sir – we can't possibly employ anyone who is mentally unstable in an explosives factory!

The agent must believe him/herself to be acting with kindness and generosity, and the victim must be desperate for the job.

Variant: a woman could be totally receptive to a suitor while hitting him with a club at unpredictable intervals.

Speech Defect Game

Two characters each believe wrongly that the other is mocking his/her articulation. They quarrel, discover the truth, and make friends. An audience that has laughed hysterically at the quarrel can weep when the characters are reconciled, and we should milk this pathos or the game may seem cruel.

I took this from a story by Wilhelm Bochert called Sysssyphusss in which the writer described a quarrel between his uncle and a waiter, each of whom was missing a piece of his tongue.

Ask the players to speak with their tongues in their cheeks. Make sure that about a quarter to a third of everything they say is unintelligible – spoken in gibberish.

I explain to the waiter that he has always had this terrible speech defect, and that although people are sympathetic – at least to his face – this is the day that a customer taunts him:

'Try not to be offended – do your job as a waiter – but the customer goes on and on until it drives you crazy and you throw her out.'

Then I explain to the customer that she's desperate for food, and that all the other restaurants are closed:

'Life is difficult because of your speech defect,' I say: 'Even though people are usually sympathetic, this waiter insists on making fun of you until eventually you can't stand it any more, and you become enraged.'

I tell them to build their antagonism to a ferocious climax and then realize that for the first time in their lives, they've met a fellow-sufferer.

Include a 'passenger' – a customer who does only the minimum that is necessary, replying if spoken to, but concentrating on ordering and eating a meal.

It's important that the first lines of dialogue do not cause offence. If the players register the 'insult' right away they'll have nowhere to go:

– Good evening, madam . . .
– Are you imitating me?

Side-coach the scene to keep it 'truthful'. To hold back the climax and to ensure that the reconciliation is passionate.

'Try to be polite to this customer!' I shout, when the waiter seems about to get belligerent. And then, 'Put up with this waiter because you are so desperately hungry. Get sympathy from the passenger when the waiter is offstage. Passenger – say less! Be non-committal! Waiter – start boiling with rage but suppress the emotion. Passenger – ask for pudding . . .' And so on until the fury is uncontainable.

'Customer – lose control . . . Burst into tears! Waiter – realize that your partner has the same affliction. No one was mocking you! Comment to the passenger. Passenger, say nothing! Waiter – ask to see her tongue. Show her yours! Pour the cognac! Get another chair and join her at the table! Weep for joy. Passenger – ask for coffee. Waiter – put the closed sign on the door . . .'

Maybe the passenger is invited to join in the celebration. Perhaps the waiter phones his mother to tell her he's not alone with his affliction. Build a climax of tremendous positive emotion. Perhaps they discover they're brother and sister.

I'm told that Bochet performed in cabaret clubs. If so, it's possible that he took this 'game' from the theatre, and that I've taken it back.

15 Technical Stuff

Judges

Function

The Judges are responsible for raising the quality of the game, and for intervening where necessary, for example:

'You accepted a challenge to a scene about nuclear power, but you're presenting a knitting competition! Do you really expect a high score for that?'

They score the scenes, adjudicate disputes and keep things moving (in the Judges' Challenge Match they also set the challenges). They should raise their scorecards quickly, even if some of their decisions are later determined to have been 'wrong'. We want them to be objective and fair, but nobody's perfect.

If a team baulks at a challenge, the Judges must uphold or deny this baulk. If a team is slow setting up a scene, the Judges must start counting them out, from five to zero.

Judges as Parental Figures

Judges should be seen as parental figures who are taking their responsibilities seriously. They can be good natured and friendly, but their task is not to be loved or to be amusing. They are there to be abused, and just occasionally to be admired. They can be pleased if a really wonderful scene occurs – but they should be too 'adult' to cheer and leap up and down with the rest of the onlookers.

Unless Judges are treated with respect, the quality of the match will suffer, and yet they're often abused, and some groups confine them to supervising the coin-toss and scoring the scenes. I've seen a team 'spin' a Judge to see who should make the first challenge. I've seen Judges dragged out of their seats and kidnapped as a 'joke'. I've seen Judges collude in their disparagement by dressing up as blind men and tapping their way across the stage. I've seen a Judge hold up the five card and then sit on it as a sign that he won't give high scores – which is ridiculous since the audience want high scores.

Everyone wants to be a comedian – the ushers, the commentator, the Judges, the people in concessions – but we should leave that to the players.

Judges should be in opposition to the players' playfulness, but they should not succeed in stamping it out.

Who Should Judge?

Some non-players make excellent judges, but in general, members of the public are too indulgent, giving almost every scene a high score. Try people out, and encourage them to express their own opinion rather than being subservient to the audience. Realize that a weak Judge may make eccentric decisions just to prove that he isn't weak. Be reluctant to use a Judge who seems weird, and who gives aberrant scores.

Celebrity Judges

Invite talk-show hosts, anchor-persons, journalists, and so on to be celebrity Judges. Appoint a warm, friendly person as their host, and give them flowers, free drinks and Theatresports memorabilia and write them a letter of appreciation afterwards.

It's wasteful to use more than one celebrity Judge, and as celebrities will almost always score everything high, it's better for the other Judges to be experts.

How Many Judges?

We use three Judges, so that there will be a third to break a tie between the other two (and in the hope that biases will cancel out).

In an emergency, you can use two Judges, or even one Judge (by agreement between the teams).

How Should They Look?

Some sort of costume may be helpful (but not a stupid one) – ours wear robes – and they should enter as a group rather than as individuals.

How to Introduce Them

I've heard commentators say, 'And here they come, these scum, these sleaze bags . . .', but if the Judges are treated this way, how can they exercise any authority? We want our audience to boo the Judges, but not to despise them. The commentator should introduce them by saying, 'And now, the traditional boo for the Judges, please!'

Where to Sit Them

If possible, sit them at the centre of the front row. This gives them a good view, allows them to relate equally to each other, and ensures that the audience can easily see the scorecards when they're held up.

Some groups place their Judges at the rear of the audience, but when Judges wish to stand up and defend some controversial decision they should be visible without the spectators having to crane their necks. (The spectators are twice as loud when screaming abuse at a Judge who has the courage to confront them.) I've seen Judges sitting onstage so that the audience could throw wet sponges at them, a horrible idea which signalled that there would be nothing worth watching and that everything would be stupid.

Nobody's Perfect

Incompetent improvisers may become enraged with what they consider a bad judgment ('we woz robbed!'), but I undermine them by saying that everyone is supposed to screw-up at least twice in every game, including the Judges.

It's difficult for some players to grasp that unpopular decisions can have a positive effect. The spectators get to discharge a lot of pent-up aggression that they might otherwise vent on their families. If referees were always perceived as 'right', sport would be less interesting.

When Theatresports is working well, it's as if the audience and the players are on one team, and the Judges are on the other. Unpopular decisions by the Judges help to consolidate this togetherness.

Weak Judges

Weak Judges will toy longingly with their rescue horns while scenes die a lingering death (a honk loses a team the stage). They're either afraid to annoy the performers or they believe that the audience is still enjoying the scene, even though it may be only friends of the cast who are laughing, or the 'groupies'.

Conversely, some weak Judges will end a scene if there's no laughter, even though it may be thrilling the spectators. A Keyboard scene presented a motorist stranded late at night near a farmhouse. He asked for a bed, and a sinister old woman showed him to a room and told him not to be alarmed if he heard strange sounds. The audience was enthralled, but their silence so unnerved a Judge that he called out, 'Ten seconds!' as a warning to them to finish. The audience booed and hissed because they wanted to know what would happen. The typist typed, in despair, 'Suddenly his head exploded,' the music improvisor threw in an explosion and the old woman stuck her head through the curtains and said, 'All right kids, supper's up!' So the scene ended wittily, but no thanks to the Judge.

Serious or melodramatic scenes, or scenes with pathos, are useful in giving the audience a breathing space, and Judges should not 'honk' them unless they're boring. A silent audience may be enthralled, as you'll find out if you trash a scene that they're absorbed in.

The Need for Strong Judges

If the audience has been enraged because a popular scene was given a warning, a weak Judge will let the next scene drag on, no matter how ghastly it is. Judges must not be quelled by the audience's antagonism.

Strong Judges do not look to see what scorecards their colleagues are about to raise before raising their own, and they do not see themselves as representatives of the audience. A scene should be thrown off when a Judge is bored – why wait until the audience is bored?

Judges who are afraid to eject teams will express their resentment by giving low scores, yet why should the audience have to endure second-rate work? A scene that is awarded a one should have been honked off. If a low score seems warranted, a Judge should consider waving down the lights or giving a Warning for Boring. Try to give high scores: it's not only the improvisers who should be taking risks.

Judges as Coaches

If the Judges are knowledgable, it's silly for them to be 'honking' scene after scene when a little advice might calm the players and set them on the right track. This is why we should never diminish their powers, or let ignorant people be Judges (except for the occasional celebrity). For example, if the players in the Hat-Game are at opposite sides of the stage, the Judges should certainly say' 'Move closer together, please!' or 'Enter a small elevator together!'

Strong Judges can say, 'We'll throw off the next scene in which the players are deliberately stupid!' or 'We'll remove Butch from the match if he's offensive one more time!' or 'We're bored with these challenges!

How about a challenge we've never seen before?' or 'We're sick of trivia. Please challenge on something that a reasonable person might care about!' or 'We're tired of every player being in every scene.'

If a team is breaking promises – working outside the frame – the Judges should bring them inside the frame; for example: 'It's been established that this scene will involve an execution – so why aren't you executing someone?' or 'You accepted the suggestion "Using jack-hammers", so why aren't you?'

During a wretched one-on-one rhyming scene a Judge stood up and said, 'There's nothing to judge. Can we please see this game with two other players?'

If a scene is distasteful – say about vomiting or dog-shit – it should be taken back to the point where the negativity took over (or to the beginning, if necessary).

Judges who intervene are affirming their responsibility for the quality of the work. Frightened Judges or emcees never intervene when things are failing.

Hell-Judges

Judges may be thinking so hard about a scene that they don't realize that they're bored (I swear this is true), or they may be itching to give a Warning for Boring and yet be anxious to give the improvisers 'one more chance'. It follows that rescue Horns are usually honked minutes late.

As a corrective to this, I place a red light in the Judges' view and place another red light in front of the lighting improvisor. These are controlled by the Hell-Judges – improvisers who are not playing in this particular match, and who are sitting at the rear of the audience. If they see a reasonable moment to fade the lights, they signal the lighting booth: if they're bored, they signal the regular Judges.

As these signals don't have to be obeyed, the Hell-Judges' responsi-bility is so minuscule that they're almost exactly like members of the audience. They're not tormented by thoughts like, Should this continue a fraction longer? and Is this becoming too negative? They just record the fact that they've seen enough.

Judges who are enjoying a scene will ignore the light even if it flashes persistently, but sometime the first gleam is enough to make them realize that they're bored too. And if a Judge is giving too many warnings, the absence of red lights can act as a restraint.

No one really knows who's making the decisions (perhaps the regular Judges are obeying every red light, but perhaps they aren't) so the players don't take harsh judgments so personally.

Technical Judges

Many years ago we used a Technical Judge, a Narrative Judge and an Entertainment Judge. This was confusing and ineffective, so we abandoned it after a few weeks, but some groups still continue with the idea, even though it doesn't work for them either.

Penalties

Penalties used to involve sitting for two minutes beside the scoreboard with your head in brown-paper supermarket bag. The audience would yell, 'Bag him! Bag him!' when a player offended them. Players with claustrophobia hated the bags (even though we cut air-holes) so I replaced them with head-shaped wicker baskets that allowed limited vision through the cracks, but cries of 'Basket! Basket!' don't have quite the same percussive quality

Some groups use paper bags and cut holes for the miscreant's face, but the punishment should involve an obliteration of the face or the effect is distracting.

Other groups punish a performer by making him/her wear a basket as a character in the next scene (uptight improvisers can't bear not being on stage), but this is no longer even a symbolic punishment since the miscreant gets the 'starring role' so don't do this.

Penalty baskets are awarded for anti-social behaviour, for the inappropriate breaking of taboos, for interfering with the work of the other team, and so on. If in doubt, consult the audience: 'Did that deserve a basket?'

Even very shy people are likely to roar loudly in response to such a question, but if the offence is blatant, the Judges should make the decision themselves. Judges who always consult the audience weaken their authority.

Even spectators can be penalized (for example, if they yell out something objectionable). There's too much peer pressure for them to refuse, but how odd to go to the theatre and be made to sit with your head in a basket.

Baskets seldom affect a team's final score. Their main purpose is to mollify anyone who might have been offended. Sitting with your head in a basket for a couple of minutes 'wipes the slate clean'. Can you devise an easier way to remove the 'bad taste' from everyone's mouth?

We asked an audience member what she'd done during the day (so that we could base a scene on it), and she told us that she was a priest and had woken up early because she had to give a sermon. Our version was unforgettable (this was a decade ago): her alarm-clock played loud church-bells, she showered still wearing her nightie, her breakfast arrived with a shower of loaves and fishes, and so on. Finally the Hindu improvisor who was embodying her gave a sermon that was passionate, impressive, hushed, condemning, affirming, and so on, but based entirely on various renditions of the word 'Bullshit!', so we awarded our first-ever 'basket for blasphemy', not because the priest might have been offended (she insisted she wasn't), but because other members of the audience might have been, or might have presumed her to be.

Whenever possible, baskets should be delayed until the scene is over. Think of them as absolution, and as yet another way to add variety.

Ejection from the Game

Baskets are reminders that certain behaviour is unacceptable, and they should be respected. A player swore, and on receiving a basket, spelled the obscenity out, letter by letter ('being funny?'). The Judges threw him out of the game.

Counting Out

Some teams waste time searching for props, or struggling into costume, or getting suggestions, or coaxing volunteers on to the stage. If the Judges or the commentator are conscious of a delay, they should 'count the team out' from five to zero. The commentator (or the audience) can begin the 'count' but the Judges are in charge of the game and can always say, 'No, no, we don't think they were wasting time.' If a scene hasn't begun by 'zero' the offenders lose the stage, but this hardly ever happens, and we wouldn't want it to.

Having only five seconds to respond to a challenge may seem absurd, but challengers go first, and the counting out should not happen until a team is perceived to be wasting time. Thirty or forty seconds, perhaps even a minute, will have passed before anyone remembers to start 'counting'. Count slowly – let them have the full five seconds.

Some groups have the audience count down before every scene. This diminishes variety and yet I like it when the audience respond as one creature so I'm in two minds about it.

There's always the danger that the trappings of Theatresports may start to take up more time than the improvisations. 'Counting out' helps to avoid this.

Waving the Lights Down

- The players onstage can wave the lights down (or up).
- So can the players on the bench – if their team has possession of the stage.
- So can the Judges.
- So can the lighting imp.

Players should not wave the lights down with an extravagant gesture that communicates, 'Wasn't that wonderful? See how great our improvisers are!' Even if the improvisers did well, this looks arrogant, but it often happens from sheer habit, even after a scene has died miserably. Be modest.

Scoring

Except for the Danish Match (which is controlled by an 'Ombud'), there are three Judges. These score each scene by holding up cards – numbered from one (for 'bad') to five (for 'excellent').

The Judges' individual scores are added together by the scorekeeper: fifteen is therefore the top score for any challenge, with the exception of one-on-one challenges, or when time-points are being used (see p. 334). Most one-on-one challenges earn the winners five points, and the Judges express this by pointing to the team whose work they preferred (they indicate a draw by pointing upwards). Best-out-of-three one-on-one Hat-Games are anomalous in that each hat taken, or successfully defended, earns three points.

Danish Games have only one Judge (the 'Ombud') and the outcome of each challenge is decided by the audience, who yell out the name of the team that they preferred. Winners get five points; losers get zero.

Some groups use massive scoreboards that have to be transported in pick-up trucks. I recommend cloth scoreboards that can be rolled up like flags (use Velcro to stick on the numbers and the team names).

Three Seldom-used Versions of Theatresports

1 No-Block Theatresports

I thought, quite wrongly, that the Ur-Theatresports that was played in my acting classes was too primitive for public entertainment, so I devised No-Block Theatresports which involved a struggle for stage-time. Challenges were not scored, but the winners of a challenge earned up to ten minutes of free-time in which to rack up points (after which the offstage team could 'challenge for the stage').

I say up to ten minutes because if a player was thought to have 'killed an idea', the offstage team would yell, 'BLOCK!', and if their claim was upheld, they took possession of the remainder of the free-time (if any). If instead of saying, 'UPHELD', the Judges said, 'OVERRULED', the offstage team would lose ten points.

No-Block Theatresports had an instability that allowed us to see more of hottest team, but a team that was inferior, or unlucky, could spend an entire game losing challenges, and end up with a score of minus a hundred and fifty. Then they'd have to kneel down and let volunteers from the audience throw custard pies at them. (I introduced the pies to discourage a losing team's 'supporters' from leaving before the end, but we haven't pied anyone for years.)

People would remember the match in which the Evil Elk never won a single challenge, or the time when they were a hundred points behind, had better luck with the challenges, and won the coveted rubber chicken.

The spectators at the very first public match screamed and cheered, and then streamed on to the stage, shaking our hands, and shouting advice: 'The Judges must never change their minds!' they cried (a burst of mass rage had so frightened our Judges that they'd reversed one of their decisions), and 'You must have penalties! You can't treat this as just a game!'

No-Block Theatresports was gradually modified: time-points became necessary, and the game was started with a challenge, rather than by allowing the spin of a coin to award ten minutes of free-time.

It's easy to attract attention when something is new and sounds hysterically funny. People looked up from their newspapers and said,

'Penalties involve sitting with the head in a paper bag! The audience throw custard pies at the losing team! This we have to see!'

Within a year No-Block Theatresports was a regular event at the Alberta Games – something that might have taken generations in other countries. I remember a 'meet' in Medicine Hat where I was surrounded by cheering people and yet the air seemed silent. I was holding a gold medal in my hand that had been awarded to an actor at a sporting event, and I felt as if I'd somehow travelled back to a point in history before theatre had branched off from sport.

2 Serious Theatresports
Teams are thrown off not only when they're boring, but when they get a laugh (what is or isn't a laugh is determined by the Judges).

This match is seldom played in public, because most players walk onstage with a miserable expression, and stand about doing absolutely nothing. Yet after they're thrown off they'll protest indignantly.

'But we were being serious.'

'Being serious isn't the same thing as looking miserable. The New Testament is serious but Jesus doesn't shuffle about looking slightly ill. The audience expects you to be altered, and to have adventures, and to build interesting relationships.'

Serious Theatresports is so difficult that it's not recommended in normal circumstances.

3 One Game Theatresports
Teams play a fifteen-minute match based on variations of one challenge. If Word-at-a-Time was chosen, teams might challenge to the best Word-at-a-Time one-on-one love scene, or to a scene in which the audience supplies every other word, or to a Word-at-a-Time in gibberish, or to a Word-at-a-Time Hat-Game. Players are forced to find new possibilities instead of grinding along the same old paths.

The Five Theatresports Matches in Current Use

1 The Regular Match
No-Block Theatresports self-destructed when the players learned not to block, so I replaced it with the Regular Game, arguing that the taboo on blocking was an irrelevancy. The teams still fought for free-time (the winner of each challenge being allowed six minutes in which to clock up

points), but in place of shouting, 'BLOCK', the Judges issued Warnings for Boring.

The players were appalled: 'Blocking *is* Theatresports!' they insisted, but I won them over.

2 The Revised Match

Jim Curry (of the Sci-fi Fingers) said, 'Why not let the winners of a challenge play just one scene?' This mutated the Regular Game into the Revised Game, and I soon realized that the challenges should also be scored (i.e. not just the free-scene). This made the event less humiliating for the losers, because even a team that lost every challenge would at least earn some points.

3 The Challenge Match

There's no free-time and no free-scene. Teams challenge each other, and the team that wins the most challenges is presented with the rubber chicken (or whatever prize is being offered).

4 The Judges' Challenge Match

This is a challenge match for beginners in which the Judges issue the challenges.

Some Judges say, 'We challenge you to . . .', but it's better to say, 'The first challenge is . . .' and then 'The next challenge is . . .', and so on.

Competent Judges can increase variety – for example, they can follow a pecking-order scene with a solo mime, or a clown scene with a serious scene. Their selection of 'challenges' can impose some control on the pace and shape of the match.

Challenges should be tailored to the abilities of the players.

5 The Danish Game

This is a challenge match in which the spectators decide the winner of each challenge. Tournus, the theatre company that I worked with in Denmark, had too few members to provide three Judges, so we introduced the 'Ombud', and let the audience cheer for the team whose work they preferred. The Ombud introduces the match, explains the penalty basket and rehearses the audience in yelling out the team names.

These names must be adapted so that they contain the same number of syllables, because if the Penguins were competing against The Fall of the Roman Empire, then you'd just hear a mass of confused shouting followed by '. . . of the Roman Empire'. To prevent this, the Ombud must say. 'Did you prefer The Penguins' escape from jail or The Romans' escape scene in which the twins were rescued by Caesarean section?'

If the Ombud is uncertain, even after a reshout, he/she can get the supporters of each team to yell separately.

Having the audience yell loudly every few minutes helps to weld it into 'one creature'.

The Ombud should write down a brief description of each scene, and should remind the audience of what it's voting on (because laughter interferes with short-term memory transfer). Such 'scene' lists are useful at the 'post-mortem'.

Ombuds can't just be passengers – they have to control the match – but nor are they emcees who are competing with the players to see who can be funniest. They're responsible for making sure that the match runs efficiently. They horn scenes, wave the lights down and say, 'Twenty seconds to finish,' or whatever. Ombuds should be friendly, but unobtrusive.

Rule of Theatresports

Rules Common to the Five Matches in Current Use

1 *Length of Games* The length of each game is decided in advance.

2 *Controlling the Game* The Judges (or the Ombud of a Danish Match) are in charge, and are responsible for quality. They must not be figures of fun.

3 *Introductions* The commentator welcomes the spectators and does a short 'warm-up'. He then introduces the Judges (or if it's a Danish Game, the Ombud) and says, 'Can we have the traditional boo for the Judges' (but he/she does not ask the audience to boo the Ombud in the Danish Game). The Judges then cross the stage to take their seats at the front of the audience.

The commentator introduces the teams one at a time, and they cross the stage to their team benches. Keep the benches out of direct light (if possible) except when there's a reason to light them – a dispute with the Judges, perhaps. Lit teams are distracting.

4 *Coaches* Coaches are optional. They can sit with the teams, and they can

join in (if extra bodies are needed), but it would be considered 'bad form' for a coach to 'star' in a game. A coach is there to assist, not to shine. Players should coach each other during the scenes when appropriate.

5 *Starting the Match* The commentator asks for a Judge and two team captains (or the Ombud) to go centre-stage. The Judge (or Ombud) supervises the coin-toss, and the winner decides which team should make the first challenge (winners of the toss often say, 'You can challenge us!'). Teams then alternate in making challenges.

If the teams agree, the coin-toss can be replaced by 'Rock-Paper-Scissors'.

6 *Counting Out* If time is being wasted in setting up the scenes, the commentator, or the Judges, or the entire audience, can start counting down from five to zero, but the Judges have the final word on whether a 'counting out' is valid.

A team that is counted out loses the stage (although this seldom happens, and we don't want it to happen). Counting out adds variety, stops the players from wasting time, and offers yet another way to get the audience involved. Only start counting a team out if time is being wasted.

7 *Warnings for Boring* A Judge who is bored by a scene should honk his/her rescue horn. This gives the dreaded Warning for Boring. Teams that are honked must end their scene immediately, yielding the stage to the opposing team. There tend to be fewer warnings in the Danish Game – the Ombud being more likely to say, 'Thank-you,' or to wave the lights down.

8 *Baskets* Penalties involve sitting beside the commentator for two minutes with your head in a wicker penalty basket (no matter which team is in possession of the stage). Penalties are awarded for obstruction, for undue obscenity, for delaying the game, for harassment of the other team, for 'distracting', and so on.

Baskets are usually awarded at the end of a scene, but in serious cases they can be imposed mid-scene.

If all the members of a team have been penalized and are therefore unable to answer a challenge, they miss the scene that they might have played (I've only known this to occur once).

The Judges can eject players from a game (this seldom happens and we should try to avoid it).

9 *Ending Scenes* If a team does not find an ending for a scene, the Judges can wave the lights down, or can say, 'Twenty seconds to end it' (or whatever), or they can use the Warning for Boring. They should not use their option of waving the lights down unless they can see a valid place to end the scene. The lighting improvisor and the players who are 'in possession' of the stage can also bring the lights down at a suitable point. The team (in possession of the stage) can wave the lights up again if they wish – but they risk a Warning for Boring.

10 *Ending the Match* If a pair of challenges are not completed (or if a section of free-time is in progress), the commentator should delay the end of the match to accommodate this. He/she can also request a 'short' challenge – for example, a one-on-one challenge. However, the Judges are in charge of the game, and they can veto any request by the commentator.

In friendly games, where the score is of no consequence, the commentator should try to end the match near the agreed time, but preferably at a high point, perhaps on a roar of laughter, or after a scene that has emotional warmth.

11 *Keeping Score* The scorekeeper keeps score on a scoreboard which is only lit between scenes (give this task to the commentator if no one else is available). He/she records the length of any time-outs, or time lost due to other interruptions, and adds this extra-time to the end of the game.

12 *Time-outs* Each team is entitled to one thirty-second time-out. Judges can take time-outs if they need them, but this is seldom necessary.

13 *Substitutions* Players can substitute out (by making a 'T' sign with their hands), or they can substitute in (by running onstage, tapping a team-mate on the shoulder, and saying, 'Substitution').

14 *Explain the Challenges* Challengers go first. If a challenge cannot be explained clearly and succinctly, it should be rejected – at the discretion of the Judges or Ombud.

15 *Refusing a Challenge* A team can 'baulk' at a challenge. If the baulk is upheld, the challengers must issue a fresh challenge. If they persist in offering unacceptable challenges, the Judges must issue a challenge on that team's behalf – although we hope this doesn't become necessary.

If a team baulks and is overruled, it can still refuse the challenge and the other team will be awarded fifteen points (five points in the Danish Game). This has never been known to happen.

Judges should baulk at a challenge that seems stupid, distasteful, unduly repetitive, or whatever.

16 *Improving the Quality* The Judges are responsible for the quality of the game. They can intrude to say things like 'We'd like to see a non-verbal challenge please,' or 'We've seen too many group scenes – we want a solo scene,' or 'We'd like a love scene!' or 'A scene with pathos,' or whatever.

Judges should not intrude any more than is necessary, and never when the match is going well.

Further Rules of the Regular Match

17 *Duration* At present we play for forty-five minutes. Recommended time – between forty and fifty minutes.

18 *Setting the Challenges* Teams challenge alternately, and the Judges point to the team that they consider 'won the challenge'. This gives the winners free-time in which to accumulate points (the challenges are not scored). If both teams have done equally well, the Judges must point into the air and issue their own challenge – preferably a one-on-one, or a short challenge.

19 *Free-time* The length of the free-time is agreed before the start of the game.

The first Theatresports games lasted for two hours and the free-times lasted for ten minutes; these days we play shorter games and the free-time is usually for six minutes.

When the limit of the free-time is exceeded the commentator (warned by the scorekeeper) says, 'End of free-time' and the Judges decide their score at that point (although the scene taking place may be allowed to finish). If a really interesting scene is cut short, the players' best strategy is to return to it later in the match as part of another challenge.

20 *Time-points* The first players of the Regular Match realized that they could win by cramming as many scenes as possible into the free-time (twenty uninspired scenes that averaged one point each could accumulate more points than one longer scene that achieved the maximum score). To prevent the Regular Match from degenerating into a series of one-liners, I said that we should multiply the Judges' points by

time-points. Every minute onstage earns one time-point, so if a scene lasts for three minutes and earns ten Judges' points, it will receive a total of thirty points, whereas a scene that's awarded twelve Judges' points, but which lasted only thirty seconds, receives six points.

This put an end to the one-liners, but when we created the Revised Match (in which the winners of a challenge present only one scene) time-points became irrelevant.

Further Rules of the Revised Match[1]

17 *The Free-scene* The team that wins a challenge gets to play a free-scene (this replaces the free-time of the Regular Match). Challenges are scored (as well as the free-scene). There are no time-points.

18 *Duration* We usually play the Revised Game for about forty-five minutes. Recommended time – between thirty minutes and fifty minutes.

Further Rules of the Challenge Match

17 *Setting the Challenges* Teams alternate in challenging each other. There is no free-time and no free-scene.

18 *Challenges Are Scored* Each challenge earns the winners five points. The exceptions are a few one-on-one games; for example, in a one-on-one, best-out-of-three Hat-Game, each hat taken, or saved from a grab, earns three points.

19 *Duration* Challenge Matches usually last for thirty minutes, but our 'rookie' matches last between ten and fifteen minutes.

Further Rules of the Judges' Challenge Match

17 *Setting the Challenges* The Judges set each challenge, choosing it with regard to the abilities of the players and the needs of the spectators.

18 *Duration* We usually play the Judges' Challenge Match for twenty minutes (or about twelve minutes if the players are beginners). Judges' Challenge Matches have never lasted for longer than half an hour, because if the players are skilled, why not let them issue their own challenges?

Further Rules of the Danish Match

17 The Ombud The Ombud honks boring scenes, waves the lights down, and so on. He/she introduces the game from centre-stage, demonstrating the penalty basket and so on, and gets the audience to practise shouting the team names.

After each pair of challenges he/she reminds the audience of the scenes that they've just watched, and invites them (on the count of three) to shout the name of the team whose work they preferred.

18 Scoring The winners of the 'shout', as determined by the Ombud, are awarded five points. One-on-one Hat-Games, and other games where the winner is self-evident, are not recommended for Danish Matches because the audience doesn't get to vote.

19 Duration Danish Matches usually last between twenty-five and forty minutes (twenty-five is more usual).

20 Team Names The names shouted out should be short, and should have the same number of syllables.

Warning: the Danish Game is not suitable for tournament use because the audience will cheer for the home team. I judged the first Sweden/Denmark game which was ruined because the Danes, who were the hosts, insisted on playing the Danish Game.

NOTES

1 I prefer this match to the Regular Match.

16 Afterthoughts

To prepare fleas for the Flea Circus (as in the Cole Porter lyric, 'Bees do it, even educated fleas do it'), cover them with a sheet of glass so that it smashes them back each time they leap. Two days of this and they'll never jump again and are described as 'educated'.

The Body

Many of us 'keep a grip' on ourselves as if we might fly apart, or as if our eyes might drop out and get stepped on. Shoulders are held high, pelvises are locked, breathing is restricted, and weight that should be carried on our bones is supported by muscle (which is why we feel lighter if our posture improves).

I've heard it argued that this decline into adulthood is as inevitable as kittens turning into cats, but whoever saw an adult cat with tight eyes? Animals move wonderfully, because there's no way that we can give them advice. If we could tell them to 'Pick up those paws up!' and 'Stiffen those whiskers!' and 'Keep that tail up!' adult cats would clump about bumping into the furniture.

Droop your head and look miserable (you can find the mood if you say things like 'I hate you, Daddy!' or 'Why can't I, Mummy?'). No one admires such a child, and the average adult will say, 'Chin up!'

Raise your chin but keep the misery (the slump). The back of your neck is now shorter, and instruction number two follows almost immediately: 'Shoulders back!'

If your head is forward the shoulders should also hang forward. Pulling them back adds more tension and emphasizes your caved-in chest: 'Chest out!'

Obey this and your pelvis tilts, allowing your abdomen to bulge: 'Stomach in!'

You feel heavier and everything admirable about your posture has now been trashed. Try to walk and what happens? Your feet drag: 'Pick your feet up!' say the adults, and then, in desperation, 'Stand up straight!'

Anyone obeying the previous instructions can't obey this one, but obedient children will try to experience 'straightness' by pressing their knees back, and this hyper-extension soon does irreparable damage.[1]

The Mind

If people are clamping their body together as if it might fall apart, perhaps the same is true of the mind. Could it be that our instructions on how to use our consciousness are as damaging as our advice about posture? Should we really be told to 'Think!' and 'Try to concentrate!' and 'Be original!' as if thought required effort, and as if originality lay somewhere outside of ourselves? Should we really think of ourselves as 'one consciousness' and force our imagination to confirm this?

It's not easy to kill the curiosity of an ape, but sitting it at a desk for year after year of organized boredom might do the trick. Our preoccupation with trivia suggests that the urge to learn is intact, but that learning anything of significance has become stressful. The Executive producer of the David Letterman show, Robert Morton, said, 'If you walk away from this show learning something, then we haven't done our job'.[2] If entertainment is designed to pass the time without teaching us anything, then I have to presume that it's a spin-off of our education system. Other cultures have feasts, celebrations and morality plays, and they may tear out hearts to ensure that the sun comes up, but I think that entertainment is peculiar to us, and many of us are entertained for most of our waking hours.

The Sexes

I soon realized instinctively that these men would be perfectly content to let me fill in the secondary slots that needed a prop female . . . I could see that they regarded Second City as a male art form, that they did not want a girl pushing in and saying, 'I can do that scene.' A girl who preceded me into Second City, Mina Kolb, once said, 'A man almost always instigates a scene, so you had to make your ideas seem like somebody else's. It was like playing with a kid.' – Joan Rivers, *Enter Talking* (1986)

Oslo Theatresports was started by women, and yet a couple of years later the men had taken over. A pity, because male-dominated Theatresports typically has no pathos, no compassion and no tenderness. Women players can provide these qualities, given the chance, and when they abandon Theatresports – as most of them do – the men thump their clubs against rocks, shouting, 'But we were treating them as equals!' I tell them not to treat women as equals because male-bonding behaviour horrifies most women, and that those who survive the put-downs and the aggression are likely to end up just as tough as the men – in which case we might as well be using men in skirts (like most comedy groups).

Men take what they can get (they even drove the women out of gynaecology), and in the average impro group the women are like nesting birds in the path of stampeding buffalo. This problem won't go away, and if it's allowed to fester there'll be no place for most women in male-dominated comedy except as mascots, or as men with breasts.

Apart from urging the men to treat women with respect, and give them a fair crack of the whip, so to speak (i.e. consciously to include 'feminine' scenes, just as action movies do, and to let women control scenes and be the heroines of stories), my suggestion is that the women should sometimes train together, away from the men, and that they should have a social life together, and should teach each other not to be ingratiating. I also recommend that both men and women improvisers become familiar with Michael Shurtleff's book *Audition* (Walker and Company, 1978), which gives excellent examples of the flight from love and affection.

A 'candid camera' confederate approached women outside an imposing office building to say that one of her heels had broken off and could she borrow their shoes for an important job interview. The 'joke' was to have been their embarrassment, but every woman agreed immediately. This seems a good example of the vast difference between male attitudes, and female attitudes.[3]

Quality

If the process is good, I assume that the end-product will be good. This stops me believing that an improvised scene has 'quality' if it resembles a written scene (as though improvisation were just a step on the road to conventional theatre).

Players are working well when:

• They're enjoying the scenes they're in (this is not the same as enjoying being onstage)
• They're giving the audience the 'future' that it anticipates (while avoiding obscene and disgusting scenes)

- They're taking care of each other and being altered by each other.
- They're daring, mischievous, humble and courageous
- The work feels 'natural', 'effortless' and 'obvious'
- No one is trying to be 'original' or to think up 'clever' ideas
- They're uniting the spectators into 'one creature'
- They're being themselves, rather than fleeing from self-revelation
- We care about the values expressed in the work
- The audience's yearnings, anxieties and fantasies are being made flesh

Players are probably working badly when they are:

- 'Shining'
- Being negative (e.g. killing ideas, presenting scenes about vomiting, and so on)
- Fighting each other for control (i.e. when they're afraid of being controlled)
- 'Planning' instead of 'attending'
- Wrecking stories for the sake of easy laughs (or for any other reason)
- Suppressing the kinetic dance
- Ignoring moral implications
- Wallowing in clichés (e.g. hunting for treasure, asking for 'household chores' to act out, and so forth)

A Theatresports team presented an incompetent weekly 'revue' at our theatre, but I refused to give them notes.

'Why not?' they said, a bit miffed.

'Because your audience kangaroo over the seats to get to the front. Because they hammer at the doors to get in. Because they pack this theatre for a late-night show even though we're out by the airport. Maybe the chaos is partly responsible. I'm not your audience!'

Ten years later they are all successful writers, script-editors, entertainers and so on. Some of them are famous.

Great Audiences

- Do not cheer uncritically
- Never sit with folded arms
- Are united with the players against the Judges
- Are benevolent (the players must do everything possible to create and sustain this benevolence)

- Laugh in huge unthinking waves, and, when silent, are absolutely silent
- Are reluctant to leave at the end of the show

Great Improvisers

A great improviser can make us laugh at any moment, and can give us moist eyes at any moment.

Great improvisers 'go with the flow', accepting that they're in the hands of God, or the Great Moose. Their attitude is the opposite of those 'beginners' for whom improvisation is very difficult and who find the demons on the stage just as threatening as those in life. When a great improviser is inspired, all limits seem to disappear. Sometimes it's as if there's extra light on the stage, and the players' outlines seem sharper. Competent improvisers give us flashes of this, but great improvisers can supply this demonic light (or heavenly radiance) for minutes at a time.

I'm describing something that all parents have seen (unless they were blinded by their intellects). Very young children can be so flooded, so pumped-up, so exploded with joy that it's as if they're streaming light into the universe. It's why some cultures regard them as gods who only gradually become human.

Great improvisers can sometimes come within spitting distance of that kind of power (as can great actors).

Getting Jaded

It's wonderful to be surfing on huge waves of laughter, but it begins to pall; you discover that your skills are no longer developing, and that most of the scenes are pointless, and that your contemporaries are drifting away to be replaced by young teenagers.

Maybe you give up, or maybe you give up only to get sucked back in again – after all, it's an interesting 'hobby'. With luck, you may eventually realize that very little of 'you' was ever present on the stage; and that verbal thinking kills spontaneity; and that the world is not six, or sixteen, or sixty seconds in the future; and that a good story is worth any amount of cheap laughs; and that the winning and losing are all ashes.

At this point, Theatresports becomes thrilling and dangerous all over again, and once more a great adventure.

NOTES

1 There are other reasons why the muscles clamp up – for example, as a way to blot out suffering. Release muscles that are chronically tense and you're likely to be overwhelmed by long-forgotten pain and misery – this is commonplace.

2 Toronto *Globe and Mail*, 22 November 1993.

3 Report in the Toronto *Globe and Mail*, 17 June 1998.

Appendix One

Fast-Food Stanislavsky Lists

Here's a selection from my current lists to use as a basis for yours. Some work for almost anyone; others have a less universal appeal. Many of the suggestions are not expected to be successful, but whether the goals are achieved or not, vivid characters can be created. These lists seem a bit negative to me; for example, there should probably be a To-be-Thought-a-Supportive-Parent list.

After I published some of these lists in the Theatresports newsletter I met groups who had found them useless. I had imagined that the longer the lists, the more the variety, but whereas in Calgary players would glance at their list and use the first suggestion that they could make truthful, players who had not worked with me would scan through as many as sixty items in an attempt to choose the very best (with dismal results).

Give beginners lists that have just five or six of the suggestions that are in bold print. The same items can be used many times in a scene, but keep saying, 'Something else on the list,' so that they are rotated. Introduce longer lists gradually.

To Give Someone a Bad Time (1)
Ape (mock) their mannerisms.
Tell them they bore you.
Be nastily polite (sarcastic).
'Bone to pick . . .'
Borrow their money, their things.
Contradict them.
Control them.
Criticize their appearance, pets, relatives, sexual prowess, blemishes, use of English, etc.
Embarrass them.
Exploit them.
Endow with stupidity, dullness, meanness, etc.
Give advice.
Groan; grind teeth; snarl; scream.
Hit them.
Invade their space.
Interrupt them.
Make faces at them.
Mishear them.
Make them lose.
Patronize them.
Repeat bad remarks (stories) made about them.
Shout at them.
Start sentences with 'You always' or

'You never'.
Spill something on them.
Tell stories to their discredit.
Tie them up.
Torture them.
Talk only about yourself.

To Give Someone a Bad Time (2)
Be offensively blunt.
Be restless, tap fingers.
Break their things.
Change the subject.
Confuse them.
Contradict them.
Cross your legs away from them.
Damage or confiscate their
possessions.
Disagree with them.
Frown; sigh; 'tut'.
Give advice.
Glare at them.
Make irritated gestures.
Laugh at wrong time.
Kill their ideas.
Know what they're about to say.
Keep looking away.
Make them work.
Only be interested in yourself.
Out-stare them.
Misunderstand them.
Poke them with finger.
Seduce then ineptly (start and give
up?).
Slander them.
Talk to them through third party.
Taunt.
Touch their head or face.

To Be Thought Beautiful
Be languid, sensual.
Check appearance (in mirror?).
Draw attention to your good points.
Glide about, dance.
Use your eyes expressively.

Smile a lot (flash teeth).
Touch and stroke yourself.
Walk tall.
Worry about figure, skin, make-up,
etc.
Ask opinions of your attractiveness.
Be a model (want to be a model?).
Exercise.
Fish for compliments.
Get bored when conversation turns
away from you.
Have a best profile.
Have (or desire) rich and/or
glamorous lovers.
Keep body open.
Look in mirror.
Make sensuous sounds.
Name drop.
One of your features is ugly.
Other people are ugly.
Panic when you find a zit.
Pose.
Show photos of yourself.

To-Show-Someone-They're-Boring
Yawn.
Interrupt.
Change subject.
Complain they always say the same
things.
Know what they're going to say.
Ignore them.
Beat head against the wall.
Ask them to leave.
Say, 'Do you ever listen to yourself?'
Phone someone; read a book,
magazine.
Tell stories about how boring they are.
Say, 'What?', 'Pardon me?'
Stare at them or avoid looking at
them.
Nod or agree too soon; i.e. you weren't
really listening.
Look at watch.

To be Thought a 'Computer'

Be efficient – everything in its right place.
Be cold and distant.
Be friendless and like it.
Be wooden.
Be insensitive to emotion (yours or other people's).
Be insensitive to pain or pleasure.
Dislike physical contact.
Express your love (or hate) as if indifferent.
Use inexpressive inflexible voice.
No time for trivialities.
Other people are slow.
Others are stupid.
Pause before answering, or snap out the answers.
Provide solutions.
Totally restrain an inner violence.

To Flirt with Someone*

Check for reactions, especially by raising eyebrows and opening eyes wide.
Emphasize points with hands more than usual.
Hold gaze longer than usual.
Face other person head on.
Find topics on which you can agree.
Keep mouth slightly open and look unconsciously at parts of other person (in sequence?).
Moisten your lips often.
Move closer than is normal.
Nod head in agreement, no matter what is being said.
Rest hand on some part of other's body.
Slight smile plus bashful look, lower eyes, look to the side, repeat.
Small touching movements.

* Based on Dr Irenaus Eibl-Elbesfeldt's instructions for the universal human flirting behaviour (Max Planck Institute, Munich).

To Give Someone a Good Time (1)

Ask questions about them and be interested in the answers.
Ask advice or their opinion.
Admire and praise their voice, their body, the way they fold a newspaper, etc.
Compliment.
Consider them first.
Endow them with humour (laugh easily).
Find them friends, sexual partners, etc.
Get them to talk about themselves (give rapt attention).
Give presents (flowers?).
Let them know that you enjoy their company.
Let them win.
Make them feel comfortable, important, at ease.
Offer food, drink, drugs, sex, money, etc.
Quote them (admiringly).
Respond promptly.
Share their sorrows, their problems.
Share a secret.
Tell nice stories about them.
Work for them (fix their car/do their laundry, etc.).

To Give Someone a Good Time (2)

Agree.
Be modest (subservient?).
Be positive (enthusiastic).
Be easy to control.
Be good natured.
Encourage (nod, make encouraging sounds, etc.).
Endow with humour.
Quote them (admiringly).
Tell stories and jokes (if appropriate).
Have a handicap and be good

natured about it.
Make their wish come true.
Praise their property, their behaviour, their pets, etc.
Shower with attention.
Stay happy when you fail (lose and be a good loser).
Suggest a holiday, a trip? A picnic? A movie? An entertainment, etc.
Support what they do or say.
Tell stories to their credit.
Touch, stroke, kiss and hug (if appropriate).
What are their three wishes?

To Accept Guilt
Apologize.
Break or ruin something.
Confess, e.g. hit and run driver; you sat on a small pet; you were unjust; you stole something; left the bath dirty, etc.
Avoid people's eyes, hang head.
Whatever you do, over-explain the reasons for it.
Embarrass someone and feel terrible.
You forgot to close fridge, gate, air-lock, etc.
Help people more than they need.
Be over-concerned.
Borrowed something and didn't return it.
Help people incompetently.
Often say, 'Is it all right?', 'Do you mind?', etc.
Set objects or people on fire.
You lied about using contraception.
You told someone's secret.
You broke a religious rule.

To Appear Happy and Contented with Everything
Behave as if you have a delightful secret.

Endow others with good intentions.
Endow others with humour.
Enjoy touching things, including yourself.
Have a pop tune inside your head.
Smile.
Laugh just from sheer pleasure.
Dance, sing.
Don't really listen.
Be confident.
Be playful.
Be very alive, healthy, awake.
Be positive.
Bodies are to give pleasure.
Have lots of time.
Indulge yourself (chocolates, drinks, etc.).
Move, laugh, stretch from sheer pleasure.
Offer to help, but don't really care.
Pet an animal.
Repeat mantras silently (e.g. 'I love everything', 'I have everything I need').
Stay happy when you fail.
Talk freely (give personal information).
Take nothing seriously.
Tease playfully.
Wreck things but feel no guilt.
Use open, unguarded body positions.
Endow playfulness.
Be unselfconscious of your body.

To Be Thought a Hero
Have a weapon.
Be on a quest.
Be attacked.
Detect dangers.
Display strength, athleticism.
Have firm resonant voice.
Have an uninhibited laugh.
Keep head still when you speak (be high status).

Smile a lot – flash teeth.
Give bold stares.
Kill something (someone).
Rescue someone.
Talk about your thrilling adventures.
Start a fight.
Show scars.
Imagine a silver ball an inch inside your chest that radiates an amazing light.*
Take risks eagerly.
Have a 'beloved'.
Guard and defend your honour.
Detect an enemy.
Issue dares.
Be relatively unaffected by pain.
People are safe when you're around.
Show trophies. medals.
Swagger.

To Humiliate Someone
Blame them.
Make unflattering comparisons.
Tell bad stories about them.
Ridicule them to other people (to the audience?).
Stare with contempt.
Make them undress, sing, attempt impossible feats.
Yawn.
Insult them.
'Over-cheer' them.
Accuse them of lying, of stealing, of coming on to you.
Make snide remarks.
Be better than them: more intelligent, sexier, etc.
Yawn – they bore you.
Tell jokes they don't get.
Lead them on and reject them.
Laugh at wrong time.
Scorn them.
Expose their shameful secrets.

* See p. 276.

Dare them to make moves on you.

To Impress Someone
Be a neurosurgeon, rock star, author, witch, murderer, athlete.
Talk about your achievements.
Demonstrate skills: yodelling? knife-throwing? hypnosis?
Detect errors.
Name drop.
Solve problems.
Know secrets.
Have famous lover.
Show awards.
Be recipient of presents, awards, etc.
Be amazingly lucky.
Receive flattering phone-call.
Be a sexual athlete.
Do magic tricks.
Be rich.
Someone is interviewing you; photographing you.
A tailor is measuring you.
Reprimand a servant.
Have incredibly obedient dog.
Animals love you.

To be Thought Intelligent
Correct people.
Know everything.
Explain baffling things.
Use complex sentences.
Use long words.
Other people are stupid/wrong.
Quote statistics (invent them).
'As Aristotle says . . .'
Use foreign phrases (gibberish?).
Interrupt.
Make thoughtful sounds, 'umms' and 'ahhhs'.
Whistle Bach.
Adopt serious attitudes.
Analyse everything.
Argue.

Be a writer, professor, doctor, etc.
Carry a calculator or a book.
Cite authorities.
Criticize.
Give abstruse information.
Lecture.
Make notes.
Name drop.
Define terms.
Steer conversation.
Stress your own brilliance.
Start sentences with 'In my opinion
. . .' or 'As I say . . .' or 'It all depends
what you mean by . . .' or 'In this
society . . .'
Talk about obscure books, artists,
films, etc.
Don't listen.
Other people are stupid.

To be Thought a Jerk
Be tactless – refer to broken love
affairs, drag up old bones.
Bad manners.
Brag.
Be a bigot.
Have chip on shoulder.
Interrupt (change subject?).
Point out people's defects. Tell them
how repulsive, smelly, stupid,
arrogant, boring, ugly, etc. they are.
Force friendliness (pester people).
Tease and irritate people.
Bully others to join in stupid or
unwise activities.
Drag everything back to sex and/or
excretion.
Get people's interest and then lose
your train of thought.
Make pointless jokes.
Offensive laugh.
Hit people.
Make a mess – be clumsy, spill stuff.
Invade people's space.

Make obvious passes.
Never take 'no' for an answer.
Pass blame on to other people.
Sing, whistle, hum (irritatingly).
Throw tantrums.
Whine when you can't get your own
way.

To be Judgmental
Accuse people.
Correct people.
Be (or try to be) higher status than
others are.
Be moralistic.
Be shocked.
Blame people.
Bossy or condescending tone of
voice.
Censor behaviour, ideas.
Criticize.
Detect wrong-doers.
Exaggerate.
Endow bad qualities – dishonesty,
treachery, perversions, etc.
Feel threatened.
Impute unworthy motives.
Interrogate people.
Offer self as a model.
Punish people.
'Tut' – make disapproving sounds.
Use 'we' instead of 'I'.
Watch people suspiciously.

To be the Life and Soul of the Party
Admire people and objects.
Agree – give total approval.
Be positive.
Be flamboyant.
Be generous.
Be loud.
Be sexy.
Be happy.
Encourage others to break rules.
Know fascinating gossip.

Remember names (and use them).
Suggest games, dancing, sing-songs, forfeits, etc.
Be fit and healthy and very relaxed.
Break taboos.
Clown.
Compliment/flatter.
Do tricks.
Draw others out.
Dress up in other people's clothes.
Forfeits; strip-poker-type games.
Get people drunk (stoned?).
Flatter.
Introduce people.
Laugh easily and a lot.
Invade personal space, playfully.
Make big entrances.
Matchmake.
Match status to partners.
Often open the eyes wide.
Offer food, drink, sex, drugs, etc.
Plan nice events, experiences, picnics, etc.
Pretend that other people are higher or lower in status for fun.
Play (invent?) musical instruments.
Put on music.
Reassure people.
Sing, strip, get others to perform.
Tell amusing stories.
Tease.
Tell jokes (get others to tell jokes).
Tickle.
Touch people.
Use lots of space.

To be Thought Mysterious
Be secretive.
Drop hints.
Receive strange presents, phone calls, etc.
Be a psychic (know things in advance).
Laugh at private thoughts.

Know secrets about other people.
Have a weapon? Skeleton keys? An enemy?
Have immense wealth? Bodyguards?
Give meaningful looks.
Significant pauses.
Secret smile.
Be going on a journey for no reason.
Be going to a laboratory, to NASA, to Tierra del Fuego, to prison – for no apparent reason.
Enter a trance.
Be 'possessed'.
Sudden swings of mood.
Suffer an attack of some kind, and try to hide it.
Expect attack (have an enemy).
Move languidly or look hunted.
Make inexplicable request.
Have no means of support.
Laugh at private thoughts.
Know things about the other person that you have no reason to know.

To be Thought a Teenage Nerd
Be enthusiastic.
Be good natured.
Be positive.
Be tactless.
Be clumsy: spill things, trip up, etc.
Talk about Mum or Dad: give their opinion on things.
Tell stupid jokes.
Laugh at stupid jokes.
Have an odd laugh.
Quick jerky movements.
Stupid arm movements.
Think you're really 'cool'.
Try to make friends with everybody.
Talk about schoolwork, grades.
Talk about chess, Dungeons and Dragons, bird watching, etc.
Clean your glasses (keep pushing them up on nose).

Often put hand to mouth, to head, etc.
Collect useless things.
Writhe with embarrassment.
Try to make friends with everybody.

To be Thought Normal
Agree with caution.
Ask dull questions.
Be a churchgoer.
Be conservative.
Check appearance, opinions.
Be concerned about the time.
Dislike bodily contact.
Don't swear unless other people do –
and then swear self-consciously.
Don't take up much space – unless
trying to imitate others.
Discuss dull things that you find
interesting (TV, weather, family,
church, garden, possessions, etc.).
Seek reassurance.
Find others strange.
Be formal.
Have a dog.
Have a slight smile, or a slight frown.
Have moderate and/or nervous voice.
Join in with caution.
Keep others at a polite distance (if
possible).
Laugh in moderation.
Listen to the most boring person.
Sit symmetrically.
Show family snap-shots.
Small concealed fidgeting.
Speak in clichés.
Try not to make the first move.
Panic momentarily and instantly
recover.
Use conventional postures in sequence.

To be Parental (a Bad Parent)
Accusation of unfeelingness.
Ask people to do stuff and then do it
yourself.

Adjust people's appearance.
Be a martyr.
Be disgusted.
Be moralistic.
Be selfless.
Be shrill.
Be protective ('you'll get raped').
Bossy or sneery tone of voice.
Correct people.
Confiscate their things.
Create obstacles.
Criticize people's appearance, morals,
personal habits, friends, etc.
Things must be done your way.
Detect misbehaviour.
Dominate.
Don't listen.
Eat leftover food.
Endow with stupidity.
Enunciate clearly.
Give advice (stupid, wrong advice?).
Give information they already have.
Gossip.
Hand out blame.
Hit people.
Hold up others (siblings? school-
mates?) as examples.
Humiliate someone publicly.
Instil guilt.
Insist on being kissed respectfully.
Impose goals.
Tell people things they already
know.
Lay down 'laws'; set limits.
Only you know the right way to do
things.
Make disapproving faces.
Make snide remarks (comment to
yourself about people).
Mock them – use sarcasm.
Nag.
Nothing they do satisfies you.
People are wasting their intelligence,
are disobedient.

Scold.

Object to people's friends, lovers, pets, laziness, etc.

Often say, 'Of course.'

Pick bones.

Pry.

Start sentences with 'You always . . .' and 'You never . . .'

Talk to people through third party.

Try to catch people out – set traps.

'Tut' – make disgusted sounds.

Things must be done your way.

'When I was young'-type hardships.

Use full names.

To Seduce a Man (1)

Ask him to dance.

Admire his taste.

Be breathless.

Be close to him.

Be suggestive.

Be vulnerable.

Caress yourself.

Laugh easily – laugh at his jokes.

Let him know he's special.

Let him know you're available.

Have mantra – 'Take me!'

Give alcohol, food, drugs.

Eat seductively.

Have low, soft, husky voice.

Hold eye contact.

Moan, sigh.

Moisten lips.

Move sensually, pose.

Play with your hair (or his hair).

Rub up against him.

Say yes a lot.

Sensual sounds.

Sit close to him with legs tucked away from him.

Touch him when speaking.

Rapt attention.

Undulate subtly.

To Seduce a Man (2)

Be close to him.

Be mysterious.

Be vulnerable.

Boost his ego.

Caress objects as if they were part of him.

Compliment him.

Candlelit dinner.

Exude happiness.

Give personal information.

Loosen clothing – expose neck.

Love cute animals; children.

Look into his eyes.

Raise arms to emphasize breasts.

Rest your head on his shoulder.

Run your foot up and down his leg.

Breathe on him (blow air through the surface of his clothes).

Sexual innuendoes – hints.

Share secrets.

Show him something in the bedroom.

Take your shoes off.

Touch him when speaking.

Massage.

Tease.

Whisper close to his ear.

You don't need a commitment.

To Seduce a Woman (1)

Be boyish, playful.

Be close to her.

Be worried you might be gay.

Be 'lonely'.

Be polite, chivalrous.

Be self-revealing.

Beg, plead, weep, grovel.

Compliment.

Discuss possibility of commitment.

Give complete attention.

Have a flaw – gay, impotent, war wound, etc.

Be ticklish.

Have mantra – 'I love you'.

Hold eye contact.
Jump on her and then apologize.
Love cute, furry animals and children.
Make her laugh.
Offer hugs.
Play with her hair.
Remove speck of dirt from her eye.
Synchronize your breathing with hers.
Soft tones in voice.
'Say that again . . .'
Touch her breasts (accidentally).
Tell her you're a virgin.
Tell her you love her.
Touch her face, etc.

To Seduce a Woman (2)

Be a hero.
Be masterful.
Be macho yet sensitive.
Be firm and confident.
Be high status (natural leader).
Be athletic (demonstrate strength, physical ability).
Control her.
Do whatever you can get away with.
Exhibit strength of character.
Get her drunk.
Give brutal advice.
Have possessions, homes, cars, aeroplanes, other women, etc.
Have insanely obedient dog.
Apologize for being roused.
Blame her because you're roused.
Have mantra – 'I hate you.'
Increase physical contact.
It's her fault you love her, want her.
Lock door.
Keep head still when you speak.
Touch her hair, head, face, etc.
You know how her mind works – what she wants.
Offer money, threaten, blackmail.
Persist, be inexorable.

Physically overpower her.
Reprimand her.
Rub against furniture, moan.
Show pornographic books, videos, etc.
Sexy voice – smoulder.
Stroke her.
Tell her you love her.
Tell her she smells good.
Take all the responsibility.
You're a fighter – you've killed someone.
Undress.

To be High Status

Take control (or fight for control).
Alternate between saying things to raise yourself and saying things to lower the other person.
Be more relaxed and stiller than your partner.
Crush any 'challenges'.
Delay before reacting.
Hold eye contact at least five seconds (never glance quickly back).
Keep head motionless when you speak each phrase.
Blink less than other people.
Suppress blinking during confrontations.
Move smoothly – often be still.
Sometimes use long 'errrr' sound before speaking.
Take lots of space.
Be very relaxed unless challenged.
Have lots of breath before you speak.
Touch other people's faces, ruffle their hair, pat their heads.
Talk in complete sentences.
Often use people's names.

To be Low Status (positive)

Admire other people's possessions, poise etc., but secretly or hesitatingly.
Answer promptly.

Bite lower lip with teeth when smiling.

Blink more than your partner.

Be wide-eyed.

Have no job, car, lover, sexual technique, but it doesn't worry you.

Be breathless when speaking.

Break eye contact but keep peeping back, hoping that your partner will look away so that you can look at their eyes.

Cheerfully tell stories that lower your status or that attempt to raise it and fail.

Disparage yourself, cheerfully, and raise your partner.

Do double-takes.

Have a hesitant (short of breath) laugh.

Have a stupid laugh.

Hands in lap fumble nervously.

Imitate your partner surreptitiously.

Laugh while moving head forward (but keep it level or raise the chin so that nape of neck shortens).

Let others control the scene.

Make nervous movements, twitch.

Often touch your face (head).

Swivel toes towards each other until they touch (heels out).

Sit low – look up to people.

Add a very short 'er' before you speak.

Take less space than your partner (but don't lean forward).

Wiggle your bottom on the seat (more characteristic of women).

Wave to someone with your elbow held tight against your ribs.

Let others control the scene.

To Get Sympathy

Sigh.

Have a brave smile.

Be clumsy.

Weep.

Be embarrassed.

Be unemployed.

Try to help but be inadequate.

Hurt yourself (spill something on self).

Admire others.

Cover face and 'weep'.

Have a handicap.

Have a terrible boss, child, sibling, mate, guru.

Punish yourself when you fail.

Tell sob story.

Have a speech defect, lisp.

Be bad at sex.

Be lonely.

Have no lover.

Get nasty phone-call, letter, etc.

You've been fired.

Tell sob story.

See yourself as a victim.

No one likes you.

Be at a loss.

Someone thrashed you.

Your pet avoids you.

Temporarily homeless.

Admire (envy) others.

Be destitute.

Appendix Two

A Selection of Tilt Lists

Some of these tilts could be used in many different lists, but it's convenient to type them out under headings.

Some have never been used (because I add more every time I type them out, and because some seem unpalatable). I have written short plays based on some that are always avoided, just to prove that they are interesting tilts.

Remove any that you find offensive, and add your own (remembering that theatre is mostly about people suffering and behaving badly).

A strong tilt presents a mystery, so I'll add any solutions that occur to me as I type. (I'll put them in italics and express them as questions to remind you that a good tilt can be solved in many ways).

A tilt is just an offer of a tilt until it's validated by someone being altered.

Babysitter
- You find photos of murdered babysitters. (*You discover your photo? The owners discover you prying among their things?*)
- Someone moving about in the house. (*Pretend to be several different people having a party?*)
- Find evidence of a satanic cult? (*The owners return? You defeat them using their own book of spells?*)
- Put on an erotic video that you find. It's you and your boyfriend. (*Find the camera?*)
- A friend of the family arrives for the weekend. You let him/her in. (*He/she is lying? Has no knowledge of the family?*)
- The sofa starts to seduce you – via a voice on the PA system. (*The sweets you found in the fridge were psychedelic? The house is a spaceship? The sofa sucks you into it?**)

Child's Bedtime
- 'Daddy, you'd better go or the thing under the bed (or in the toy-cupboard?) will get you!' (*The cupboard sucks Daddy in? Child enters the toy cupboard and disappears? Daddy orders the thing out and punishes it?*)
- 'I can't sleep, Mummy, because the demons make me work for them.' (*Notice blisters on the child's hands?*

* Keith sofas have a concealed entrance in the back.

The demons make the parents work for them as well?)

● 'The other kids say you're a witch.' (*Take revenge by sticking pins into a doll? Teach the child to fly? Teach it to teleport objects?*)

● 'The monsters said that if I told you about them, they'd take you away.' (*It happens? Fight the monsters? Capture one? Punish the child for lying and the monsters seize you? Recognize the monsters as the ones from your own childhood? Have a party?*)

● 'I said my prayers, and God told me he had a message for you.' (*Education is evil? God wants you to take over the universe?*)

Crime

● 'I ran over a pedestrian and drove on.' (*Get someone else to confess to being the driver? Ghost of victim appears but is only visible to the driver?*)

● Interrupt a burglar. (*He/she was your best friend at school? It's an antique dealer from the future?*)

● 'Let's see that scar (tattoo, birthmark, etc.)' (*You're the one who raped/mugged/robbed/kidnapped me?*)

Dating

● You tell a friend that they're not attractive enough to take to the party. (*He/she slashes wrists? Attacks you? Scars your face? Takes you to a party full of ugly monsters? Becomes an angel who was testing you?*)

● Your date is a taxidermist planning to stuff you. (*You find stuffed murdered people in her apartment?*)

● You discover that your lover is an alien from outer space. (*Is a serial killer? Has come to save the earth?*)

● 'I'm only dating you because it gives me the chance to see your brother. (Your sister? Your mum? Your dad?)' (*Torment the deceiver? Call your sibling, mum, dad, etc.?*)

Family

● You interview your father for a school project. (*You find that you knew nothing about him? You discover a terrifying secret among his papers?*)

● A child confronts the parent who rejected him/her. (*Parent seduces it? Parent asks for a loan?*)

● You discover that your close relative is a whore? Is a serial killer? A drug-dealer? A black magician? Is gay? (*You hand them over to the authorities? To the Church? To the mental hospital? To the Klan? To the deprogrammers? You join them?*)

● A bed-ridden teenager. (*Asks Dad or Mum to arrange a call girl or a rent boy? An angel cures him – it was a dream? The voice of God gives him a purpose?*)

● 'It's time I told you about the family curse.'

● Your child is a racist? (*Tell him he's Jewish, black, Chinese – whatever's appropriate?*)

Hitch-hiker

● He/she won't let you stop when the police flag you down.

● He/she forces you to take a road that keeps descending until it arrives in hell.

● Because he/she has a seed of marijuana, your car plus the boat that you are towing is confiscated at the US border.

● The hitch-hiker (or the driver) is

Death. Or Jesus. Or Don Juan. Or the hitch-hiker's lost parent.
- The driver asks the hitch-hiker to abduct a family member.
- The driver wants the hitch-hiker to murder him/her so that someone can collect the insurance.

Honeymoon
- Honeymoon. (*Spouse has arranged for valet or servant to perform the sex – 'I'll just get you started'? Spouse is Bluebeard?*)
- Find spouse wearing your clothes.
- The groom is a magician. (*Find his wands?*)
- The motel is a spaceship – your spouse is an alien? A ghost? A magician? Is the 'honeymoon murderer'? A werewolf? Was meek but becomes a psychotic control freak?

Horror
- A killer is stalking you and you don't know why. (*It's your sibling who wants the inheritance? It's a patient you 'cured' of his mental illness? It's your future self?*)
- The book you are reading describes events that are actually happening. (*Someone is breaking into the house? Tear out the pages? Cross out paragraphs and rewrite?*)
- Marooned alone on a desert island. (*Try to persuade an invisible companion that you're sane? The island starts talking to you? Orders you off?*)
- Your hand feels numb. (*It grabs the doctor? Strangles people? It attacks you? Writes you notes?*)
- 'Dad – the kids at school said I came from an egg.' (*Explain that you're reptiles? Become reptilian?*)

Hunting/Camping
- You are hunting for mimes. (*A mime uses mime to trap you?*)
- 'You may wonder why I brought you out here, so far from civilization.' (*He/she wants your soul? Unzips his/her skin and emerges as the creature you were hunting? Is going to leave you here to toughen you up?*)
- Hunters shoot a man in mistake for a bear. (*Flee, and find his corpse in your truck; throw it in the ditch; see it at the roadside trying to thumb a lift; go to a shrink and the shrink is the corpse; go to confession and the corpse is the priest; be making love and the corpse replaces your lover; be admitted to mental hospital – the corpse is one of the attendants; arrive in heaven – the corpse is in charge of admissions, etc?**)
- Wounded or trapped animal pleads for its life. (*Offers you immortality? Three wishes?*)
- 'Actually the animals enjoy the sport!' (*Someone, or something, starts shooting at you?*)
- Shoot an animal. (*Your partner says, 'I didn't think you earthlings were serious' – gives you a running start?*)
- You're hunting animals who escaped from the research lab. (*They shoot back? You get the disease you gave them? A UFO captures you for its research lab?*)
- Arrive at a gingerbread house. (*Capture the witch? Steal her book of spells? Steal her broom?*)

Party
- Drunk friend insists on driving. (*Tie him/her up? Steal the car keys? Go

* This 'sequence' can last for at least twenty minutes, if the players are inspired.

as passenger to make sure he/she is safe?)
- Your penis urges you to talk to someone – or not to talk to someone? (*Their sex organ talks back?*)
- Your lover's birthday party. (*Realize that all the other guests are dead, although still partying?*)
- You make a pass at a woman who becomes furious. (*You just made love to her but failed to recognize her?*)

Park Bench (Strangers)
- One demonstrates his/her control over the weather. (*And loses control of it?*)
- One wants the other's soul.
- 'God (or Satan) sent me to find you.' (*You're dead? God or Satan wants to make a deal?*)
- 'God said you have a message for me.' (*Torture someone to make them give you the message?*)
- Old people – strangers. (*They discover that they were friends or enemies in their youth? Members of the same impro group? One dies?*)
- 'I'm from the future.'
- 'This was my favourite place before I died.'
- Discover that you were lovers in a previous life. (*Then remember the betrayal?*)
- 'I'm a bounty hunter!'
- One is a psychic who always knows what the other will do or say. (*Murder the psychic?*)
- Realize you were at school together. (*The bullied one wreaks revenge? One committed the crime for which the other was expelled?*)
- 'Will you throw sticks for me?' (*It's a werewolf?*)

Power
- 'I married you for your money.'
- 'I faked every orgasm.' (*'So did I'?*)
- One will abandon the other unless a condition is met.
- 'You don't realize it, but I've already made love to you.'
- The maid/housekeeper bosses the new wife about: 'What are you doing in my kitchen?'
- 'Make love to me or I'll say you attacked me.'
- 'Queasy? That's because I've drugged you.'
- 'I can read your mind.' (*Every example is accurate?*)
- A stranger knows the most intimate details about you. (*It's an angel? A demon? Jesus? A stalker? A mind-reader? A burglar who read your diary?*)

Prison
- Scorn a religious prisoner who prays. (*God rescues him? Rescues you both?*)
- 'I'll protect you from the queers in this place.' (*A kiss?*)
- The executioner offers to escape with you. (*He/she is in love with you? It's a kindly way to execute you?*)
- The guard arrives with a present – for your birthday? For Xmas? (*The prisoner is allowed to beat the guard up? It's an inflatable prisoner? It's a bullet in the back of the neck?*)
- A beautiful, mysterious, gentle, sweet person appears in your cell. (*As he/she leads you out, you look back and see your lifeless body?*)

Religion and Death
- Saint cures a cripple. (*The saint limps off, crippled? Uncures him when he finds the cripple is Jewish?*)

- At a grave. (*Realize it's your own grave? The dead person arrives to comfort you, or for revenge?*)
- You discover an evil or good spirit inside you. (*Good and bad consciences appear and harangue you and each other?*)
- You hire someone to beat up your spouse who won't follow the religious rules. (*Thug beats you up? Spouse runs off with the thug?*)
- A poor Indian wants to sell his tribe's religious secrets to a professor. (*They were printed in books generations ago? Put a spell on the professor? The professor is a member of the tribe?*)
- Your date always wears gloves. (*He/she removes them to show the wounds of Christ?*)
- Your boss wants you to join his religion. (*So that you won't be so uppity? Your God fights it out with his God?*)
- 'I work miracles.' (*Do some?*)
- A Christian ends up in the wrong heaven through a clerical error. (*He's really in hell but they're teasing him?*)
- Heaven is wonderful until you discover you've no sex organs. (*Get an orgasm when you cross yourself?*)
- You're refused entry into heaven – or hell. (*Your pet speaks up for you? A lab rat speaks up for you? Your pet speaks against you?*)
- 'We're closing hell down!' (*Desperately search for someone you know? Be left alone and light a fire?*)

Revenge

- A woman tracks down the person (people) who raped her. (*Destroy them? Forgive them? It's the wrong person?*)
- A stranger stalks you. (*It's someone you bullied at school? It's someone you taught at school? It's your date's parent?*)
- You are prepared for surgery. (*Realize the surgeon is an old enemy?*)
- Old enemy buries hatchet by inviting you to posh hunting party. (*You discover that you are the creature to be hunted?*)
- Judge asks dominatrix to pretend to execute him. (*She really does it? He condemned her parent/lover/sibling/child?*)
- The person who has tied you to the bed is revealed as an old enemy. (*They've mistaken you for someone else?*)
- You recognize the person who did you a terrible injury. (*Drug him/her? Invite him/her to your parents' estate so that you can be avenged?*)

Room-mates

- Discover room-mate is from another planet/time-period. (*His flying saucer crashed? He/she abducts you to another planet? Captures you for his zoo?*)
- 'Someone is trying to kill me!' 'Is stalking me!' (*Say, 'It's me!'?*)
- Discover your room-mate (or whoever) has been replaced by an impostor.*
- 'This isn't an apartment! This is a mental hospital!' (*Room-mate is another patient?*)
- Why do you need the apartment to yourself on Friday nights? (*Room-mate invites you to stay? Is a monster? Introduces you to his imaginary playmate? Opens a door into another universe?*)

* This has clinical name – it's called Capgra's syndrome.

- 'I've been secretly in love with you, and it's driving me crazy!'
- 'I've sold you.'
- 'You really believe that you met me for the first time when I answered the advertisement?'
- Enraged room-mate is collecting his/her things, i.e. moving out after a quarrel. (*Scene ends when you reconcile?*)

Science Fiction

- 'Mother was impregnated by aliens, Father: that's why I can do THIS!'
- Your child can read minds? Can teleport things? Can control you mentally?
- Family. (*You discover that your parents are robots? You discover that you are a robot?*)
- An elevator sticks between floors. (*The computer that works the elevator is taking over the building?*)
- Park bench. (*Stranger asks for help to repair his/her spaceship?*)
- 'I'm from a parallel universe and I need to mind-swap with you.' (*Time-cop arrives and arrests the wrong body?*)
- 'Pat is out philandering. I'm a robot built as an exact replica.' (*Live happy with robot for ever – move scene forty, sixty years ahead: you're ancient, but the robot is unchanged?*)
- Astronauts on new planet. (*They drill into the ground and the planet roars in agony? It turns them into trees? They meet cute alien creature – it disappears inside one of them?*)
- You discover a second brain clamped to your date's spine. (*Make love anyway, and when you kiss something alive wriggles into your mouth?*)

Sex/Romance

- Couple making love in bed. (*A priest climbs in the window?*)
- I'm my twin. (*Both twins always secretly share lovers?*)
- A man with poor eyesight discovers that the boy he is trying to seduce is a girl.
- Someone describes a sexual exploit. (*You recognize your spouse from the description?*)
- Your penis escapes from you and you hunt it down. (*It attacks you and you take flight? It attacks audience members? Lure it with pornography?*)
- New wife/husband is shocked to discover that her/his spouse can only make love in front of an audience. (*Sell tickets? Discover people hiding under the bed? In the wardrobe?*)
- Someone becomes romantically involved with a 'forbidden' person (*A priest? There's a clap of thunder whenever they touch each other?*)
- Elderly seducer chases you around. (*Be so worried he'll have a heart attack that you give in.*)
- The call girl or rent boy arrives. (*It's a family member?*)
- Perfect date becomes a monster when not being looked at – i.e. a version of the Making Faces Game.
- 'I found these panties under the pillow. They aren't my size.' (*Husband says, 'They're mine'?*)

Someone Climbs in Through the Window When You're Asleep

- It's the person who's been stalking you.
- It's someone who needs a kidney.
- It's the writer/artist whose work you reviewed?

- It's the mad tattooist.
- It's an autograph hunter.
- 'I'm your homeless person!' (*Billeted on you by the government.*)
- It's a fanatic who wants to convert you.
- It's the soul that never found you when you were born. (*It's why life has seemed so cruel and meaningless?*)

The Small Voice Game*

- A cockroach, frog, bird, snail, beetle, scorpion, etc. wants you to:
  - Help it get its poems published.
  - Kill its enemy.
  - Accept its surrender.
  - Kill it.
  - Let it live with you for the winter. (*All its friends arrive?*)
  - Give it some rules to live by. (*Because it thinks you're God?*)
- A tiny human is a scientist who was conducting experiments. (*On losing weight?*)
- A tiny human is a driving instructor who failed a witch.

A Stranger is Invited Home

- 'Don't you recognize me?' (*It's the kid you terrorized at school? It's a ghost? It's a character from your novel? It's someone you betrayed? It's your younger/older self?*)
- 'Last night, you asked for a sign from God. Here I am.'
- The stranger is a magical being who rewards you for your kindness
- He/she confesses to a crime against God? Against Satan? (*Is pursued by demons?*)
- He/she proves you are the guest. (*You realize that it's true and that you have to leave?*)

* See p. 115.

- 'I've been stalking you.'

Teacher–Student

- The teacher shows the parent the child's obscene drawings. (*The parent drew them?*)
- Bored student has an amazing adventure. (*It was just a day-dream? Characters from the dream arrive in the classroom?*)
- 'I'll do anything to get an A in this class!' ('*Anything?*')
- 'Give me an A or I'll say you fondled me.'

Vampire/Werewolf

- Vampire (Werewolf) wants to be cured. (*Aversion therapy? Werewolf eats the therapist?*)
- Police station or park bench. (*Vampire or Werewolf wants a 'deal' so he/she can surrender?*)
- Teacher/parent: 'Where exactly is it you go during the day, Oliver?'
- 'Chain me up and don't come back until daylight.' (*Do it, and then insist on staying to watch?*)
- 'That's about the fourth time today you've shaved.'
- 'Will you throw a stick for me?'

Miscellaneous

- Exploring a giant. (*You're a surgical team? Or find the brain and control it?*)
- The boss is firing you. (*Synchronize speech with the boss and then exchange roles – Security arrive and throw the boss out?*)
- Reading a book. (*Your teacher has stolen your work and published it? You realize it's your life story – dare to look at the end?*)
- You visit the camp where your son

is a Nazi doctor. (*Discover accidentally the terrible research that the son is involved in?*)

● Blue-eyed people are being massacred. (*Will you protect your blue-eyed friend?*)

Appendix Three

More Filler Games

Activity to Music
Typically a household task is requested.
'Vacuuming!'
The improviser 'vacuums to music'. and then the music changes pace and the vacuuming becomes frenetic or romantic, or whatever. The audience laugh, but it's the improvisational equivalent of muzak.

Had the vacuum-cleaner sucked in the carpet, the cat, the furniture, the house, the city, the world, the sun, the moon the entire universe, and had a furious God arrived only to get sucked in as well (and I once saw a player mime this successfully) there'd have been something worth remembering.

Alliteration
(Not my game and not recommended.) Ask the audience for a letter, and then play a scene using as many words beginning with that letter as you can manage, (don't accept 'impossible letters'). This is pure filler, and not a patch on the No 'S' Game (see p. 188).

Variant: give each player a different letter to alliterate on – this is not an improvement.

Alphabetical Sentences
(Origin unknown.) The first sentence of the scene begins with an 'A', and next with a 'B', and so on. For example:
'Andrew!'
'Brian!'
'Can I come in!'
'Dear fellow, no one is more welcome!'
'Eating supper already?'
'Freida has saved a place for you?'
'Great!'
'Have a drink.'
'I'd love one.'
And so on (with the improvisers 'locked in' for twenty-six sentences). The game is offered as a display of 'skill', i.e. 'see how difficult this game is,' but the risk is minimal. Use it as a novelty. Keep it short.

Backward Scenes (Scene in Reverse)

These were a way of forcing players to work 'in the present' by agreeing that when a coach shouts, 'Now!' everything would go into reverse (and unless the players have attended to what's happening, how can they reverse it?). The Theatre Machine applied this technique to murder scenes so often that it was often referred to as 'Murder in Reverse'. Sometimes the dialogue sounded like a tape being played backwards, and at other times the words were spoken in the reverse order.

This backward technique was useful in allowing me to return a failing scene to some earlier point and run it forward in some more profitable direction.

These days the 'forward' part of the game has been lopped off – something we would never have done – and the game is 'invented' backward, starting with a murder victim who immediately springs back to life. I've never seen this version be of any interest – apart from the novelty.

Balancing the Stage

Imagine that the stage is pivoted at the centre, and that the actors have to keep it in balance. (This is not a performance game.)

Beginners are often so afraid of the audience that they retreat until they are pressed against the rear wall in a sort of Egyptian Frieze Theatre (even experienced improvisers move upstage when they get 'rattled'). Balancing the Stage is a corrective for this that was inspired by Antony Stirling's art-games that encouraged children to use all of the paper.

Gregor knocks at a mimed door, stage left: Hilda appears opposite:

'Did someone knock?'

'Only me!' says Gregor, entering. This forces Hilda to move forward to greet him (to 'keep the balance'). They embrace, centre-stage:

'Like a drink?' she says, moving upstage to open an invisible cupboard.

'Great heavens! What a wonderful view!' he says, forced downstage and justifying it by looking out of an imaginary window. 'Actually, I would like a drink,' he says, and then moves stage-right. 'This isn't a real Matisse, is it?'

'A gift from the artist,' she says, moving stage-left to answer a mimed phone (still holding Gregor's drink). 'It's for you!' she says, refusing to move, so that he's forced to stay where he is.

'It's that dreadful woman!' he says, justifying his behaviour. 'I won't talk to her!'

And so on.

Balancing the Stage is usually 'pure filler', but it adds variety, and it forces the players to attend to what's happening. If you are challenged to this game (which I hope you aren't) ask for the challenge to be reissued as a 'one-on-one'. This is not a game that you'd want to see twice in a row.

Bob Fosse

(Origin unknown.) An excellent warm-up game. A largish group faces front. A player steps forward and the others imitate whatever crazy dance movements this leader does. Then he/she shouts the name of another player who becomes the new leader, and so on.

Create a Commercial
This was a Theatre Machine game but it must have been used by earlier groups. It's usually issued as a challenge, with the audience being asked to suggest the product – but it's more useful as a way of ending scenes ('. . . and now, over to these important messages'). Beginners like this game, but it needs wit and imagination.

Cutting Room
A director constructs a story by cutting from one scene to another: 'And now, back at the ranch . . .', and so on.

In theory, this is a narrative game, but in practice the directors get laughs by cutting to somewhere stupid and/or 'original': 'Meanwhile, in Tanganyika . . .'. These leaps typically occur when some interaction is about to occur.

When I coached the Theatre Machine I cut forward instead of sideways (as a way to avoid bridging). If someone was proposing marriage, I might say, 'Scene two – a honeymoon hotel in the West Indies.'

If someone was feeling depressed I might say, 'Cut to a window-ledge high above the street.'

Saying, 'Meanwhile, back at the ranch . . .' is tedious and 'safe' compared with thrusting the characters directly into the future.

Dictionary
Someone in the audience is asked to close their eyes and point at a page in a dictionary that is held open for them. A scene is then based on the word selected. Use a small dictionary – larger ones contain more abstruse words, and these aren't so much fun.

Emotional Quadrants
Not recommended.

The stage is quartered, each quadrant endowing 'fear', 'pride', 'suspicion', or whatever. As you change areas, so you change emotion, and the audience will laugh.

This almost certainly derives from systems for blocking the moves of actors in relation to areas of the stage that are wrongly believed to be associated with different emotions.

Emotional Replay
Okay for occasional use. The same situation is played several times, using different emotions.

The Theatre Machine would present a short fragment of a scene; perhaps a daughter would announce that she was leaving home, the common emotion being 'anger'. Then we'd repeat this with a different emotion – fear, perhaps – extending the scene so that the parents could discover that she intends to be an actor. Then we might repeat the scene with happiness, or lust, and we'd add that she'd already been accepted at drama school.

These days – as part of the flight from narrative – most groups just repeat the first sequence, and some shorten it each time. They'll also 'lock themselves in' by announcing that they'll play a scene three (or four) times using different emotions, whereas I wouldn't have explained anything.

Variant: gag version. Repeat the scene quicker each time e.g.: do it in sixty seconds, thirty seconds, fifteen seconds . . . Silly, but guarantees a laugh.

Emotional Transitions
Recommended as a training game, especially on text.

Called Emotional Hurdles in David Shepherd's *Impro Olympics*.

The players are compelled to switch emotion by people outside the scene who shout, 'Anger!', 'Lust!', 'Despair!' and so on.

This game always gets some sort of a laugh (audiences like transitions) but it's unlikely to create any narrative. It's just occurred to me that this may be a safe form of It's Tuesday (see p. 110).

Great Moments in History with the Central Person Missing
It's a reasonable assumption that the issuing of this challenge will be more entertaining than the execution of it.

Headline
Not recommended. The audience is asked to invent an imaginary newspaper headline; the players then act out this news item. Ninety-nine times out of a hundred the suggestion will get a laugh, but the scene will be pathetic.

It would be better to select real headlines, preferably from today's newspaper, or to bring a TV in and act things straight off the news (don't get sued).

The Invention of . . .
The audience suggest an object – a Boeing 747, a meringue, clockwork false-teeth, who knows? Then the improvisers present a scene that shows how the object was invented. This is usually taken as yet another opportunity to be stupid, but it can be charming if the players are playful and good natured and choose an object that inspires them.

Last Sentence
Not recommended. This involves getting a 'sentence' from the audience (almost always something silly), and then playing a scene that ends with that sentence. Frightened improvisers love this game because it tells them where they're heading; i.e. it encourages bridging.

The Theatre Machine would sometimes ask for a sentence to start a scene with, and then head off in whatever direction fate took them. This may seem perverse to improvisers who want to be safe but I've always seen improvising as firing an arrow into the darkness, rather than aiming at an agreed target.

Madrigals, etc.

(Not my game.) Each player sings an agreed phrase, sentence or word. One player starts, and the others chime in whenever a 'conductor' points at them.

Teams who have no skill at singing seem impelled to challenge to madrigals, and I've even seen beginners substitute sounds instead melody: they went 'whoooo whoooo' or 'oink oink'. The audience laughed (moderately), but why pay money to see that?

Audiences are courteous to singers, and are amazed at their ability to improvise songs. It follows that 'songs' and 'musicals' are relatively safe, and are likely to proliferate (because technical proficiency can substitute for inspiration). Improvised musicals are likely to be more interesting than madrigals – because we may get a story – but when the Judges permit the eighth singing challenge in a row (as happened at a tournament recently) it might be better to advertise the match as a musical event and let MusicSports build its own clientele.

Most Uses of Object Chosen by Opposing Team.

A good example of a very simple but useful filler game. Perhaps a shoelace is thrown on to the stage and becomes a snake, a ring for a flea circus, a fuse for a bomb, a tightrope for a pair of fingers, a whip for a pet mouse, and so on, until an agreed time limit, usually one minute, is reached (at fifty-five seconds start a five-second fade).

One to Ten

One word, then two words, then three words – up to ten and then back.

– John!
– Yes, Lord?
– All those humans!
– You created them, Lord.
– Well I'm proud of them.
– I think we all are, Lord.

And so on.

A typical example of a game designed to display the improvisers' cleverness.

Sit/Stand/Lie

Three players are onstage, plus some furniture; one is sitting, one is standing, and one is lying on the floor. This arrangement should look natural, and has to be maintained. If a player stands up, then whoever is standing must sit down, or flop to the floor – and attempt to justify this action. And if you're lying on the floor when someone else lies on the floor, you'll have to sit or stand.

Not my game, and not from Loose Moose, but an entertaining justification game that forces the actors to respond to each other.

Change position to force a change in the other players. Justify the change *after* you make it or the game will be too slow.

Variant: sit, stand, lie, enter. Only three players can be onstage at any one time, i.e. when a fourth enters, someone has to leave (and vice versa).

Variant: sit/stand. A two-player version for beginners.

Variant: sit/stand/lie/kneel – usable.

Spoon River

Corpses sit up in their graves and talk about their lives – essentially undramatic. (Unless they were to change each other but I've never seen it used this way.) Not recommended except for audiences of intellectuals.

Strange Bedfellows

Not recommended. .

Two famous characters – usually historical – interact together. I've never seen this game create anything of value:

'Who would you like us to be?'

'Donald Duck . . .'

'And somebody else!'

'Charlemagne!'

'Charlie who?'

Stunt Doubles

Whenever any strong physical action is called for, the players say, 'Stunt doubles!' and actors waiting at the side run on and replace them. I wouldn't use the game often (it's just a gag) but it can be very funny; for example:

– I think I'll run upstairs and get my book. Stuntman!

  [*A stuntman mimes running up and down-stairs.*]

– Oh dear, wrong book!

  [*A stuntman mimes running up the stairs to fetch the right one.*]

– Darling. I want you to kiss me like I've never been kissed before!

– Certainly dear. Stuntman!

Subtitles

A gibberish scene is played while other players provide the 'translation', running across the front of the stage as they do this – being 'subtitles'.

Good for a laugh, but it works best when it's a novelty.

Time Jump

This is where filler games meet narrative. It's very likely to create something memorable.

Two characters meet. Show them half an hour later? Then a year later? Then twenty years later? Then fifty years later? Then a thousand years later? Reincarnated?

Time Warp
Move a scene into another era, in the past or the future. When 'Time warp' is called the players freeze and then continue in the new era. I doubt that this can work successfully.

What are You Doing?
A is sweeping the floor. B says, 'What are you doing?' A says, 'Looking through a telescope!' B looks through a telescope. A says, 'What are you doing?' B says, 'Changing a diaper.' A then changes a diaper, and so on, ad infinitum. Good as a warm-up. Not my game, but fun.

Who? What? Where?
The audience are asked who the actors are, where they are, and what their problem, or purpose is. This might be okay if the suggestions are sensible but they won't be; for example:
'Who are we?'
'Penguins!'
'What are we doing?'
'Walking on stilts!'
'And where are we?'
'Crossing the Sahara!'
This game is popular with actors who want the audience to share the blame. I banned it at the Studio because even if the suggestions were serious, I didn't want to reinvent conventional theatre.

Appendix Four

Notes I've Given

My pockets are often stuffed with paper that's covered in notes I've given. Here are some of them.

- Warm up by singing, by playing football, or tag (but not enough to tire you). Sprawling about in the green room and cracking jokes means that you'll probably be a lot less funny when you get onstage.
- Practise physical skills.
- Whether you were audible is not the point: the voice has to be a whip to 'discipline' the audience.
- A small group of fans were cheering everything and they seduced you into being stupid.
- Don't let audience members volunteer their friends.
- Gibberish: X is unchanged when listening, but alters himself when he speaks – he seems less talented this way.
- X declared his love but his legs were crossed away from her. The director should have corrected this.
- Word-at-a-Time was followed by One Voice: not enough contrast.
- Asking for a household implement to commit suicide with is a terrible cliché – nothing good will come of it except cheap laughs.
- After half an hour think about getting audience volunteers.
- I'm sick of fingers being used as guns.

- Be fit. Be athletic. Be sensual. Dress attractively. If the audience wants to take you home, they'll buy more tickets.
- If audience volunteers speak too quietly, pretend deafness.
- If someone plays several characters each with a different hat, why not have someone hand the hats to him?
- Be knowledgeable about current events. Know that the government plans to allow billboards along all the major highways. Know that people are going bananas about Viagra. Know that millions of people in India have been crippled by the UN's 'Decade of Water' programme.
- When you feel uninspired, just be efficient. If you try to do your best, you'll be unable to cooperate with anyone.
- Be clean. Who knows what intimate postures you may have to assume?
- Dirty old denims put people off. Think about costume. Officials should never look disreputable.
- Don't make gags in love scenes!
- Don't crash into love scenes as other characters unless you're really needed.
- The set-up for the Speech-When-in-Physical-Contact scene was

baffling: a Judge or the commentator should have explained.

- Don't habitually use a funny voice.
- Don't always come on weird.
- Never lower a volunteer's status.
- When children are onstage – please, please avoid anything sexual.
- We need variety: why were there no one-on-one challenges?
- Mustn't depend on audience to inspire you.
- You can always get a laugh by biting the plastic fruit but why bother?
- Don't have two scenes onstage at the same time – except in very special situations.
- Other things being equal, if you mime washing a window, don't stand sideways on to the audience.
- If you're going to act out a story told by an audience member, get additional information – how would she describe herself? If parents or lovers are involved, get adjectives that describe them.
- Gorilla Theatre – ordering players to cry three times in one show is too much.
- When you have no idea what to do, just say confidently, 'I know just what to do!'
- Why bother to explain what a three-word-sentence scene is?
- Don't enter as a gardener if we just had a gardening scene.
- Commentator forgetting to emphasize the score.
- Too many people were onstage. We needed a quiet love scene, or a solo mime to music, anything but more funny stuff.
- Two players entered a 'bus' – someone should have provided seats for them.

- Not everything has to be improvised, especially formal announcements.
- If you reject a suggestion saying, 'a good idea, though!' it sounds patronizing.
- Some churl in the audience suggested picking scabs as an activity: never accept disgusting suggestions.
- Keep still when dubbing your partner's voice. We don't want our eyes to be drawn to you.
- A Word-at-a-Time about a tin of peaches – who cares?
- Something on the stage was reflecting into the audience and dazzling people.
- Don't go for a stupid laugh by saying that your salary as a brain surgeon is five dollars a month.
- The best resistance is the truth.
- Let the audience decide what's funny.
- If a coach tells you what to say, repeat it identically and the audience will laugh; alter the instruction and there'll be less response.
- When he said, 'Do you juggle?' you should have agreed even though you can't – you could have mimed it.
- In general, always supply furniture when audience volunteers are onstage (in dubbing games, for example).
- The snoggers should provide scenography before it's asked for. If it's rejected, the audience will enjoy their frustration as they drag it off.
- Make sure that sheets are tucked into the bed so that we don't see shoes sticking out.
- The 'serenade an audience member' forfeit is embarrassing. Throw it out.
- An onlooker, or scorekeeper, must

keep a list of scenes played (to remind us of what happened when we meet after the performance).

- Avoid jargon. Don't say, 'We challenge you to a Boris Scene,' say 'We challenge you to an interrogation.'
- How about teams of nuns versus teams of Hell's Angels, or teams of right-wing bigots versus teams of left-wing bigots?
- Four Person Pecking Order with two audience volunteers – they should have been cast as Number One and Number Four, not as Numbers Two and Three.
- Don't touch the carpet when you mime brushing the mud from it. Don't touch shoes when you mime brushing them.
- Don't flap the carpet unless you know it's not dusty.
- What-Comes-Next is a bad challenge after Word-at-a-Time – too similar.
- Don't quench hecklers by using comedy-club put-downs ('You live under power-lines, do you?' or 'Of all those millions of sperm it's amazing that you were the fastest,' etc.).
- When X became inspired you should have become a passenger and let him take over the scene.
- Detect and remove unnecessary tension (or we won't see you as charming). Experiment with how little tension you need on a stage.
- The Die Game is an audience warm-up game. Don't end with it.
- The commentator never mentioned the score, never treated the game as a sporting event.
- Fear and ego are the enemies. Conquer the first and the second may still get you.

- Don't make moves on other players until you're outside the building. Don't grope other players in the black-outs. Don't slip them the tongue if you kiss them in a scene.
- Scenographer hurled a pillow at actor in bed. Be respectful. Place the pillow under the actor's head.
- Don't snap the lights in and out, do fades.
- Always play music when scenography is being set.
- Always check mike levels – the sound was brutally loud.
- Percussive music and/or songs are bad under speech.
- If you invite the audience to come closer, don't say they'll hear better, say they'll have a better time.
- Ushers should move slowly. Even the air you displace can disturb people.
- Ushers should not wear squeaky shoes.
- 'Anyone never seen improvisation before? Good, come up on stage.' Never 'hook' unwilling volunteers this way.
- If a scene is about nothing of any interest, bring the lights down as soon as possible.
- Commentator read out name on wallet and then made the owner walk to him to get it. Someone should have taken it to her.
- Commentator – never make jokes at the audience volunteer's expense.
- Moving Bodies scenes need furniture, but a Judge should have rejected the bench as too unstable.
- Excellent that the Judge said that they weren't doing the challenge, and started them again.
- If Judges are booed for an

unpopular decision, they should stand up and explain why.

• I was so grateful when the Judge said 'Too many scenes with guns'.

Index of Games

The games in **bold** are the ones that I recommend you to teach first. Those in [square brackets] are the ones that seem unimportant to me.

Activity to Music 362
[Adjective] 205
Advancing/Not Advancing 248–54
   Staying With It 249–53
Alliteration 362
Alphabetical Sentences 362
Animal Games 278–9
The Arms 202–4
   Loading the Pockets 204
The Audience Speak 175–6
Avoiding the Wolf 133

Backward Scenes (Scenes in Reverse) 363
[Balancing the Stage] 363
Balloons, Hitting with 254–60
   Fights 257–8
   Master-Servant 258–9
   The Spontaneous Balloon 259
   Wheel of Tension 256–7
Battle of the Sexes 200
Beep-Beep 230, 260–2
Bell and Buzzer 302
Blind Offers 192–3, 241
Blocking Games 101–13
   Accept but Make Negative Offers 109–10
   Both Accept (Gibberish) 106
   Both Accept (Mime) 106–7
   Both Block 102–3
   Both Block (Two Realities) 103–4
   First to Block Loses 104–5
   It's Tuesday 110–12
   One Blocks/One Accepts 108–9
   Remove the Blocks 105
   'Sounds Good to Me' 107–8
   Tag Version 106
   No-blocking Games 112–13
Bob Fosse Game 363–4
Body image *see* Image Games
Boring the Audience 211
Boris Game 145–51
Breaking the Routine 84–9
Bum Tag 161

Chain Endowments 186

Changing the Body Image 276–7
Changing the Object 304–6
Changing Real Objects 306
Circles of Expectation 79–80
Commercial, Create a 364
Cutting Room 364

Danish Game 4-5, 19, 327, 330–1
Death in a Minute 121–3
Dennis's Puppet Show 304
[Dictionary] 364
Die Game 183–4
Drawing games 112
Dubbing 171–8
   Lip-Sync 176–8
   One Voice 171–4
   The Audience Speak 175–6
   The Professor 174–5
   Two-way Lip-Sync 177–8
The Dwarf 204–5

Emotional Goals 184–5
[Emotional Quadrants] 364
Emotional Replay 364–5
Emotional Sounds 268–70
Emotional Transitions (Emotional Hurdles) 365
Endowments 185–6
   Chain Endowments 186
   Invisibility 178–80
   Party Endowments 233–6
The Expert Game 123
The Eyes 112

Faces *see* Making Faces
Fast-food Laban 237, 283–4
Fast-food Stanislavsky 237, 285–301
   Lists 287–301, 343–53
Fight for Your Number 228, 237
Filler Games 183–91, 362–8
Fingers, Scenes with 302–3
Flashlight Theatre 36
[Freeze Games] 186–7

Gag-Police 127
Gaskill's Samurai Game 161–2
The Gerbil 125–7
Ghost Game 181–2, 221
The Giant 205
Gibberish 171, 185–6, 214–19
    Both Accept 106
    Guess the Situation 217–19
    He Said/She Said 198
    Jokes 217
    Subtitles 367
Gibberish Cards 214–15
Gibberish/English 216
Giving Presents 58–9
Gorilla Theatre (My-Scene Impro) 42–9
Gossip to Interaction 119–20
Grandmother's Footsteps 163
[Great Moments in History] 365
Group-Yes 34–6
Guess the Phrase 187–8
Guess the Situation 217–19

Hand on Knee 310–14
Hat Games 19, 156–61
    blindfold 160
He Said/She Said 195–9
[Headlines] 365
Hitting with Balloons see Balloons, Hitting
    with

I Love You – I Hate You (Mantra) 272–3
Image Games 276–7
    Changing the Body Image 276–7
    Endowments 185–6, 233–6
Instant Death 280–2
The Invention of . . . 365
Invisibility 178–80, 181
It's Tuesday 110–12

Justify the Gesture 193–5

Keep the Servant on the Hop 163–7
Keyboard Games 151–4
The King Game 237–40
    Pecking-order version 239–40
The Klutz 246–8
Knife Game 308–10

Laban, Fast-food 237, 283–4
[Last Sentence] 365–6
Leave for the Same Reason 169–71
Link the Items 144
Lip-Sync 176–8
    with Audience Volunteers 178
    from Offstage 178

    see also Dubbing
Lists
    Fast-food Stanislavsky 287–301, 343–53
    Non-Sequential 142–3
    Tilts 96–100, 354–61
Love Scenes 265–7
Machines 277
Madrigals/Musicals 366
Making Faces 162–8
    in fives 167–8
    in pairs 168
    Pecking Orders 168
    The Vampire 168–9
    in threes 163–7
Mantras 270–4

Master-Servant Games 240–1
    Blind Offer version 241
    Hitting with Balloons 258–9
    Keep the Servant on the Hop 163–7
    King Game 237–40
    Lip-Sync 176–8
    Making Faces, 163–8
    Piggy-Back version 241
Mega-Death (footnote) 129
Micetro Impro 49–54, 90, 93
Moral choices 78–9
Most Uses of an Object 366
Mouse Police 279
Moving Bodies 200–2
Mysteries 82–4

No Adjectives or Buts 133–4
No Laugh Impro 127
No 'S' Game 6, 188
No-Block Theatresports 328–9

Non-sequential Lists 142–3
Objects, Changing 304–6
Objects, Most Uses of 366
Obsessions 280–3
One Game Theatresports 329
One to Ten 366
One Voice Games 171–7
    in pairs 174
    The Audience Speak 175–6
    The Professor 174–5
One-word Sentences, Speaking in 68, 155–6
Over-accepting Offers 110–12

Paper-flicking 316–17
Party Endowments 233–6
Pecking Orders, Making Faces 168
    King Game 239–40
People Machines 277–8

People as Objects 303–4
Phrase substitution 264–5
Present Tense Only 120
Presents, Giving 58–9
The Professor 174–5
Puppet Shows 200–2
Dennis's 304

Rejection Game 225–6
Reversal Game 226–7
Routine, Breaking the 84–9

Samurai Game 161–2
Sandwiches 236–7
A Scene without . . . 189–90
Scenes in Reverse (Backward Scenes) 363
Seen Enough 36–9
Self Up/Partner Down 228–9
Serious Scenes 264–74
    Emotional Sounds 268–70
    Love Scenes (Love and Hate) 265–7
    Mantras 270–4
    Substituting Phrases 264–5
Serious Theatresports 329
Sideways Scenes 189–90
Sit/Stand/Lie 366–7
Slow-motion Commentary 241–5
Small Voice Game 115–17
Snake Police 279
Sounds, Emotional 268–70
Sounds Good to Me 107–8
Soundscape 208–9
Spasms 314
Speech Defect Game 317–19
Spoon River 367
Stanislavsky, Fast-food 285–301
    Lists 287–301, 343–53
Status games 219–31
    Challenges 223
    Equal Status 227–8
    Fight for your Number 228, 237
    King Game 237–40
    Low-Status Trick Presentation 230–1
    Master-Servant 240–1
    Parties 221–2
    Rejection Game 225–6
    Reversal 226–7
    Sandwiches 236–7
    Self Up/Partner Down 228–9
    Transitions 224
    Two-person Games 223–4
    Wrong Status 229–30
    see also **Master-Servant Games**
Stealing 307–8

Story Games 130–54
    Boris Game 145–51
    Keyboard Games 151–4
    Link the Items 144
    Verbal Chase 144–5
    What Comes Next? 134–42
    Word-at-a-Time 114–15, 131–4, 329
Straight Men 213–14
[Strange Bedfellows] 367
Stunt Doubles 367
Substitution Impro 199–200
    Battle of the Sexes 200
Subtitles 367

Tag 59–60
    Blocking Game 106
    Bum Tag 161
    in Pairs 59–60
Tag-team Impro 200
Tempo 207–8
Theme and Forfeit 39–42
Three-word Sentences, Speaking in 68, 155, 198
Tilting 89–100
    arbitrary 100
    forcing 95–6
    lists 96–100, 354–61
    negating 94–5
Time Jump 367–8
Time Warp 368
Timing the Spasms 315–16
Tug-o'-War 57–8
Two Realities 103–4
Two Voice Game 176–7
Two-way Lip-Sync 177–8

The Vampire 168–9
Verbal Chase 144–5
Verse 245–6

Wallpaper Drama 212–13
What Are You Doing? 368
What Comes Next? 134–42
    committee version 139–41
    Paradoxical 142
Wheel of Tension 256–7
[Who? What? Where?] 368
Wide Eyes 205–6
Wide Mouth 206–7
Word-at-a-Time 114–15, 131–4, 329

Yes! And . . . 36, 191
Yes-But 190–1
You're Interesting 209–11